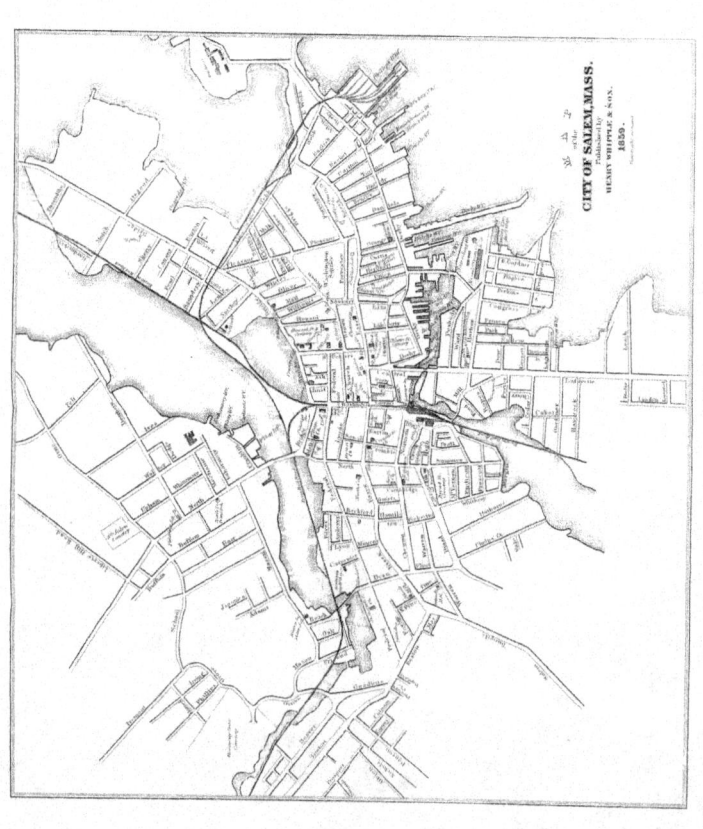

D. B. BROOKS & BRO.,
Publishers & Booksellers,
STATIONERS
AND
MUSIC DEALERS.

Having extended our store, and possessing increased facilities for our business, we are prepared to offer great inducements to buyers, both at

WHOLESALE AND RETAIL.

We are agents for the best

WRITING AND PRINTING PAPERS,

Which we can furnish at manufacturers' prices.

ALSO, FOR

Dawson's & Warren's Celebrated Gold Pens,

MELODEONS,

Of PRINCE, and other approved makers.

BLANK BOOKS

Made to order, for Corporations.

Our PAPER ROOMS, in rear of store, we keep stocked with

WRAPPING PAPERS AND TWINES

OF ALL DESCRIPTIONS;

Particular sizes and weights made to order.

The Old Stand, 193 Essex Street,

And Allen's Block, South Danvers.

HENRY WHIPPLE & SON,

Booksellers & Stationers,

190 ESSEX STREET, SALEM,

Offer constantly for sale

A COMPLETE
ASSORTMENT OF BOOKS,

In all departments of Literature.

English, French, and American

STAPLE AND FANCY STATIONERY

OF EVERY VARIETY.

DEPOT FOR PERIODICALS

AND

PAMPHLETS OF ALL DESCRIPTIONS,

AND

SUBSCRIBERS PROMPTLY FURNISHED

AT THE

VERY LOWEST RATES.

Blank Books made to order,

AND PAGED.

CHARTS OF ALL PARTS OF THE WORLD.

☞ **Nautical Works of all kinds.** ☜

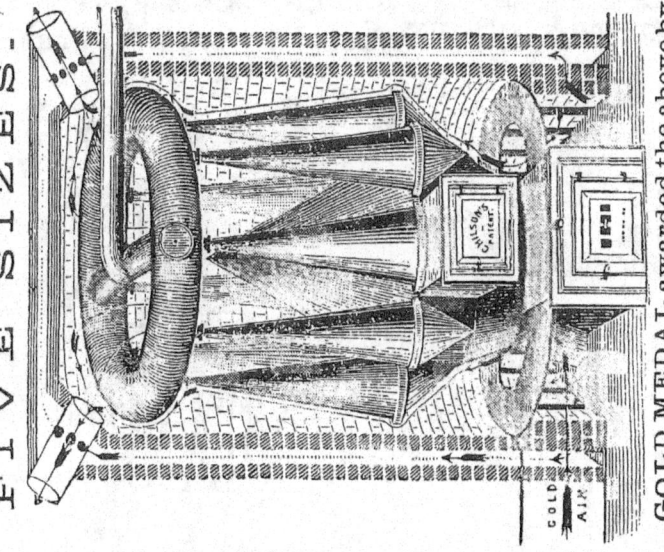
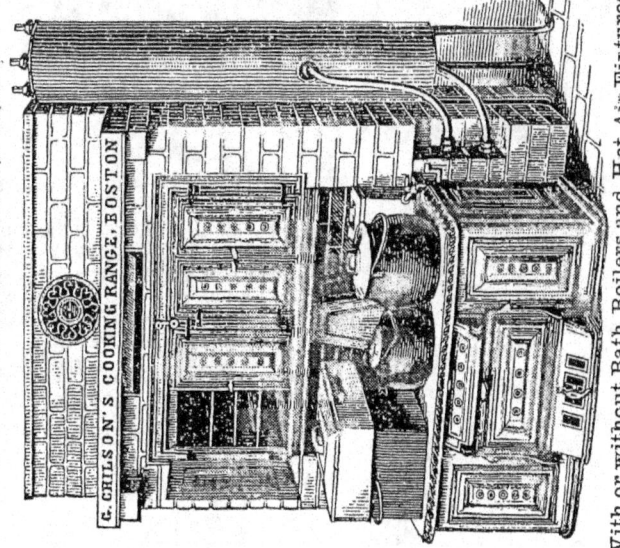

A CHALLENGE TO THE WORLD!

CHILSON'S PATENT TRIO STOVE.

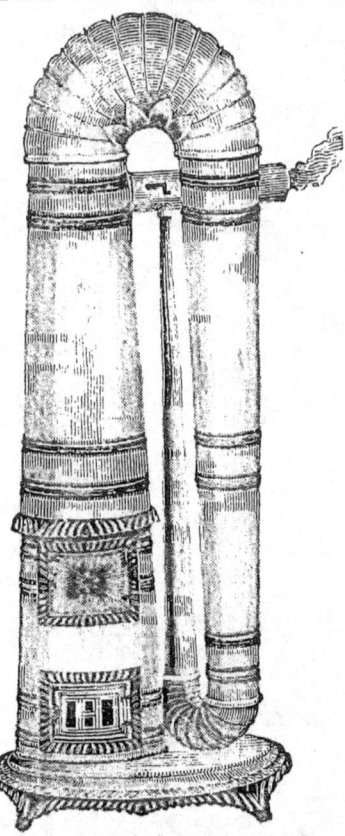

SIX SIZES.

The cut of this remarkably economical Stove will enable every intelligent mind to comprehend, at once, the great economy in fuel secured by this strictly philosophical invention. Its extensive use has *proved*, and we can safely *warrant* a saving of *fifty per cent.* in fuel over any other plan of stove known.

CHILSON'S PATENT Trio Portable Furnace.

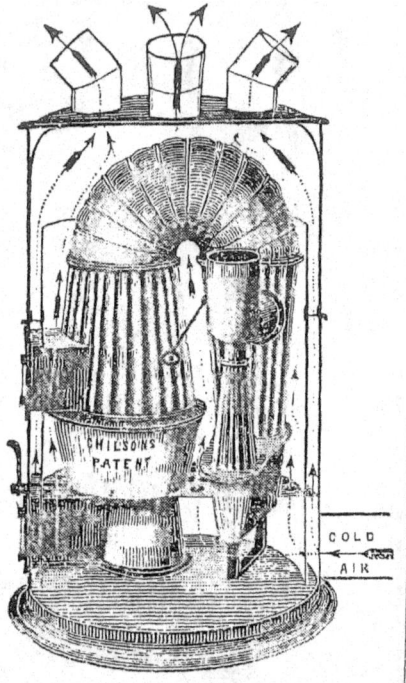

THREE SIZES.

This Furnace is the same in principle as the Trio Stove. We warrant a saving of *fifty per cent. in fuel* over the common Portable Furnaces. It is made of substantial heavy castings, and is not liable to rust and burn out, or leak gas, as is the case with the common portable furnaces, made partially of sheet iron.

Stoves, Furnaces, Ranges, Mantels, Grates, Registers, Ventilators, &c., as usual.

Special attention given to warming and ventilating buildings.

GARDNER CHILSON,
99 and 101 Blackstone Street, . . Boston

WENTWORTH & FIFIELD,
No. 15 ST. PETER STREET,

Manufacturers of and dealers in

HOT-AIR FURNACES, COOKING RANGES, KITCHEN, PARLOR, OFFICE, & STORE STOVES.

We are prepared to furnish the following list of FURNACES, at the manufacturers' lowest prices, viz.:

Hawkes's Brick and Portable, Macgregor do., Herman's, Seavey's, Spence's, and Union.

Also, the following patterns of RANGES:

Carpenter's Double Oven, 8 sizes (see cut), Seavey's Gothic, Chilson's, Pond's Improved, Spence's do., &c., &c.

Also, Furnace Fixtures, consisting of Registers, Ventilators of various patterns, Soap Stones, &c. Kitchen, Parlor, Office, and Store Stoves in great variety. A complete assortment of Tin Ware (of the best quality) constantly on hand. Also, Tin, Sheet Iron, and Copper work of all kinds done to order, in a faithful manner.

THE SALEM
[MASSACHUSETTS]
DIRECTORY

CONTAINING THE
NAMES OF THE CITIZENS,
CITY OFFICERS,
a Business Directory,
GENERAL EVENTS OF THE YEARS 1856 AND 1857,
AND AN
ALMANAC FOR 1859

Also, a Business Directory of South Danvers

Adams, Sampson & Company
PUBLISHERS OF THE BOSTON DIRECTORY, MASS. REGISTER, NEW ENGLAND
BUSINESS DIRECTORY, NEW YORK STATE BUSINESS DIRECTORY, ETC.
OFFICE, 91 WASHINGTON STREET, BOSTON

HERITAGE BOOKS
2015

HERITAGE BOOKS
AN IMPRINT OF HERITAGE BOOKS, INC.

Books, CDs, and more—Worldwide

For our listing of thousands of titles see our website
at
www.HeritageBooks.com

A Facsimile Reprint
Published 2015 by
HERITAGE BOOKS, INC.
Publishing Division
5810 Ruatan Street
Berwyn Heights, Md. 20740

Copyright © 2002 Heritage Books, Inc.

Originally published
Salem:
Henry Whipple & Son
190 Essex Street
1859

— Publisher's Notice —

Pages 5, 6, 19 and 20 are missing, as are the tops of pages 21 and 22. No significant text has been lost.

In reprints such as this, it is often not possible to remove blemishes from the original. We feel the contents of this book warrant its reissue despite these blemishes and hope you will agree and read it with pleasure.

International Standard Book Numbers
Paperbound: 978-0-7884-2101-3
Clothbound: 978-0-7884-6180-4

PREFACE.

The ninth edition of the Salem Directory, with a Business Directory of South Danvers, is now presented to the citizens, with the assurance that its value will be fully equal to any of its predecessors.

Although the general depression of business during the past year has affected Salem to some extent, there is at the present time an increasing activity in all branches of industrial pursuits.

The following figures show that there has been a considerable increase in the number of names, during the two years, and also the great number of changes which take place in the same time, in even as permanent a population as reside in Salem.

The number of names added is 1,669; struck out, 1,232; other changes, 2,323.

The number of names in last edition was 6,130, in the present, 6,567; making an increase of 437.

The publishers return their thanks to all who have assisted and encouraged them in the work, and hope it will meet the wants of the public.

LIST OF CONTENTS.

Abbreviations, ... 47	Insurance Companies; . . . 225
Advertising Department, follows 252	Justices of the Peace, . . . 249
Almanac for 1859, ... 6	Loan Fund Associations, . . 225
Banks in Salem, . . . 222—225	Masters in Chancery, . . . 247
British Consular Agent, . . 221	Military, ... 241
Business Directory, ... 196	Names of the Inhabitants, . . 49
Census of Essex County, . . 245	Newspapers, ... 239
Churches, ... 217—220	New York State Directory, . 48
City Government, 1858, . . 211	Notaries Public, ... 247
Clergymen, ... 198	Odd Fellows and Masons, . . 239
Commissioners for other States, 247	Physicians, ... 206
Commissioners of Insolvency, 246	Plummer Hall, ... 252
Congressional Districts, 6 & 7, 245	Police Court, ... 249
Counsellors, ... 199	Post Office, ... 221
Counting-Room Almanac, 1859, 5	Railroads, ... 250
Counting-Room Almanac, 1860, 30	Reading Rooms, ... 221
Court Sessions. . See Calendars.	Savings Bank, ... 224
Courts in Essex County, . . 246	Schools and Teachers, . 214—217
Custom House, ... 220	Societies and Companies, 227—241
Eastern Railroad, ... 250	Sons of Temperance, . . . 241
Essex County Officers, . 246—249	Stages, ... 244
Expresses, ... 243	Streets, Courts, and Places, . 45
Fire Department, ... 213	Taxation in Salem, ... 245
General Events of 1856-7, . . 31	Ward Boundaries, ... 48
Halls, Buildings, &c., . . . 48	Wharves, ... 47

South Danvers Business Directory, &c., follow Salem Advertisements.

Index to Advertisements, see page 253.

PIANO-FORTE MANUFACTORY,

NO. 484 WASHINGTON STREET,

BOSTON,

Originated A. D., 1828, in the firm of Currier & Gilbert.

We have manufactured near EIGHT THOUSAND. Particular attention is called to our

PARLOR GRANDS,

As superior to all others now manufactured, and the most desirable PARLOR INSTRUMENT that can be found for

POWER,

Nearly equal to the Full Grand, yet occupying less space on the floor than the Large, common-form,

SQUARE PIANO-FORTE.

We keep on hand, and manufacture to order, every variety, including SQUARES, FULL GRAND, and ORTHEONS, all made with

IRON FRAMES,

In the most substantial manner, and of thoroughly seasoned materials, with

SUPERIOR ACTION,

Which requires less regulating than any other now in use, is unsurpassed for simplicity of construction, ease of execution, and adaptation to every variety of climate. In these and all other desirable qualities, is superior to any other now known.

☞ *All orders by mail, or otherwise, faithfully executed, and warranted satisfactory, or purchase-money refunded.*

WM. H. JAMESON,   1858.   T. GILBERT & CO.

IMPORTANT TO GENTLEMEN!

Gentlemen wishing to purchase a good article of CLOTHING are invited to call at

Nichols's Old Establishment,

Which was the first custom establishment opened in Boston, where cash customers could save 25 per cent, as nothing is taken here to offset bad debts. Now this establishment will be found to take the lead, as formerly, in regard to prices, work, and style.

This is the central point for STUDY or DRESSING GOWNS and BREAKFAST JACKETS (a neat, rich garment).

☞ Purchase your clothing here this year, and see if it is a place where you wish to trade in future.

GEO. N. NICHOLS.

96 WASHINGTON STREET, ... BOSTON.

MEMORANDA FOR FEBRUARY, 1859.

12	22	1	Clear Cloudy
29	22	2	Cloudy Snow
30	30	3	Cloudy Snow Storme all day
30	36	4	Clear Pleasant
32	36	5	Clear Pleasant
16	36	6	Cloudy Snow Storme
20	30	7	Cloudy
20	08	8	Cloudy
30	29	9	Cloudy rainy
26	30	10	Cloudy Clear
16	21	11	Cloudy Snow
18	22	12	Cloudy Snow Storme all
8	20	13	Cloudy
16	24	14	Clear Pleasant Storm
24	15	15	Cloudy rainy
20	16	16	Clear Pleasant
30	17	17	Cloudy
30	26	18	Cloudy rainy
30	8	19	Cloudy foggy
20	6	20	Cloudy rainy
24	31	21	Cloudy Clear high wind
	32	22	Clear Pleasant
22	30	23	Clear Pleasant
32	32	24	Cloudy rain Snow Clear
12	2	25	Cloudy Clear
	26	26	Cloudy Snow Storme
2	4	27	Clear Pleasant cloudy
26		28	Clear Pleasant cloudy

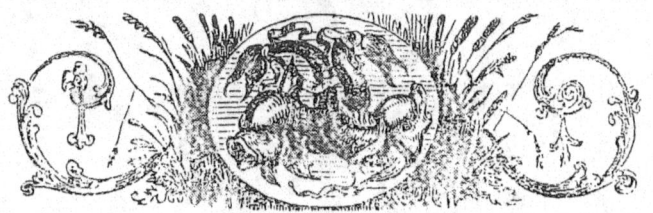

FEBRUARY, 1859.

MOON'S PHASES.

New Moon, 2d day, 8h. 20m. afternoon.
First Quarter, 10th day, 2h. 56m. afternoon.
Full Moon, 17th day, 5h. 58m. morning.
Last Quarter, 24th day, 9h. 37m. morning.

D. of Mo	Days of week.	SUN Rises.	Sets.	Moon rises.	HIGH WATER. Morn.	Eve.	COURTS.
		h. m.	h. m.	h. m.	h. m.	h. m.	
1	Tuesday	7 14	5 14	6 58	10 36	11 2	
2	Wednesday	7 12	5 15	sets	11 21	11 39	
3	Thursday	7 11	5 17	5 48	11 57	11 57	
4	Friday	7 10	5 18	6 51			
5	Saturday	7 9	5 19	7 54	0 53	1 10	
6	SUNDAY	7 8	5 21	8 57	1 27	1 45	
7	Monday	7 7	5 22	10 3	2 4	2 23	Feb. 7th, C. C. P. Fitchburg. (Civil.)
8	Tuesday	7 6	5 24	11 9	2 42	3 4	
9	Wednesday	7 5	5 25	morn	3 22	3 45	
10	Thursday	7 3	5 26	0 17	4 9	4 40	
11	Friday	7 2	5 27	1 16	5 11	5 43	
12	Saturday	7 1	5 29	2 35	6 15	6 53	
13	SUNDAY	7 0	5 30	3 44	7 31	8 8	
14	Monday	6 58	5 31	4 51	8 45	9 18	Feb. 14th, C. C. P. Cambridge. (Criminal.)
15	Tuesday	6 57	5 32	5 39	9 51	10 21	Feb. 15th, S. J. C. Dedham. (Jury Term.)
16	Wednesday	6 55	5 33	6 18	10 50	11 14	
17	Thursday	6 54	5 34	rises	11 38	11 59	
18	Friday	6 52	5 36	7 29			
19	Saturday	6 51	5 37	8 45	0 44	1 5	
20	SUNDAY	6 49	5 39	10 1	1 26	1 47	
21	Monday	6 48	5 40	11 18	2 8	2 30	Feb. 21st, C. C. P. Northampton. (Civil.)
22	Tuesday	6 47	5 41	morn	2 51	3 13	
23	Wednesday	6 45	5 43	0 14	3 37	4 1	
24	Thursday	6 43	5 44	1 17	4 25	4 58	
25	Friday	6 42	5 45	2 20	5 27	5 57	
26	Saturday	6 41	5 46	3 13	6 28	7 0	
27	SUNDAY	6 39	5 47	4 6	7 30	8 1	
28	Monday	6 37	5 48	4 58	8 30	8 59	Feb. 28th, C. C. P. Lenox. (Civil.)

By different nations, each day in the week is set apart for public worship,—Sunday by Christians, Monday by Greeks, Tuesday by Persians, Wednesday by Assyrians, Thursday by Egyptians, Friday by Turks, and Saturday by Jews.

MEMORANDA FOR FEBRUARY, 1859.

12	32	1	Clear Cloudy
22	32	2	Cloudy Snow
36	30	3	Cloudy Snow Storm all day
30	36	4	Clear Pleasant
32	36	5	Clear Pleasant
16	26	6	Cloudy Snow Storm
20	30	7	Clear
20	10	8	Cloudy
30	29	9	Cloudy rainy
35	30	10	Cloudy Clear
6	26	11	Cloudy Snow
18	28	12	Cloudy Snow Storm all
8	30	13	Cloudy
16	30	14	Clear Pleasant Storm
24	35	15	Cloudy rainy
30	36	16	Clear Pleasant
30	40	17	Cloudy
30	36	18	Cloudy rainy
30	38	19	Cloudy foggy
24	36	20	Cloudy rainy
30	31	21	Cloudy Clear high wind
20	32	22	Clear high wind Pleasant
22	30	23	Clear Pleasant
32	34	24	Cloudy rain snow Clear
12	25	25	Cloudy Clear
18	26	Cloudy Snow Storm
24	42	27	Clear Pleasant Cloudy
36	28	Clear Pleasant Cloudy

MARCH, 1859.

MOON'S PHASES.

New Moon, 4th day, 2h. 56m. afternoon.
First Quarter, 11th day, 11h. 55m. afternoon.
Full Moon, 18th day, 5h. 1m. afternoon.
Last Quarter, 26th day, 4h. 43m. morning.

D. Mo	Days of week.	SUN Rises. Sets.	Moon rises.	HIGH WATER. Morn. Eve.	COURTS.
		h. m. h. m.	h. m.	h. m. h. m.	
1	Tuesday	6 35 5 50	5 35	9 33 9 47	March 1st, Superior Court for Suffolk Co. Boston.
2	Wednesday	6 33 5 51	5 57	10 9 10 31	March 7th, C. C. P. Worcester. (Civil.)
3	Thursday	6 32 5 53	6 19	10 52 11 13	March 1st, S. J. C. Boston. (Law Term.) For Suffolk and Nantucket.
4	Friday	6 30 5 54	sets	11 29 11 45	March 14th, C. C. P. Springfield. (Civil.)
5	Saturday	6 29 5 55	6 46		March 14th, C. C. P. Taunton and Lowell. (Civil.)
6	SUNDAY	6 27 5 56	7 52	0 19 0 37	March 21st, C. C. P. Lawrence. (Civil.)
7	Monday	6 26 5 58	8 59	0 55 1 13	March 21st, C. C. P. Greenfield.
8	Tuesday	6 24 5 59	9 36	1 32 1 58	
9	Wednesday	6 23 6 0	11 14	2 14 2 36	
10	Thursday	6 21 6 1	morn	2 59 3 25	
11	Friday	6 19 6 2	0 33	3 52 4 24	
12	Saturday	6 17 6 3	1 39	4 56 5 32	
13	SUNDAY	6 15 6 5	2 45	6 9 6 47	
14	Monday	6 14 6 6	3 31	7 25 7 57	
15	Tuesday	6 12 6 7	4 16	8 29 9 2	
16	Wednesday	6 10 6 8	4 47	9 35 10 1	
17	Thursday	6 9 6 9	5 18	10 28 10 50	
18	Friday	6 7 6 10	rises	11 12 11 32	
19	Saturday	6 5 6 11	7 26	11 53	
20	SUNDAY	6 3 6 13	8 34	0 34	
21	Monday	6 2 6 14	9 42	0 55 1 16	
22	Tuesday	6 0 6 15	10 47	1 38 2 0	
23	Wednesday	5 59 6 17	11 51	2 22 2 45	
24	Thursday	5 57 6 18	morn	3 10 3 35	
25	Friday	5 55 6 19	1 12	4 1 4 28	
26	Saturday	5 53 6 20	1 58	5 1 5 33	
27	SUNDAY	5 52 6 21	2 43	6 1 6 28	
28	Monday	5 51 6 22	3 29	6 59 7 28	
29	Tuesday	5 49 6 23	3 56	7 59 8 20	
30	Wednesday	5 47 6 24	4 23	8 44 9 9	
31	Thursday	5 45 6 25	4 51	9 31 9 52	

O SQUARE THYSELF FOR USE! a stone that may
Fit in the wall is not left in the way.
Alger's Poetry of the East.

MEMORANDA FOR MARCH, 1859.

20	91	1	Clear very blustering
6	62	2	Clear pleasant
14		3	
21	14	4	
		5	
	446	6	cl
28	417	7	Cloudy clear ...
38	348	8	very blustering snow ...
30		9	Clear pleasant
32	1810	10	Clear very ...
26	511	11	Clear cloudy
36	412	12	Cloudy rainy day
26	513	13	Clear ... pleasant
30	414	14	Clear cloudy
40	515	15	Very rainy day and night
32	816	16	
36	6017	17	
	18	18	
		19	
		20	
		21	
		22	
		23	
		24	
		25	
		26	
		27	
		28	
		29	
		30	
		31	

APRIL, 1859.

MOON'S PHASES.

New Moon, 3d day, 5h. 33m. morning.
First Quarter, 10th day, 6h. 37m. morning.
Full Moon, 17th day, 4h. 22m. morning.
Last Quarter, 25th day, 0h. 1m. morning.

D. Mo	Days of week.	SUN Rises. Sets.	Moon rises.	HIGH WATER. Morn. Eve.	COURTS.
		h. m. h. m.	h. m.	h. m. h. m.	
1	Friday	5 43 6 26	5 1	10 14 10 33	
2	Saturday	5 41 6 27	5 24	10 51 11 10	
3	SUNDAY	5 40 6 28	sets	11 28 11 46	
4	Monday	5 38 6 29	7 59		
5	Tuesday	5 36 6 30	9 10	0 26 0 47	April 5th, C. C. P. Barnstable.
6	Wednesday	5 34 6 31	10 21	1 9 1 32	April 11th, C. C. P. Plymouth.
7	Thursday	5 32 6 32	11 32	1 56 2 22	April 12th, S. J. C. Lowell. (Jury Term.)
8	Friday	5 30 6 33	morn	2 49 3 18	April 12th, S. J. C. Worcester. (Jury Term.)
9	Saturday	5 29 6 34	0 39	3 47 4 20	April 19th, S. J. C. Northampton. (Jury Term.)
10	SUNDAY	5 27 6 35	1 30	4 53 5 28	April 19th, S. J. C. Taunton. (Jury Term.)
11	Monday	5 25 6 36	2 7	6 4 6 38	April 25th, C. C. P. Dedham.
12	Tuesday	5 24 6 37	2 44	7 12 7 43	April 26th, S. J. C. Salem and Springfield. (J.T.)
13	Wednesday	5 22 6 38	3 21	8 14 8 42	
14	Thursday	5 21 6 39	3 44	9 10 9 34	
15	Friday	5 19 6 40	4 7	9 59 10 21	
16	Saturday	5 17 6 41	4 31	10 44 10 56	
17	SUNDAY	5 16 6 42	rises	11 5 11 30	
18	Monday	5 15 6 43	8 47		
19	Tuesday	5 13 6 44	9 46	0 27 0 48	
20	Wednesday	5 12 6 46	10 45	1 11 1 34	
21	Thursday	5 10 6 47	11 45	1 58 2 22	
22	Friday	5 8 6 48	morn	2 46 3 10	
23	Saturday	5 6 6 49	0 47	3 35 4 1	
24	SUNDAY	5 4 6 51	1 16	4 28 4 55	
25	Monday	5 3 6 52	1 45	5 22 5 50	
26	Tuesday	5 2 6 53	2 14	6 13 6 43	
27	Wednesday	5 1 6 54	2 42	7 9 7 35	
28	Thursday	4 59 6 56	3 0	7 59 8 23	
29	Friday	4 57 6 57	3 22	8 45 9 7	
30	Saturday	4 56 6 58	3 44	9 29 9 52	

Good striving
Brings thriving.
Better a dog who works
Than a lion who shirks.

MEMORANDA FOR APRIL, 1859.

1.
2.
3.
4.
5.
6.
7.
8.
9.
10.
11.
12.
13.
14.
15.
16.
17.
18.
19.
20.
21.
22.
23.
24.
25.
26.
27.
28.
29.
30.

MAY, 1859.

MOON'S PHASES.

New Moon, 2d day, 5h. 28m. afternoon.
First Quarter, 9th day, 0h. 15m. morning.
Full Moon, 16th day, 4h. 23m. afternoon.
Last Quarter, 24th day, 6h. 5m. afternoon.

D. Mo	Days of week.	SUN Rises.	Sets.	Moon rises.	HIGH WATER. Morn.	Eve.	COURTS.
		h. m.	h. m.	h. m.	h. m.	h. m.	
1	SUNDAY	4 54	6 59	4 28	10 14	10 37	
2	Monday	4 53	7 0	sets	10 58	11 26	
3	Tuesday	4 51	7 1	8 3	11 42		
4	Wednesday	4 50	7 2	9 11		0 29	
5	Thursday	4 49	7 3	10 19	0 54	1 21	
6	Friday	4 48	7 4	11 28	1 48	2 17	
7	Saturday	4 47	7 5	morn	2 46	3 14	May 3d, Superior Court for County of Suffolk, Boston.
8	SUNDAY	4 46	7 6	0 14	3 43	4 14	May 3d, S. J. C. Barnstable, for Barnstable and Dukes. (Jury Term.)
9	Monday	4 45	7 7	0 49	4 45	5 16	May 9th, C. C. P. Worcester. (Criminal.)
10	Tuesday	4 44	7 8	1 16	5 48	6 18	May 10th, S. J. C. Lenox and Plymouth. (Jury Term.)
11	Wednesday	4 43	7 9	1 43	6 48	7 16	May 16th, C. C. P. Springfield. (Criminal.)
12	Thursday	4 42	7 10	2 9	7 45	8 11	May 23d, C. C. P. Newburyport. (Criminal.)
13	Friday	4 41	7 11	2 38	8 37	9 2	May 30th, C. C. P. Edgartown.
14	Saturday	4 40	7 12	3 7	9 27	9 50	
15	SUNDAY	4 39	7 13	3 35	10 14	10 57	
16	Monday	4 38	7 14	rises	11 0	11 22	
17	Tuesday	4 37	7 15	8 46	11 44		
18	Wednesday	4 36	7 16	9 42		0 27	
19	Thursday	4 35	7 17	10 38	0 51	1 15	
20	Friday	4 35	7 18	11 22	1 38	2 1	
21	Saturday	4 34	7 19	11 56	2 24	2 47	
22	SUNDAY	4 33	7 20	morn	3 9	3 31	
23	Monday	4 32	7 21	0 23	3 53	4 16	
24	Tuesday	4 31	7 22	0 45	4 40	5 4	
25	Wednesday	4 30	7 23	1 7	5 27	5 52	
26	Thursday	4 29	7 24	1 28	6 17	6 42	
27	Friday	4 28	7 25	1 50	7 7	7 33	
28	Saturday	4 28	7 26	2 12	7 58	8 23	
29	SUNDAY	4 27	7 27	2 23	8 48	9 14	
30	Monday	4 26	7 28	3 5	9 40	10 6	
31	Tuesday	4 25	7 29	3 17	10 32	10 59	

Mahomedans say that one hour of justice is worth seventy years of prayer. One act of charity is worth a century of eloquence.

MEMORANDA FOR MAY, 1859.

1.
2.
3.
4.
5.
6.
7.
8.
9.
10.
11.
12.
13.
14.
15.
16.
17.
18.
19.
20.
21.
22.
23.
24.
25.
26.
27.
28.
29.
30.
31.

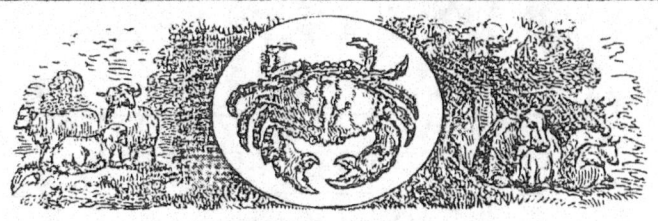

JUNE, 1859.

MOON'S PHASES.

New Moon, 1st day, 2h. 26m. morning.
First Quarter, 7th day, 6h. 3m. afternoon.
Full Moon, 15th day, 5h. 34m. morning.
Last Quarter, 23d day, 9h. 48m. morning.
New Moon, 30th day, 9h. 57m. morning.

D. Mo	Days of week.	SUN Rises.	Sets.	Moon sets.	HIGH WATER. Morn.	Eve.	COURTS.
1	Wednesday	4 25	7 29	sets	11 25	11 52	
2	Thursday	4 24	7 30	9 13			
3	Friday	4 24	7 30	9 46	0 47	1 15	
4	Saturday	4 23	7 31	10 19	1 44	2 11	
5	SUNDAY	4 23	7 32	10 52	2 37	3 5	
6	Monday	4 23	7 33	11 26	3 31	3 57	June 6th, C.C.P. Northampton (Civil) and Nantucket.
7	Tuesday	4 22	7 33	morn	4 24	4 56	June 6th, C.C.P. Concord. (Civil.)
8	Wednesday	4 22	7 34	0 16	5 19	5 46	
9	Thursday	4 22	7 35	0 39	6 14	6 41	
10	Friday	4 22	7 35	1 2	7 8	7 35	
11	Saturday	4 22	7 36	1 26	8 3	8 31	
12	SUNDAY	4 22	7 37	1 59	8 58	9 24	
13	Monday	4 22	7 37	2 32	9 50	10 15	June 13th, C.C.P. Springfield. (Civil.)
14	Tuesday	4 22	7 38	3 6	10 40	11 3	June 13th, C.C.P. New Bedford.
15	Wednesday	4 22	7 38	rises	11 27	11 48	June 13th, C.C.P. Northampton. (Criminal.)
16	Thursday	4 22	7 38	8 17			
17	Friday	4 23	7 39	9 8	0 32	0 54	
18	Saturday	4 23	7 39	9 59	1 15	1 37	
19	SUNDAY	4 23	7 39	10 50	1 57	2 18	
20	Monday	4 23	7 39	11 11	2 37	2 57	June 20th, C.C.P. Salem. (Civil.)
21	Tuesday	4 23	7 39	11 28	3 17	3 37	June 20th, C.C.P. Worcester. (Civil.)
22	Wednesday	4 23	7 40	11 50	3 57	4 17	
23	Thursday	4 23	7 40	morn	4 39	5 1	
24	Friday	4 24	7 40	0 10	5 26	5 51	
25	Saturday	4 24	7 40	0 37	6 18	6 45	
26	SUNDAY	4 24	7 40	1 4	7 13	7 42	June 27th, C.C.P. Concord (Criminal) and Lenox (Civil.)
27	Monday	4 25	7 40	1 31	8 13	8 45	
28	Tuesday	4 25	7 40	2 20	9 15	9 46	
29	Wednesday	4 25	7 40	3 9	10 17	10 48	
30	Thursday	4 25	7 40	sets	11 16	11 44	

A jewel is a jewel still, though lying in the dust;
And sand is sand, though up to Heaven by the tempest thrust.
Alger's Poetry of the East.

MEMORANDA FOR JUNE, 1859.

1.
2.
3.
4.
5.
6.
7.
8.
9.
10.
11.
12.
13.
14.
15.
16.
17.
18.
19.
20.
21.
22.
23.
24.
25.
26.
27.
28.
29.
30.

JULY, 1859.

MOON'S PHASES.

First Quarter, 7th day, 1h. 10m. morning.
Full Moon, 14th day, 8h. 9m. afternoon.
Last Quarter, 22d day, 10h. 42m. afternoon.
New Moon, 29th day, 5h. 0m. afternoon.

D. Mo	Days of week.	SUN Rises.	SUN Sets.	Moon sets.	HIGH WATER. Morn.	HIGH WATER. Eve.	COURTS.
		h. m	h. m.	h. m.	h. m.	h. m.	
1	Friday	4 26	7 40	8 43	0 5	0 5	
2	Saturday	4 26	7 40	9 14	0 30	1 0	
3	SUNDAY	4 27	7 40	9 45	1 30	1 55	
4	Monday	4 27	7 39	10 16	2 20	2 43	
5	Tuesday	4 28	7 39	10 47	3 6	3 25	
6	Wednesday	4 29	7 39	11 7	3 53	4 18	
7	Thursday	4 29	7 39	11 28	4 44	5 11	
8	Friday	4 30	7 38	11 55	5 38	6 7	
9	Saturday	4 31	7 38	morn	6 36	7 6	July 5th, Superior Court for Suffolk at Boston.
10	SUNDAY	4 31	7 38	0 26	7 36	8 4	July 5th, S. J. C. Nantucket. (Jury Term.)
11	Monday	4 32	7 37	1 11	8 33	9 1	July 4th, C. C. P. Lenox. (Criminal.)
12	Tuesday	4 33	7 37	1 56	9 29	9 55	
13	Wednesday	4 34	7 36	2 42	10 22	10 45	
14	Thursday	4 35	7 36	rises	11 9	11 30	
15	Friday	4 36	7 35	8 29	11 51		
16	Saturday	4 37	7 35	8 48		0 30	
17	SUNDAY	4 38	7 34	9 7	0 49	1 8	
18	Monday	4 39	7 33	9 26	1 26	1 44	
19	Tuesday	4 39	7 32	9 41	2 2	2 20	
20	Wednesday	4 40	7 32	9 57	2 37	2 57	
21	Thursday	4 41	7 31	10 13	3 16	3 36	
22	Friday	4 42	7 30	11 29	3 56	4 17	
23	Saturday	4 43	7 29	11 56	4 43	5 9	
24	SUNDAY	4 44	7 28	morn	5 38	6 7	
25	Monday	4 45	7 27	0 53	6 40	7 13	
26	Tuesday	4 46	7 26	1 36	7 48	8 24	
27	Wednesday	4 47	7 25	2 29	8 59	9 34	
28	Thursday	4 48	7 24	3 3	10 5	10 37	
29	Friday	4 49	7 23	sets	11 5	11 33	
30	Saturday	4 50	7 22	7 49		11 57	
31	SUNDAY	4 51	7 21	8 17	0 21		

Who learns and learns, but acts not what he knows,
Is one who ploughs and ploughs, but never sows.

9	
10	
11	
12	
13	
14	
15	
16	
17	
18	
19	
20	
21	
22	
23	
24	
25	
26	
27	
28	
29	
30	
31	

New Moon, 26th day, 9h. 12m. morning.

D. Mo	Days of week.	SUN Rises.	SUN Sets.	Moon rises.	HIGH WATER. Morn.	HIGH WATER. Eve.	COURTS.
		h. m.	h. m.	h. m.	h. m.	h. m.	
1	Thursday	5 24	6 36	8 26	2 8	2 31	Sept. 5th, C. C. P. Lowell. (Civil.) Sept. 6th, Superior Court for Suffolk Co., Boston. Sept. 6th, S.J.C. Springfield. (J.T.); C.C.P. Barnstable. Sept. 12th, C. C. P. Taunton. Sept. 13th, S.J.C. Lenox (L.T.) and Greenfield (J.T.). Sept. 19th, C.C.P. Newburyport and Dedham. (Civil.) Sept. 26th, S.J.C. Northampton (Law Term) for the Counties of Hampshire, Franklin, and Hampden. Sept. 26th, C. C. P. Edgartown.
2	Friday	5 25	6 35	9 6	2 54	3 18	
3	Saturday	5 26	6 33	9 47	3 43	4 11	
4	SUNDAY	5 27	6 31	10 27	4 39	5 10	
5	Monday	5 28	6 30	11 25	5 41	6 13	
6	Tuesday	5 29	6 28	morn	6 45	7 16	
7	Wednesday	5 30	6 26	0 29	7 47	8 14	
8	Thursday	5 31	6 25	1 29	8 42	9 6	
9	Friday	5 32	6 23	2 32	9 31	9 57	
10	Saturday	5 33	6 21	3 24	10 14	10 33	
11	SUNDAY	5 34	6 19	4 37	10 53	11 10	
12	Monday	5 35	6 17	rises	11 27	11 44	
13	Tuesday	5 36	6 16	6 47			
14	Wednesday	5 37	6 14	7 5	0 16	0 36	
15	Thursday	5 39	6 12	7 24	0 54	1 13	
16	Friday	5 40	6 11	8 2	1 34	1 55	
17	Saturday	5 41	6 9	8 40	2 16	2 37	
18	SUNDAY	5 42	6 7	9 37	3 2	3 28	
19	Monday	5 43	6 5	10 34	3 57	4 27	
20	Tuesday	5 44	6 4	11 33	5 2	5 37	
21	Wednesday	5 45	6 2	morn	6 13	6 49	
22	Thursday	5 46	6 0	0 50	7 24	8 0	
23	Friday	5 47	5 58	2 7	8 32	9 3	
24	Saturday	5 48	5 56	3 24	9 31	9 58	
25	SUNDAY	5 49	5 54	4 43	10 23	10 48	
26	Monday	5 50	5 52	sets	11 9	11 31	
27	Tuesday	5 51	5 50	5 56	11 51		
28	Wednesday	5 53	5 49	6 29		0 34	
29	Thursday	5 54	5 46	7 3	0 56	1 19	
30	Friday	5 55	5 45	7 36	1 42	2 4	

"How," said Mr. M. to Mr. Y., "do you accomplish so much in so short a time? Have you any particular plan?" "I have. When I have anything to do, I go and do it."

MEMORANDA FOR SEPTEMBER, 1859.

1.
2.
3.
4.
5.
6.
7.
8.
9.
10.
11.
12.
13.
14.
15.
16.
17.
18.
19.
20.
21.
22.
23.
24.
25.
26.
27.
28.
29.
30.

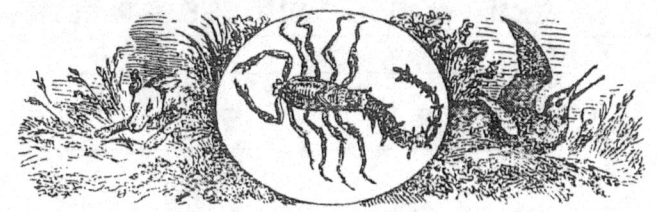

OCTOBER, 1859.

MOON'S PHASES.

First Quarter, 3d day, 3h. 48m. afternoon.
Full Moon, 11th day, 7h. 8m. afternoon.
Last Quarter, 19th day, 0h. 59m. morning.
New Moon, 25th day, 7h. 49m. afternoon.

D. Mo	Days of week.	SUN Rises.	SUN Sets.	Moon rises.	HIGH WATER. Morn.	HIGH WATER. Eve.	COURTS.
		h. m.	h. m.	h. m.	h. m.	h. m	
1	Saturday	5 56	5 43	8 51	2 30	2 55	
2	SUNDAY	5 57	5 42	10 2	3 21	3 48	
3	Monday	5 58	5 40	11 13	4 15	4 44	
4	Tuesday	5 59	5 39	morn	5 14	5 44	
5	Wednesday	6 1	5 38	0 25	6 14	6 42	
6	Thursday	6 2	5 36	1 31	7 10	7 36	
7	Friday	6 3	5 34	2 36	8 3	8 27	Oct. 3d, C. C. P. Springfield (Civil); Nantucket.
8	Saturday	6 4	5 33	3 42	8 51	9 12	Oct. 4th, S. J. C. Worcester. (Law Term.)
9	SUNDAY	6 5	5 31	4 48	9 33	9 53	Oct. 10th, C. C. P. Lawrence. (Criminal.)
10	Monday	6 6	5 29	5 54	10 13	10 32	Oct. 18th, S. J. C. Cambridge. (Law Term.)
11	Tuesday	6 8	5 28	rises	10 52	11 11	Oct. 17th, C. C. P. Lowell and Worcester. (Criminal.)
12	Wednesday	6 9	5 26	5 38	11 30	11 49	Oct. 17th, C. C. P. Northampton. (Civil.)
13	Thursday	6 10	5 24	6 22			Oct. 24th, C. C. P. Lenox and Fitchburg. (Civil.)
14	Friday	6 11	5 22	7 6	0 28	0 49	Oct. 25th, S. J. C. Plymouth (Law Term) for the Counties of Bristol, Plymouth, Barnstable, and Dukes.
15	Saturday	6 12	5 20	7 51	1 12	1 35	
16	SUNDAY	6 13	5 19	8 46	2 1	2 26	
17	Monday	6 14	5 17	9 41	2 54	3 21	
18	Tuesday	6 15	5 16	10 35	3 51	4 22	
19	Wednesday	6 16	5 14	11 51	4 55	5 28	
20	Thursday	6 18	5 13	morn	6 1	6 35	
21	Friday	6 19	5 11	1 8	7 7	7 39	
22	Saturday	6 21	5 10	2 22	8 7	8 33	
23	SUNDAY	6 22	5 8	3 30	9 2	9 28	
24	Monday	6 23	5 7	4 51	9 52	10 17	
25	Tuesday	6 24	5 5	sets	10 40	11 3	
26	Wednesday	6 25	5 4	4 52	11 25	11 48	
27	Thursday	6 27	5 2	5 36			
28	Friday	6 28	5 1	6 20	0 33	0 56	
29	Saturday	6 29	5 0	7 5	1 20	1 45	
30	SUNDAY	6 31	4 58	7 48	2 9	2 36	
31	Monday	6 32	4 57	8 22	3 3	3 27	

Avoid a villain as you would a brand
Which lighted burns, extinguished smuts the hand.

Alger's Poetry of the East.

MEMORANDA FOR OCTOBER, 1859.

1
2
3
4
5
6
7
8
9
10
11
12
13
14
15
16
17
18
19
20
21
22
23
24
25
26
27
28
29
30
31

NOVEMBER, 1859.

MOON'S PHASES.

First Quarter, 2d day, 11h. 34m. morning.
Full Moon, 10th day, 9h. 21m. morning.
Last Quarter, 17th day, 8h. 23m. morning.
New Moon, 24th day, 8h. 59m. morning.

D. Mo	Days of week.	SUN Rises.	Sets.	Moon sets.	HIGH WATER. Morn.	Eve.	COURTS.
		h. m.	h. m.	h. m.	h. m.	h. m.	
1	Tuesday	6 33	4 55	10 8	3 49	4 14	
2	Wednesday	6 34	4 54	11 9	4 40	5 6	
3	Thursday	6 35	4 53	morn	5 33	5 58	
4	Friday	6 36	4 52	0 4	6 24	6 49	
5	Saturday	6 37	4 50	1 12	7 14	7 8	
6	SUNDAY	6 39	4 49	2 15	8 2	8 23	
7	Monday	6 40	4 48	3 18	8 48	9 9	
8	Tuesday	6 41	4 47	4 21	9 31	9 53	
9	Wednesday	6 43	4 45	5 25	10 16	10 38	Nov. 1st, Superior Court for Suffolk, Boston.
10	Thursday	6 44	4 44	rises	11 1	11 23	Nov. 1st, S. J. C. Dedham. (Law Term.)
11	Friday	6 45	4 43	5 19	11 45		Nov. 8th, S. J. C. Salem. (Law Term.)
12	Saturday	6 47	4 42	6 23		0 33	Nov. 14th, C. C. P. Greenfield.
13	SUNDAY	6 48	4 41	7 26	0 58	1 26	Nov. 8th, S. J. C. New Bedford. (Jury Term.)
14	Monday	6 49	4 40	8 30	1 53	2 20	Nov. 15th, S. J. C. Boston. (Jury Term.)
15	Tuesday	6 51	4 39	9 43	2 47	3 15	
16	Wednesday	6 52	4 38	10 56	3 43	4 11	
17	Thursday	6 53	4 37	morn	4 41	5 10	
18	Friday	6 54	4 36	0 9	5 39	6 9	
19	Saturday	6 55	4 36	1 22	6 38	7 7	
20	SUNDAY	6 56	4 35	2 35	7 35	8 4	
21	Monday	6 58	4 34	3 47	8 31	8 58	
22	Tuesday	6 59	4 33	4 59	9 24	9 50	
23	Wednesday	7 0	4 33	6 12	10 15	10 40	
24	Thursday	7 1	4 32	sets	11 4	11 28	
25	Friday	7 3	4 31	4 51	11 51		
26	Saturday	7 4	4 30	5 52		0 37	
27	SUNDAY	7 5	4 29	6 53	1 2	1 25	
28	Monday	7 6	4 29	7 54	1 48	2 11	
29	Tuesday	7 7	4 28	8 57	2 34	2 55	
30	Wednesday	7 9	4 28	10 1	3 17	3 39	

Ten poor men sleep in peace on one straw heap, as Saadi sings;
But the immensest empire is too narrow for two kings.
Alger's Poetry of the East.

MEMORANDA FOR NOVEMBER, 1859.

1.
2.
3.
4.
5.
6.
7.
8.
9.
10.
11.
12.
13.
14.
15.
16.
17.
18.
19.
20.
21.
22.
23.
24.
25.
26.
27.
28.
29.
30.

DECEMBER, 1859.

MOON'S PHASES.

First Quarter, 2d day, 9h. 5m. morning.
Full Moon, 9th day, 10h. 29m. afternoon.
Last Quarter, 16th day, 4h 32m. afternoon.
New Moon, 24th day, 1h. 3m. morning.

D. Mo	Days of week.	SUN Rises. Sets.	Moon sets.	HIGH WATER. Morn. Eve.	COURTS.
		h. m. h. m.	h. m.	h. m. h. m.	
1	Thursday	7 10 4 29	11 1	4 0 4 22	
2	Friday	7 11 4 29	morn	4 45 5 8	
3	Saturday	7 12 4 28	0 3	5 31 5 55	
4	SUNDAY	7 13 4 28	1 2	6 19 6 43	
5	Monday	7 14 4 28	2 13	7 8 7 34	
6	Tuesday	7 15 4 28	3 17	8 0 8 26	
7	Wednesday	7 16 4 28	4 21	8 52 9 18	
8	Thursday	7 17 4 28	5 25	9 45 10 12	
9	Friday	7 18 4 28	rises	10 39 11 6	Dec. 5th, C. C. P. (Criminal.) Worcester. (Civil.) Springfield. (Criminal.) Plymouth. Dec. 12th, C. C. P. (Civil.) Cambridge. (Civil.) Dec. 12th, C. C. P. (Civil.) New Bedford. Dec. 19th, C. C. P. (Civil.) Salem. (Criminal.) Dedham. Northampton.
10	Saturday	7 19 4 28	5 3	11 32 11 58	
11	SUNDAY	7 20 4 28	6 17		
12	Monday	7 21 4 28	7 31	0 50 1 17	
13	Tuesday	7 22 4 28	8 44	1 43 2 10	
14	Wednesday	7 22 4 29	9 56	2 35 3 0	
15	Thursday	7 23 4 29	11 8	3 25 3 50	
16	Friday	7 24 4 29	morn	4 16 4 42	
17	Saturday	7 24 4 29	0 26	5 10 5 38	
18	SUNDAY	7 25 4 29	1 38	6 7 6 31	
19	Monday	7 25 4 29	2 50	7 6 7 35	
20	Tuesday	7 26 4 29	4 2	8 3 8 31	
21	Wednesday	7 26 4 29	5 12	9 59 9 27	
22	Thursday	7 27 4 30	6 15	10 54 10 22	
23	Friday	7 27 4 30	7 18	11 47 11 12	
24	Saturday	7 28 4 30	sets	11 35 11 59	
25	SUNDAY	7 28 4 30	5 41		
26	Monday	7 29 4 31	6 45	0 41 1 2	
27	Tuesday	7 29 4 31	7 49	1 23 1 43	
28	Wednesday	7 29 4 32	8 52	2 3 2 22	
29	Thursday	7 29 4 33	9 51	2 4 3 0	
30	Friday	7 30 4 34	10 50	3 18 3 37	
31	Saturday	7 30 4 35	11 50	3 57 4 17	

There is no ointment for the wolf's sore eyes
Like clouds of dust that from the sheep arise.
Alger's Poetry of the East.

MEMORANDA FOR DECEMBER, 1859.

1
2
3
4
5
6
7
8
9
10
11
12
13
14
15
16
17
18
19
20
21
22
23
24
25
26
27
28
29
30
31

W. S. DAMRELL & FRANK C. MOORE,
Book, Job, and Card Printers,
16 DEVONSHIRE ST., BOSTON.

1860 COUNTING-HOUSE ALMANAC. 1860

	Su.	Mo.	Tu.	We	Th.	Fri.	Sat	Su.	Mo.	Tu.	We	Th.	Fri.	Sat	
JAN.	1	2	3	4	5	6	7	1	2	3	4	5	6	7	**JULY.**
	8	9	10	11	12	13	14	8	9	10	11	12	13	14	
	15	16	17	18	19	20	21	15	16	17	18	19	20	21	
	22	23	24	25	26	27	28	22	23	24	25	26	27	28	
	29	30	31	..	..	..	..	29	30	31	..	..	..	..	
FEB.	..	..	..	1	2	3	4	..	..	..	1	2	3	4	**AUGUST.**
	5	6	7	8	9	10	11	5	6	7	8	9	10	11	
	12	13	14	15	16	17	18	12	13	14	15	16	17	18	
	19	20	21	22	23	24	25	19	20	21	22	23	24	25	
	26	27	28	29	..	..	..	26	27	28	29	30	31	..	
MARCH.	..	..	..	..	1	2	3	..	..	..	..	..	..	1	**SEPT.**
	4	5	6	7	8	9	10	2	3	4	5	6	7	8	
	11	12	13	14	15	16	17	9	10	11	12	13	14	15	
	18	19	20	21	22	23	24	16	17	18	19	20	21	22	
	25	26	27	28	29	30	31	23	24	25	26	27	28	29	
APRIL.	..	..	..	..	..	..	..	30	..	..	..	..	..	..	**OCT.**
	1	2	3	4	5	6	7	..	1	2	3	4	5	6	
	8	9	10	11	12	13	14	7	8	9	10	11	12	13	
	15	16	17	18	19	20	21	14	15	16	17	18	19	20	
	22	23	24	25	26	27	28	21	22	23	24	25	26	27	
	29	30	..	..	..	..	..	28	29	30	31	..	..	..	
MAY.	..	..	1	2	3	4	5	..	..	..	..	1	2	3	**NOV.**
	6	7	8	9	10	11	12	4	5	6	7	8	9	10	
	13	14	15	16	17	18	19	11	12	13	14	15	16	17	
	20	21	22	23	24	25	26	18	19	20	21	22	23	24	
	27	28	29	30	31	..	..	25	26	27	28	29	30	..	
JUNE.	..	..	..	..	..	1	2	..	..	..	..	..	..	1	**DEC.**
	3	4	5	6	7	8	9	2	3	4	5	6	7	8	
	10	11	12	13	14	15	16	9	10	11	12	13	14	15	
	17	18	19	20	21	22	23	16	17	18	19	20	21	22	
	24	25	26	27	28	29	30	23	24	25	26	27	28	29	
	..	..	..	..	..	..	..	30	31	..	..	..	..	..	

GENERAL EVENTS IN 1856.

JANUARY.

2d. A severe shock of an earthquake is felt at San Francisco.

5th. A violent snow storm extends from Washington, D. C., to Halifax, N. S. Travelling on the railroads is much obstructed for some days.

6th. The packet ship St. Dennis founders at sea. The captain, three passengers, and part of the crew are lost. The survivors are picked up by the ship Naples, Capt. Lovell, and conveyed to New York.

8th. The Potomac river is frozen across from shore to shore; many persons cross on foot with safety.

11th. A meeting is held in New York by the Emmett Monument Association, at the Tabernacle, the object of which is to procure the liberation of Ireland from British rule, by the force of arms.

18th. The Ladies' Seminary, at Auburn, N. Y., is destroyed by fire.

21st. The casting of the collossal statue of Washington, modelled by H. K. Brown, is completed at Chicopee, at the foundry of the Ames Company.

23d. The President of Nicaragua suspends all official communication with Mr. Wheeler, minister resident of the United States, because the Government of the United States, " in opposition to the sentiment of that country," have refused to receive Parker H. French, the accredited minister to that country.

24th. President Pierce communicates a message to Congress upon the affairs of Kansas, giving his statement of the causes of the difficulties there.

29th. In Washington, D. C., Albert Rust, member of Congress, from Arkansas, assaults Horace Greely, the editor of the Tribune, and beats him with his fist in the capitol grounds, and again near National Hotel.

30th. The Chilian war steamer Cassado foundered at sea, and over 300 persons perished.

30th. The Southern Commercial Convention assembled at Richmond, Va.

FEBRUARY.

2d. Nathaniel P. Banks, Jr., of Massachusetts, is elected Speaker of the House of Representatives, after a contest of nine weeks.

3d. In Kansas the thermometer sinks as low as 30 deg. below zero. The cold extends over the United States, and in some parts to a degree unknown before.

5th. A destructive fire consumes Patten's building, in Manchester, N. H., which is occupied with printing offices, lawyers' offices, and stores.

6th. The ship Great Duke, of Boston, on the passage from New Orleans to Liverpool, is totally lost, at Poolslaughter bay; 29 of the crew, including the captain, are drowned, and 3, including the chief mate, are saved.

7th. There is a severe gale on the English coast, in which many vessels suffer injury, among which are several from the United States

10th. A decree is promulgated at the city of Granada, by President Rivas, claiming and annexing the whole Musquito territory as an integral portion of the State of Nicaragua, and nullifying the Kinney purchase.

11th. President Pierce issues a proclamation in regard to Kansas matters, warning all persons against unlawful combinations against the constituted authority of the territory.

15th. The United States forces in Kansas are put by the Secretary of War under the requisition of the governor of that territory.

15th. A severe shock of an earthquake is felt at San Francisco.

19th. The ship John Rutledge, from Liverpool to New York, encounters an iceberg, and is found to be in a sinking condition. Five boats leave the ship, but only one is found, which contains Thomas W. Nye, the only survivor. He was picked up by the ship Germania, Capt. Wood.

22d. The National American Convention assembles in Philadelphia, and nominates Millard Fillmore, of New York, for President, and Andrew J. Donaldson, of Tennessee, for Vice President.

24th. Owing to the breaking up of the ice in the Ohio river, six steamers and several barges were sunk, causing a great loss of property.

25th. The Peace Conference at Paris holds the first meeting, at which Count Walewski presides.

29th. Delegates from the belligerent armies in the Crimea meet to concert measures to carry out the armistice.

MARCH.

1st. Col. William H. Garland, the city treasurer of New Orleans, is found to be a defaulter to the amount of $150,000, and attempts to escape by the river, but is arrested and brought back.

1st. Hon. Geo. M. Dallas sails from New York for London, to take the place of Mr. Buchanan, as American Minister to England.

2d. A destructive earthquake occurs in the Island Great Saugor, one of the Moluccas, by which 2,806 lives are lost.

4th. The Free State Legislature of Kansas is organized at Topeka.

5th. The Covent Garden Theatre is burned.

6th. The Essex Cotton Mill, in Newburyport, is destroyed by fire.

7th. A. H. Reeder and J. H. Lane are elected U. S. Senators by the Free State Legislature at Topeka.

11th. Costa Rica declares war against Nicaragua.

15th. The steam ferry boat New Jersey, while running from Philadelphia to Camden, takes fire, is burned, and many lives are lost.

16th. The Empress Eugenie gives birth to a son.

18th. The Cunard steamer Curlew is wrecked near the Bermudas.

20th. Col. Schlessinger, with a party of Gen. Walker's men, is attacked at Santa Rosa by Gen. Mora, with 500 Costa Ricans, and entirely defeated.

25th. The Court of Appeals of New York decides the Search and Seizure clause of the New York Liquor Law to be unconstitutional.

31st. The propeller Arctic arrives at New York, after an unsuccessful search for the Pacific.

APRIL.

2d. The news of the signing of the Treaty of Peace reaches the allied armies in the Crimea.

6th. Gov. Clark, of New York, pardons Dr. Graham, who was sentenced to 7 years' imprisonment for killing Col. Loring.

7th. The steamship Adriatic, the largest steamer afloat, is launched at New York. She was modelled by George Steers, Esq.

7th. The Costa Ricans take possession of Rivas with 2000 men. On the 11th, Walker, with 600 men, attacks them, and after a contest of 17 hours, they leave the city.

12th. Gerrish Market and two adjoining buildings, in Boston, are destroyed by fire. The adjacent buildings are scorched. The steam fire engine works efficiently for 12 hours.

13th. A violent tornado visits

GENERAL EVENTS. 33

Philadelphia, and unroofs many houses.

14th. Gov. Wells, of Maine, removes Woodbury Davis from the office of Justice of the Supreme Judicial Court of Maine.

15th. An affray occurred at Panama between the American transit passengers and the natives, by which the former had thirty killed, and 40 wounded.

19th. Sheriff Jones arrests S N. Wood, in Lawrence, Kansas, but is prevented from carrying him away. He returns, April 20, with assistants to make arrests, but effects nothing. On the 23d, returns with the U. S. troops and makes arrests. 24th, while sitting in a tent, is shot at and wounded, which act is publicly condemned by the Free State men, and a reward of $500 is offered for the apprehension of the offender. 25th, Col. Sumner arrives at Lawrence with his whole command.

23d. Grand naval review takes place at Spithead, in presence of the Queen, foreign ministers, and members of Parliament. The fleet was led by Vice Admiral Sir George Seymour, in the Royal George.

29th. Proclamation of peace is made at London with the mediæval ceremonies.

MAY.

1st. A fire in the station house of the Harlem and New Haven railroad, in New York city, destroyed property to the amount of nearly $100,000.

5th. A convention of delegates from the principal Typographical Unions in the United States meet in Philadelphia, Pa.

5th. An accident on the Panama railroad occurs, by which 43 persons are killed, and 60 wounded.

8th. P. T. Herbert, member of Congress from California, kills Thomas Keating, a waiter at Willard's Hotel, at Washington.

9th. There is much excitement in Detroit, because of the arrest of persons under the "liquor law."

10th. Gov. Robinson, while leaving Kansas, is detained at Lexington, on the ground that he was fleeing the territory to avoid arrest on an indictment for treason.

14th. In San Francisco a man named Casey shoots James King, editor of the Bulletin. Casey is arrested and carried to jail. On the 18th, the Vigilance Committee go to the jail, demand Casey, and Cora, the murderer of Richardson, carry them to the committee rooms, where they are tried and sentenced to be hung on the day of the funeral of Mr. King.

14th. Padre Vigil at Washington presents his credentials, and is recognized by the President.

15th. The St. Louis City Hospital was destroyed by fire. Several of the inmates were burned to death, and others severely injured.

21st. Mr. Fillmore, in Paris, France, accepts the nomination of the American Party for President.

21st. The Emigrant Aid Society's Hotel, at Lawrence, and the Herald of Freedom Printing Office are destroyed, and houses are sacked and plundered by Sheriff Jones and his posse. Two of the pro-slavery men are killed accidentally.

22d. Chas. Sumner, Senator from Massachusetts, while seated at his desk in the Senate Chamber, engaged in writing, after the adjournment of the Senate, is assaulted and beaten to the floor by Preston S. Brooks, who is accompanied by L. M. Keitt, both members of the House, from South Carolina.

29th. Senator Wilson, in a manly, sensible letter, declines to fight a duel with Mr. Brooks.

30th. There is a storm of snow on the Baltimore and Ohio Railroad.

JUNE.

2d. The House Committees at Washington report in favor of the

GENERAL EVENTS.

expulsion of Mr. Brooks. There being at first fewer than the requisite number of votes, the House refuses to expel Mr. Brooks, upon which he defends his conduct and resigns his seat.

2d. The Democratic National Convention assembles at Cincinnati, Ohio, and June 6th, on the 17th ballot, nominated James Buchanan, of Pa., as President, and John C Breckenridge, of Ky., Vice President.

5th. The Postmaster General instructs the Postmaster of New York, whenever a letter is deposited unpaid, to send a circular to the person addressed, informing him of the fact, and that it will be forwarded on the receipt of the amount due for postage, in postage stamps.

5th. Gov. Johnston, of California, declares the city of San Francisco to be in a state of insurrection, and calls upon all persons subject to military duty to hold themselves in readiness for orders from the commander-in-chief.

6th. Osauatomie, in Kansas, is sacked. Destructive floods occur in France, especially in the neighborhood of Lyons. In some places whole villages are swept away, and many lives lost. The railway station at Tours was ten feet under water.

14th. Mr. Marcy, Secretary of State, formally notifies the Danish minister that the United States will not make forcible resistance to the collection of the Sound dues for a year from this day.

16th. The Grand Trunk Railway is opened to Guelph, 87 miles from Toronto.

17th. The National Republican Convention meets at Philadelphia, and on the first ballot John Charles Fremont of California is nominated for President, and William L. Dayton, of New Jersey, is nominated for Vice President.

19th. The new steam frigate Colorado is launched at Norfolk, Va.

24th. A destructive fire occurs in Portland, Me.

25th. Senator Wilson presents in the Senate, the memorial of the New England Emigrant Aid Society, asking compensation for their property destroyed in Lawrence.

27th. A company of emigrants from Worcester, Mass., for Kansas, are stopped on the Missouri River, and disarmed. A company from Chicago had been previously so treated, and other emigrants are subsequently detained and disarmed.

JULY.

1st. There is a heavy gale on the coast of Labrador, and 29 vessels out of a fleet of 30 are driven ashore and lost.

2d. A destructive fire occurs at St. Louis, Missouri. Six steamboats are destroyed.

3d. The House pass a bill for the admission of Kansas, with the Topeka Constitution, into the Union as a State.

4th. Both branches of the Kansas Free State Legislature meet at Topeka, but are dispersed by Col. Sumner with the United States troops.

4th. The difficulties between Spain and Mexico are peacefully arranged.

8th. Preston S. Brooks is sentenced to pay a fine of $300 for his assault upon Senator Sumner.

12th. The Submarine Telegraph cable is laid across the Gulf of St. Lawrence, Cape Redcore, Newfoundland, and Ashby Bay, Cape Breton, a distance of 85 miles, and messages are freely transmitted.

16th. A collision takes place on the North Pennsylvania road. One train is from Philadelphia with a large party of Sunday School children on board; 40 persons are killed, and many more are injured.

GENERAL EVENTS. 35

17th. The steamer Northern Indiana is burned on Lake Erie. Many passengers are lost.

17th. At Salonica, Turkey, while a fire is raging, a terrific explosion of gunpowder occurs, killing and wounding 700 persons. Among the wounded are the Russian, Dutch, and Sardinian Consuls.

21st. Mr. Burlingame, in reply to a note from Mr. Brooks, states that any difference between them can be settled on the 26th of July, at the Clifton House, Niagara Falls. Mr. Brooks declines the meeting.

27th. The steamer John Jay takes fire on Lake George, and is consumed. Several lives are lost.

28th. Preston S. Brooks and Lawrence M. Keitt are re-elected members of Congress from South Carolina.

29th. Jefferson Block, in North street, Boston, is destroyed by fire. Eighty families are burned out, and nine lives lost.

AUGUST.

1st. The House of Representatatives, by 110 yeas and 92 nays, decide that Mr. Whitfield is not entitled to a seat as delegate from Kansas; and also reject Mr. Reeder by 88 yeas to 113 nays.

6th. There have been upwards of 80 cases of yellow fever at quarantine in New York, since June 11.

10th. Last Island, a summer resort in the Gulf of Mexico, is destroyed during a terrific storm which raged three days. The island is entirely submerged, and every house on the island gives way. 173 persons are known to have perished. The effects of the storm are felt greatly at New Orleans.

12th. The Free State men in Kansas capture the town of Franklin, after a contest of a few hours.

12th. Mr. David S. Hoyt, a native of Deerfield, Mass., is brutally murdered in Kansas.

16th. F. McMullen, of Virginia and A. P. Granger, of New York, both members of Congress, had an altercation in an omnibus in Washington, D. C., and McMullen strikes Granger.

18th. The first session of the 34th Congress terminates by adjournment. The army bill fails of its passage. The President calls an extra session to meet on the 21st August.

21st. The laying of the submarine telegraphic cable to Nantucket is successfully completed.

21st. The old Charter Oak, at Hartford, Conn., fell early this morning with a tremendous crash. Crowds of citizens are visiting the ruins, each one bearing away a portion of the venerable tree. A dirge was played at noon over the fallen tree, and the bells of the city tolled at sundown.

25th. The first anniversary of the opening of the Tufts College in Somerville, was celebrated in that town, with appropriate exercises.

27th. The New Industrial School for Girls at Lancaster is opened.

28th. Advices from California state that Brace and Hetherington, two murderers, were tried and executed on 29th inst., by the Vigilance Committee. Several thousand troops were under arms in the vicinity of the gallows.

30th. The extra session of Congress, called by the President, to meet on the 21st, adjourn to-day, the House having agreed to the Senate amendment, striking out the Kansas proviso in the army, by 101 yeas to 97 nays.

SEPTEMBER.

2d. Telegraphic advices from Kansas announce that Gov. Shannon has declared Kansas to be in a state of insurrection, and called upon law-abiding citizens for assistance.

6th. Late intelligence from Kansas states that Free State settlers are

GENERAL EVENTS.

driven from their claims by the invaders, and that all the Free State men have been driven from Leavenworth at the point of the bayonet.

8th. The President announces his intention to obtain order and quiet in the Territory, and a requisition for a militia force is made upon the governors of Kentucky and Illinois.

9th. The late election in Maine results in the election of Hamblin, the Republican candidate for governor, by over twenty thousand majority.

12th. Hon. Anson Burlingame, M. C., is made the subject of a public reception at the Tremont Temple, Boston.

17th. The bronze statue of Benjamin Franklin is inaugurated with much eclat in Boston.

17th. A Whig National Convention meet in Baltimore. The nomination of Millard Fillmore for the Presidency is endorsed. The convention comprise delegates from twenty-six States.

20h. Gov. Geary, the new governor of Kansas, in his inaugural address promises to do justice to all, without regard to party considerations.

24th. A distressing occurrence happened on Lake Michigan,— the burning of the steamboat Niagara. There were about 160 passengers on board, of whom 50 or 60 are lost.

27th. Three Frenchmen are arrested in New York, being guilty of swindling the Northern Railway of France to the amount of nearly three millions of francs.

29th. Advices from Kansas state that 3000 invaders from Missouri made an attack upon Lawrence on the 19th inst., and were dispersed by Gov. Geary.

30th. An important arrest of seventy-eight gamblers was made in Boston last evening.

OCTOBER.

5th. Four riots occur in Baltimore, caused by a rumor that the democrats had imported some New York roughs to do the fighting at the polls next Wednesday. Fire arms are freely used, though but one man is killed. Two political headquarters are mobbed.

7th. The Fourth annual fair of the U. S. Agricultural Society opens successfully at Philadelphia, and continues one week.

9th. Geo. Peabody, Esq., the eminent London banker, after an absence of more than twenty years, visits his native town of Danvers, and is cordially welcomed by a public reception.

10th Gov. Geary officially proclaims peace in Kansas Territory.

13th. The State election in Pennsylvania takes place. Victory is claimed and congratulated upon by both parties, but the election finally results by a small majority in favor of the democrats. This State has been the battle ground of the present presidential campaign, wherein much effort and money have been expended.

21st. A grand Horse Show opens under favorable auspices on the ground of the U. S. Agricultural Society, Boston.

28d. Intelligence from Nicaragua indicates that a severe battle has been fought there, in which Gen. Walker was victorious.

NOVEMBER.

3d. Hon Charles Sumner receives a public reception in Boston, on his return home.

4th. The 18th Presidential election takes place to-day. The result is 19 States with 174 electoral votes go for Buchanan and Breckinridge; 11 States with 114 electoral votes go for Fremont and Dayton; and 1 State (Maryland), with 8 electoral votes goes for Fillmore and Donaldson. The popular vote is as fol-

GENERAL EVENTS. 37

lows:—Buchanan, 1,850,960; Fremont; 1,334,553; Fillmore, 855,960. Henry J. Gardner is again re-elected Governor of Massachusetts.

10. A disastrous fire in Warren st., New York, involves a loss of over $500,000, mostly insured.

——. Lady Byron evinces her sympathy with the Free State people of Kansas by forwarding a check for £65 to be applied to their relief.

——. The publication of the Kansas Herald of Freedom is resumed after a suspension of six months, its office having been mobbed, and its press thrown into the river by the border ruffians.

17th. Intelligence from Nicaragua states that affairs in that country are quiet. Gen. Walker waiting for recruits.

20th. Thanksgiving day is very generally observed in the South and West, also in Kansas.

23d. A large party of recruits for Gen. Walker's army in Nicaragua leave New York by the steamship Texas.

24th. A banquet in honor of the re-election of Hon. Anson Burlingame to the U. S. House of Representatives is held at Faneuil Hall.

DECEMBER.

1st. The second session of the 34th Congress convenes. The first debate is upon the admission of Mr. Whitfield as delegate from Kansas. After a long discussion, the House refuses to admit, 94 to 104.

1st. The new missionary brig, Morning Star, sails from Boston on her first cruise, destined for the Sandwich Islands.

3d. The electoral college of Massachusetts meet at the State House, and cast the unanimous electoral vote of the State for Fremont and Dayton.

5th. The jury in the case of Baker, on trial for the murder of William Poole, in New York, being unable to agree upon a verdict, are discharged. They stand 6 to 6.

8th. Municipal elections occur in six of the cities of Massachusetts. Alexander H. Rice is re-elected Mayor of Boston.

——. Considerable excitement exists in various parts of the South concerning rumored insurrections of the slaves. A number of supposed ringleaders are seized and executed.

13th. The news from Nicaragua is important. Gen. Walker is reported to have gained decisive victories, both by land and sea, over the Costa Ricans.

15th. A terrific gale passes over a part of New York State. One of the towers at Lundy's Lane is blown over, and great fears were entertained for the safety of the Suspension Bridge.

15th. Mr Galen C. Walker, Deputy Warden of the State Prison at Charlestown, is brutally murdered by James Magee, one of the convicts under his charge.

18th. Another report from Nicaragua states that Gen. Walker was experiencing reverses of fortune, and that his men were suffering from want and disease.

18th. Congress votes to confer medals upon Dr. Kane and his party of Arctic explorers.

22d. A bill explanatory of the resolution making General Scott Lieut. General by brevet, so as to give him the same rate of pay that was allowed to Gen. Washington, is passed by Congress.

——. Major Buford, the famous leader of the southern army of invasion in Kansas is reported to have declared that he has lost upwards of $10,000 by the *enterprise*.

29th. Another shocking murder is committed at the State Prison. Solon H. Tenney, the Warden, is stabbed by a convict by the name of Charles L. Cater, and almost instantly expires.

GENERAL EVENTS IN 1857.

JANUARY.

3d. Thalberg gives his first concert in Boston in the Music Hall.

3d. William S. Tuckerman, late Treasurer of the Eastern Railroad, is found guilty in the Municipal Court, Boston, of embezzling $2000 of the funds of that corporation. Questions of law are reserved for the Supreme Court.

6th. The Vermont State Capitol at Montpelier is destroyed by accidental fire. The building was begun in 1833 and finished in 1837, at a cost of $132,077.

7th. The Free State Legislature of Kansas meets at Topeka. Gov. Robinson having resigned, and Lieut. Governor Roberts being absent, Judge Curtis, the President of the Senate, acts as Governor. Seven members of the Legislature are arrested by the United States Marshal.

9th. Charles Sumner is re-elected by the Legislature of Massachusetts, Senator in Congress, by a vote of 333 to 12 for others.

17th—21st. A term of severe cold weather from Washington to Bangor. A snow storm prevails over Canada, New Brunswick, and within the northern United States. The railroads are blocked. The East river is frozen over.

19th. "North College," one of the buildings at Amherst College, Mass., is destroyed by fire.

23d. A destructive fire at Lee, Mass., destroys a large amount of property in the centre of the village.

23d—25th. Another severe term of cold weather. The mercury is from 12 to 24 degrees below zero throughout New England, railroads are obstructed by blowing snow, and Boston harbor is frozen over.

27th. Hon. Preston S. Brooks, of South Carolina, dies suddenly in Washington, of acute inflammation of the throat.

30th. Dr. Harvey Burdell, dentist, is found murdered in his house in Bond street, New York. There are marks of strangulation about the neck, and fifteen stabs on his body. Mrs. Cunningham, her daughters, and some of the inmates of the house are placed under arrest.

FEBRUARY.

2d. George Peabody has a "grand reception" at Baltimore, Md., by the City Government and others.

7th—8th. Great damage is done by freshets in western Massachusetts, New York, Pennsylvania, and some of the western States.

10th. Abigail Gardner, of Hingham, Mass., is arrested and brought before a magistrate, charged with the murder of her husband, Hosea J. Gardner, by poison.

10th. Hon. Albion K. Parris, a distinguished citizen of Maine, died suddenly in Portland, aged about 72 years.

12th George Peabody gives $300,000 to trustees to establish and endow an Institute in Baltimore, Md.

16th. Dr. Elisha Kent Kane dies in Havana, aged 35. The authorities of the Island attend his funeral. His country mourns his loss, and throughout its borders honors his memory.

16th. The navigation of Long Island Sound—interrupted by the ice—is resumed, the boats commencing their regular trips.

25th. The iron steamship "Le Voyageur de la Mer," built in Boston for the Pasha of Egypt, is successfully launched.

26th. Charles Sumner takes his seat in the United States Senate for the first time since the outrage upon him.

MARCH.

3d. A resolution complimentary to Speaker Banks passes the House of Representatives, by a vote of 119 to 25.

4th. James Buchanan, of Pennsylvania, is inaugurated President of the United States.

5th. The Senate of Rhode Island refused, by 2 majority, to restore capital punishment, except in case of murder committed in the State Prison.

6th. Chief Justice Taney, of the U. S. Supreme Court, delivers the opinion of the Court in the Dred Scott case. The points decided are, that Scott is not a citizen—that he was not manumitted by being taken by his master, when a slave, into the then Territory of Illinois, and that the Missouri Compromise was an act unconstitutionally passed by Congress. Justices McLean and Curtis dissented from the majority.

——. Mrs. Mary A. Patten, the heroic wife of the captain of the ship Neptune's Car, who, while her husband was prostrate with fever, and in spite of the mutinous conduct of the first officer, navigated the ship for upwards of thirty days, safely to its destination, San Francisco, is presented with $1000 by the New York underwriters.

14th. Gov. Geary resigns the governorship of Kansas. Supposed cause, neglect of the Federal administration to remove office holders who have been embarrassing to his administration.

22d. A man by the name of Waldo Wood is fatally and mysteriously stabbed, in Harrison avenue, Boston, early this morning.

23d. The act to incorporate the city of Chelsea is accepted by the voters of that town, by the decisive vote of 733 to 107.

26th. Hon. Robert J. Walker accepts the office of Governor of Kansas.

——. News from Nicaragua report Walker's position as desperate, 125 of his men having deserted in a most destitute condition. The Costa Rican government had the humanity to pay their passage from San Juan. Walker had barricaded himself at Rivas with 600 men, indifferently supplied with provisions.

3). The 19th regiment of Native Infantry is disarmed and disbanded at Barrackpore, India, for mutinous conduct. Troops are concentrated at the place to prevent an outbreak.

30. W. W. Drummond, one of the Justices of Utah Territory, resigns his Judgeship, assigning as reason the impossibility of executing the laws of Utah, and giving numerous instances of notorious violations of law and of outrages by Brigham Young and his followers.

APRIL.

11. The allies (Costa Ricans, &c.) attack Walker in his intrenchments at Rivas, but are repulsed with loss.

14. A fire in Baltimore, Md. consumes property on Charles and Lombard streets to the amount of over $400,000. Fifteen persons are buried in the ruins.

22. The U. S. steam frigate Niagara sails from New York on her trial trip, and returns April 24. The ship and her machinery work well.

27. The steamer Empire City arrives in New Orleans with 100 of Gen. Walker's men.

MAY.

1. Gen. William Walker, surrounded by the Costa Rican forces, agrees with Capt. Davis of the U. S. frigate St. Mary's to leave Nicara-

gua upon Capt. Davis's pledge of safety to him and his men; and Rivas is surrendered to Capt. Davis.

May 1. The three amendments to the Constitution of Massachusetts are adopted by the people. They provide that no person shall vote who cannot read and write; that the House of Representatives shall consist of 240 members chosen by districts; and that the Senate shall consist of 40 members, chosen from 40 single districts.

May 9. The trial of Mrs. Cunningham, in New York, for the murder of Dr. Burdell, ends by a verdict of Not Guilty.

May 9. At Meerut, India, 85 men of the cavalry corps are imprisoned for refusing to handle greased catridges. General mutiny ensues, with murder and horrible barbarity. The King of Delhi is proclaimed Sovereign of India. The mutiny is widely extended.

May 10. About sixty of the convicts at the Sing Sing prison, New York, overpower the guard, separate into two parties, and attempt to escape, but are all caught.

May 13. The 250th anniversary of the settlement of Jamestown, Va., is celebrated at that place. Ex-President Tyler delivers the oration.

May 25. The new cents are distributed from the mint in Philadelphia.

May 27. Robert J. Walker, Governor of Kansas, arrives at Lecompton, and reads his inaugural.

June. Gen. Wm. Walker arrives at New Orleans, from Nicaragua, and receives a reception from his sympathizers.

June 1. At the municipal election in Washington, D. C., there is a serious riot, occasioned chiefly by "Plug Uglies," from Baltimore. The police being overpowered, the marines are called in from the Navy Yard—are fired upon, and return the fire. Five men are killed and seventeen wounded.

June 11. Governor Robinson delivers a message to the Free State Legislature of Kansas, convened at Topeka from their adjournment in January last.

June 17. The statue of General Joseph Warren, erected on the battle ground of Bunker Hill, is inaugurated with much ceremony.

June 26. An appalling disaster occurs on the river St. Lawrence. The steamer Montreal takes fire and is destroyed. Nearly 250 passengers perish by the flames or by drowning. Among the number lost is Hon. Stephen C. Phillips of Salem. A majority of the passengers were emigrants from Scotland.

June 29. Benjamin Peirce, Louis Agassiz, B. A. Gould, Jr., and E N. Horsford, a committee appointed to investigate the controversy between the Boston Courier and Dr. H F. Gardner, in regard to "spiritual manifestations," give it as their opinion, derived from observation, that any connection with spiritualistic circles, so called, corrupts the morals and degrades the intellect."

June 30. The gun sent by the citizens of Boston to Sardinia reaches Geneva.

July 1. The number of legal voters in Massachusetts by the recent census is in round numbers 212,000.

July 4. During the display of fireworks on Boston Common a mortar bursts, killing four persons, among whom is George P. Tewksbury, late Harbor Master of Boston; others are wounded.

July 4. The corner-stone of the monument to Henry Clay is laid at Louisville, Kentucky.

July 4 There is a riot in New York City between the Five-Pointers and the Bowery Boys. Eight are killed and about thirty wounded. In minor riots throughout the city during the day, two persons are killed and from twenty to thirty badly wounded. July 5, the riots are renewed. Nine persons are taken to the hospital seriously wounded. The military are called out, quiet is restored.

July 13. There is a riot in the Seventeenth Ward of New York City between some foreigners and the Metropolitan Police. Some of the military are under arms.

July 13. Gen. Havelock defeats the rebels at Futtepore. July 16, he defeats Nena Sahib and recaptures Cawnpore, which was surrendered to Nena Sahib June 27. He finds in the city the bodies of women and children recently and most barbarously mutilated and murdered.

July 14. A mob in Powesheik County, Iowa, takes a man from the court-house, where he is about to be tried for murder, and hang him. The previous week two men, horse-thieves, were taken from the jail or court-house near Tipton and hung.

July 15. Gov. Walker, of Kansas, issues a proclamation to the people of Lawrence, censuring their conduct in forming a city charter, and threatening to employ the United States forces to prevent them from carrying it into effect.

July 16. The citizens of Rockland county, N. Y., celebrate the anniversary of the storming of Stony Point by Gen. Wayne. The corner-stone of a monument commemorative of the gallant conduct of that hero is laid with appropriate ceremonies.

July 19. The main body of troops destined for the Utah expedition, take up their line of march from Leavenworth.

July 21. The house of Ezra Taft in Uxbridge, Mass., is struck by lightning, and his daughter, 19 years of age, killed.

July 24. In Tewksbury, Mass., there is a violent and destructive tornado, which lifts a man, a horse, and wagon in the air, unroofs houses, uproots trees, and causes other damages.

July 25. A violent thunder-shower, with much wind and hail, passes over Albany, inundating a part of the city; the pavements in many streets are torn up, and deep gullies are made.

July 26. A thunder-shower of unusual violence passes over Hartford, Conn., and a very great quantity of rain falls, flooding the streets and inundating cellars.

July 31. The portions of the Atlantic Sub-marine Telegraph Cable on board the Niagara and Agamemnon are joined, and messages are sent through the distance of 2,500 miles in less than one second.

July 31. The special session of the Massachusetts Legislature, convened to district the State in accordance with the recent amendments to the Constitution, adjourn after a session of eighteen days.

August. A cane and spy-glass, formerly belonging to Washington, are sold at auction in Baltimore, for $205. They are purchased by the ladies of the Mount Vernon Association, as a gift to Edward Everett, in token of appreciation of his valuable services in aid of the objects of the association.

Aug. 3. The United States steam frigate Roanoke arrives at New York with 204 of General Walker's late army in Nicaragua, and, August 18, the steamer Tennessee brings 275 more.

Aug. 4. Mrs. Cunningham is arrested in New York for attempting to produce a false heir to the Burdell estate.

Aug. 4. A hundred Mormons, former disciples of Brigham Young, having deserted him, reach Kansas after a laborious journey of more than sixty days. They say that many more have also left Utah in disgust.

Aug. 5. The shore end of the Atlantic submarine telegraph cable

GENERAL EVENTS.

is received from the United States steam frigate Niagara, with much ceremony at Valentia Bay, Ireland, by the Lord-Lieutenant of Ireland, and is made fast.

Aug. 7. The Agamemnon and Niagara, with their attending vessels, leave Valentia Bay, the Niagara paying out the cable.

Aug. 8. During the month of July, eighty-three emigrant carrying vessels arrived at New York, bringing 27,192 emigrants, being 10,000 more than were landed here during the corresponding month of last year. Of this number, but 415 were first class passengers.

Aug. 10. A Southern Commercial Convention meets at Knoxville, Tenn., and continues in session four days. A resolution is passed by 64 yeas to 27 nays, recommending the abrogation of the 8th article of the Ashburton Treaty, which requires the United States to keep a certain naval force on the coast of Africa. Maryland, North Carolina, and Tennessee vote in the negative.

Aug. 11. The Atlantic submarine telegraph cable breaks after 335 miles have been paid out; the fracture not being "in the least degree attributable to any one connected with the Niagara."

Aug. 13. Miss Harriet G. Hosmer, the famous American sculptress, returns from Europe. One of her best works is on its way to this country, having been shipped in a sailing packet.

Aug. 14. Sir Colin Campbell, the new Commander-in-chief of the forces of India, arrives in Calcutta.

Aug. 15. A collision takes place on Long Island Sound, between the Metropolis and the propeller J. N Harris. The latter sinks in a few minutes. About fifteen lives are lost.

Aug. 15. Mr. Bostwick, late Secretary of State to Gen. Walker, states that no less than 5700 filibus-

ters have found their graves in Nicaragua.

Aug. 24. The Surrogate decides against Mrs. Cunningham's claim to the Burdell estate, and gives it to the blood relations of the deceased.

Aug. 24. The Ohio Life and Trust Company suspend payment. It is considered to be the heaviest financial calamity that has ever occurred in this country, and likely to cause great embarrassment and distress.

Aug. 24. The Vanderbilt steamer claims to be the champion of the seas, having made the voyage to Liverpool in 9 days and 1 hour. The quickest passage heretofore made was by the Persia in 9 days 1 hour and 30 minutes.

Sept. A portion of the army for Utah is retained in Kansas as a *posse comitatus* to aid in executing the laws of the alleged bogus Legislature.

Sept. 4. A fireman's muster in Worcester passes off with good success, five prizes are awarded in the following order—Torrent 5 of Manchester, N. H.; Merrimac 4 of Lowell; Torrent 6 of Roxbury; Independence 6 of North Bridgewater; and Barnicoat 11 of Boston—the greatest height played is 180 feet.

Sept. 7. In Boston the bells are rung and cannon fired at sunrise, noon, and sunset, to commemorate the centennial anniversary of the birth of Lafayette.

Sept. 7. The Free State party are victorious in the municipal election at Leavenworth, Kansas.

Sept. 12. The California steamship Central America, with 500 souls on board, founders at sea, when four days out from Havana. Forty-four passengers are rescued by the Norwegian barque Eloise, others are afterwards from time to time picked up, lastly three in a boat reduced to the point of death by starvation and thirst. About 400 are lost, among whom is her

GENERAL EVENTS.

heroic commander, Capt. Herndon. The amount of treasure lost is $1,595,000.

Sept. Financial excitements are occurring all over the country; failures, and accounts of runs on banks, are the news of the day.

Sept. 14. The steamer Norfolk, from Philadelphia, bound to Norfolk, having sprung a leak is abandoned, the passengers and crew taking to four small boats, three of which are fallen in with by the Joseph Whitney of Boston. Much credit is given Capt. Kelley, through whose noble conduct all on board are saved.

Sept. 25. The Bank of Pennsylvania suspends payment, and is followed by the Girard and Commercial Banks; there is also a heavy run on all the banks of Philadelphia, the Presidents of which meet and decide to suspend specie payment on checks and notes exceeding $10.

Sept. 26-28. Banks in various parts of the South suspend specie payment.

Sept. 28. Rhode Island Banks suspend specie payment.

Sept. 30. To relieve in a measure the financial pressure the Boston Banks unite in the policy of making discounts to the amount of ten per cent. of their capital (about $3,000,000) within five days.

Oct. 2. A large meeting of the business men of Boston and vicinity is held at the Merchan's' Exchange to devise and commend such measures as may alleviate the present pecuniary distres s.

Oct. 4. Steamer Star of the West arrives from California with $1,268,734 in specie, which tends to give encouragement to the public.

Oct. 12. The steamer Empire State, of the Fall River line to N. York, is wrecked and sunk in the night, at Hell Gate. Her passengers, including 150 ladies, are saved.

Oct. 13. The day is a very exciting one in financial matters; fifteen banks in New York city suspend.

Oct. 14. The Boston Banks suspend specie payment, and are followed by many of the country banks throughout New England. Many of the manufacturing establishments cease to run on full time.

Oct. 17. There is an improved feeling in commercial circles. The general impression is that the monetary crisis has reached its height, and that there will be a gradual restoration of confidence and buiness.

— During the past two months the increase of business of the Telegraph Companies has averaged almost 100 per cent. In one day the number of messages sent from and received in N. York city reached nearly 5000.

Oct. 18. Early this morning, Ezekiel W. Hodsdon, police officer, is shot in East Boston, while in discharge of his duty, by some person unknown.

— Advices from the Utah expedition state that they arrived at Fort Laramie September 5-7. The cattle of the government train were dying fast, and the mules were breaking down. Grass was scarce

— Gov Walker, of Kansas, throws out the illegal votes of Oxford and Johnson County precincts, and evinces a determination to have justice observed.

Nov. Advices from Utah state that the Mormons are loud in their denunciations against the U. S. Government, and that they will resist the troops to the last extremity.

Nov. 4. Hon Nathaniel P. Banks is elected Governor of Massachusetts.

Nov. 9. A negro woman named Betty, a slave, on a visit with her master's family to Lawrence, Mass., is brought before Chief Justice Shaw, Boston, on a writ of habeas corpus. Judge Shaw held an interview with her, and she preferring to return to Tennessee with her master, he announces that she is at liberty to do so.

— The unemployed in New York city congregate each day in front of the City Hall, and participate in idle and riotous demonstrations.

Nov. 11. Gen. Walker again successfully leaves the country with 300 filibusters for Nicaragua, the U. S steamer Fulton, stationed in the Mississippi river, being outwitted.

Nov. 13. Intelligence is received that the English had taken Delhi, India, after a siege of six days.

Nov. 14. Intelligence is received of the burning of three government trains, consisting of 78 wagons, by the Mormons.

— Attempts are made in England to launch the great steamer Leviathan.

Nov. 20. A public reception is given to Hon. Neal Dow, the temperance reformer, at Tremont Temple, Boston.

Nov. 25. Thanksgiving Day in Massachusetts, as well as in twenty other States.

— Gov. Walker arrives in Washington. He is opposed to the action of the Kansas Constitutional Convention; the President approves of it. Senator Douglas upholds the views of Walker.

Nov. 29. Wm. S. Tuckerman, the defaulting treasurer of the Eastern Railroad, out on bail, is detected in robbing the mail between New York and Boston.

Dec. 1. The Scots Charitable Society celebrate their two hundredth anniversary by a supper at the Revere House, Boston.

Dec. 5. The funeral of Thomas Crawford, the American sculptor, who died in London, Oct. 10, takes places in New York city.

Dec. 8-9. The President's message is communicated to Congress. Senator Douglass dissents from the views of the President on the Kansas affairs, and advocates the right of the people of Kansas to vote upon the proposed constitution.

Dec. 10. The U. S. District Attorney at New Orleans is discharged for want of diligence in preventing the escape of Gen. Walker.

Dec. 12. The Boston Banks resume specie payment.

Dec. 15. Gov. Walker, of Kansas, resigns his office.

Dec. 20. A Treasury Note Bill is passed in Congress, providing for the issue of notes to the amount of $20,000,000, of no less denomination than $100; its operations are limited to Jan. 1, 1859.

Dec. 24. A conflict occurs at Fort Scott, Kansas; five pro-slavery men are shot, and twenty Free State men are taken prisoners.

Dec. 27. Intelligence is received of the failure of Walker's last expedition. On the 8th inst., Commodore Paulding, of the U. S. frigate Wabash, landed with a force at Nicaragua and compelled Walker and his followers to surrender; he is taken to Washington as a prisoner, but is informed by Secretary Cass that he is not considered as such by the Government.

STREETS, COURTS, AND PLACES.

Aborn, from 161 Boston to Silsbee
Adams, from opp. 65 Mason
Albion, from South end of Prospect
Allen, from 17 English to Webb
Andover, fr. 24 Beckford to 8 Lynn
Andrew, fr. 18 Pleasant to Webb
Ash, from 14 Federal to 155 Bridge
Barr, from 20 Mason to 17 School
Barton court, from Barton street
Barton st. fr. 65 Bridge to Collins's cove
Barton square, fr. 15 Washington
Beach, fr. 75 Mason to North River
Beaver, from Grove to Boston
Beaver court, rear Beaver st.
Beaver lane, from 134 Boston
Becket st. from 23 Essex to 44 Derby
Becket avenue, from 25 Becket to 38 Derby
Beckford, fr. 346 Essex, to River st.
Bentley, fr. 51 Essex to 84 Derby
Blaney, fr. 47 Derby to Webb's whf.
Boston, from 410 Essex to So Danvers line
Bott's court, from 343 Essex to 18 Chestnut
Bridge, fr. Beverly bridge to North
Briggs, fr. 15 Pleasant to Webb
Broad, from 42 Summer
Brown, fr. 20 Pleasant to St. Peter
Bryant, fr. North to 48 Buffum
Buffum, from 12 Mason to Danvers line
Cabot, from Cedar to Hancock
Cambridge, from 321 Essex to 10 Broad
Carlton, fr. 33 Essex to 52 Derby
Carpenter, from 134 Federal
Cedar, fr. 58 Lafayette to Mill Pond
Cedar court, from Cedar
Central, fr. 185 Essex to Lafayette
Charter, fr. 150 Derby to Central
Cherry, from Porter to Cedar
Chestnut, fr. 34 Summer to Flint
Church, fr. 23 St. Peter to Wash.
Conant, from 56 Bridge
Congress, from 44 Harbor
Creek, from 16 Mill to 35 Summer
Crombie, fr. 277 Essex to 26 Norman
Cross, from Lemon to Conant

Cross street ct. from Cross
Curtis, fr. 89 Essex to 116 Derby
Daniels, fr. 59 Essex to the water
Dean, fr. 388 Essex to North River
Dearborn, fr 88 North to the river
Derby, from Neck to Central
Derby square, fr. 209 Essex to Front
Dodge, fr. 12 Walter to Southwick
Dodge's court, fr. 18 Lafayette
Dow, from 47 Lafayette to 14 Salem
Downing, fr. 13 Margin to Prescott
East Webb, east fr. 9 Webb
Elm, fr. 125 Essex to 162 Derby
Endicott, fr. 36 Mill to 15 Winthrop
English, fr. 13 Essex to 28 Derby
Essex, from Webb to Turnpike
Everett, fr. 55 Lafayette to Salem
Federal, fr. 23 St. Peter to 36 Boston
Federal court, fr. 91 Endicott st.
Felt, fr. Dearborn to Orne
Flint, from 389 Essex to Broad
Forrester, from 20 Essex to 14 Newbury
Fowler, from 18 Boston
Foye's court, from Webb
Franklin, from 46 North
Friend, fr. 89 Mason to North River
Front, fr. 22 Central to 12 Wash'n
Gardner, fr. 74 Lafayette to E. R.R.
Gardner court, from 14 March
Gardner street (East), fr. 70 Harbor
Gedney court, fr. 47 Summer to 20 High
Gerrish place, from 15 Essex
Goodhue, from 60 Boston to Frye's Mills
Green place, 1st west from Phelps court
Grove, from 96 Boston to junction School and Tremont
Hamilton, from 353 Essex to 22 Chestnut
Hancock, from 82 Lafayette
Hanson, from 93 Boston
Harbor, fr. 67 Mill to the water
Hardy, fr. 45 Essex to the water
Harmony, from 27 Buffum to Barr
Harrod, from Tremont to Harmony Grove
Harrison ave. fr. 6 Everett to La'rge

Hathorne, fr. 31 Broad to the water
Herbert, from 99 Essex to 128 Derby
Higginson sq. between Wash'n. st. and Derby square
High, fr. 26 Mill to 51 Summer
High street court, from 13 High
Hollingsworth Hill, on the Neck
Holly, from 98 Lafayette
Howard, fr. 20 Brown to 131 Bridge
Irving, from Grove to Harrod
Ives, fr. above 33 Dearborn to rear of the Laboratory
Ives ct. fr. 24 Brown to 38 St. Peter
Jackson place, 2d west fr. Phelps ct.
Japonica, Mason Hill
Jeffrey ct. opens 50 Washington
Laboratory, fr. 69 North to Laboratory buildings
Lafayette, fr. Central to Marblehead
Lagrange, from 69 Lafayette
Laurel, from 98 Lafayette to Linden
Lawrence place, cor. of Washington and Front
Leach, fr. 103 Lafayette street east
Lemon, from 96 Bridge street
Lemon court, from 20 Lemon
Liberty, from 141 Essex to Derby
Liberty Hill, near North and Nursery streeets
Liberty Hill Road, from 180 North
Linden, from Holly to Laurel
Lummus court, from 183 Federal
Lynde, from Wash'ton to 16 North
Lynn, from 124 Federal to 20 River
Mall, from 8 Brown to Bridge
March, from 30 Bridge
Margin, from Summer to Winthrop
Market court, from 217 Essex south
Mason, from 55 North to Grove
Mason court, from 9 Liberty
Mason Hill, on Adams, rear Mason
May, from 11 Boston to 416 Essex
May street court, from 10 May st.
Mechanic, from 72 North to Walter
Melcher court, opens 79 North
Milk, from 18 Pickman to Andrew
Mill, from 3 Norman to Lafayette
Mill street court, rear 36 Mill
Monroe, from 366 Essex to 125 Federal
Mount Vernon, from 64 Summer to 9 Winthrop
Neck, eastern section of the city

Newbury, fr. 124 Essex to 12 Brown
Nichols, from 103 Boston
Norman, fr. 1 Wash. to 29 Summer
North court, from 149 Bridge
North Pine, fr. 400 Essex to Fowler
North, fr. 310 Essex to Danvers line
Northey, from 104 Bridge
Nursery, from above 144 North
Oak, from 81 Mason to North River
Odell sq. fr. 30 North to 58 Federal
Oliver, from 6 Brown to Bridge
Orange, from 85 Essex to 114 Derby
Ord, from 3 Aborn
Orne, from 108 North to Orne's Point
Osgood, from 31 Bridge
Palfrey court, from 100 Derby
Park. from 30 Harbor
Parker's court, from 35 Pleasant
Peabody, from 25 Lafayette to 55 Harbor
Pearl, from 64 Bridge to the river
Perkins, from 57 Harbor
Phelps court, from 51 Broad to the water [line
Phillips, from Grove to So. Danvers
Pickering, from 25 Chestnut to Broad
Pickman, from 17 Winter to Webb
Pine, from 401 Essex to Warren
Pingree, from 64 Harbor
Pleasant, fr. 68 Essex to 85 Bridge
Pleasant street avenue, fr. 23 Pleasant to Winter
Pond, from 58 Mill to Mill Pond
Pope's court, from 49 Boston
Porter, fr. 48 Lafayette to Mill Pond
Porter court, from 8 Porter
Pratt, from 18 High to 30 Endicott
Pratt street court, from 4 Pratt
Prescott, from 23 Winthrop to Margin
Prince, from 34 Harbor
Proctor court, from 61 Boston
Prospect, from Nichols to Aborn
Putnam, fr. Hanson to Proctor ct.
Randall, from 83 North to Buffum
River, fr. 29 Beckford to 13 Lynn
Ropes, from 70 Mill
Rust, from 18 Federal to Bridge
Salem, from 24 Harbor to Lagrange
Salem turnpike, from 428 Essex to Lynn line

SALEM DIRECTORY.

Saunders. from 78 Bridge
School, from 105 North to Grove
Sewall, from 284 Essex to 17 Lynde
Shillaber, from Aborn, South Danvers
Silsbee, from Aborn to Washington street, Danvers
Skerry, from Bridge to North River
Southwick, from opp. 31 Dearborn to Dodge
Spring, from 28 Pleasant to Webb
St. Peter, from 170 Essex to Bridge
St. Peter court, from 4 St. Peter
Summer, fr. 384 Essex to Mill Pond
Summit, from Prospect Hill
Sutton, fr. Aborn to Salem turnpike
Thorndike, from Bridge, n. Beverly Bridge
Tremont, from junction of Grove and School to South Danvers
Turner, fr 39 Essex to Salem harbor
Union, fr. 109 Essex to South Salem
Union place, from 102 North
Upham, from 9 Dearborn to Orne
Vale, from Phelps court
Varney, from Nichols to Putnam
Ward, from 29 Lafayette to Peabody
Walnut, from 117 Essex to Charter
Walter, from Laboratory to Orne
Warren, fr. Pickering to Turnpike
Warren court, rear 57 Warren
Washington, fr. R. R. D to Bridge
Webb, from 1 Derby to 85 Bridge
West place, rear of Mansion House
Whittemore, fr. 11 Mechanic to 10 Dearborn
Williams, from 9 Brown to Bridge
Winter, fr. 5 Brown to 101 Bridge
Winthrop, fr. 19 Broad to Mill Pond
Woodbury's court, from 15 Northey

WHARVES.

Bancroft's, opens at 199 Derby
Bowker's, opens at 227 Derby
Brookhouse, opens 53 Derby
Brooks, opposite 190 Derby
Brown's, near North Bridge
Buffum's, opens at 9 and 13 Front
Burley & Briggs's, 18 to 36 Peabody
Carlton's, opens on Franklin
Central, opens at 117 Derby
Cushing's, 183 Derby
Derby, opp. Custom H., Derby st.
Dodge's, from 16 Lafayette
Faben's, opens 211 Derby
Farnham's, opens at 221 Derby
Felt's, near Orne's Point
Flint's, opens on Franklin
Frothingham's, opens at 25 Front
Hatch's, 113 Derby
Hunt's, opens at 53 Derby
Laboratory, opens on Franklin
Leech's, opens at 205 Derby
Market, opens at 19 Front
Mill, opens at Mill street
Moore's, opens 225 Derby
Naumkeag, opens on Peabody
North, near the North Bridge
Peabody's, 165 Derby, foot of Elm
Perkins, 153 Derby
Pierce's, opens at 171 Derby
Phillips, or India, opens 29 Derby
Putnam's, opens 157 Derby
Sanborn's, 115 Derby
Smith's, near Railway, South Salem
Tucker's, from 101 Derby
Ward's, 121 Derby
Waters's, opens on Franklin
Webb's, from 45 Derby
White's, foot of Carlton
Whipple's, foot of Turner
West's, opens 15 Peabody
West's, opens 215 Derby

ABBREVIATIONS.

St. street; pl. place; ct. court; sq. square: l. lane; n. near; r. rear; fr. from; ft. foot; opp. opposite; c. or cor. corner; b. or bds. boards; h. house; (B.) Boston; (Cal.) California.

HALLS, PUBLIC BUILDINGS, ETC.

Almshouse, on the Neck
Arrington building, Washington, n. Depot
Asiatic building, 32 Washington
Athenæum, in Plummer Hall
Bowker building, 150 Essex
City Fish Market, rear 21 Front
City Hall, 44 Washington
City Market, Derby square
City Mills, 35 to 43 Mill street
City Scales, Bridge, near St. Peter
City Watch House, 21 Front
Court House, Federal, cor. Wash'n
Creamer's building, 243 Essex
Custom House, 112 Derby
East India Marine Hall, 165 Essex
Essex Institute, in Plummer Hall
Franklin Market, 14 Newbury
Franklin building, Newbury, cor. Essex
Frye's Mills, junction of Goodhue & Beaver
Hamilton Hall, Cambridge, corner Chestnut
Lyceum Hall, 35 Church
Lynde Hall, 157 Essex
Mechanic Hall, 285 Essex
Museum, 165 Essex
Nonantum Hall, 47 Warren
Perkins Hall, in Franklin building
Phœnix building, Lafayette, corner Front
Phœnix Hall, in Phœnix building
Plummer Hall, 134 Essex
Post Office, 32 Washington
Town Hall, Derby square

BOUNDARIES OF WARDS.

WARD 1. That portion of the city south of Essex street, east of Washington street, excepting South Salem.
WARD 2. All north of Essex street, east of Washington street.
WARD 3. All west or south of Washington, Essex, and Boston streets, as far as the town bridge.
WARD 4. Includes all north of Essex street, west of Washington street (excepting North Salem), and all above the town bridge on Boston street.
WARD 5. All of South Salem.
WARD 6. All of North Salem.

THE NEW YORK STATE
BUSINESS DIRECTORY,

Similar in character to the New England Business Directory,

WILL BE ISSUED

Early in the Year 1859,

By ADAMS, SAMPSON & Co.,

No. 91 WASHINGTON ST.,
BOSTON, MASS.

GENERAL DIRECTORY.

AARL JOHN, currier, house 8 Lynn
Aaron John, cabinet maker, house 10 Broad
Abbot Benjamin, teamster, 30 Front, h. 57 Bridge
Abbot Daniel, insurance agent, house 38 Church
Abbot Daniel C. house 10 Ward
Abbot Frederick, clerk at W. P. Phillips's, b. at Beverly
Abbot Philip, house 20 Williams
Abbot Philip jr. painter, rear 9 Church, house 20 Williams
Abbot Robert, truckman, house 4 Downing
Abbot Robert B. ticket master, E. R. R. house 9 Barton sq.
Abbott Adolphus, baker, house 32 Essex
Abbott Alfred A. counsellor, 224 Essex, h. at South Danvers
Abbott Anice, widow, house 6 Fowler
Abbott Eliza K. Miss, house 56 Harbor
Abbott George B. mariner, house 97 Bridge
Abbott George F. fireman, house 23 Warren
Abbott Israel C., Market Hotel, 11 and 12 Market square, h. 53 Charter
Abbott John H. 12 Market square, boards 53 Charter
Abbott Joseph, peddler, boards 1 Sewall
Abbott Lydia Mrs. house 13 Winthrop
Abbott Mary A. widow, house 97 Bridge
Abbott *(Nathaniel)* & Dummer *(John S.)*, fish, oysters, and produce, Philips wharf, house 53 Derby
Abbott Samuel C., Danvers & Salem express, 7 Washington, house at South Danvers
Aborn Joseph H. currier, house 136 Boston
Aborn Rebecca, widow, house 136 Boston
Aborn Sarah S. widow, house 136 Boston
Adams Charles H. house 7 at the F. R. Lead Mills
Adams *(Charles H.)* & Foster *(William K.)*, pearl glass signs, 24 Washington, boards 7 Central
Adams Charles, tanner, house 46 Beaver
Adams Charles, boards 16 School
Adams Eleanor Mrs. house 59 Mill
Adams George W. mariner, house 59 Mill

SALEM [A] DIRECTORY.

Adams Harriet M. Miss, house 44 Warren
Adams Henry, mariner, house 10 High
Adams John, currier, house rear 67 Mason
Adams *(Joseph)*, Richardson *(C. M.)*, & Co. *(H. E. Jocelyn)*, hardware, cutlery, and agricultural tools, 207 Essex, house Pine street, North Danvers
Adams Oliver, house 7½ St. Peter
Adams Rebecca G. Mrs. house 16 School
Adams Rebecca & Sarah Misses, house 3 Federal
Adams Thomas, house 16 Church
Agge Jacob, blacksmith, 51 Harbor, house 96 Federal
Ahearn David, house 6 F. R. Lead Mills
Aiken Wm. B. mariner, house 18 Howard
Alden Lott Mrs. house 13 Walnut
Aldrich Moses, overseer Naumkeag Mill, house 68 Harbor
Aldrich Moses H. operative, house 68 Harbor
Alexander Charles, mariner, house 50 Derby
Allard Almon B. farmer, house foot of Orne
Allen Benjamin B. tanner, Goodhue, boards 92 Boston
Allen Charles H. captain, house 24 Hardy
Allen Charles H. mariner, house 4 Andover
Allen David, cabinet maker, house 8 Carlton
Allen Edward, merchant, house 24 St. Peter
Allen Edward L. currier, house 30 Hathorne
Allen Ephraim, measurer of leather, house 191 Federal
Allen Ephraim W. Rev. house 1 Northey
Allen George H. clerk, 14 Asiatic building, boards 24 Hardy
Allen George W. currier, house rear 59 Warren
Allen Ira G. engineer, house 6 Beaver
Allen Israel, shoemaker, house rear 264 Essex
Allen John, blacksmith, house 56 Broad
Allen John E. Mrs. house 57 Warren
Allen John F. grapery, Dean, house 31 Chestnut
Allen Joseph, mariner, boards 19 Webb
Allen Joseph H. tanner, boards 30 Beaver
Allen Joseph P. stonecutter, house 20 Ward
Allen Laura W. fancy goods, 368 Essex, house do.
Allen Nathaniel K. house 30 Lafayette
Allen Sarah Mrs. house 7 Webb
Allen Wm. C. (B.), house 3 Ward
Allen Wm. E. carpenter, boards 7 Webb
Alley Margaret C. Mrs. house 12 Howard
Almon Andrew B. counsellor, 214 Essex, house 79 Lafayette
Almy James F. dry goods, 156 Essex, house 280 do.
Ames Ebenezer, cooper, boards 5 Allen
Ames Edward B. painter, 3 Crombie, house 45 St. Peter

SALEM [A] DIRECTORY.   51

Ames George L. house 10 Williams
Ames Jeremiah, carpenter, 32 St. Peter, house do.
Ames Mary L. Mrs. house rear 169 Essex
Ames Mary S. Mrs. house 10 Williams
Ames Peter, house 11 Curtis
Amidon Augustus R. tailor, 178 Essex, house 6 Union
Amory Elizabeth, boards 33 Summer
Anderson Augustus M. clerk, 116 Derby, boards 61 do.
Anderson Jacob, laborer, house 61 Derby
Anderson James H. tailor, 9 Central, house 13 St. Peter
Anderson John, upholsterer, house St. Peter
Anderson John M. gluemaker, r. Salem turnpike, h. do.
Anderson Mary Mrs. house 14 Turner
Anderson Mary C. house 306 Essex, cor. North
Anderson Wm. confectionery, 3 Arrington building
Andrew Eunice W. dressmaker, house 218 Essex
Andrew John, printer, boards 10 Curtis
Andrew John F. Mrs. house 9 Newbury
Andrew Martha Mrs. house 10 Curtis
Andrew Samuel G. mariner, house 10 Curtis
Andrews Caroline, boards 393 Essex
Andrews Christopher, peddler, house rear 19 Daniels
Andrews Daniel, house 24 Lynde
Andrews Dolly Ann, house 24 Lynde
Andrews Eliza, house 24 Lynde
Andrews Esther H. Mrs. house 78 Mill
Andrews George, counsellor, 150 Essex, house 393 do.
Andrews Gilman, blacksmith, 27 Beach, house 5 Oak
Andrews Hiram, pattern maker and house joiner, h. 20 Salem
Andrews Howard, shoemaker, boards 7 Prince
Andrews James H. merchant (B.), house 119 Lafayette
Andrews Jane, widow, house 26 Mill
Andrews John P. house 393 Essex
Andrews Joseph, merchant (B.), house 38 Chestnut
Andrews Joseph, currier, house 56 Charter
Andrews Mary Ann Mrs. house 26 Church
Andrews Mary, widow of Nehemiah, house r. 101 Lafayette
Andrews Samuel P. clerk Police Court, 150 Essex, h. Flint, n. Warren
Andrews Solomon, shipcarpenter, house 62 Harbor
Andrews ———, musician, boards 1 Sewall
Anketell Edward, boarding house, 176 Derby
Annable Ephraim Mrs. house 73 North
Annable E. Augustus, clerk, 228 Essex, boards 73 North
Annable John U. millwright, house 177 Boston
Anthony Harriet M. widow, house 16 High

Appleton George B. watchmaker & jeweller, 179 Essex, house 5 Everett
Appleton Nathaniel, coffin wareroom, 80 Derby, h. 14 Northey
Ara Victor, carver, house 10½ Turner
Archer *(Augustus J.)*, Downing *(T. W.)*, & Co., dry goods & carpetings, 173 Essex, house 134 Federal
Archer Deborah Mrs. house 134 Federal
Archer Dolly R. house 6 River
Archer Elizabeth S. tailoress, house 12 Carlton
Archer Fidelia W. Mrs. house 6 Carpenter
Archer George N. 179 Essex, boards 120 Bridge
Archer Henry Mrs. house 26 Williams
Archer James N. house rear 140 Essex
Archer John, house 6 Daniels
Archer Lydia, vestmaker, house 23 Pleasant
Archer Lydia Miss, house 25 North
Archer Mary M. Mrs. house 40 Essex
Archer Rufus P. mariner, house 67 Mill
Archer Sarah, nurse, house rear 28 Church
Archer William, secy. Salem & Danvers Loan and Fund Association, 16 Wash. house 67 Lafayette
Archer Wm. jr. auctioneer and commission merchant, 18 Washington and 34 Front, house 67 Lafayette
Archer Wm. H. mariner, house 10 Howard
Archer William H. carpenter, house 33 Essex
Archibald Matthew, currier, house 16 Flint
Armstrong Eliza, h. 175 Bridge
Armstrong John, boarding house, 24 Charter
Arnold Edward B. morocco manuf. 3 Pope's ct. h. 87 Boston
Arnold James A. wheelwright, house 405 Essex
Arnold Mary, house 10 Herbert
Arnold Mary J. Mrs. house 69 Boston
Arnold Michael P. morocco dresser, house 70 Boston
Arnold Nicholas, laborer, house 428 Essex
Arnold Patrick, servant at 9 Newbury
Arnold Peter, laborer, house rear 19 Daniels
Arnold Thomas A. morocco dresser, boards 87 Boston
Arnold William Mrs. house 38 Derby
Arrington Benjamin, printer, house 8½ Turner
Arrington Benjamin R. painter, house 17 Beaver ct.
Arrington George S. watchman, house 10 High
Arrington George S. jr. painter, boards 10 High
Arrington James, house 6 Andover
Arrington John, fisherman, house 9 Creek
Arrington Joseph Mrs. house 43 Lafayette
Arrington Walter R. painter, house 84 Summer

Arvedson George, clerk, 216 Essex, house 12 Broad
Arvedson Hannah Mrs. house 12 Broad
Arvedson Wm. blacksmith, house 12 Broad
Ashby Elias W. currier, house 188 Federal
Ashby John J. boots and shoes, 276 Essex, house 96 do.
Ashby Josephus, carpenter, house Union place
Ashby Robert R. shoemaker, house 21½ Salem
Ashby Thomas, carpenter, house 18 Barr
Ashby Thomas W. gardener, house 7 Dean
Ashton Francis M. captain, house 4 Walnut
Ashton Francis P. house 5 Dearborn   [h. 20 Central
Ashton William B. clothing and furnishing goods, 211 Essex,
Ashton William F. clerk, 211 Essex, boards 20 Central
Atkins James, carpenter, house Southwick, near Dearborn
Atkins William, house 13 Ash
Atkinson Betsey Mrs. house 125 Essex
Atwell Josiah R. Mrs. house 26 Turner
Atwill Isaac, ropemaker, house 4 Barton
Atwood Solomon L. coachman, boards 61 Harbor
Austin Eleazer, lumber, 16 Lafayette, house 58 do.
Austin Elizabeth D. widow, house 10 Ash
Austin Francis, mariner, house 41 Buffum
Austin George F. lumber, 16 Lafayette, house 58 do.
Austin James L. tanner, house 59 Warren
Austin Josiah, watchmaker, boards 59 Warren
Austin Richard H. painter, house 8 N. Pine
Austin William, currier, rear 46 Boston, house 13 do.
Averell *(Nathaniel P.)* & Low *(A. T.)*, boots and shoes, 76
   Boston, house 79 do.
Averell Nathaniel S. currier, boards 79 Boston
Averill Benjamin, cooper, house 8 Herbert
Averill Benjamin jr. distiller, house 8 Herbert
Averill Charles A. blacksmith, house 5 Upham
Averill Edward A. engineer, house 10 May
Averill Eliza H. Mrs. house 8 Herbert
Averill James W. painter, house 8 Herbert
Averill John J. carpenter, City Mills, house 2 Downing
Averill Lucy A. seamstress, house 8 Herbert
Averill Moses A. watchman, house 5 Upham
Avery Mark B. superintendent almshouse at the Neck
Ayers Daniel, laborer, house 27 Beaver
Ayer Orpha, widow, house 17 Saunders
Ayers James, miller, 1 Front, house 20 Porter
Ayers Peter, captain, house 23 Forrester
Ayers Thomas, currier, house 89 North
Aylward George G. currier, house 9 High

SALEM [B] DIRECTORY.

BABBIDGE BENJAMIN, boatbuilder, house 106 Essex
Babbidge Benjamin A. Mrs. house 7 Elm
Babbidge Christopher, shipwright, house 21 Essex
Babbidge Eunice Mrs. house 52 Essex
Babbidge Francis, captain, house 43 Broad
Babbidge John, house 106 Essex
Babbidge Lydia, teacher, house 7 Carpenter
Babbidge Sarah, widow, house 5 Mall
Babcock Cecelia (*Remond & B.*), hairwork, 188½ Essex, h. 13 [School
Babcock Charles, hairdresser, 214 Essex, house 13 School
Babcock David, currier, house 23 Albion
Babcock James, house 13 School
Babcock John F. tanner, boards 2 Goodhue
Bacon Sarah, variety store, 371½ Essex, house do.
Badger Abigail Mrs. nurse, house 5 Woodbury court
Badger Bartholomew S. laborer, house 5 Woodbury court
Badger George A. medicine peddler, house 2 Everett
Bagnall James R. tel. operator, E. R. R. depot, bds. 9 Wash.
Bailey Catherine, widow, house 133 Boston
Bailey Edward, shoemaker, boards 15 Salem
Bailey Edwin A. dyer, house Cambridge, corner Broad
Bailey Elisha K. carpenter, house 30 Buffum
Bailey George C. tanner, house 10 Beach
Bailey George E. captain, house 32 Dearborn
Bailey Mary C. Mrs. house 31 Boston
Bain James, currier, house Grove, above Mason
Baizley Charles, seaman, house 91 Derby
Baker Mrs. boarding house, 9 Washington
Baker Charles, carpenter, house 24 Lafayette
Baker Eugenia, house Rubber Factory, Ward [Harbor
Baker Ezra F. (*E. K. Noyes & Co.*), grocer, 6 Front, house 39
Baker Harriet, dressmaking, 3 North
Baker Martha, widow, house 181 Bridge
Baker Mary T. millinery, 3 North, house 7 River
Baker William H. painter, house 12 Herbert
Balch Benjamin, watchmaker, 234 Essex, house h. 25 Lynde
Balch Benjamin jr. captain, house Cherry, corner Cedar
Balch Harriet J. widow, house 89 Federal
Balcomb George, carpenter, boards 8 Phillips
Balcomb Henry W. carpenter, house 8 Phillips
Baldwin Ann Mrs. house 15 Pleasant
Baldwin Benjamin, carpenter, house 15 Essex
Baldwin Joseph, carpenter, house 64½ North
Baldwin Sarah Mrs. house 72 North
Ball George, shoemaker, house Pingree
Ball John, city missionary, office 8 Franklin building, h. 26 St. [Peter
Ball Mary Mrs. house 67 Mill

Ball N. Franklin, upholsterer, house 48 Charter
Ball Wm. baker and flour merchant, 22 Central, h. 34 Charter
Ballard Barzillai, fisherman, house 16 March
Ballard Henry A. captain, house 28 St. Peter
Ballard James, house 96 Lafayette
Ballard James C. captain, house Linden
Bancroft George C. at Gas Works office, house 108 Boston
Bancroft James B. boots and shoes, 108 Boston, boards do.
Bancroft Sydney C. counsellor, 27 Washington, h. So. Danvers
Bancroft Thomas S. boots, shoes, and crockery, 108 Boston, house do.
Barker Benjamin, baker, house 158 Bridge
Barker Benjamin F. stonecutter, boards 12 Harbor
Barker Henry M. shipwright, house 17 Beckett
Barker Jacob, carpenter, 39 North, house 14 Walter
Barker Joseph W. wheelwright, 29 Liberty, house 4 Pearl
Barker Ruth Mrs. house 11 Curtis
Barker Sarah, house 9 Turner
Barlow Lydia A. widow, house Green place
Barlow John, boots and shoes, 149 Essex, house 10 Pleasant
Barlow Joseph H. mariner, house Green place
Barnard Edward, captain, house 1 Cambridge
Barnard Samuel, gum copal works, house 14 Allen
Barnes Alice A. Mrs. house 319 Essex
Barnes Joseph, shoemaker, Bridge, c. Williams, h. 162 Bridge
Barnes Thomas H. principal Hacker School, b. 9 Washington
Barnett Michael, currier, house 16 Beaver court
Barney Daniel, laborer, house 170 Desby
Barney Laura, widow, house 14 Derby
Barney Samuel Mrs. house 9½ English
Barr Eunice, house 21 Lynde
Barr Robert, flagman, house 13 Mason
Barr Robert Mrs. house 3 Daniels
Barrenson Abraham Mrs. house 15 Essex
Barrett Edward, tanner, house rear 67 Mason
Barrett John, laborer, house Tucker's wharf
Barrett Levi, overseer, boards 66 Harbor
Barrett Matthew, clerk, 3 High, house 19 Herbert
Barrett Martha O. milliner, 168 Essex, house at South Danvers
Barrett Mary, widow, house 9 Cherry
Barrett Peter, laborer, house 170 Derby
Barrett Patrick, laborer, house 2 Tucker's wharf
Barrett Patrick, laborer, house 27 Daniels
Barrett William, laborer, house foot Ives
Barrett William, currier, house 148 Boston
Barron Franklin S. blacksmith, house 48 Charter
Barron Laura A. teacher, house 48 Charter

Barron Phœbe H. Mrs. nurse, house 48 Charter
Barry Edward, laborer, house 6 Tucker's wharf
Barry James (Cal.), house 8 Ropes
Barry James, laborer, house 28 Peabody
Barry James, teamster, house foot of Ives
Barry James, shoemaker, house 23 North
Barry John, laborer, house 7 Ropes
Barry John, laborer, house 20 Carlton
Barry Michael, laborer, house Adams, near Mason
Barry Thomas, shoemaker, house foot Pingree
Barstow Anstiss S. Mrs. house 25 Chestnut
Barstow Benjamin, counsellor, 159½ Essex, house 25 Chestnut
Bartlett Alexander, grocer, 82 Derby, house 2 Palfrey court
Bartlett Fred. B. *(Smith & B.)*, cigar manufacturer, 132 Derby, house 2 **Palfrey** court
Bartlott Hiram P. dentist, 208 Essex, boards 14 Elm
Barton Gardner, apothecary, 124 Essex, house 88 Bridge
Barton William C. ice dealer, 8 Brown, house 2 Williams
Bassett John A. clairvoyant physician, house 14 Webb
Bassett John B. captain, house 8 Lemon
Bassett Robert C. Mrs. house 9 Mechanic
Bassett Robert C. boards 9 Mechanic
Batchelder Anna & Mary, dry goods, 202 Essex, house 200 do.
Batchelder Charles J. clerk (B.), boards 28 Brown
Batchelder Charles M. machinist, house 67 North
Batchelder Cyrus D. teamster, house 9 Lagrange
Batchelder David G. foreman F. R. Lead Co. house 3 Holly
Batchelder Elizabeth Mrs. house 55 Broad
Batchelder George E. clerk, house 147 Bridge
Batchelder George H. fireman, house 1 Carlton
Batchelder George W. liquors, 10 Derby square, h. 23 Union
Batchelder Increase, laborer, house Pingree, near Harbor
Batchelder Jacob, principal High School, house 28 Brown
Batchelder John D. shoemaker, house Phelps court
Batchelder John H. dentist, 20 Washington, house do.
Batchelder Joseph, wheelwright, 18 Creek, house 13 Ward
Batchelder Mary A. teacher, boards 28 Brown
Batchelder Richard, freight master, Lawrence R. R. h. 71 Fed-[eral
Batchelder Samuel L. house 3 Cedar
Batchelder Sarah Mrs. house 7 Herbert
Batchelder William, farmer, house near 123 Lafayette
Batchelder William L. sash and blind maker, house 47 Endicott
Bateman Thomas, laborer, house 206 Derby
Bates Elizabeth H. Mrs. house 2½ Federal
Bates Charles H. (B.), house 2½ Federal
Bates Sarah Ellen Miss, house 2½ Federal
Bates Thomas, currier, house rear 40 St. Peter

SALEM [B] DIRECTORY. 57

Bates William B. captain, house 76 Bridge
Bates William M. dentist, 208 Essex, house 69 do.
Bathrick Josiah, laborer, house 86 Mill
Battis George J. cigar maker, house 6 Cambridge
Battis *(James H.)* & Brown *(Willard H.)*, tobacconists and cigar manufacturers, 110 Derby, house 23 Liberty
Battis John, cooper, 147 Derby, house 21 Union
Battis Lucy Mrs. boards 56 Harbor
Baxter Charles, laborer, house 127 Derby
Beadle John, mast and spar maker, house 17 Turner
Beadle John jr. sparmaker (B.), house 10 Hardy
Beadle Joseph, calker, house 17 Turner
Beadle Josiah, shoemaker, 3 Lemon, house 102 Bridge
Beadle Josiah jr. calker, house 21 Turner
Beaman Charles C. Rev. house 80 Bridge
Beard James Mrs. house 39 Summer
Beaver James, mariner, house 29 Becket
Becker P tailor, boards Mansion House
Becket *(Daniel C.)* & Fellows *(George)*, boat builders and spar makers, foot Daniels, house 42 Derby
Becket George, laborer, house 172 Derby
Becket Hannah Miss, house 21 Union
Becket Hannah Mrs. house 18 Carlton
Becket Jane H. Mrs. house 42 Derby
Becket Samuel Mrs. house 18 Carlton
Beckford Asa N. tanner, house rear 385 Essex
Beckford Eben, currier, house 70 Boston
Beckford Jefferson A. tanner, boards rear 385 Essex
Beckford John M. tanner, house 51 Broad
Beckford *(Josiah)* & Hanson *(J. V.)*, grain and meal, 1 Front and Grove, house 18 School
Beckford Melinda R. Mrs. nurse, house 24 Union
Beckford Penson, laborer, house rear 385 Essex
Beckford Sarah R. Mrs. house 2 Rust
Beckford Thomas F. grocer, Pleasant, c. Bridge, h. 8 Saunders
Bedee John F. shoemaker, house 12 Ward
Bell Charlotte, widow, house 12 Cedar
Bell Elizabeth Mrs. house 18 Becket
Bell John H. carpenter, house 7 Lynn
Bell Mary, widow, house 7 Lynn
Bellow Catherine, widow, house 17 Harbor
Bennard Andrew A. cooper, house 6 Curtis
Bennett Abraham, clothing, &c. 33 Lafayette, house 35 do.
Bennett Geo. W. harness maker, 321 Essex, h. 8 Beckford
Bennett Philip K. machinist, house 65 Harbor
Benson Charles A. mariner, house foot Cedar
Benson Emery K. clerk (B.), house 52 Forrester

Benson George W. clerk (B.), house 52 Forrester
Benson John H. boards 52 Forrester
Benson Samuel, captain, house 52 Forrester
Benson Samuel, captain, house 131 North
Benson William C. mariner, house 52 Forrester
Bentley George, house 18 High
Bentley John, boards 18 High
Berg Nancy Mrs. nurse, house 5 Woodbury court
Berick Francis H. Rev. house 6 Cross
Berick Francis H. jr. student at law, 243½ Essex, b. 6 Cross
Bermingham C. variety store, 30 Norman, house do.
Bermingham George, laborer, house 30 Norman
Bermingham Maurice, at oil works, house Pingree, n. Harbor
Berry Aaron W. captain, house 12 Conant
Berry Anna D. widow, house 8 Congress
Berry Betsy Mrs. house Phelps court, opp. Green place
Berry Charles H. rigger, 20 Derby wharf, house 6 North court
Berry Charles H. mariner, house 23 Essex
Berry Eben, captain, house Union place
Berry Edward A. ropemaker, house 5 High
Berry George A. currier, house Phelps ct. opp. Green place
Berry George E. captain of the watch, house 41 Essex
Berry George F. baker, 2 Front, house foot Skerry
Berry Jacob, turnkey at the jail, house 8 Congress
Berry James, laborer, house 28 Peabody
Berry John, currier, boards 3 Boston
Berry John C. captain (*H. E. Jenks & Co.*), house 30 Harbor
Berry Lawrence, F. R. L. mill, house 5 Park
Berry Nathaniel, house 37 St. Peter
Berry Oliver, 279 Essex, house Phelps ct. opp. Green place
Bertram John, merchant, Central wharf, house 370 Essex
Bertram Joseph H. M. house 370 Essex
Beston James, shoemaker, house 411 Essex
Bettis John B. book agent, house 29 Pleasant
Bezarsne M. E. waiter, 136 Essex
Bigelow Charles A. sawyer, house 11 Norman
Bigelow Lewis A. shoemaker, house 11 Norman
Bird Ann, widow, house 2 High street court
Bird Benjamin M. painter, house 9 High
Bird Sarah, widow, house 8 Park
Bivors Charles, cigar maker, house 16 Williams
Bixby H. M. clerk, 155 Essex, boards at Beverly
Black Jessie, widow, house 210 Derby
Blaisdell Samuel R. Mrs. house 20 Park
Blake Augustus S. carpenter, 29 Liberty, house Green place
Blake George T. furniture dealer (B.), house 406 Essex
Blake Jethro, laborer, house 16 Sewall

Blanchard Asa, distiller, house 24 Liberty
Blanchard E. Ripley, teacher of music Normal School, house at Boston
Blanchard Lorenzo A. musician, boards Mansion House
Blethen True G. boards 20 Ward
Blinn George H. carpenter, house 55 Federal
Blinn John F. carpenter, house North, near Nursery
Blodgett Pearl D. (*Steele, Blodgett & Co.*), flour and produce, 26 Front, house Harrison avenue
Blunt Thomas, laborer, house 18 Salem
Boardman Benjamin S. currier, house 15 Mason
Boardman Daniel, grocer, 39 Derby, house 11 Prescott
Boardman Daniel W. musician, boards 62 North
Boardman Francis G. clerk, 56 Derby, bds. 31 Williams
Boardman William H. carpenter, boards 16 Sewall
Bodwell Frederick L. painter, house 76 Summer
Bodwell George H. carpenter, house 41 Buffum
Bogue John Mrs. house Pingree
Boles John, currier, house Green place
Bond Lewis, tanner, Goodhue, house 6 Boston
Bos-on (*Abraham F.*) & Glover (*George D.*), boots and shoes, 14 Lafayette, house 3 Salem
Boswell John C. clerk, boards 4 Buffum
Boswell William W. wood and bark, house 4 Buffum
Bott James, tanner, rear 27 Boston, house 27 do.
Bott James B. leather finisher, house 27 Boston
Bott John C. currier, 9 Pope's court, house 95 Boston
Bott Thomas, shoemaker, 46 Derby, house 20 Becket
Bousley (*Joseph*) & Locke (*M. P.*), carpenters, 16 Mill, house 14 Cedar
Bousley Joseph H. carpenter, house 14 Cedar
Bovey Nicholas, gardener, house 27 Charter
Bowditch Daniel C. shipwright, head Phillips' whf. h. 6 Hardy
Bowditch Francis M. mariner, house 17 Andrew
Bowditch George, house 11 Bentley
Bowditch George jr. mason, house 9 Bentley
Bowditch Harriet Mrs. boarding house, 5 Barton square
Bowditch William A. crockery and glass ware, 221 Essex, h. 196 Derby
Bowdoin David W. photographic artist (B.), house 10 Federal
Bowdoin Sarah, widow, house 7 Dean
Bowdoin W. L. dentist, 208 Essex, house 57 Washington
Bowen John, currier, house rear 79 Boston
Bowen Thomas, shoemaker, house Chestnut, cor. Cambridge
Bower Antoine, tailor, boards Mansion House
Bowker Brothers (*George & Charles*), flour, grain, and salt, 227 and 229 Derby

Bowker Charles *(Bowker Brothers)*, house 9 Crombie
Bowker George *(Bowker Brothers)*, house 9 Crombie
Bowker Joel, merchant, house 9 Crombie
Bowland Hannah, teacher, 1 Walnut
Bowman James, shoemaker, 5 Endicott, h. 15 High st. court
Boyce Hugh, tanner, house Varney
Boyce Hugh, house 325 Essex
Boyce James, tanner, house Varney
Boyce Jonathan H. shoemaker, house 15 Warren
Boyer Charles, captain, house 4 Howard
Boye ———, currier, boards 62 North
Boyle Edward, morocco beamster, house 18 Beaver court
Boyle Mary, widow, house 82 Mason
Boylston Peter (Cal.), house 30 Norman
Boynton Oliver H. (*Pray & B.*), eating room, 25 Front, house rear 36 Mill
Braden James, currier, 47 Boston, house 169 Federal
Bradley Hugh, shoemaker, boards 90 Derby
Brady Edward, shoemaker, boards 53 Warren
Brady Patrick, shoemaker, house 26 Ward
Brackett Thomas, teamster, house 16 Dow
Bradford Benjamin W. cabinet maker, house 31 Turner
Bradford George P. teacher, 1 Cambridge, bds. 4 Broad
Bradford John W. laborer, house 103 North
Bradley John, Naumkeag Mill, house 7 Herbert
Brady Thomas, cooper, house 88 Derby
Brady Thomas, shoemaker, boards 59 Harbor
Bragg Hartson, laborer, house 9 Turner
Brainard Walter, farmer, house foot of Orne
Brand John, hairdresser, 214 Essex, house 9 Hardy
Bra don Martin, varnisher, house 2 Conant
Branigan Arthur, shoemaker, house 3 Pond
Branigan James, shoemaker, house 21 Buffum
Bray Ann R. dry goods, 76 Federal, house do.
Bray Benjamin, patent balance curtain spring manufactory, 2 Franklin building, house 17 Carlton
Bray Olive P. teacher at Normal School, h. at W. Gloucester
Breed George J. house 8 Mall
Breed Holton J. captain, house 8 Mall
Breed Rebecca Mrs. dressmaker, house 57 Summer
Breed Rebecca S. teacher, house 57 Summer
Breen John, laborer, house Lafayette, opp. lead works
Breller Andrew, tobacconist, boards Orange, cor. Derby
Brennan Ann, widow, house 121 Boston
Brennan Bernard, laborer, house 12 Goodhue
Brennan George, currier, house 148 Boston
Brennan James, laborer, house 143 North

SALEM [B] DIRECTORY.   61

Brennan Richard, currier, house 121 Boston
Brennan Walter, laborer, house 132 North
Brennan Walter, laborer, house 83 Mason
Brewster Ethan A. boards 43 North
Brewster George I. (*Ira A. Brewster & Son*), house 13 Mason
Brewster Ira A. & Son (*G. I. Brewster*), tanners and curriers, 11 Franklin, house 43 Forth
Brick Ellen, widow, house 10 Herbert
Brickley Honora, widow, house 92 Derby
Briggs Charles C. carpenter, house 11 Gardner court
Briggs Charles N. at laboratory, house 12 Lynn
Briggs Edward T. 15 Lafayette, house 5 Barton square
Briggs George W. Rev. house 9 Summer
Briggs James B. Mrs. house 38 Forrester
Briggs James C. house 38 Forrester
Briggs John F. currier, house 22 Albion
Briggs Joseph B. shoemaker, boards 77 North
Briggs Lydia Mrs. house 77 North
Briggs Nancy Mrs. house 97 Boston
Briggs Richard, marble worker, boards 1 Sewall
Briggs Susan A. Mrs. house 24 Lafayette
Briggs William A. shoemaker, house 14 Albion
Bright Mary Mrs. house 12 Becket
Brimblecomb Philip H. mariner, house 7 Federal
Brittan John, tanner, boards 29 Beaver
Brittney Jane Mrs. house 86 Boston
Broadrick Bridget, widow, house foot of Pingree
Broadrick Dennis, laborer, house Odell square
Broadrick Thomas, laborer, house 73 Mason
Brogan Patrick, laborer, house 8 Whittemore
Brookhouse Elizabeth T. Mrs. house 19 Oliver
Brookhouse Mary H. Mrs. house 23 High
Brookhouse Robert, merchant, 16 Asiatic building and Phillips wharf, house 51 Washington
Brookhouse Robert jr. merchant, 16 Asiatic building and Phillips wharf, house 13 Lynde
Brooking Thomas, blacksmith, 21 Mason, house 17 Barr
Brooks Alfred R. teamster, 107 Derby, house 12 Hardy
Brooks Asa, hardware, crockery, and paper hangings, 143 Essex, house 11 Andrew
Brooks Augustus T. flour, coal, &c. 117 Derby, h. 20 Federal
Brooks D. Brainerd & Brother (*L. B. Brooks*), books, stationery and music store, 193 Essex, h. 30 Brown
Brooks E. M. R. Miss, music and French teacher, boards 112 Lafayette
Brooks George P. (B.), boards 11 Andrew

Brooks Henry M. clerk and treasurer Forest River Lead Co. 243½ Essex, house 112 Lafayette
Brooks Isaac C. *(Dodge & B.)*, carpenter, Derby wharf, h. 11 Andrew
Brooks James, carpenter, house rear 11 Andrew
Brooks James L. shipjoiner, house 14 Carlton
Brooks John Mrs. house 7 Lemon
Brooks John G. Mrs. house 11 Andrew
Brooks Joseph H. mariner, boards 11 Andrew
Brooks Lovina Mrs. house Jackson place
Brooks Luke (89 Commercial street, Boston), house 7 Briggs
Brooks Luke jr. grocer, 178 Derby, house 11 Oliver
Brooks Lyman B. *(D. B. Brooks & Brother)*, house 40 Summer
Brooks Nathaniel H. grocer, 178 Derby, house 10 St. Peter
Brooks Samuel Mrs. house 192 Derby
Brooks Susan, fancy goods, 8 Elm, house do.
Brooks *(Timothy)* & Noyes *(Isaac S.)*, grocers, 121 Essex, h. 7 Liberty
Brooks William A. apothecary, 33½ Lafayette, h. 11 Andrew
Brophy Martin, currier, house 93 Mason
Brown Alexander, laborer, house 10 Derby
Brown Ann Mrs. house 12 Northey
Brown A. Parker, clerk, boards 28 St. Peter
Brown Augustus S. clerk Naumkeag S. Co. boards 114 Essex
Brown Benjamin Mrs. house 61 Essex
Brown Benjamin, cabinet maker, house 11 Rust
Brown Catharine, widow, house Congress, west side
Brown Catharine H. milliner, house 15 Crombie
Brown Charles, ship carpenter, house 86 Bridge
Brown Charles Dudley, clerk, 243 Essex, boards 15 Crombie
Brown Charles E. mariner, house 13 Becket
Brown Charles E. painter, 42 Charter, house 13 Briggs
Brown Daniel jr. baker, 10 Mill, and grocer, 16 Mill, h. 8 do.
Brown Daniel, gate keeper at workhouse, at the Neck
Brown Daniel, shoemaker, boards 78 Mill
Brown Edmund Mrs. house 5 Woodbury's court
Brown Edward, captain, house 118 Bridge
Brown Elbridge K. clerk, 4 Newbury, h. Pleasant, c. Andrew
Brown Elizabeth L. Miss, seamstress, house 61 Essex
Brown Eppes, house 15 Crombie
Brown Ephraim, Register of Deeds, Court House, h. 11 Winter
Brown Frances S. Miss, tailoress, house 61 Essex
Brown Francis, treasurer Salem Gas Light Co. 23 Northey, h. 5 Brown
Brown George, carpenter and stairbuilder, 49 St. Peter, h. do.
Brown George, currier, house 11 May

Brown George, clerk. 30 Front, house 9 Northey
Brown George jr. stairbuilder, North, n. Bridge, h. 8 Northey
Brown George jr. mariner, boards 59 Bridge
Brown George A. & Theodore, carpenters, 158 Derby, house 59 Bridge
Brown George T. wrapping paper, bags, &c. 33 Lafayette, h. 11 Salem
Brown George F. & S. lumber, wood, bark and hay, 33, 35, and 37 North, house 31 Dearborn
Brown George W. elder, house 24 Brown
Brown Hannah Mrs. house 11 Oliver
Brown Harvey, house 44 Forrester
Brown Henry, mason, house 7 Turner
Brown Henry jr. painter, house 42 Derby
Brown Henry 3d, bootmaker, house Phelps court
Brown Henry A. clerk, 26 Washington, h. 18 Winthrop
Brown Henry F. carpenter, house 11 Elm
Brown Jacob F. principal of Browne School, house 13 Cedar
Brown James, seaman, house 90 Derby
Brown James M. carpenter, Bridge, opp. St. Peter, h. 23 Mall
Brown John, laborer, house foot Lagrange
Brown John B. umbrella maker, 159 Essex, h. 8 Albion
Brown John D. cooper, house 11 Carlton
Brown John M. (Australia), house 21 Salem
Brown John W. tanner, house 3 Beaver court
Brown Jonathan Mrs. house rear 14 Webb
Brown Jonathan, 40 Washington, house 34 St. Peter
Brown Joseph A. baker, house 8 Mill
Brown Judith Mrs. house 408 Essex
Brown Lawrence, refreshments, Arrington's building, house do.
Brown Lawrence, house 42 Harbor
Brown Leander C. trader, house 6 Boston
Brown Leonard, clerk, 145 Derby, boards 114 do.
Brown Lucy Mrs. house 16 High
Brown Martha A. teacher, house 44 Forrester
Brown Mary C. Mrs. house 8 Cross
Brown Mary, widow, house 1 High st. court
Brown Mary, widow, house 16 Summer
Brown Nathaniel, merchant, house 22 Brown
Brown Nathaniel jr. captain, house 52 Lafayette
Brown Nehemiah, coroner and constable, house 2 Beckford
Brown Parker, captain, house 28 St. Peter
Brown Phebe Mrs. boards 53 Lafayette
Brown Robert L. painter, 159½ Essex, boards 49 St. Peter
Brown Samuel, tanner, house 40 Beaver
Brown Samuel *(G. F. & S. Brown)*, h. Upham, c. Dearborn
Brown Sarah Augusta, teacher, house 44 Forrester

Brown Silas, currier, house 163 Federal
Brown Stephen, blacksmith, house rear 93 Boston
Brown Theodore *(Geo. A. & T. Brown)*, house 114½ Bridge
Brown Thomas, currier, house 34 Beaver
Brown Thomas W. shoemaker, house 1 Beach
Brown Timothy, tanner, house 1 High street court
Brown Willard H. *(Battis & Brown)*, cigar manuf. 110 Derby, house 35 Charter
Brown William, laborer, house Jackson place
Brown William, mariner, house 8 North court
Brown William, laborer, house Jackson place
Brown William B. *(Perkins & Brown)*, clothing, 137 Derby, h. 86 Bridge
Brown William D. (Cal.), house 15 Webb
Brown William H. house 2 Beach
Brown Winthrop, wool puller, house 13 Aborn
Brown —— Mrs. house 17 Conant [cor. Summer
Browne Albert G. merchant (33 Comm'l. st. B.), house Broad,
Browne Anna M. tailoress, house 30 Andrew
Browne *(Benjamin F.)* & Price *(Charles H.)*, druggists and apothecaries, 226 Essex, house 1 Hamilton
Browne J. Vincent, merchant, house 13 Pleasant
Browning George B. Mrs. house 56 Harbor
Browning Geo. F. mariner, house 56 Harbor
Browning John P. clerk, 154 Essex, boards 56 Harbor
Bruce Daniel, captain, house Linden
Bruce Francis, currier, house 51 Warren
Bruce George W. currier, 63 Boston, house 65 do.
Bruce Robert P. carpenter, house 19 Winthrop
Bruce Sarah Mrs. house 51 Warren
Bruce Sarah H. nurse, house 24 Derby
Bryant Hiram K. shoemaker, house 8 Carpenter
Bryant J. Johnson, shoemaker, 27 Norman, house do.
Bryant John, shoemaker, house Bryant, rear North
Bryant John, currier, boards 4 Oak
Bryant John jr. mariner, house Bryant, n. Buffum
Bryant Lydia, nurse, house 14 Norman
Bryant Timothy, merchant, house 31 Charter
Buchanan George, laborer, house rear 17 Lafayette
Buckley Cornelius, laborer, house Phillips, near Grove
Buckley David, laborer, house 30 Peabody
Buckley Edmund, Naumkeag Mill, h. n. foot of Pingree
Buckley James, clerk, 1 Washington
Buckley John, laborer, house 123 Boston
Buckley Lawrence, farmer, house 30 North
Buckley Margaret, widow, house 30 North
Buckley Michael, shoemaker, house 30 North

Buckley Michael, blacksmith, house 141 Boston
Buckley Michael, laborer, house 7 Ward
Buckley Patrick, carver, house 123 Boston
Buckley Timothy, currier, house Adams
Buckley William, laborer, house 27 Daniels
Buckley William, laborer, house rear 170 Derby
Buckmaster William, boarding house, 129 Derby
Buffington James, captain, house 115 Boston
Buffum Caleb, shoemaker, house 18 Buffum
Buffum Caroline, millinery, 255 Essex, house 149 Bridge
Buffum Charles C. steam planing, house 149 Bridge
Buffum Charles S. cabinet maker, house 39 Summer
Buffum David, lumber and steam planing, 9 Front, house 149 Bridge
Buffum Edward, saddler, 23 Buffum, house 21 do.
Buffum George, carpenter, house 21 Buffum
Buffum James R. house 62 Washington
Buffum Joshua, house 39 Summer
Buffum Sarah Mrs. house 1 Chestnut
Buffum William, clerk, 9 Front, boards 3 Pleasant
Buffum William P. shoemaker, house 25 Buffum
Bullock George, house 73 Derby
Bullock Isaac S. house 73 Derby
Bullock Martha, widow, house 158 Boston
Bullock Mary Ann, house 15 Carlton
Bullock Preserved, dressmaker, house 100 Federal
Bunker Asa F. trader, boards 14 Flint
Bunker Eli, teamster, house Everett, corner Salem
Bunker Lyman W. currier, house 6 N. Pine
Burbank Charles G. carriage painter, 3 Cambridge, h. 3 Camb.
Burbank David H. machinist, house 12 Sewall
Burbank Eben G. carriage painter, West place, h. 6 Buffum
Burbank E. Augustus, carriage painter, house 6 Buffum
Burbank Eunice Mrs. boards 29 Brown
Burbank George W. merchant tailor, 235 Essex, h. 33 Salem
Burbank Hannah, nurse, house 31 Norman
Burbank Jonathan M. blacksmith, house Ives court
Burbank Moses T. house 30 Derby
Burbank Silas, coach painter, 3 Cambridge, house do.
Burbeck Lydia, widow, house 75 North
Burbeck William H. merchant tailor, 249 Essex, h. 75 North
Burchmore Zachariah, house 7 Northey
Burchstead Job, shoemaker, house 52 Buffum, above Bryant
Burding Henry W. Mrs. house Beaver lane, corner Beaver
Burding William Mrs. house 122 Boston
Burding Thomas, house 15 High street court

Burgess James, fisherman, house 26 Turner
Burgess James jr. mariner, boards 26 Turner
Burgess Joseph, Naumkeag Mill, house Perkins
Burgess William, machinist, house 68 Harbor
Burgess William H. machinist, boards 68 Harbor
Burke Israel H. trader, house 8 Carpenter
Burke Mary, widow, house 6 Beach
Burke Mary Mrs. house 19 Herbert
Burke Michael, currier, house 6 Beach
Burke William, laborer, house 24 Charter
Burkinshaw George, horsenail maker, Proctor's ct. h. 24 High
Burley John, house 4 Lynde
Burnham Charles F. mariner, house 21 Becket
Burnham Ebenezer, house 33 Dearborn
Burnham Elizabeth G. Mrs. nurse, house 20 Northey
Burnham Franklin C. mariner, house 21 Becket
Burnham George A. baker, house 20 Northey
Burnham John T. secretary Holyoke and Hamilton Mutual Fire Insurance Companies, 27 Wash. house 12 Williams
Burnham Joseph, mariner, house 21 Becket
Burnham Lydia P. Mrs. house Ives court
Burnham Martha Mrs. house 58 Federal
Burns Daniel, laborer, house 2 Pratt st. court
Burns Eunice, widow, house 49 Derby
Burns John Mrs. house rear 6 Essex
Burns Mary, widow, house 40 Union
Burns Michael, currier, boards 1 Sewall
Burns Nancy Mrs. house 2 Lynde
Burns Peter, gum copal worker, house 2 English
Burr Ephraim, captain, house 34 Charter
Burrill John, currier, house 23 Beaver
Burrill Josiah S. clerk, 245 Essex, house 385 do.
Burrill Mary Mrs. nurse, house 7 Becket
Burt David W. currier, house 44 Beaver
Burt Sarah H. teacher, house 44 Beaver
Bush Charles Mrs. house 45 Endicott
Bush Charles, currier, house 45 Endicott
Bush Mary A. dressmaker, 255 Essex, house 45 Endicott
Buster James, tanner, house 23 Beaver
Buswell Eben, boots and shoes, 196 Essex, house 54 Lafayette
Buswell Eben W. boards 54 Lafayette
Butland John, shoemaker, house 8 Nursery
Butland Mary, widow, house 8 Nursery
Butler Benjamin, currier, house 4 May
Butler Daniel, currier, house 21 Warren
Butler Edward E. currier, house 13 Williams

Butler James S. stonecutter, boards 102 Lafayette
Butler John S. shoemaker, 10 Boston, house 4 May
Butler Pierce, currier, house rear Adams
Butler Thomas, currier, house Fowler
Butman Elizabeth Mrs. tailoress, house 14 Central
Butman Francis C. merchant, 130 Commercial st. (B.), house Pleasant, corner Andrew
Butman Luther C. shoemaker, house 14 Allen
Butterfield Hiram, Naumkeag Mill, house Cabot, c. Hancock
Buttrick Samuel B. bookkeeper, Commercial Bank, h. 54 Mill
Buxton Alonzo D. house 19 Summer
Buxton Augustus, tanner, house 15 Friend
Buxton Charles H. currier, house Irving, near Grove
Buxton Edward, shoemaker, house Aborn
Buxton Eleanor, house 68 Boston
Buxton Elizabeth, house 7 Friend
Buxton George, house 19 Summer
Buxton George, gardener, house Ord
Buxton Henry, tanner, house 8 Friend
Buxton Joseph, house 14 Friend
Buxton Joseph jr. tanner and currier, h. 1 Beach, c. Mason
Buxton Joseph S. watchman, house 15 Friend
Buxton Seth S. painter, house 8 Friend
Buxton Thos. millinery and lace, 256 Essex, h. at So. Danvers
Byard Charles, cooper, house 20 Oliver
Byors James, house 7 Park
Byrne Anna E. variety store, 352 Essex, house do.
Byrne Clifford C. teamster, 117 Derby, house 152 do.
Byrne Cornelius, baker, 162 Boston, house do.
Byrne Luke, currier, house Green place
Byron Eunice D. widow, house 5 Salem

CABAN LYDIA, widow, house rear 18 Beckford
Cabeen John, teamster, 198 Derby, house 14 Central
Cabeen William, coal and wood, 211 Derby, house 14 Central
Cabot Joseph S. president Asiatic Bank, house 365 Essex
Cabot Rebecca, house 365 Essex
Cagin Eunice, widow, house 47 Derby
Cahill Thomas, mariner, house 6 Tucker's wharf
Cahoon Reuben, house at the Fort
Caldwell Elizabeth W. Mrs. house 23 Turner
Caldwell Terrence, shoemaker, house 18 Congress
Calef John, grocer, 26 Washington, house 126 Federal
Call Samuel L. mariner, house 4 Endicott
Call Thomas A. Mrs. house 119 Essex
Call Thomas S. cooper, house 119 Essex
Callahan Dennis, laborer, house 24 High

Callahan Eugene, laborer, house 21 High
Callahan Hannah, widow, house 160 Bridge
Callahan John, tanner, house rear 13 Lynn
Callahan John, laborer, house 4 High street court
Callahan Margaret, widow, house 432 Essex
Callahan Patrick, currier, house 15 River
Callaher Jeremiah, laborer, house 24 Peabody
Callaher John, laborer, house Adams
Caller James M. leather dealer, house 146 Boston
Calley Jane Mrs. house 50 Mill
Calley Mary Mrs. house 5 Rust
Calley Samuel, painter, 74 Washington, house 11 Rust
Calley William, blacksmith, house 5 Rust
Callum Edward, house 4 Pratt
Calnan Jeremiah, laborer, house 1 High street court
Campbell Catharine, widow, house 11 Aborn
Campbell Charlotte Mrs. house 20 Conant
Campbell Francis, laborer, house 89 North
Campbell Richard, tanner, house 11 Aborn
Campion John, glovemaker, house 71 Mason
Campion Misses, millinery and gloves, 74 Federal, h. 71 Mason
Cann Wm. captain, boards with J. H. Carty, Pingree
Canney Sylvester G. engineer, house 14 Barr
Cannon John, currier, house 407 Essex
Canty Charles, laborer, house rear 35 Harbor
Canty John, laborer, house rear 35 Harbor
Capela William, mariner, house 15 Pond
Capulla Joseph, cabinet maker, house 166 Essex
Caraway Catharine S. variety store, 58 Derby
Caraway Edward A. boards 58 Derby
Carey Daniel, currier, house Phelps court
Carey Jeremiah, laborer, house Phillips, near Grove
Carey Joseph W. painter, 7 Boston, h. Fulton st., S. Danvers
Carey Mary, widow, house Phelps court
Carey Patrick, laborer, house 21 High
Carey Patrick, laborer, house Tucker's wharf
Carey Patrick, laborer, house 26 Mill
Carey Thomas, laborer, house 26 Mill
Carey William, painter, house Barr, beyond School
Carey William, house 26 Mill
Carigan James, tanner, house 12 Friend
Carleton Edward F. tanner, 14 Franklin, house 15 Mason
Carleton Frazer, tanner, 14 Franklin, house 42 Federal
Carleton Henry W. tanner, house 16 Buffum
Carleton Joseph G. S. clerk, 207 Essex, house 384 do.
Carleton Mary I. teacher, house 4 Lynde
Carleton William J. clerk, 63 Union, house 384 Essex

SALEM [C] DIRECTORY. 69

Carley John, laborer. house 6 Tucker's wharf
Carlile Horace D. bookkeeper (B.), house 392 Essex
Carlile Nathaniel D. merchant (Commercial wharf, B.), house 392 Essex
Carlin Samuel, shoemaker, boards 25 Harbor
Carlton David, carpenter, house 19 Upham
Carlton Elizabeth, house 21 Union
Carlton Henry, tanner, house 16 Buffum
Carlton John, variety store, 158 Essex, house 88 Federal
Carlton John W. currier, boards 7 Friend
Carlton Jonathan F. carpenter, house 7 Friend
Carlton Lewis, machinist, Naumkeag Mill, house 25 Salem
Carlton Michael Rev. house 30 Charter
Carney Catharine, widow, house 31 Boston
Carney Joanna, widow, house 7 High street court
Carney Mary, widow, house 8 Ropes
Carney Morris, currier, house 7 High street court
Carney Thomas, laborer, house 11 Flint
Carpenter Ann P. widow, house 8 Barton square
Carpenter David P. clothing and furnishing store, 205 Essex, house 8 Barton square
Carpenter Irving S. clerk, house 8 Barton square
Carpenter Isaac W. gum copal worker, boards 22 Becket
Carr Andrew, mariner, house 8 Lagrange
Carr Dennis, Essex Railroad, house 151 Bridge
Carr Eliza, widow, house 8 Lagrange
Carr Honora Mrs. house 130 North
Carr John, currier, house Grove
Carr John, gum copal worker, house 3 English
Carr Patrick, house 2 F. R. L. Mills
Carr Patrick, currier, house Jackson place
Carr Simon, gum copal worker, boards 3 English
Carroll Edward, shoemaker, house 12 Odell square
Carroll Hannah, house 183 Bridge
Carroll Joanna, house Congress, west side
Carroll John, peddler, house 19 Daniels
Carroll Mary, widow, house 149 Boston
Carroll Michael, tanner, house 68 Mason
Carroll Michael, currier, house 24 Beaver
Carroll Owen, machinist, boards 4 North Pine
Carson Matthew, laborer, house 4 High street court
Carson Robert, currier, boards 29 Beaver
Carson William L. carriage maker, boards 9 Higginson square
Carter George S. painter, house rear 23 Cedar
Carter Jacob *(J. Perley jr. & Co.)*, bookbinder, 191 Essex, house 6 Broad
Carter James, switchman, house 53 St. Peter

Carter John C. farmer, house 86 Boston
Carter Oliver Mrs. fruit and confectionery, 15 Central, h. do.
Carter Robert, hostler, house Grove, near Mason
Carty James H. shoemaker, on Union Bridge, house Pingree
Casey James, laborer, house 6 Carlton
Casey Thomas, laborer, house 34 Derby
Casey William, currier, house 25 Beaver
Casey William, weaver, house foot of Pingree
Cashman Joanna, widow, house 24 Peabody
Cashman Jeremiah, laborer, house Grove, above Mason
Casmay John, house 36 Mill
Cass James, house 11 Whittemore
Cass James jr. currier, house rear 11 Whittemore
Cass John, currier, house Phillips, near Grove
Cass Michael, currier, house Phillips, near Grove
Cass Walter, currier, house Irving, near Harrod
Cassell Edward P. waiter, house 6 Ropes
Cassell John, currier, house Putnam, near Hanson
Cassell John M. hairdresser, 7½ Wash. house foot of Cedar
Cassidy Hugh, laborer, house 140 Derby
Cassidy James, Naumkeag Mill, house 13 Charter
Cassidy Thomas, peddler, house 204 Derby
Cassidy Patrick, laborer, house High street court
Cassin Edmund, tanner, house rear Adams
Cassin Robert, currier, boards at Edmund Cassin's
Cassino John T. decorative upholsterer, 279 Essex, h. at Essex
Cassody Michael, carpenter, house 7 Prospect
Caswell Edmund, wheelwright, house 29 Barr
Cate Aaron J. steamplaner, house 17 Crombie
Cate James S. Mrs. house 6 English
Cate John H. mariner, house 6 English
Cate Mary E. nurse, house 19 Warren
Cate Samuel A. mariner, house 19 Warren
Caulfield Anthony A. captain, house 16 Andrew
Caulfield Anthony D. captain, house 16 Andrew
Caulfield James C. mariner, house 16 Andrew
Caulfield Wm. Henry, captain, house 16 Andrew
Cavanaugh Mary, widow, house Warren court
Chadwick Ann & Catharine, house 396 Essex   [Chestnut
Chadwick John, cashier Exchange Bank, 172 Essex, house 20
Chadwick John C. (B.), house 17 Brown   [86 Summer
Chamberlain Benj. M. *(Smith & C.)*, jeweller, 201 Essex, h.
Chamberlain Charles, apothecary, 138 Derby, cor. Union, house
   13 Williams
Chamberlain Edward W. clerk (B.), boards 116 Federal
Chamberlain Hazen, house 40 Buffum

SALEM [C] DIRECTORY. 71

Chamberlain Henry P. clerk (50 State B.), h. 12 Crombie
Chamberlain *(James)*, Harris *(James jr.)*, & Co. *(John Chamberlain)*, grocers, 24 Front, house 16 Lynde
Chamberlain James A. clerk, 47 State (B.), boards 16 Lynde
Chamberlain John *(Chamberlain, Harris & Co.)*, h. 1 High
Chamberlain Jos. W. apothecary, 1 Boston, b. 1 High
Chamberlain Luther L. currier, house 81 Boston
Chamberlain Richard H. hosiery, &c., 236 Essex, h. 40 Buffum
Chamberlain Samuel Mrs. house 1 High
Chamberlain Samuel D. house 116 Federal
Chamberlain *(Samuel)* & McKenzie *(R. A.)*, merchant tailors, 29 Wash. h. 116 Federal   [house 1 High
Chamberlain Samuel G. fruit and vegetables, 22 Derby square,
Chamberlin Thomas, distiller, Charter, cor. Derby, h. in Boston
Chambers George, laborer, house foot of Ropes
Chambers James, laborer, house foot of Ropes
Chambers William, laborer, house 26 Peabody
Chandler Abby B. boarding house, 20 Norman
Chandler Gardner L. house 8 Mount Vernon
Chandler James P. 4 Washington, house 9 Mt. Vernon
Chandler John, clerk, 106 Federal, house 7 River
Chandler John, baggage master S. R. R. R. house 14 School
Chandler Joseph, 3 City wharf (B.), house 7 River
Chandler Joseph D. grocer, 106 Federal, house 7 River
Chandler Joseph D. confectioner, house 135 North
Chandler Joseph S. shoemaker, house 135 North
Chandler Luther & Co. *(Irving Stone)*, periodicals and newspapers, 4 Washington, house 50 Broad
Chandler *(Luther)* & Haskell *(Orin S.)* grocers, 391 Essex
Chaney George L. house 14 Liberty
Chaney James, house 14 Liberty
Chaney James H. captain, house 14 Liberty
Chapman Francis R. cooper, boards 28 Williams
Chapman George R. 54 City Exchange (B.), house 103 Federal
Chapman Isaac N. captain, house 38 Pleasant
Chapman *(John)* & Palfray *(Charles W.)*, publishers "Salem Register," 185 Essex, house 103 Federal
Chapman John O. printer, 185 Essex, house 20 Beckford
Chapman William H. boots, shoes, and rubbers, 210 Essex, h. 3 Harrison avenue
Chapple John D. tobacconist, house 20 Howard
Chapple William F. police, house 2 Bentley
Charles John, hairdresser, boards 13 School
Charnce James, Indian physician, $23\frac{1}{2}$ Union, house 12 Cedar
Chase Abigail, widow, house 23 Becket
Chase Abigail L. house 13 North

Chase Abijah Mrs. house 21 Federal
Chase Benjamin E. carpenter, house 37 Salem
Chase Charles H. Mrs. house 26 Derby
Chase Esther, widow, boards 56 Broad
Chase Francis A. painter, boards 8 Barton
Chase George C. agent Forest River Lead Company, 243½ Essex, house 69 Lafayette
Chase George H. shoe manufacturer at Lynn, h. 85 Federal
Chase Hannah B. widow, house 6 Andrew
Chase Jacob C. mariner, house Osgood
Chase James, stonemason, house 8 Barton
Chase James C. sashmaker, boards 63 Harbor
Chase Lydia H. Miss, house 83 Federal
Chase Lyman H. cooper, house 23 Becket
Chase Nathaniel, carpenter, house 13 Ash
Chase *(Nathaniel E.)* & Co. *(A. M. Chipman)*, stoves and tin ware, 8 Lafayette, house 7 Central
Chase Nathaniel S. overseer Naumkeag Mill, h. 62 Harbor
Chase Samuel, porter at Essex House
Chase Stephen A. house 138 Federal
Chase Thorndike, boards 69 Lafayette
Chase Wm. hardware and stoves, 206 Essex, house 22 Federal
Chase Wm. W. ropemaker, house 19 Briggs
Chautard Leon *(B.)*, house 16 Williams
Cheever Abigail Mrs. house 11 Ash
Cheever Benjamin Mrs. house 400 Essex
Cheever George N. Mrs. house 20 Winter
Cheever Joseph, captain, house 8 Federal
Cheever Joseph C. gasfitter, 273 Essex, house 64½ North
Cheever Mary P. Mrs. nurse, house 371 Essex
Cheever William, currier, boards 186 Federal
Chenery Henry, mariner, house 20 Mall
Cheney Joseph H. cigar maker, house 3 Hardy
Cheney William H. mariner, house 20 Becket
Chesley Charles H. watchman, Naumkeag Mill, h. 22 Cedar
Chesman Charles H. mariner, house Everett, n. Salem
Cheswell Samuel, cabinet maker, boards 20 Crombie
Chever D. Augustus, house 137 Essex
Chever George F. counsellor, 150 Essex, house 137 do.
Chever James W. Mrs. house 137 Essex
Chever William J. captain, house 33 Summer
Chew Nancy J. Mrs. house 2 Barton court
Childs William F. clerk, 173 Essex, b. at S. Danvers
Chipman Andrew A. tinsmith, boards 10 Winthrop
Chipman Andrew M. *(Cha·e & Co.)*, tinware, &c. 8 Lafayette, house 10 Winthrop

Chipman Andrew T. currier, house 424 Essex
Chipman Anstiss, house 424 Essex
Chipman Caroline, dressmaker, house 8 Hardy
Chipman Eleazer M. tinsmith, house 347 Essex
Chipman Ellen, teacher, house 424 Essex
Chipman George T. clerk, 240 Essex, house 8 Williams
Chipman Hannah, widow, house 424 Essex
Chipman Henry G. tinplate worker, house 347 Essex
Chipman John M. Mrs. house 8 Williams
Chipman Richard M. tinplate worker, 347 Essex, house do.
Chisholm Eliza, house 7 Pond
Chisholm Joseph, line and twine factory, 68 Mill, h. 7 Pond
Chisholm William, currier, house Warren court
Choate David, physician, house 18 Church
Choate Francis & Co. *(F. W. L. Huntoon)*, dry goods, 222 Essex, boards 19 Lynde
Choate George, physician, 251 Essex, house 257 do.
Choate George F. *(Northend & C.)* Judge of Probate and Insolvency, 20 Asiatic building, boards 9 Washington
Choate Wm. G. counsellor, 25 Asiatic building, h. 257 Essex
Christian Elmira G. boarding house, 1 Sewall
Church Hannah Mrs. house 15 Salem
Church Jonathan R. shoemaker, house foot of Ropes
Church Lemuel, engineer, house 15 Salem
Church P. R. Miss, teacher, house 31 Broad
Church Samuel, blacksmith, 5 Laboratory, house 4 do.
Church William, house Ropes
Churchill Abigail H. tailoress, boards 2 Conant
Churchill Charles S. machinist, house 1 Ward
Churchill George, machinist, house 9 Salem
Churchill Wm. mariner, house 2 Conant
Churchill Wm. H. shoemaker, house 2 Conant
Chute Calvin, carpenter, house Harrod, opp. Phillips
Chute Edward, carpenter, house Irving, near Harrod
Chute Isaiah, carpenter, house Harrod, opp. Phillips
Chute James E. shoestitcher, house 17 Barr
Claggett James, laborer, house 13 Charter
Clancy Martin, currier, house 79 Mason
Clapp Dexter Rev. house 105 Bridge, corner Winter
Clapp Luther, sawing and turning, 5 Front, h. 8 Williams
Clarence Joseph Mrs. house Melcher court
Clark Albion J. clerk, 57 Harbor, boards 70 do.
Clark Andrew, laborer, house 13 Prince
Clark Asa, teamster, house 8 North court
Clark Betsey, widow, house 20 Mill [Harbor
Clark Charles S. *(Wiggin & C.)*, wood, &c. 29 Peabody, h. 70

Clark Cornelius, hostler, house 11 Church
Clark Elizabeth Mrs. house 4 Daniels
Clark George C. carpenter, house 110 Bridge
Clark Henry, tobacconist, house Putnam
Clark James, horseshoer, West place, house 75 North
Clark James A. tobacconist, house 17 Salem
Clark John, house 24 Becket
Clark John Mrs. house 4 Chestnut
Clark John D. captain, house 22 Andrew
Clark John F. printer, boards 53 Lafayette
Clark John S. mariner, house 33 Essex
Clark John W. bookkeeper (B.), house 53 Lafayette
Clark Mary, widow, house 35 Harbor
Clark Nathan T. granite, 25 Peabody, house 9 Ward
Clark Patrick *(Heeney & C.)*, coal, 169 Derby, h. rear 76 Federal
Clark Samuel C. painter, 112 Essex, house 5 Winter
Clark Sarah, widow of John, house 5 Winter
Clark Sarah F. variety store, 18 Mill, house 20 do.
Clark William, peddler, house 98 Derby
Clark Wm. B. mariner, boards 53 Lafayette
Clarke Nicholas A. insurance agent, 27 Wash. h. 116 Bridge
Clarridge Ruth, widow, house Phelps court
Cleaveland Ebenezer, blacksmith, house 16 Northey
Cleaves Eunice, widow, house 59 Buffum
Cleaves Joshua, boards Essex House
Cleaves Nathaniel, weigher and guager (B.), h. 26 Pleasant
Cleaves N. Porter, insurance broker (B.), house 26 Pleasant
Clement Henry, currier, house 11 Prescott
Clement James, peddler, house Lemon court
Clement Mary, nurse, house 181 Bridge
Cleveland Lucy H. Mrs. house 62 Lafayette
Cleveland William S. Treasurer Salem Turnpike Co. 42 Wash. house 62 Lafayette
Clifford Dan A. ambrotypist (B.), house 17 Saunders
Clifford Dennis, tailor, house 41 St. Peter
Clifford Hannah Mrs. house 7 English
Clifford Israel, book agent, house 14 Williams
Clifford John H. laborer, house 7 English
Clough Andrews, mariner, house 65 Essex
Clough Benjamin P. mariner, house 97 Essex
Clough Daniel E. trader, boards 113 North   [Federal
Clough Robert P. *(Kinsman & C.)*, currier, Franklin, house 90
Clough Thomas, mariner, house 48 Essex
Clough William H. captain, house 97 Essex
Clough William H. shoemaker, house 140 Bridge
Cloutman Charles E. expressman, house 8 Congress

Cloutman George W. pilot, house 22 High
Cloutman Joseph, city clerk, City Hall, house 10 Union
Cloutman Sally and Priscilla, tailoresses, house 15 Carlton
Cloutman Stephen, captain, house 45 Essex
Cloutman Thomas T. 10 Derby square, house 106 Essex
Cloutman William R. mariner, boards 10 Union
Clyne Joseph, tailor, boards 21 Lafayette
Clynes Thomas, laborer, house 4 River
Coburn George, laborer, boards 144 North
Cochran Daniel, Naumkeag Mill, house 14 Congress
Cochran James, currier, house Grove, corner Phillips
Cochran James, Naumkeag Mill, house 16 Congress
Cochran James, clothing, 101 Derby, house do.
Cochran Jeremiah, laborer, house 28 Peabody
Cochran Patrick, laborer, house Becket avenue
Cochran Robert, Naumkeag Mill, house 63 Harbor
Cochran William (B.), house 14 High street court
Cody Edmund, mariner, house 407 Essex
Cody Thomas, currier, house Hanson
Coff William, laborer, house 21 Fowler
Coffee John, laborer, house 24 Ward
Coffin Calvin, shipwright, S. Railway, Gardner st. h. 61 Mill
Coffin James, captain, house 6 Everett
Coffrain Mary E. widow, house 7 South Pine
Cogswell Eliza T. teacher, boards 26 Federal
Cogswell Epes, housewright, house 24 Derby
Cogswell John E. watchman, Naumkeag Mill, house 66 Harbor
Cogswell Martha Mrs. house 8 Hardy
Cogswell Robert Mrs. house 26 Federal
Cohan Lawrence, laborer, house 172 Derby
Coker Elizabeth Mrs. house 11 Union
Coker John J. agent (in Africa), house 11 Union
Colbert Edmund, laborer, house 42 Peabody
Colburn Rebecca Mrs. nurse, house 14 Howard
Colby Hannah Mrs house 10 Broad
Colby Isaac N. tanner, house 175 Boston
Colby James T. calker and graver, house 4 Prince
Colby John W. variety store, 46 Peabody, house do.
Colby William C. calker and graver, house 91 Federal
Colcord Joseph A. coachman, 212 Essex, house rear do.
Cole George, coachman, Essex House, house 9½ St. Peter
Cole John F. clerk (B.), boards 10 Hathorne
Cole John W. city watchman, house 3 March
Cole Mary A. Mrs. house 10 Hathorne
Cole Nicholas, fisherman, house 10 March
Cole Solomon D. peddler, house 12 Park

Cole Thomas Mrs. house 28 Chestnut
Collier Charles D. cabinet maker, house 43 Bridge
Collier Edward T. carpenter, boards 16 Conant
Collier Hannah, widow, house 16 Conant
Collier John H. sash and blind maker, house 9 Buffum
Collier John, baker, boards 89 Essex
Collier Lois Miss, house 7 North court
Collier Perry, varnisher, boards 16 Conant
Colligan Patrick, teamster, house 13 Lynn
Collins Andrew, currier, house Grove
Collins Charles, clerk, 44 Derby, house 7 Orange
Collins Charles H. boards 14 English
Collins Daniel, laborer, house 13 Prince
Collins Daniel, provisions, 5 Charter, house do.
Collins Dennis, laborer, house 155 Boston
Collins Edward, assistant city marshal, house 31 Turner
Collins Edward jr. clerk, boards 31 Turner
Collins George B. cooper, boards 14 English
Collins James, ropemaker, house 14 English
Collins Jeremiah, saloon, 89 Derby, boards do.
Collins Joanna, widow, house 16 Crombie
Collins John, house 16 Daniels
Collins John, currier, house rear 11 Whittemore
Collins John, laborer, house 90 Derby
Collins John, house 85 Derby
Collins Lucy Mrs. house 7 Monroe
Collins Michael, farmer, house Phillips
Collins Patrick, oysters, 1 Phoenix building, house 5 Charter
Collins Patrick, laborer, house 170 Derby
Collins Simon, tanner, boards 184 Federal
Collins Thomas, laborer, house 85 Derby
Collins Thomas, shoemaker, 107 Derby, house do.
Collins Timothy, currier, house Varney, near Hanson
Collins Timothy T. laborer, house East Webb
Colman Benjamin, auctioneer, 9 Derby square, h. 3 Winter
Colman Benjamin F. clerk, 9 Derby square, boards 3 Winter
Colman Bernard G. currier, house 39 Beaver
Colman Fanny O. Mrs. dressmaker, 242½ Essex, h. Cross st. ct.
Colman George B. hairdresser, 175½ Essex, house 12 Porter
Colman John, Naumkeag Mill, house 4 Elm
Colman Michael, laborer, house Odell square
Colman M. A. Miss, teacher, house 3 Winter
Colman Sarah, widow, house 12 Porter
Colman Simon Mrs. house 140 Derby
Comaford Catharine, widow, house 405 Essex
Comer John, teamster, house Oak, near Beach

Conant Herbert, mason, house 3 Mount Vernon
Conant John, mason, house 23 Harbor
Conboy George, laborer, house 1 Derby
Condon Richard, shoemaker, house 19 Beaver court
Condon Thomas, shoemaker, house opposite 22 Congress
Cone George R. conductor, house 10 Buffum
Conlan Thomas, laborer, house opposite 22 Congress
Conlon John, gardener, house 24 Briggs
Connell Cornelius, laborer, house 5 Buffum
Connell Martin, harness maker, house 14 Williams
Connell Patrick, currier, house 46 Beaver
Connell Patrick, laborer, house rear 89 North
Connelly John, laborer, house 10 River
Connelly Patrick, shoemaker, house 9 Cross
Conner Charles T. mariner, house 4 Cabot
Conner James F. mason, house 30 Albion
Conners Bartholomew, laborer, house 34 Derby
Conners William, currier, house 166 Federal
Connolly Michael, Naumkeag Mill, boards 59 Harbor
Connors Dennis, laborer, house 38 Peabody
Connors Ellen, widow, house rear 35 Harbor
Connors Michael, hostler, house 47 Washington
Connors Owen, laborer, house 26 Peabody
Connors Timothy, watchman, house 47 Beaver
Connors ——, upholsterer, boards 9 Norman
Connors ——, Mrs. house 20 Park
Conrey James H. currier, Buffum, house 98 North
Conroy Bernard, confectionery, 2 Washington
Convers Abigail Mrs. boarding house, 196 Derby
Converse Charles F. shoemaker, boards 118 Boston
Converse Francis T. shoemaker, house 1 N. Pine
Converse Josiah, shoemaker, house Ord
Converse Robert, shoemaker, house 118 Boston
Conway Chaplin, captain, house 20 Beckford
Conway Edward A. clerk, house 7 Herbert
Conway Hugh, currier, 69 Mason, house 3 Oak
Conway James H. carpenter, house 7 Beach
Cook Arial, refreshments, Eastern R. R. depot, house 20 Mill
Cook Barnabas, mariner, house 68 Essex
Cook Caleb, student, house 5 Hathorne
Cook Eliza A. widow, house 36 Pleasant
Cook Elizabeth P. house 44 Charter
Cook George T. fish dealer, North, near the bridge, house 36 Buffum
Cook Hannah G. widow, house 12 St. Peter
Cook Henry, cooper, house 18 Walnut

Cook Humphrey, hats, caps, and furs, 233 Essex, and 33 Washington, house Union place
Cook James P. merchant, house 64 Bridge
Cook John, house 36 Pleasant
Cook Mary, house 44 Charter
Cook Samuel, merchant, house 142 Federal
Cook Simon L. tailor, 189 Essex, house 44 Charter
Cook William, house 12 Carlton
Cook William, house 36 Pleasant
Cook William Mrs. house 5 Hathorne
Cook William Rev. author Ploughboy & Neriah, h. 44 Charter
Coombs Frederick, harness maker, 81 North, house 3 Mechanic
Coombs Lydia Mrs. house 51 North
Coomer Vincent, laborer, house 51 Derby
Copeland George A. millinery, 250 Essex, h. 9 Washington
Copeland Robert M. carpenter, 8 North, house 16 Norman
Corbett Dennis, currier, boards 14 Oak
Corcoran Joseph, clerk, house 27 Dearborn
Corcoran Mary, widow, house 27 Dearborn
Corgin Timothy, laborer, house foot of Park
Cornelius Alonzo G. merchant tailor, 178 Essex, h. 4 Cross
Corning Martha E. widow, house 161 Boston
Cornish Humphrey, blacksmith, house 19 Upham
Cornwell Francis, currier, boards 59 Harbor
Costello Margaret, widow, house 86 Derby
Cotter Edmund, laborer, house 23 Carlton
Cotter Simon, laborer, house Tucker's wharf
Cottle Alfred, cooper, house 33 Derby
Cottle Hannah Mrs. seamstress, house 50 Derby
Cottle Michael, laborer, house 99 Derby
Cottle William, house 32 Essex
Cottle William H. shipwright, house 32 Essex
Cottrell James K. (Cal.), boards 158 Bridge
Cottrell Judith Mrs. house 158 Bridge
Couch Daniel, baker, 2 Front, house 7 Whittemore
Couch Francis A. carpenter, house 58 Federal
Coughlin Daniel, laborer, house Herbert
Coughlin Jeremiah, laborer, house 8 Pratt
Coughlin Maurice, laborer, house foot Park
Coughlin Michael, tailor, house Parker's court
Coughlin Michael, laborer, house 5 Creek
Coughlin Patrick, laborer, house 8 Pratt
Coughlin Timothy, tailor, house Parker's court
Courtis Hannah Miss, house 17 North
Courtis Nancy Miss, house 117 Federal
Cousins Thomas, mariner, house 8 English
Cousins Thomas jr. clerk, 152 Essex, house 8 English

Cowee George L., Laboratory, house 66 North
Cowley John, laborer, house S. Prospect, corner Pingree
Cox Andrew, mariner, house 14 Becket
Cox Benjamin, merchant, house 21 Norman
Cox Benjamin jr. physician, house 23 Norman
Cox Edward S. house 21 Norman
Cox Francis, com. merchant, 17 Doane (B.), house 1 Chestnut
Cox Francis R. blacksmith, Bridge, cor. North, h. 19 Upham
Cox Mary G. Mrs. nurse, house 16 High
Crafts George, junk, 43 Derby, house 22 Forrester
Crahan Dennis, teamster, house rear 8 Pratt
Craig Catharine Mrs. house 38 Essex
Craig George B. 3 Lafayette, house 20 Liberty
Craig Samuel, provisions, 3 Lafayette, house 14 Central
Craig Winnifred, widow, house 6 Peabody
Crandell John, sailmaker, rear 41 Derby, house 12 Becket
Crandell Joseph H. sailmaker, house 12 English
Crandell William H. mariner, house 10 Turner
Crane Lizzie D. milliner, 168 Essex, house at South Danvers
Crane Mary E. 168 Essex, house at South Danvers
Craney John, laborer, house 422 Essex
Craney Mary, widow, house 422 Essex
Crary William T. musician, boards 3 Pleasant
Cread Daniel, laborer, house Adams
Cread James, tailor, house Parker's court
Creamer Benjamin Mrs. house 361 Essex
Creamer Frederick M. house 71 Lafayette
Creamer Geo. bookseller & stationer, 243 Essex, h. 1 Newbury
Creamer Hannah Mrs. house 12 Walnut
Creamer Henry, machinist, boards 4 North Pine
Creamer Jeremiah, laborer, house 28 Congress
Creamer Matthew, laborer, house 20 Carlton
Creamer Michael, stevedore, house 7 Allen
Creasy Charles, superintendent Harmony Grove, h. 8 Grove
Creesy Mehitable, widow, house 14 Central
Credon John, laborer, house 36 Peabody
Credon Mary, widow, house 4 High street court
Cresoe Henry, boards 17 Pond
Cresoe Michael, ropemaker, house 17 Pond
Crierie Archelaus, mariner. house 17 Creek
Crocker Josiah, house 18 Mall   [cor. Front, h. at Ipswich
Crocker Samuel P. foreign and domestic fruit, 12 Washington,
Cronan Daniel. currier, house 10 Beaver court
Cronan Ellen, widow, house 14 Congress
Cronan Hannah, widow, house 53 St. Peter
Cronan John, house 16 Congress
Cronan John, laborer, house 82 Mason

Cronan Michael, currier, house 10 Beaver court
Cronan Patrick, laborer, house Pingree
Cronan William, currier, house Green place
Cronan William, harness maker, h. South Prospect, n. Pingree
Crooks Paul, shoemaker, house 118 Boston
Crosby Alpheus, principal Normal School, house 24 Lynde
Crosby George W. root beer manuf. 10 Derby sq. h. 14 Winter
Crosby Josiah H. cooper (Cuba), house 51 Harbor
Crosby Sarah, nurse, house 14 Norman
Cross Charles B. shoemaker, house 4 Friend
Cross Hannah and Lucy, house 9 Liberty
Cross Henry J. librarian at Plummer Hall, h. Liberty Hill Road
Cross James, Naumkeag mill, house 28 Ward
Cross Joseph S. clothing, 198 Essex, house 11 Central
Cross Joshua H. tinplate worker, house 50 Lafayette
Cross Martha F. house 27 Summer
Cross Mary A. teacher, house 13 Liberty
Cross Parker, farmer, house Liberty Hill Road
Cross Sarah E. teacher, boards 27 Summer
Cross Susan, house Liberty Hill Road
Cross William Mrs. house 13 Liberty
Crotty Alice Mrs. house rear 40 St. Peter
Crotty Richard, laborer, house 18 Charter
Croughwell John, currier, house rear Shillaber
Croughwell William, currier, house rear Shillaber
Crowdis George R. currier, house 6 Friend
Crowell Abigail Mrs. house 148 Bridge
Crowell Hannah Mrs. house 148 Bridge
Crowley John, E. R. R. depot, house 7 Ropes
Crowley John H. laborer, house 7 Ropes
Culberston John H. clerk, 228 Essex, house 54 Endicott
Cullen James, laborer, house 76 North
Culliton Bridget, widow, house 105 Mason
Culliton John, tanner and currier, Milldam, house 9 Friend
Cummings Barney, laborer, house 41 North
Cummings Edward D. sailmaker, house 2 Turner
Cummings John, currier, house Grove, above Mason
Cunningham Anastatia, widow, house 2 High st. court
Cunningham Eliza, house foot Phelps court
Cunningham John, harness maker, 17 Daniels, h. 93 Derby
Cunningham Patrick, currier, boards 29 Beaver
Cunningham Peter, currier, boards 8 Ward
Curran Catherine, widow, house 18 Charter
Curran Hannah Mrs. house 22 Dearborn
Curran James, laborer, house Tucker's wharf
Curran John, tanner, boards 29 Beaver
Curran Stephen, chemist, house 22 Dearborn

SALEM [D] DIRECTORY.

Curran Susan Mrs. house 12 Mall
Currier Daniel, laborer, house 11 Walnut
Currier Edward A. cooper, boards 11 Walnut
Currier George H. dentist, 208 Essex, house 1 Ward
Currier *(Seth S.)* & Miller *(B. R.)*, furniture, 259 & 261 Essex, house 17 Barton square
Currin Francis, tanner, house 21 Fowler
Currin John A. clerk, P. O. house 12 Mall
Curtain John, currier, house rear 67 Mason
Curtan Fanny Mrs. house 53 St. Peter
Curtin Jeremiah, currier, house 129 Boston
Curtin Mary, widow, house 15 Flint
Curtin William, currier, boards 15 Flint
Curtis Austin, clerk, 228 Essex, boards 7 Prince
Curtis Elizabeth, cook, house 15 Pond
Curtis Emanuel, trader, house 101 Federal
Curtis Lydia Mrs. house 7 Prince
Curtis Richard, currier, boards at Daniel Shea's
Curtis Stephen W. shoemaker, house 45 Derby
Curtis Thomas, tanner, boards at Daniel Shea's
Curwen George R. clerk Register of Deeds, house 21 Lynde
Curwen James B. merchant, Central wharf, house 331 Essex
Curwen Priscilla B. Mrs. house 21 Lynde
Curwen Samuel R. captain, house 333 Essex
Cushing Abner, shoemaker, boards 63 Harbor
Cushing Isaac, merchant, 183 Derby, house 21 Union
Cushing Maria, teacher, house 183 Bridge
Cushing Nancy P. Mrs. house 183 Bridge
Cushman Joseph S. mason, house 8 Broad
Cutler William, dry goods, 138 Boston, house 105 do.
Cutts Benjamin, blacksmith, 8 Sewall, house 32 Beckford
Cutts Richard, blacksmith, Endicott, c. Mill, h. 45 Endicott

DADY WILLIAM, laborer, house 411 Essex
Dailey Robert, city express, 5 Arrington building, h. 8 Porter
Dakin Rachel Mrs. dressmaker, house 77 Summer
Dakin Timothy H. house 77 Summer
Daland Edward, boards 132 Essex
Daland Joanna Mrs. house 12 and 14 Beckford
Daland Joanna, carpet market, house 12 and 14 Beckford
Daland John, boards 132 Essex
Daland Mary, tailoress, house 12 and 14 Beckford
Daland Tucker Mrs. house 132 Essex
Daley Catharine, widow, house 4 Pingree
Daley Daniel, currier, house 10 High st. court
Daley Daniel, currier, house 30 North
Daley James, Naumkeag Mill, house Congress, west side

Daley Jeremiah, laborer, house 18 Charter
Daley Jeremiah, laborer, house Congress, west side
Daley John, baker, house 7 Creek
Daley John, currier, boards 1 Friend
Daley Mary, widow, house Adams
Daley Matthew, tanner, house 1 Friend
Daley Michael, baker, boards 11 High
Daley Michael, baker, boards 7 Creek
Daley Timothy, currier, house Adams
Daley William, laborer, house Thorndike
Dalrymple James, asst. city marshall, house 6 Herbert
Dalrymple John J. clerk, Post Office boards 6 Herbert
Dalrymple Sarah Mrs. house 10 Essex
Dalrymple Simon O. cooper, 4 Derby wharf, house 99 Essex
Dalrymple Simon O. boards 6 Herbert
Dalrymple William H. clerk, Post Office, boards 6 Herbert
Dalton Charles H. currier, house 55 Forrester
Dalton David, currier, house Pope's court
Dalton Edward A. calker, boards 65 Essex
Dalton Edward E. tailor (B.), house 16 Mechanic
Dalton Edward H. clerk, house 65 Boston
Dalton Eleazer M. house 55 Forrester
Dalton Eleazer M. jr. currier, house 5 Friend
Dalton John, currier, house Fowler
Dalton John C. coachman (B.), house 4 Everett
Dalton Joseph A. tanner, 61 Mason, house 75 Boston
Dalton Lucy, widow, house 163 Boston
Dalton Patrick, shoemaker, house 15 Park
Dalton Sarah N. Mrs. house 65 Essex
Dalton William T. currier, house 41 Boston
Daluhary Daniel, oil mill, house 49 Mill
Daluhary David, laborer, house 49 Mill
Dane Joseph F. shoe dealer (B.), house 31 Summer
Danforth Edward F. carpenter, house 2 Downing
Danforth Henry F. 14½ Front, boards 19 Summer
Danforth John K. house 78 Essex
Danforth Joseph A. carpenter, 46 Union, house 43 Forrester
Danforth N. G. Mrs. house 3 Margin
Danforth Samuel G. carpenter, 33 Endicott, h. 13 Winthrop
Danforth Wm. H. printing press manuf. 46 Union, b. 98 Federal
Daniels Charles H. clerk, 70 Federal, house 46 do.
Daniels John, shoemaker, house 125 Lafayette
Daniels John B. shoemaker, house Lafayette, n. F. R. L. Mills
Daniels Lucy Mrs. house 64 Broad
Daniels Stephen, provisions, 70 Federal, house 68 do.
Daniels William, shoemaker, house 64 Broad
Davenport William, shoemaker, house 16 Central

Davidson Henry, tanner, house 47 Broad
Davidson John, tanner, house 75 Mason
Davidson Moses, coach painter, 134 Boston, house 20 Albion
Davidson Thomas F. painter, house 20 Albion
Davis Alice N. Mrs. house 27 Forrester
Davis Augustus, tanner, boards 15 Friend
Davis Benjamin T. carpenter, house 142 Bridge [Dodge
Davis Charles H. painter and glazier, 35 North, h. Walter, cor.
Davis Christopher C., E. R. R. house 60 North
Davis David W. shoemaker, house 64 North
Davis Dudley B. captain, house 14 Osgood
Davis Eliza B. boards 33 Summer
Davis Hannah L. fancy goods, 142½ Essex, house do.
Davis Horatio G. coachman, 212 Essex, house 199 Bridge
Davis Jacob, laborer, house 12 Cedar [Walnut
Davis Jacob P. *(Moulton & Davis)*, express, 10 Wash. house 18
Davis James, house Phelps court
Davis James B. tailor, house 56 Broad
Davis James D. shoemaker, boards 29 Buffum
Davis John, mariner, house 26 Peabody
Davis John Mrs. house 55 North
Davis John H. junk, house 20 Pickman
Davis Jonathan, mason, boards 12 Upham
Davis Mary, widow, house 4 Palfrey court
Davis Mary Mrs. house 408 Essex
Davis Paine M. shoemaker, house 64 North
Davis Richard, merchant, house 19 Hardy
Davis Rodman J. dancing master, house Phelps court
Davis Sally, widow, house 5 May
Davis Stephen W. clerk, 12 Washington, house 15 Creek
Davis Susannah, widow, house 64 North
Davis Sylvester P. fireman, house 80 North
Davis Joseph W. at laboratory, house 12 Upham
Davis Warren P. currier, house 17 Warren
Dawes Mary, widow, house 375 Essex
Dawson George, shipkeeper, house 22 Carlton
Day Albert, carpenter, 228 Derby, house 3 Mt. Vernon
Day Amos P. *(Goldthwait & D.)*, house 14 Harbor
Day Aziel, currier, house 9 Albion
Day Edward A, clerk, 188 Essex, boards 14 Harbor
Day James, farmer, house Phillips, near Grove
Day John, captain, house 15 North
Day Margaret, widow, house 123 Boston
Day Margaret Mrs. house 15 Becket
Day Mary, widow, house 8 Beaver
Day Samuel, house 57 Washington
Day Thomas, farmer, house Grove, near School

Day Thomas H. shoemaker, boards 7 Prince
Dayton Isaac, carriage trimmer and harness maker, 4 Sewall, house do.
Dean Desire Miss, house 112 Bridge
Dean George, mariner, house 51 Summer
Dean James, laborer, house 22 Northey
Dean Mary, widow, house 172 Derby
Dean Sarah B. widow, house 120 Bridge
Dean William H. captain, house 11 Warren
Dearborn Charles A. stable, Wash. c. Church, h. 6 Laboratory
Dearborn Charles H. 156 Essex, boards 17 Washington
Dearborn Henry, tinplate worker, house 11 Beaver
Dearborn John R. laborer, house 7 Nursery
Dease Lawrence, tailor, 244 Essex, house 24 Charter
Dease Thomas, tailor, 244 Essex, house 24 Charter
Debaker Victor F. captain, house 36 Essex
Decker Robert M. carver, house 55 Endicott
Dee David, overseer Naumkeag Mill, house 69 Harbor
Dee Eliza, widow, house 8 Ropes
Deffel Joseph, mariner, house 51 Derby
Deforest Daniel, laborer, house Buffum
Defreace Joseph, turner (B.), boards 11 Prescott
Defreace Margaret, widow, house 7 Endicott
Deland Charles, mariner, house 113 Essex
Deland Harriet Miss, house 9 Newbury
Deland Judith, house 15 Whittemore
Deland Mary, variety store, 157 Bridge, house do.
Deland Robert, house 113 Essex
Deland Samuel D. shoemaker, house 155 Bridge
Deland Susan, house 69 North
Deland Susan Miss, house 2 Church
Delaney John, blacksmith, house 11 Beaver
Delaney Thomas, currier, house Hanson
Delany Thomas, currier, house 29 Boston
Dempsey James, tanner, boards 123 Boston
Dempsey Patrick, currier, house 10 Aborn
Denehy Michael, shoemaker, house 22 Congress
Denehy William, laborer, house 24 Ward
Dennett Ruth, widow, house 28 Harbor
Dennigan William, currier, house Adams
Dennis Devereux, carpenter, 8 Lafayette, h. 15 Dearborn
Denny Timothy, laborer, house foot Perkins
Derby Abigail Mrs. house 4 Blaney
Derby Caroline R. Miss, house 122 Lafayette
Derby Charles, watchmaker, 242 Essex, house 14 Howard
Derby Charles, Naumkeag Mill, house 22 Ward
Derby Charles W. watchmaker, house 10 Saunders

Derby E. Hersey Mrs. house 122 Lafayette
Derby Henry, inspector custom house, house 59 Federal
Derby H. Matilda Miss, house 122 Lafayette
Derby John H. clerk, 42 Washington, boards 59 Federal
Derby Marianne B. Miss, house 122 Lafayette
Derby Martha Mrs. house 8 Beckford
Derby Mary, artist, house 4 Blaney
Derby Mary E. widow, house 20 Boston
Derby Perley, dentist, house 15 Northey
Derby Putnam T. tinplate worker, house 6 Andrew
Derby Samuel Mrs. house 116 Federal
Derby Susan A. nurse, house 2 Dow
Desent Elizabeth, widow, house 40 St. Peter
Desmond John, shoemaker, 42 Union, house do.
Devereux Arthur F. clerk (B.), boards 19 School
Devereux George H. counsellor, 24 Washington, h. 19 School
Devereux Humphrey, merchant, boards 33 Summer
Devereux John F. student at law, 24 Washington, b. 19 School
Devine Catharine, widow, house 36 Mill
Devine James, Naumkeag Mill, house 49 Harbor
Devine Jeremiah, shaver, boards 41 North
Devine John, laborer, house 3 Tucker's wharf
Devlin Jane Miss, house 5 Park
Devlin ———, peddler, boards 5 Park
Dewing Dolly, dressmaker, house 2 Lynde
Dewing Joseph Mrs. house 28 Beckford
Dewing Josiah, captain, house 93 Federal
Dewire Jeremiah, laborer, house 27 Daniels
Dewire Mary, widow, house Grove
Dexter Benjamin W. Mrs. house 8 Church
Dickerson George, laborer, house rear 8 Whittemore
Dickey Isaac, mastic roofer, boards 7 Central
Dickson Thomas, tanner, house 2 Mason
Dickson Walter S. tanner, boards 2 Mason
Dignan Patrick, servant at 22 Union
Dike John & Co. *(R. C. Manning)*, coal, wood, &c. 183 Derby,
    house 52 Federal
Dike Nathaniel, clerk, 183 Derby, boards at Beverly
Dimond Abigail Mrs. house Botts court
Dimond Abigail, dressmaker, house Botts court
Dimond Benjamin, mariner, house Botts court
Ditmore Sarah, widow, house 12 Oliver
Dix Asa C. dry goods, 245 Essex, house 50 Federal
Dix Daniel, mariner, house 2 Carlton
Dix Edward D. mariner, house 83 Summer
Dix George A. currier, house 424 Essex
Dix Thomas M. clerk, house 84 Summer

Dockham Eliza, house 402 Essex
Dockham Elizabeth, nurse, house 34 Essex
Dockham Mary Ann, dressmaker, 402 Essex
Dockham William S. job wagon, house Parker's court
Dodd John, hostler, house 12 Ash
Dodd John, switchman E. R. R. house 49 Mill
Dodd Patrick, laborer, house 30 Peabody
Dodd Patrick, oil mill, house 49 Mill
Dodd Thomas, switchman E. R. R. house 31 Mill
Dodge Allen W. county treasurer, Court House, h. at Hamilton
Dodge Clara, house 12 Summer
Dodge *(David)* & Brooks *(Isaac)*, carpenters, Derby wharf, house 5 Orange
Dodge Ebenezer, surveyor Custom House, house 4 Federal ct.
Dodge Ellen M. teacher Normal School, house 5 Lemon
Dodge Emeline Miss, nurse, house 48 Charter
Dodge Emma C. Mrs. house 47 Essex
Dodge Francis A. mariner, house 22 Hardy
Dodge George, grocery and clothing store, 122 Derby, house 2 Brown
Dodge George A. mariner, house 8 Conant
Dodge George A. (Cal.), house 28 Church
Dodge George F., Wash. Bank (B.), boards 2 Brown
Dodge Hannah, widow, house 93 Bridge
Dodge Hannah, widow, house 19 Salem
Dodge Jacob L. wood and coal, 17 Lafayette, house 18 do.
Dodge *(James A.)* & Jones *(J. S.)*, flour, grain, and plaster, Pierce's wharf, house 4 Federal court
Dodge John N. carpenter, house 24 Derby
Dodge John W. carriage maker, 20 Peabody, h. 93 Bridge
Dodge Joseph S. tanner, house 4 Beaver court
Dodge Josiah, carpenter, house 8 Conant
Dodge Josiah S. mariner, house 8 Conant
Dodge Leverett, painter, boards 8 Conant
Dodge Lucy, widow, house 18 Lafayette
Dodge Mary Mrs. house 7 Turner
Dodge Mary Ann Mrs. seamstress, house 113 Essex
Dodge Peter S. (B.), boards 20 Cedar
Dodge Sarah, upholsteress, house 8 Williams
Dodge Temple, painter, house 28 Dearborn
Dodge Thomas F. carpenter, house 177 Boston
Dodge Thomas S. coachman, house 10 Sewall
Dodge William, house 3 North court
Dodge William H. mariner, house 8 Conant
Dodge William M. shoemaker, 3 Lemon, house 5 do.
Doggett William, laborer, house 2 Pratt street court
Doherty Charles, laborer, house 27 Ward

Doherty Lawrence, laborer, house 21 Ward
Doherty Thomas, currier, house Green place
Doherty Patrick, laborer, house rear 6 Essex
Dolan Edward, laborer, house rear Adams
Dolan John, grocer, 171 Derby, house 55 Warren
Dolan John jr. farmer, house 55 Warren
Dolan Morris, laborer, house 30 North
Dolan Owen, laborer, house High street court
Dolan Patrick, laborer, house 12 Beach
Dolan Patrick, shoemaker, house 3 Aborn
Dolan Timothy, laborer, house 28 Peabody
Dolan William, gardener, house 160 Bridge
Doland James H. tinsmith, house 18 Howard
Dole William S. shoemaker, house 31 Bridge
Dolliver John, shoemaker, house rear 28 Church
Dominick Joseph, carpenter, boards 310 Essex
Dominick Michael, laborer, house 30 Essex
Donahoe John, laborer, house 10 Derby
Donahoe John J. printer, 185 Essex, house Warren court
Donahoe Michael, shoemaker, house 8 Ropes
Donahoe Michael, laborer, house 21 Ward
Donahoe Patrick, currier, house Warren court
Donahoe Thomas, laborer, house 11 Lynn
Donahoe William, Naumkeag Mill, house 26 Union
Donaldson Alexander, pump and block maker, 141 Derby, house 99 Bridge
Donaldson James, currier, house 20 Mason
Donaldson John, pump and block maker, house 99 Bridge
Donally John, laborer, house 172 Derby
Donovan Catharine, widow, house Becket ave.
Donovan Jeremiah, laborer, house 2 Tucker's wharf
Donovan John, laborer, house 40 Peabody
Donovan John, laborer, house 20 Carlton
Donovan John, laborer, house 7 Charter
Donovan Mary, widow, house 153 Bridge
Donovan Michael, house 23 Charter
Donovan Michael, shoemaker, 168 Derby, house 23 Charter
Donovan Patrick, laborer, house 25 Liberty
Doody Bartholomew, laborer, house Mason, opp. Rosin works
Doody John, currier, house 14 Oak
Doran William, currier, boards 8 Ward
Dore Edmund, teamster, house Dodge, near Southwick
Doret Stephen, 164 Derby, house 29 Turner
Douglass George W. mariner, boards 5 Gedney court
Douglass William, laborer, house 48 Derby
Douglass William C. mariner, house 10 Church
Dow Edward A. mariner, house 19 Summer

Dow Milo, rags and junk, house 25 Pickman
Dow William W. confectioner, 170 Essex, house do.
Dow Zilpha M. Mrs. house 17 Mason
Dowbridge Andrew, rigger, house 9 Gardner court
Dowbridge Andrew jr. mason, house 51 Bridge
Dowbridge Henry, mason, house 11 Gardner court
Dowling Thomas, boards 21 Lafayette
Downes Mary Mrs. house 216 Derby
Downing Catharine, widow, house 22 Williams
Downing Charles M. cook, house 68 North
Downing John H. captain, house 20 Brown
Downing John P. clerk Naumkeag Bank, boards 14 Salem
Downing John W. Mrs. house 14 Dow
Downing Thomas, merchant, house 20 Brown
Downing Thomas W. (*Archer, Downing & Co.*), dry goods and carpetings, 173 Essex, house 20 Brown
Dowst David, baker, boards 23 North
Dowst David B. teamster, Charter, cor. Central, h. Dodge's ct.
Dowst Joseph A. expressman, boards 15 Creek
Dowst Joshua D. painter, house 6 Creek
Dowst Richard, expressman, house 15 Creek
Dowst Richard jr. carpenter, house Green place
Dowst William, baker, house 6 Creek
Doyle Edward, laborer, house 3 Pratt street court
Doyle John, currier, house 27 Albion
Doyle John, laborer, house 99 Derby
Doyle Thomas, house 33 Summer
Draper Arnold, millinery, 260 Essex, house do.
Drew Mary A. Mrs. house rear 40 St. Peter
Drew Thomas, waiter and tender, house rear 1 Ropes
Drinan John, charcoal, house foot Ives
Driscoll Bridget Mrs. house Dodge's court
Driscoll Daniel, laborer, house 6 Carlton
Driscoll Dennis, laborer, house 101 Derby
Driscoll Jeremiah, laborer, house Fowler
Driscoll John, laborer, house E. Webb
Driscoll John, laborer, house 10 Herbert
Driscoll Maurice, tanner, house 8 River
Driscoll Patrick, laborer, house Fowler
Driscoll Patrick Henry, mariner, house 14 Union
Driscoll Peter, laborer, house 26 Congress
Driscoll Timothy, laborer, boards P. Driscoll's, Fowler
Driver George, shoecutter, 16 Washington, h. Cedar, c. Cherry
Driver John S. student at law, 27 Washington
Driver Stephen and Co. (*Stephen P. Driver and Lucius Wells*), shoe manufacturers, 16 Wash. and 34½ Front, house Beaver Brook, N. Danvers

Driver Stephen P. *(S Driver & Son)*, house 51 Essex
Drown Peter, horse shoer, Lummus court, house 18½ Beckford
Drown William P. carriagesmith, boards 18½ Beckford
Duchow John C. Mrs. house 13 Allen
Duffee John, currier, house 11 Beaver
Dugan Bernard, laborer, house 20 River
Dugan Dennis, laborer, house 28 Peabody
Dugan Michael (Cal.), house 15 River
Dugan William, laborer, house rear 31 Derby
Dukes Edward, currier, boards 148 Boston
Dukes James, currier, house 148 Boston
Dummer John S. *(Abbot & D.)*, fish, Phillips Wharf,, boards 53 Derby
Dunbar Alvah, ship carpenter, boards 16 Dow
Duncan William, captain, house 89 Federal
Duncklee E. milliner, 295 Essex, house 121 North
Dunham John, captain, house 28 Derby
Dunham John S. captain, house 28 Derby
Dunn Margaret A. teacher Bentley School, house 19 Becket
Dunn Martin, carpenter, house 7 Creek
Dunn Thomas C. captain, house 43 North
Dunney John, currier, house 24 High
Dunzack Daniel N. painter, house 7 Winter
Duperre Julius, currier, house Adams, Mason hill
Durgan Mary Mrs. house 77 Federal
Durgin John, peddler, house 97 Derby
Durvin Ellen, widow, house 204 Derby
Dutch Mary, house 13 Federal
Dutra Francis, mariner, house 8 Pearl
Duvall Mitchell Mrs. house 84 Derby
Dwinell Israel E. Rev. house 65 North
Dwyer Hannah Mrs. house 27 Turner
Dwyer John, merchant (B.), house 336 Essex
Dwyer John F. captain, house 336 Essex

EAGAN CATHARINE Mrs. house Putnam
Eagan Martin, currier, house Lummus court
Eagan Patrick D. currier, house 5 Beach
Eagan Richard, currier, house 153 Boston
Eagan William, hostler, house 15 Ash
Eagleston John H. captain, house 48 Lafayette
Earl Charles H. carpenter, house 2 Bentley
Earl John, currier, house 8 Lynn
Easson William Henry, carpenter, house 8 Beach
Easterby Thomas, cigar maker, house 101 Derby
Eastman Nancy, widow, house 131 North
Eastman William H. currier, boards 73 North

Eaton Elizabeth G. Mrs. house 5 Cross [36 do.
Eaton John D. tinplate and sheetiron worker, 40 North, house
Eaton Nathaniel J. baker, 29 Brown, house do.
Eaton William B. artist, house 5 Cross
Edds William M. house 50 Charter
Edgerly John F. overseer Naumkeag Mills, house 7 Lagrange
Edgerly Samuel, captain, house 14 Odell square
Edgerly Samuel B. laborer, house E. Webb
Edgerly Peter Mrs. house 15 Federal
Edwards Abraham, paper hanger, house 21 Creek
Edwards Abraham jr. Naumkeag Mill, house 57 Harbor
Edwards Benjamin, merchant tailor, 224 Essex, house 1 Harrison avenue
Edwards Charles W. paper hanger, house 8 Creek
Edwards Henry, mariner, house 19 Northey
Edwards Jesse B. carpenter, house 6 Cross
Edwards John B. house 9 Andrew
Edwards John L. mariner, house 16 Williams
Edwards John S. carpenter, 8 North, house 49 Summer
Edwards Jonathan Mrs. house 71 Federal
Edwards Lowell S. (Cal.), house 16 Williams
Edwards Mary Mrs. house 13 Curtis [Leach
Edwards Richard, principal Normal School at St. Louis, house
Edwards William, painter, house 3 North court
Edwards William (Cal.), house 4 Curtis
Egan William, hostler, 212 Essex
Ehions Charles, mariner, house 14 Peabody
Elliot Isaac B. provisions, 3 & 4 Market House, house at South Danvers
Ellis John, shipkeeper, house 11 Herbert
Ellis John (Cal.), house 50 Derby
Ellis John, shoemaker, house 16 Derby
Elwell *(Charles B.)* & Potter *(J. F.)*, carpenters, 38 Peabody, house 6 Pond
Emerson Brown Rev. D.D. house 377 Essex
Emerson Elizabeth Mrs. house 23 Albion
Emerson George B. house 377 Essex
Emerson George F. shoemaker, house 74 Federal
Emerson Gilbert B. clerk 4 Newbury, boards 51 St. Peter
Emerson Henry W. mariner, boards 12 Park
Emerson Hiram G. & N. grocers, 134 Boston, house Prospect, near Summit
Emerson Huldah & Olive Misses, house 25 North
Emerson Jane H. Mrs. house 23 Norman
Emerson Nathan *(H. G. & N. Emerson)*, house 173 Boston
Emerton Hannah M. Mrs. house 1 Elm
Emerton James, apothecary, 123 Essex, house 1 Elm

SALEM [F] DIRECTORY.

Emery Charles, carver, house 4 Turner
Emery Charles, carver, house 7 Mall
Emery Samuel, nautical instrument maker, 162 Derby, house 131 Federal
Emmerton Daniel S. mariner, house 13 Summer
Emmerton Edward P. house 13 Summer
Emmerton Ephraim, merchant, house 13 Summer
Emmerton George R. clerk (B.), house 13 Summer
Emmerton James A. physician, house 13 Summer
Emmerton William, house 114 Essex
Emmerton *(Wm. H.)* & Foster *(J. C.)*, architects and engineers, 26 Asiatic building, house 13 Summer
Endicott Aaron Mrs. house 90 Bridge
Endicott Caroline Mrs. house 331 Essex
Endicott Charles *(Phippen & E.)*, merchant, 61 Union, house 3 Brown
Endicott Charles E. house 35 Warren
Endicott Charles M. house 35 Warren
Endicott Wm. C. *(Perry & Endicott)*, counsellors, 182 Essex, house 359 do.
Endicott William P. house 359 Essex
English Philip, curled hair factory, Bridge, house 11 Northey
English William G. manuf. curled hair, house 19 Pickman
Entwistle Thomas, shoemaker, house foot East Gardner
Estes George W. restorator, 10 Newbury, house 8 Howard
Estes George W. jr. 10 Newbury, house 8 Howard
Estes Nathaniel K. shoemaker, house Barr, beyond School
Estes Joshua P. ketchup maker, house Thorndike
Estes J. Frank, clerk, 175 Essex, house at S. Danvers
Esty Jeremiah A. restorator, 17 Derby sq. house at Middleton
Esty Warren A. 17 Derby sq. boards at Middleton
Eustis Betsey, house 154 Boston
Eustis Nancy, teacher, house 154 Boston
Evans Alvah A. currier, rear 9 Mason, house 11 Mason
Evans Alvan A. currier, house 11 Mason
Evans Andrew, teamster, house 16 Carlton
Evans Lucy Ann, widow, house 19 Daniels
Evans William A. cigar maker, boards 23 Forrester
Evans William H. mariner, house 19 Daniels

FABENS BENJ. merchant, 211 Derby, house 87 Lafayette
Fabens B. F. merchant, boards 9 Washington
Fabens Charles H. merchant, 211 Derby, house 81 Lafayette
Fabens Elias W. Mrs. house 16 Williams
Fabens John, porter, Market House, house 61 Broad
Fabens John W. shoemaker, house rear 61 Broad
Fabens Joseph Mrs. house 30 St. Peter

Fabens Mary T. Mrs. house 33 Summer
Fabens Samuel E. merchant, house 81 Lafayette
Fairbrothers Marsena C. building mover, house rear 9 Aborn
Fairclough Thomas, Naumkeag Mill, h. Pingree, n. Harbor
Fairfield Hesther Mrs. house 11 Warren
Fairfield James, captain, house 7 Carlton
Fairfield James jr. carpenter, 29 Essex, house 5 Carlton
Fairfield Margaret Mrs. house 67 Essex
Fairfield Samuel W. machinist, house Phelps court
Fairfield Samuel G. cooper, house 4 Becket
Fairfield William, shoemaker, house 9 Upham
Fallon Anthony, laborer, house Grove, above Mason
Fallon Ellen, widow, house 89 North
Fallon James, shoemaker, house 16 Ward
Fallon Malachi, laborer, house 12 Beach
Fallon Thomas, currier, house Grove, near the Cemetery
Fanning James, currier, r. 46 Boston, house Hanson
Farless James A. hardware and cutlery, 186 Essex, house 25 Norman
Farless Thomas, merchant, house 120 Derby
Farley Charles M. cooper, house 25 Cedar
Farley George G. cooper, house 27 Cedar
Farley Henry, cooper, house Cabot, cor. Hancock
Farley John, laborer, house 28 Ward
Farley Joseph L. cooper, 22 Cedar, house 5 Everett
Farley Rebecca Mrs. house 25 Cedar
Farmer James D. shoemaker, house 13 Flint [h. 47 North
Farmer *(Joseph)* & Harris *(Walter S.)*, masons, 72 Wash.
Farmer Joseph P. mason, house Southwick [Pearl
Farmer Moses G. telegraphic engineer (156 Wash. B.), h. 11
Farnham Jonathan M. lumber and lime, 221 Derby, h. 8 Lynde
Farnham Wm. H. P. clerk, 173 Essex
Farnsworth Elizabeth Mrs. house 9 Cedar
Farnum George W. currier, house Summit
Farnum Henry, currier, house Irving, near Grove
Farnum Henry A. carpenter, house 11 School
Farnum Joseph Mrs. house 143 Federal
Farnum Joseph jr. dentist, 251 Essex, house 143 Federal
Farnum Nathan, clerk, 10 Washington, h. 13 Winthrop
Farnum Thomas, house 11 School
Farrell Ellen, widow, house 22 Congress
Farrell Eugene, currier, house Warren court
Farrell James, currier, house 100 Mason
Farrell Robert, shoemaker, 7 Congress, house 9 Congress
Farrell Sylvester, laborer, house 170 Derby
Farrell Thomas, gardener, house Jackson place
Farrington Eben, overseer, Naumkeag Mill, b. 62 Harbor

SALEM [F] DIRECTORY.

Farrington Edward, shoemaker, house 12½ Hathorne
Farrington George P. druggist, 310 Essex, h. 114 Federal
Farrington George P. jr. clerk, 310 Essex, h. 114 Federal
Farrington Timothy, farmer, house rear 9 Aborn
Faulkner Joseph, morocco dresser, boards 65 Mill
Fausel George, shoemaker, house 317 Essex
Faxon Elisha J. carpenter, house 15 Warren
Faxon James, shoemaker, house rear 15 Warren
Fay Nicholas, laborer, house 10 Derby
Fearing E. P. *(Presby & F.)*, dry goods, 228 Essex, b. Essex House
Feeley James, currier, house 8 Lynn
Feeley Michael, currier, house Varney
Fellows Eliza Mrs. house 22 Becket
Fellows George *(Becket & F.)*, boatbuilder, foot Daniels, house 17 Lynde
Fellows Israel, furniture warehouse, 199 Essex, h. 13 Andrew
Fellows Oliver, calker, house 16 Crombie
Fellows Thomas, laborer, house 18 Lemon
Felt Augusta and Caroline, house 13 Norman
Felt Benjamin Mrs. house 118 Derby   [Curtis
Felt Benjamin, pump and block maker, 118 Derby, house 8
Felt Benjamin W. cigar maker, boards 110½ Derby
Felt Betsey Mrs. house 19 Lynde
Felt Catherine Miss, house 113 Federal
Felt Charles H. clerk, 245 Essex, boards 31 Turner
Felt Charles W. student, house 8 Norman
Felt Dorcas Mrs. house 16 Curtis
Felt Edward A. mariner, boards 110½ Derby
Felt Edward B. Mrs. house 110½ Derby
Felt Eliza and Martha Misses, house 32 Charter
Felt Ephraim, farmer, house 142 North
Felt Ephraim, ticket office E. R. R. house 8 Norman
Felt George R. bookkeeper, Naumkeag Bank, h. Summit
Felt George W. cooper, house 31 Turner
Felt John (Cal.), house 118 Derby
Felt John, city liquor agent, 25 Wash. house 6 Federal ct.
Felt John, cooper, house 31 Turner
Felt John G. painter, 27 Front, house 2 Church
Felt John H. house 2 Church
Felt John V. clerk, 22 Central, house 1 Hardy
Felt Jonathan P. office 118 Essex, house 6 Federal court
Felt Joseph, house 113 Federal
Felt Lucy, widow of Ephraim, house 31 Turner
Felt Rebecca, house 12 Summer
Felt Samuel Q. clerk, house 2 Church
Felt Sarah Miss, house 113 Federal

Felt Susan, house 12 Summer
Felt William H. clerk, 193 Essex, boards 2 Church
Felton Francis A. sailmaker, house 17 Essex
Felton George W. supt. rubber factory, Malden, h. 10 Broad
Felton Harriet S. teacher, boards 20 Winthrop
Felton John S. house 144 Federal
Felton Nancy Mrs. house 20 Howard
Fenollosa Manuel, music teacher, 7 Central, h. 5 Chestnut
Ferguson Edward A. machinist (B.), boards 10 Carpenter
Ferguson George, confectioner, boards 269 Essex
Ferguson George B. machinist, boards 10 Carpenter
Ferguson Hannah Mrs. house 343 Essex
Ferguson James B. painter, 341 Essex, house 6 Monroe
Ferguson John F. painter, 9 Beckford, house 10 Carpenter
Ferguson Mercy L. widow, house 10 Carpenter
Ferguson Samuel, soap manufacturer, house 164 Boston
Ferguson Thomas B. boots, shoes, and rubbers, 2½ Norman, h. 4 Bott's court
Ferguson Wesley B. tanner, house 4 Bott's court
Fern Otis L. house 31 Norman
Fernald Giles C. currier, boards 13 Warren
Fernald Isaac, carpenter, house 24 Harbor
Fernandez Manuel, cigar maker, boards 21 Lafayette
Fernandez William D. cabinet maker, house Skerry
Ferran Joseph, carver, 199 Essex, boards 21 Lafayette
Ferrin Sarah S. widow, house 14 High
Fettyplace Thomas Mrs. house 16 Winter
Field Charles, shoemaker, house Irving, n. Harrod
Field Louisa Mrs. nurse, house 112 Bridge
Field Lucinda B. house 17 Upham
Field M. E. milliner, 264 Essex, house do.
Field Marshall, currier, house Grove
Field Patten, carpenter, house 112 Bridge
Field Robert M. shoemaker, h. Harrod, opp. Phillips
Field Sally Mrs. house 17 Upham
Field Winnie C. Mrs. house 18 Northey
Fifield Charles H. (*Wentworth & F.*), stoves, &c. 15 St. Peter, house 11 Williams
Fifield George W. salesman, 29 Peabody, boards 18 March
Fifield Perkins, house 5 Salem
Fifield Richard, farmer, house 18 March
Filene William & Co. embroidery and trimmings, 146 Essex, house 33 Brown
Findull James H. trader, Beach, c. Oak, h. Harrod, n. Tremont
Finley Ruth R. widow, house foot of Northey
Finn Patrick, currier, house 11 Beaver
Finn Richard, charcoal, boards foot of Ives

Finnegan Mary, house 30 North
Finton Dennis, boards 21 Ward
Fischer William F. tailor, boards 21 Lafayette
Fisher Caroline, seamstress, house 10 Lafayette
Fisher George A. clerk, 173 Essex, boards 115 Federal
Fisher Margaret, widow, house 32 North
Fisher Thorpe, house 115 Federal
Fisk Augustus, mariner, house 31 Mason, cor. Buffum
Fisk John B. captain, house 31 Mason, cor. Buffum
Fisk Joseph E. dentist, 11 Washington, house do.
Fitton Francis Mrs. house 168 Derby
Fitz Daniel P. merchant, 5 Derby whf. house 13 Harbor
Fitz Joseph L. shipjoiner, house 21 Forrester
Fitz Josiah, house 10 Curtis
Fitz Mary Jane, teacher Bentley School, house 10 Curtis
Fitz Gerald Edward, physician and surgeon, house 25 Lafayette
Fitzgerald John, currier, house Grove
Fitzgerald Margaret, widow, house 22 Odell square
Fitzgerald Michael, grocer, 86 Derby, house do.
Fitzgerald Michael, currier, boards 89 Derby
Fitzgerald Morris, laborer, house 41 Union
Fitzgerald Thomas, currier, house 411 Essex
Fitzgerald William, laborer, house 142 Bridge
Fitzgibbon James, currier, house 202 Derby
Fitzpatrick Cornelius, laborer, house Tucker's wharf
Flakefield John, sailmaker, house 11 Cross
Flakefield John jr. ropemaker, boards 11 Cross
Flaherty Hugh, laborer, house 34 Derby
Flaherty Patrick, laborer, house 5 Creek
Flanders Richard, boards 144 North
Flannigan Nicholas, laborer, house 9 Herbert
Fleet George E. shoemaker, house 24 Cedar
Fletcher Henry, mariner, house 31 Bridge
Fletcher R. C. Mrs. millinery, 168 Essex, house 166 do.
Flinn Edward P. hostler, house 55 Warren
Flinn James, laborer, house 105 Derby
Flinn Jeremiah, laborer, house 8 Pratt
Flinn Michael, laborer, house 15 Turner
Flinn Thomas, hostler, house 13 St. Peter
Flint Charles F. farmer, house 12 Laboratory
Flint George, farmer, house 12 Laboratory
Flint Harrison O. boots, shoes and rubbers, 210 Essex, house 8 Prescott
Flint John F. farmer, house 12 Laboratory
Flint Nancy, widow, house 12 Laboratory
Flint Samuel P. house 12 Laboratory
Flint Simeon, mason, 223 Derby, house 3 Harbor

Florentine Nicholas, carpenter, house 11½ English
Floto John Henry, physician, house 10 Liberty [Winthrop
Flowers Thomas B. agent S. I. P. Association, 37 Endicott, h. 17
Flowers Wm. H. cabinet maker, house 6 High
Floyd Abigail, Elizabeth E., Hannah, and Sarah, h. 18 Crombie
Floyd Reuben H. expressman, house Phelps court
Floyd Samuel P. trader, house 56 Bridge
Flynn James, 165 Derby, h. E. Gardner, cor. S. Prospect
Flynn Mary, widow, house 22 Charter
Flynn Peggy Mrs. house 76 Bridge
Flynn Thomas, laborer, house 204 Derby
Fogerty Hannah, widow, house 30 Peabody
Fogg John M. teamster, house 83 Derby
Fogg Stephen, house 4 Flint
Folan Bridget, widow, house 10 Odell square
Foley Catharine Mrs. house 2 High street court
Foley Cornelius, laborer, house 383 Essex
Foley Edward, painter, 32 Endicott, house 6 Ward
Foote Caleb, editor of "Salem Gazette and Essex County Mercury," 191 Essex, house 44 Warren
Foote Frazier C. teaming, house rear 93 Boston
Foote John C. currier, boards rear 93 Boston
Foote Moses F. teamster, boards rear 93 Boston
Forbush Jonathan C. provisions, 7½ Winter, h. 67 Bridge
Ford Jeremiah L. laborer, house 18 Fowler
Ford Jeremiah L. jr. currier, boards 18 Fowler
Ford John F. morocco dresser, house 18 Fowler
Ford Mary, widow, house 21 Creek
Ford Thomas, currier, house Varney, near Hanson
Fornis Sally Mrs. house 7 Cross
Forrester Charlotte Mrs. house 9 Oliver
Forsyth Ezra R. captain, house 81 Summer
Forsyth William, laborer, house 166 Federal
Foster Charlotte, teacher, boards 9 Dean
Foster Charles S. mariner, boards 62 North
Foster Clementine and Adaline Misses, house 23 Summer
Foster Elijah, lobsters, house 31 Bridge
Foster Isaac P. grocer, 109 Derby, house 12 Charter
Foster Isaac P. jr. 109 Derby, house 14 Walnut
Foster John M. house 7 Buffum
Foster John S. (Cal.), house 22 High   [357 Essex
Foster Joseph C. *(Emmerton & Foster)*, 26 Asiatic building, b.
Foster Joshua L. constable, house 4 Turner
Foster Josiah, cooper, house 10 Mechanic
Foster Lydia, widow, house 62 North
Foster Mary Mrs. house 7 Buffum
Foster Matilda L. milliner, 263 Essex, house 119 do.

SALEM [F] DIRECTORY. 97

Foster Samuel R. (41 Federal, B.), house 12 Andrew
Foster Thomas A. (Cal.), house 20 Derby
Foster William Mrs. house 119 Essex
Foster William, blacksmith, house 14 Derby
Foster Wm. H. cashier Asiatic Bank, 32 Wash. h. 357 Essex
Foster William B. *(Adams & F.)*, pearl glass signs, 24 Wash. boards 7 Central
Foster William J. teller Asiatic Bank, house 357 Essex
Fountain Nancy, widow, house 166 Bridge
Fountain James W. hairdresser, house 14 Porter
Fowler Charles B. clerk, 27 Washington, b. 18 Endicott
Fowler Edwin K. baker, 36 St. Peter, house do.
Fowler George, house 2 St. Peter court
Fowler George P. mason, house 2 St. Peter court
Fowler Hannah Mrs. house 29½ North
Fowler Joseph, baker, house 18 Endicott
Fowler Joseph H. cigar maker, house 36 St. Peter
Fowler Newton G. house 30 Mill [16 do.
Fowler Sarah J. and Elizabeth B. variety store, 14 Boston, h.
Fowler William T. sawyer, City Mills, house 30 Mill
Fox Ebenezer, mason, house 11 Creek
Foye Deborah, teacher, house 4 Lynde
Foye Samuel, house 75 Derby
Foye William, ropemaker, house East Webb
Francis Anthony jr. billiard hall, 243½ Essex, house 3 Turner
Francis Augustus B. mariner, house 10 Pearl
Francis Ephraim F. stove polisher, house Barton
Francis John, captain, house 29 St. Peter
Francis John E. mariner, house 29 St. Peter
Francis Joseph, cigars, 140 Essex, house do.
Francis Lucy Mrs. variety store, 13 Flint, house do.
Francks Rachel Mrs. house 16 Becket
Francois Dorlice J. mariner, house 9 Pond
Fraser John W. currier, boards 15 Friend
Frazier John, mariner, house 4 Poabody
Fredrickson Wm. F. currier, house 4 Beach
Freeman Andrew T. laborer, house Rubber factory, Ward
Freeman Sylvester, laborer, house 27 Daniels
Freese Noah L. tanner, boards 16 March [Crombie
French H. P. Miss, telegraph operator, Asiatic building, h. 15
French John W. overseer Naumkeag Mill, boards 69 Harbor
Friend Franklin, house 72 Summer
Frothingham D. T. Mrs. house 179 Boston
Frothingham Josiah A. house 179 Boston
Frothingham Nathaniel Mrs. house 23 Church
Frothingham N. & T. H. *(Nathaniel & Thomas H.)*, stoves and tinware, 29 and 31 Front, N.'s house 12 Federal

Frothingham Thomas H. (*N. & T. H. Frothingham*), house 75 Summer
Frye Abigail, widow, house 91 Boston
Frye Alfred, currier, boards 2 Beaver
Frye Benjamin, house 32 Beckford
Frye Caroline, Elizabeth, and Marion Misses, h. 19 Daniels
Frye Daniel, currier, Beaver, house 4 do.
Frye Frederick A. tanner, foot of Beach, house 91 Boston
Frye George W. clerk (B.), house 90 Boston
Frye Henry L. engineer, house 91 Boston
Frye James, tanner, Goodhue, house 8 Beaver court
Frye John N. house 11 Daniels
Frye Joseph S. bark grinding mill, Goodhue, h. 90 Boston
Frye Nathan, captain, house 354 Essex
Frye Nathan A. merchant, 16 Asiatic building and Phillips wharf, house 356 Essex
Frye Nathaniel L. currier, house 37 Boston
Frye Sally, house 137 Federal
Frye Stephen N. tanner, Beaver, house 30 do.
Frye Thomas, house 95 Boston
Frye William, house 2 Beaver
Frye William jr. tanner, house 163 Boston
Full Joseph, hairdresser, 22 Washington, b. 33 Salem
Full Marena Mrs. house 33 Salem
Full William, teamster, house 75 Derby
Fuller Benjamin B. & Co. (*Nath'l Fuller*), wood, coal, and lumber, 13 Front, house 7 South Pine
Fuller Christopher G. house 8 Ash
Fuller David, porter, house 16 Porter
Fuller Elijah Mrs. house 67½ Essex
Fuller Enoch P. carpenter, N. Pine, cor. Fowler, h. 7 S. Pine
Fuller Joseph, currier, boards 5 May
Fuller Joseph, shoemaker, house 2 May street ct.
Fuller Mary A. house 20 Andrew
Fuller Nancy, widow, house 23 High
Fuller Nathaniel (*B. B. Fuller & Co.*), house 13 Union
Fuller Samuel, inspector at Custom House, house 59 Mill
Fuller Thomas jr. mariner, house 13 Mt. Vernon
Fuller Wm. P. stoves and tinware, 43 Wash. h. 12 Howard
Fullerton John W. ambrotype artist, 224 Essex
Fullum William, laborer, house 95 Derby

GAFFNEY ELLEN, widow, house 27 Ward
Gafney Mary, house Adams
Gaffield James, currier, house 49 Warren
Gage Andrew jr. painter, 71 Derby, house 18 Hardy
Gahagan Patrick, tanner, house Pope's court

Gahagan William, currier, house 19 Fowler
Gaharty William, laborer, house 99 Derby
Gale Mary, widow, house 10 Mill
Gallagher John, laborer, house 4 Elm
Gallagher Michael, currier, house 15 River
Gallagher Patrick, laborer, house 156 Bridge
Gallagher William, bootmaker, boards Mansion House
Gallison Joseph, shoemaker, boards 26 Derby
Gallivan Edward, currier, house 62 Mason
Gallivan John, currier, house Mason, cor. Friend
Gallivan John, tanner, house 27 Albion
Gallivan Michael, tanner, house Salem Turnpike
Ganey Catharine, house 6 High st. court
Gannan John, laborer, house 18 River
Gannon Margaret, widow, house 18 River
Gannon Thomas, currier, house 6 May
Gardner Barnard W. clerk, Merchants Bank, b. 5 Barton sq.
Gardner Benjamin, hairdresser, 4 Central, house 99 Federal
Gardner Benjamin B. stairbuilder, boards 21 Lafayette
Gardner Benjamin S. shoemaker, house 7 Federal
Gardner Daniel B. merchant, house 21 Washington
Gardner Daniel B. jr. *(M. C. Reynolds & Co.)*, grocer, 20 Front, boards Mansion House
Gardner David, mason, house 5 Cambridge
Gardner Edward E. laborer, house 7 Federal
Gardner George A. house 14 Margin
Gardner George W. overseer, house 33 Charter
Gardner Henry, merchant, 1 Market ct. house at N. Danvers
Gardner James W. carpenter, boards 99 Federal
Gardner John, grocer, 3 and 5 High, house 28 Winthrop
Gardner John Francis, house 33 Brown
Gardner John jr. carpenter, house 33 Charter
Gardner Jonathan, cooper, house rear Adams
Gardner Joseph jr. house 19 Crombie
Gardner Joseph 2d (17 N. Market, B.), house 13 Margin
Gardner Lucy F. Mrs. house 67 North
Gardner Martha, cloak and dressmaker, house 59 Mill
Gardner Richard, clerk Gas Light Co. boards 5 Barton sq.
Gardner Samuel, sale stable, Endicott, cor. Margin, house 24 Endicott
Gardner Sarah Mrs. house 7 Federal
Gardner Simon, baker, 24 Turner, house do.
Gardner Stephen W. currier, boards 67 North
Gardner Thomas (B.), house 21 Washington
Gardner T. N. (B.), house 21 Washington
Gardner William C. harness maker, boards 20 Norman
Gardner William F. Mrs. house 72 Lafayette

Gardner William H. shoemaker, house 7 Federal
Gardner Wm. F. carpenter, 6 Pine, house 55 Endicott
Garney Nancy, house 1 Federal
Garrett John, laborer, house rear 39 Derby
Garrett John E. mariner, house 17 Lemon
Garrigan Henry, rubber worker, house 156 Derby
Garrigan Henry, upholsterer, house 142 Bridge
Garrity John G. (Cal.), house rear 8 English
Gass James, stonecutter, house 317 Essex
Gauss Ruth, widow, house 36 Derby
Gauss Stephen, cooper, house 36 Derby
Gavett Charles (10 Summer, B.), house 21 Turner
Gavett Henry, currier, house rear 8 Whittemore
Gavett Jonathan, house 19 North
Gavett William F. (27 Federal, B.), boards W. R. Gavett
Gavett Wm. R. dry goods, 192 Essex, h. Turner, cor. Derby
Gay Charles B. currier, house 13 Warren
Gayle Edward Mrs. house 12 Brown
Gayle Edw. F. W. bookkeeper, at W. P. Phillips's, h. 12 Brown
Gearring James B. currier, house 51 Broad
Geary Daniel J. variety store, 3 Newbury, boards 18 High
Geary John, laborer, house 18 High
Geary John, currier, boards 411 Essex
Geary John jr. trunkmaker, boards 18 High
Geary Owen E. harness maker, boards 18 High
Gebow John, laborer, house 4 Essex
Gerrish Elizabeth Mrs. house 11 Boston
Gerrish Lavinia, house 45 Summer
Gerrish Margaret C. house 77 Summer
Gersdoff B. physician, 49 Washington, house do.
Getchell Alfred W. carpenter, house Summit, n. Prospect
Getchell Benj. W. cooper, head Phillips wharf, h. 9 Carlton
Getchell George F. cooper, house 17 Webb
Getchell Josiah W. superinten't Marine Railway, h. 17 English
Getchell Nicholas, currier, boards 1 Sewall
Getchell Stephen O. carpenter, house 140 Boston
Getchell William, laborer, house 17 English
Getchell Wm. Henry, musician, house 10 Beckett
Gibbon James (Cal.), house 16 Turner
Gibney John, tanner and currier, Beach, house 14 do.
Gibney John A. tanner, boards 11 Beach
Gibson John F. mariner, house 25 Charter
Gifford George G. brass founder and finisher, head Phillips' whf.
    boards 55 Derby
Gifford James B. *(T. J. Gifford & Co.).* house 33 Mason
Gifford Rufus B. carpenter, Dean, house Federal, cor. Dean
Gifford Thomas S. carpenter, house rear 59 North

Gifford Thomas J. & Co. *(J. B. Gifford)*, carpenters, rear Carpenter st. house 35 Mason
Gilbert Elizabeth Mrs. house 8 Creek
Gilbert James, captain, house 3 Spring
Giles Charles, mariner, house 24 Cedar
Giles Lydia G. Mrs. house 28 Lynde
Gillispie James, bootmaker, 34 Boston, house Lummus court
Gill Catharine, washerwoman, house 16 Congress
Gill Henry H. mariner, house rear 10 Church
Gill Robert, currier, house 80 Boston
Gillan John, captain, house 4 Prescott
Gilligan John, Naumkeag Mill, house Perkins
Gillis James A. *(Phillips & G.)*, counsellor, 22 Asiatic building, house 32 Forrester
Gillis Lydia D. Mrs. house 32 Forrester
Gilman Daniel, ropemaker, house 5 English
Gilman Daniel, shoemaker, house Phelps court
Gilman Joseph, laborer, house 5 English
Gilman Joseph jr. ropemaker, boards 5 English
Gilmartin Patrick, tanner, boards 123 Boston
Gilmore P. S. leader Salem Brass Band, 5 Washington, boards Essex House
Glazier Charles H. shoemaker, house 11 Lagrange
Glazier Ezra, auctioneer, Charter, cor. Central, h. 11 Lagrange
Glazier George W. mason, boards 11 Lagrange
Glazier John, carpenter, boards 11 Lagrange
Glazier John M. shoemaker, house 11 Lagrange
Gleason John, currier, boards 14 Oak
Glidden Bethuel, trader, house 144 North
Glidden Joseph P. Mrs. house 99 Federal
Gloss Abraham, laborer, house rubber factory, Ward
Glover Deborah M. Mrs. house foot of Hancock
Glover George D. *(Bosson & G.)*, shoes, 14 Lafayette, house Hancock
Glover Isabella, variety store, 43 Essex, house do.
Glover John H. captain, house foot of Hancock
Glover John P. painter, house 4 Pearl
Glover Joseph E. station agent, E. R. R. house 46 Endicott
Glover Joseph N. Endicott, cor. Margin, house 15 Hathorne
Glover Nancy, widow, house 15 Hathorne
Glover Nathaniel S. house 86 North
Glover Sally, widow, house 46 Endicott
Glover Susan Mrs. house 86 North
Glover William H. painter, house 86 North
Goff Walter, shoemaker, house 8 Lagrange
Goldsmith Albert, Naumkeag Mill, boards 62 Harbor
Goldsmith George W. cabinet maker, house 33 Buffum

Goldsmith James T. carpenter, house 13 English
Goldsmith John, captain, house 68 Bridge
Goldsmith John, Naumkeag Mill, boards 62 Harbor
Goldsmith John H. mariner, house 14 Church
Goldthwait *(Aaron and Aaron jr.)* & Day *(Amos P.)*, carpenters, 20 Peabody, house 43 Broad
Goldthwait Aaron jr. *(Goldthwait & Day)*, house 7 Cedar
Goldthwait Charles, carpenter, house Phelps court
Goldthwait Edward A. shoemaker, house Phelps court
Goldthwait Francis, carpenter, house Phelps court
Goldthwait George C. painter, house 3 Woodbury's court
Goldthwait James G. carpenter, house 3 Woodbury's court
Goldthwait Joseph A. *(Savory & Co.)*, Boston express, 7 Wash. boards Mansion House
Goldthwait Joseph W. shoemaker, house 3 Woodbury's court
Goldthwait Luther Mrs. house 27 Andrew
Goldthwait Luther, tanner, house 111 North
Goldthwait Mary Mrs. house 5 Cross
Goldthwait Moses jr. clerk, 223 Essex, house 12 Church
Goldthwait Samuel F. shoemaker, house 3 Woodbury's court
Goldthwait Willard, dry goods and carpets, 155 Essex, house 10 Margin
Goldthwait William J. tinsmith, house 27 Andrew
Goldthwait William W. clerk, 14 Newbury, house 22 Forrester
Gomes Charles H. clerk, 10 Lafayette, boards 8 Cherry
Gomes Joseph, boots and shoes, 10 Lafayette, house 8 Cherry
Gomes Joseph C. hairdresser, 22 Washington, boards 8 Cherry
Goodell Abner C. & Son *(Zina Goodell)*, machinists, 16 Lafayette, house 4 Federal
Goodell A. C. jr. register of Court of Insolvency, Court House, house 4 Federal
Goodell Zina *(A. C. Goodell & Son)*, boards 4 Federal
Goodhue Abner jr. Mrs. house 2 Liberty
Goodhue Charles H. clerk at Essex House
Goodhue Elizabeth, house 4 Butts court
Goodhue Frances Mrs. house 345 Essex
Goodhue George C. clerk (B.), house 2 Liberty
Goodhue Jas. B. blacksmith, 3 Cambridge, house 6 Hathorne
Goodhue Joseph, feather bed renovator, 274 Essex, house 19 Lemon
Goodhue Priscilla, dressmaker, house 55 Washington
Goodhue Robert W. shoemaker, house 12 Winthrop
Goodhue Samuel B. clerk (B.), boards 51 Essex
Goodhue Sarah Mrs. house 47 Broad
Goodhue Thomas A. carpenter, house 55 Washington
Goodhue William, house 22 Liberty
Goodhue William jr. trader, 4 Cambridge, house Melcher ct.

SALEM [G] DIRECTORY. 103

Goodhue William P. ship chandler and grocer, 44 Derby, house 51 Essex
Goodrich Charles R. teamster, 43 Derby, house 24 Union
Goodridge George A. periodicals and papers, 4 Washington, boards 46 Peabody
Goodridge John W. captain, house 8 Becket
Goodridge Mary L. Mrs. house 8 Becket
Goodwin Enoch, grocer, Derby, cor. Carlton, house 81 Derby
Goodwin Isaac, cooper, house 7 Hardy
Goodwin James B. mariner, house 3 Ash
Goodwin Paul, cooper, house 5 Carlton
Goodwin Thomas, teamster, house 24 Mechanic
Gordon George E. seaman, boards 23 Daniels
Gordon Hiram E. dyer, house 33 Barr, near School
Gordon Mary, widow, house 93 Mason
Gordon Michael, laborer, house 93 Mason
Gordon Oliver A. mariner, house 24 Derby
Gordon Patrick, currier, house 93 Mason
Gordon Rufus L. wood and bark measurer, 2 Lafayette, house 23 Daniels
Gordon William F. machinist, boards 23 Daniels
Gorman James, cigar maker, boards 63 Harbor
Gorman Joanna, widow, house 17 Harbor
Gorman John, laborer, house 23 Charter
Gorman John, laborer, house 4 Elm
Gorman Patrick, laborer, house 2 High street court
Goss Daniel F. A. currier, house 62 North
Goss Ezekiel, furniture & upholstery, 279 Essex, h. 15 Chestnut
Goss Francis, gum copal worker, house 28 Turner
Goss Francis P. plumber, 7 St. Peter, house 24 Hardy
Goss Polly, nurse, house 62 North
Goss Richard G. baker, 87 North, house do.
Gosslin John, currier, house 106 Boston
Gould Charles P. house 15 Dearborn
Gould Charles P. jr. house 15 Dearborn
Gould Robert W. measurer, Custom House, h. 10 Monroe
Gould Solomon, carpenter, house 63 Essex
Gould William C. boards 63 Essex
Gove Hiram, physician, 265 Essex, house 26 Lynde
Gove Obadiah P. 14½ Front, boards 70 Summer
Gove Squire, house 15 Margin
Gove Thomas N. shoemaker, house 70 Summer
Gower George, ropemaker, house 7 Herbert
Gowen William, saloon, 16 Derby sq. house at Lynnfield
Gracia Henry A. mariner, house Barr, near Mason
Gracia Henry R. clerk, 10 Derby square, bds. Barr, n. Mason
Grady Henry, laborer, house 82 Mason

Grady James, laborer, house rear 67 Mason
Grady Jeremiah, laborer, house 3 Church
Grady Julia, widow, house 3 Church
Grady Peter, laborer, house rear 67 Mason
Graham Asa S. ship carpenter, house 210 Derby
Graham George, carpenter, house 210 Derby
Graham John, laborer, house 22 River
Graham Thomas, mariner, house 24 Peabody
Graham Thomas, shoemaker, boards 64 Mill
Graham William, currier, house rear 36 Mill
Grant Benjamin H. painter, house 31 Union
Grant Franklin, paper box manufacturer, 5 Mer. Row (B.), b. 26 Williams
Grant Frederick, clerk, 273 Essex, house 31 Union
Grant Henry, house 9 Boston
Grant John, grocer, 18 Boston, house do.
Grant John C. cabinet maker, 15 Lafayette, house 14 Creek
Grant Joshua B. cabinet maker, 51 Boston, house 3 Fowler
Grant Samuel, inspector, Custom House, house 31 Union
Grant Samuel jr. machinist, house 31 Union
Grant William H. saddler, boards 29 Beaver
Graves Joseph B. fish peddler, house 2 Everett
Graves William B. captain, house 114 Federal
Gray Benjamin (Cal.), house 72 Derby
Gray Benjamin A. public administrator and insurance agent, house 13 Mall
Gray Charles, livery stable, Church, boards 16 Allen
Gray Daniel C. seaman, boards 16 Allen
Gray Everard, cooper, boards 16 Allen
Gray Elizabeth Mrs. house 25 Williams
Gray John, cooper, boards 16 Allen
Gray Nathaniel A. clerk, boards 16 Allen
Gray Susan P. Mrs. house 57 Federal
Gray William, clerk, 44 Derby, house 16 Allen
Gray William B. grocer, 15 English, house 16 Allen
Greeley William E. merchant (B.), house 33 Chestnut
Greeley William H. merchant (B.), house 33 Chestnut
Green Alexander, captain, house 40 Lafayette
Green Charles, overseer, house 25 Lafayette
Green Eliza Mrs. house 15 Lemon
Green James, shoemaker, house rear foot E. Gardner
Green Joseph H. cigar maker, house 35 Essex
Green Rebecca, widow, house Jackson place
Green Thomas, shoemaker, boards 36 Mill
Greenleaf Mary V. Mrs. house 23 Becket
Greenman Mary A. Mrs. house 6 River
Greenman William B. veterinary surgeon, 10 Boston, house do.

Greenough Caroline, dressmaker, house 12 Daniels
Greenough Daniel S. shoemaker, house 12 Daniels
Greenough John W. carpenter, house 3 Park
Greer Samuel, shoemaker, boards Orange, corner Derby
Griffen Ebenezer, shipping master and dealer in clothing, Liberty, corner Charter, house 26 Charter
Griffen Ebenezer jr. shipping master, 38 Charter, house 45 do.
Griffen John S. clerk, 38 Charter, house 45 do.
Griffen Thomas J. shipping master and clothing, 32 Derby, h. 7 Pratt
Griffin Bridget, widow, house 25 Ward
Griffin Hosea B. cutter, 267 Essex, house 8 Lynde
Griffin James, currier, house 20 Beaver
Griffin John, laborer, house foot Perkins
Griffin John, tanner, house Beaver lane
Griffin John, shoemaker, house 101 North
Griffin Nathaniel, house 1 Winter
Griffin Thomas, currier, boards 20 Beaver
Griffin Timothy, currier, house 20 Beaver
Griffin William, laborer, house 6 Tucker's wharf
Grimes Oliver, laborer, house Thorndike
Grimes Robert, fisherman, house rear 6 Church
Grindal Stover, roller coverer, house 6 Everett
Griswold Benoni L. sewing machines, 17 Central, h. 27 Charter
Grogan James, Naumkeag Mill, house 4 Elm
Grover Albert, teamster, house 1 Carlton
Grover Augustus, clerk, house rear 18 Becket
Grover Benjamin F. surveyor, house 28 Norman
Grover James, currier, house 55 North
Grover John, wood and coal, Brookhouse & Hunt's wharf, house 18 Becket
Grover John jr. teamster, house 1 Allen
Grover Susan, nurse, house 23 Winthrop
Grover William B. civil engineer, boards 20 Norman
Groves Henry B. (65 State, B.), house 21 Winter
Groves Ruth Mrs. house 58 Federal
Grush Benjamin S. mason, house 13 Pickman
Grush Michael, mason, house 15 Williams
Guilford Elbridge, shoemaker, house 14 Central
Guilford Elbridge G. constable, house 19 St. Peter
Guilford William H. H. musician, boards 19 St. Peter
Gunner Frederick Rev. house 346 Essex
Guion Sylvanus D. cooper, house 24 Becket
Gwinn Edward A. ropemaker, house 1 Parker's court
Gwinn James F. twine factory, 38 Bridge, house 3 Barton ct.
Gwinn James S. *(T. W. & J. S. Gwinn)*, house 57 Warren
Gwinn Mary A. millinery, 294 Essex, house 2 Margin

SALEM [H] DIRECTORY.

Gwinn Thomas W. & James S. grocers, 410 Essex, h. 408 do.
Gwinn William, baker, boards 89 Essex

HADDOCK JAMES M. mariner, house 11 Congress
Hadley Francis E. tanner, house 44 Boston
Hadley George S. tanner, Goodhue, house 5 Albion
Hadley Willis, currier, house 5 Albion
Hafey William, currier, house 407 Essex
Haffernan Catharine, house 18 Odell square
Hagan William H. laborer, house 38 Essex
Hagerty Bartholomew, laborer, house Hanson
Hagerty Cornelius, tanner, house Hanson
Hagerty Daniel, harness maker, 25½ Boston, house do.
Hagerty Dennis, laborer, house 5 Gerrish place
Hale Eliza Mrs. house 58 North   [Essex, house 12 Northey
Hale Henry, hardware, cutlery, and agricultural tools, 215
Hale Henry A. clerk, 215 Essex, boards 12 Northey
Hale Joseph, house 101 Mason
Hale Joseph jr. mariner, boards 101 Mason
Hale Pemberton, grocer, 27 Summer, house 11 Cambridge
Hale William H. baker, house 17 Essex
Haley Bridget, widow, house rear 28 Beaver
Haley Dennis, tanner, house Grove
Haley James, tanner, house 6 Aborn
Haley Shillaber, carpenter, 5 Prince, house 23½ Harbor
Hall Andrew, house 12 Mall
Hall David, blacksmith, house Melcher's court
Hall Eliphalet, carpenter, house 97 Boston
Hall Gilman B. currier, house 97 Boston
Hall Henry C. laborer, house 7 Central
Hall John, lather, house 23 Cedar
Hall Mary Mrs. house 12 Mall
Hall Thomas, shoemaker, house 101 North
Hall William H. captain, house 84 Derby
Hallahan Hannah, widow, house 1 Pratt
Hallahan Ellen, widow of Edward, house 8 Whittemore
Halliscy John, gardener, house 20 Congress
Halliscy Thomas, marble worker, house 24 High
Ham Joseph, mason, boards 21 Lafayette
Hamblett Malvina L. widow, house 18 Williams
Hamilton Alexander Mrs. house 34 Mill
Hamilton Alexander, laborer, house 34 Mill
Hamilton George P. mariner, house 6 Webb
Hamilton John C. at laboratory, house Mill, corner Endicott
Hamilton Joseph R. laborer, house 34 Mill
Hamlett Henry H. laborer, house Adams
Hammond Daniel, laborer, house 8 Whittemore

Hammond Daniel, painter, house 6 Prescott
Hammond Hannah Mrs. nurse, house 12 Winthrop
Hammond John, captain, house 12 Conant [h. 17 Cambridge
Hammond *(John D.)* & Tuttle *(F. W.)*, dry goods, 167 Essex,
Hammond John L. Mrs. house 10 Barr
Hammond Joseph, captain, house 10 Barr
Hammond Joshua F. mastic roofing, 153 Derby
Hamond William C. carpenter, 127 Derby, house 14 Carlton
Hancock John, mariner, house 8 Webb
Hanley Margaret, widow, house rear foot E. Gardner
Hanley Patrick (Cal.), house 22 Congress
Hannam Thomas, tailor, 64 Boston, house Hanson, c. Varney
Hannan Catharine, house 21 Ward
Hannan Dennis B. homœopathic physician, house 122 Boston
Hannan John, gardener, house 39 Dearborn
Hannan Patrick, currier, boards 411 Essex
Hanscom James Mrs. house 42 Buffum
Hanscom William R. machinist, house 16 Central
Hanson Caleb H. house 6 Curtis
Hanson Charles J. clerk, 6 Front, boards 31 Harbor
Hanson Elijah A. tanner, 13 Grove, house 96 Boston
Hanson Job V. *(Beckford & H.)*, house 4 Beaver
Hanson John, miller, boards 4 Beaver
Hanson John B. captain, house 103 Lafayette
Hanson Joseph, teamster, 64 Union, house 31 Harbor
Hanson Joseph H. merchant, 16 Asiatic building and Phillpis wharf, house 23 Federal
Hanson Lydia S. Mrs. house 22 River
Hanson Tobias, butcher, house 32 Beaver
Haraden Abigail Mrs. house 14 Curtis
Haraden Andrew, Boston express, basement Asiatic building, house 6 Barton square   [ton
Haraden Jonathan, basement Asiatic building, h. 19 Washing-
Haraden Stephen, captain, house 3 Ash
Harden John, laborer, house 23 Carlton
Harden William, laborer, house 23 Turner
Harding David, horsehoer, rear 25 Front, house 29 Union
Harding James (B.), house 6 Ward
Harding Margaret T. dressmaker, house 29 Union
Harding Patrick, carpenter, boards East Gardner, n. Harbor
Hardy Abner H. painter, house 121 North
Hardy Augustus, doors, sashes, and blinds, 26 Front, house 65 Federal
Hardy Charles F. farmer, boards 1 Aborn
Hardy Granville, shoemaker, boards 6 River
Hardy Harrison, shoemaker, boards 1 Aborn
Hardy Temple, grocer, 72 Federal, house do.

Hardy Temple jr. 26 Front, house 74 Federal
Harrigan Matthew, currier, house rear 67 Mason
Harrigan Michael, laborer, house 77 Derby
Harrigan Patrick, laborer, house rear 21 Becket
Harrington Charles, currier, 428 Essex, house 397 do.
Harrington Francis, clerk (B.), boards 12 Beaver
Harrington George, captain, house Ives court
Harrington Henry, clerk, 428 Essex, house 153 Federal
Harrington Jonas B. gardener, house 12 Beaver
Harrington Leonard B. currier, 428 Essex, house 153 Federal
Harrington Patrick, marketman, house 26 Congress
Harrington Richard, tanner, r. 9 Mason, house 7 Buffum
Harrington Samuel B. currier, house Salem turnpike
Harrington William H. *(Maloon & H.)*, house 116 Boston
Harris Daniel Mrs. house Walter
Harris *(Daniel M.)* & Hutchings *(Augustus)*, carpenters, 36 North, house 12 Upham
Harris Elizabeth B. Mrs. house 7 Carpenter
Harris Esther, widow, house 8 Whittemore
Harris Israel P. *(Parks & Harris)*, grocer, 4 St. Peter, h. 14 do.
Harris James, ship carpenter, house 17 Hardy
Harris James jr. *(Chamberlain, Harris & Co.)*, grocer, 24 Front, house 86 Bridge
Harris Jerome, physician, house 22 Washington
Harris John, currier, house Adams   [North
Harris Walter S. *(Farmer & Harris)*, mason, 72 Wash. h. 84
Harris William B. teamster, house Walter
Harrison Eunice Mrs. house 19 Federal
Harrod Benjamin C. on Eastern R. R. house 24 School
Hart Ann, widow, house 69 Summer
Hart Daniel, laborer, house 16 Turner
Hart David, boatbuilder, head Phillips wharf, h. 24 Carlton
Hart David, shipcarpenter, boards 24 Carlton
Hart Timothy, currier, house rear 8 Whittemore
Hart Winnifred, widow, house 28 Ward
Hartney Michael Rev. house 22 Union
Hartney Michael, tanner, house rear 56 Broad
Hartwell Lydia B. widow, house 7 Park
Haskell Alfred W., Front, cor. Derby sq. b. 13 Norman
Haskell Charles Mrs. house 100 Derby
Haskell Charles, clerk, boards 100 Derby
Haskell Daniel C. currier, 71 Mason, house 174 Federal
Haskell Edward B. currier, boards 100 Derby
Haskell Elijah, U. S. N. house 17 North
Haskell Jacob, ice, 2 Lafayette, house 18 Ward
Haskell *(Jacob S.)* & Longee *(Joseph)*, cabinet makers, 296 Essex, house 325 do.

Haskell John jr. clerk, 391 Essex, b. at O. S. Haskell's
Haskell John M. mariner, boards 100 Derby
Haskell Mark, clerk, 172 Essex, house 9 Ash
Haskell Mark H. house 9 Ash [place
Haskell Orin S. *(Chandler & H.)*, grocer, 391 Essex, h. Green
Haskell Reuben R. 173 Essex, boards 1 Rust
Haskell Samuel C. restorator, Front, c. Derby sq. h. 13 Norman
Haskell Susan J. house 9 Ash
Haskell William, variety store, 5 Lynn, house 19 Warren
Haskell William H. shoemaker, house 15 Hathorne
Haskell William R. (Cal.), house 402 Essex
Haskins Susan L. Mrs. millinery and fancy goods, 147 Essex, house 72 Mill
Haslam Joseph, teamster, 56 Harbor, house 16 Ward
Hatch Elizabeth A. teacher, house 15 Andrew
Hatch Henry J. machinist, house 21 Cedar
Hatch Lemuel B. wood and coal, 113 Derby, h. 15 Andrew
Hatch S. stonecutter, house 16 Peabody
Hathaway Eleazer, baker, 68 Washington, house do.
Hathaway James, currier, house 9 May
Hathaway Samuel R. shoemaker, house 12 Essex
Hathorne Ebenezer, nurseryman, house Hollingsworth Hill
Hause Carl, teacher of music, boards 9 Washington
Hawes Augustus G. R. shoemaker, boards 21 Lafayette
Hawes Henry, tanner, boards 34 Beaver
Hawes John Q. carpenter, house 34 Beaver
Hawes Nancy, widow, h. at Samuel B. Harrington's
Hawes William, carpenter, 127 Boston, house 34 Beaver
Hawkes John, clerk, 144 Essex, boards do.
Hawkes Louisa M. teacher, house 20 Andrew
Hawkes Timothy *(Needham & H.)*, fruit, &c. 144 Essex, h. do.
Hay John A. bootmaker, 35 Brown, house 12 Pearl
Hayden Mary, widow, house Phelps ct. n. Jackson pl.
Hayes Bartholomew, laborer, house 23 Carlton
Hayes Dennis, laborer, house 6 Tucker's wharf
Hayes James, laborer, house 2 Tucker's wharf
Hayes Jeremiah, laborer, house 26 Peabody
Hayes John, laborer, house 24 Peabody
Hayes John, laborer, house Tucker's wharf
Hayes John, laborer, house 23 Carlton
Hayes John jr. laborer, house 2 Tucker's wharf
Hayes Julia, widow, house 405 Essex
Hayes Michael, laborer, house rear 39 Derby
Hayes Michael, laborer, house 16 Turner
Hayes Morris, laborer, house 23 Carlton
Hayes Morris, laborer, house Becket avenue
Hayes Patrick, laborer, house Tucker's wharf

Hayfield James, laborer, house 10 Herbert
Hayford Asa, provisions, 91 Essex, house do.
Hayford William B. clerk, 91 Essex, house 1 Turner
Hayman John, captain, house 42 Essex
Hayman John (Cal.), house 14 Church
Hayward Aaron, mason, house 82 Summer
Hayward Charles E. teamster, boards 63 Harbor
Hayward Charles H. (clerk Columbian Bank, B.), boards 82 Summer
Hayward Cyrus, stage proprietor, house 13 River
Hayward Cyrus L. clerk, 173 Essex, boards 13 River
Hayward George, trader, boards 138 North
Hayward Josiah, mason, house 120 Federal
Hayward William, trader, house 138 North
Hayward William P. teacher Pickering School, h. 183 Bridge
Hazeltine Stephen, captain, house 3 Ash
Hazelton Andrew, currier, house 20 Fowler
Hazelton Augustus, tanner, house 7 May
Hazelton John, tanner, May, house 15 do.
Hazelton Joseph, currier, house 15 May
Hazelton Lucy, widow, house 15 May
Heard Mary Mrs. house 10 Church
Heard Mary, widow, house Adams
Heard Nathaniel, mariner, house 24 Dearborn
Heard, see Hurd
Heath Sarah A. widow, house 34 Summer
Heburn Mary, widow, house East Gardner
Heeney Bridget, widow, house opposite 19 Daniels
Heeney *(Patrick)* & Clark *(Patrick)*, coal, wood, and bark, 169 Derby, house 16 Elm
Heeney Richard, currier, house Adams, near Mason
Heferern Michael, laborer, house 20 Lemon
Helt Benjamin G. cigar maker, house 17 Daniels
Henderson Benjamin I. painter, boards 9 Williams
Henderson Daniel, painter, 6 Newbury, house 9 Williams
Henderson Elizabeth Mrs. house 9 Williams
Henderson F. A. Miss, music teacher, 14 St. Peter
Henderson John S. carpenter, house 6 Prescott
Henderson Joseph, hardware (B.), house 9 Williams
Henderson Margaret Miss, house 27 Liberty
Henderson Mary E. dressmaker, boards 17 Brown
Henderson Samuel, boots and shoes, 21 St. Peter, house 14 do.
Henderson S. Goodhue, clerk, 207 Essex, house 14 St. Peter
Henderson *(Thomas)* & Kimball *(S. T.)*, furniture dealers, 38 & 40 Washington, house 11 Mt. Vernon
Henderson William C. bookbinder, house 57 Mill
Hendley John, shoemaker, house 136 Boston

Henfield Amos (B.), house 4 High
Henfield John, house 32 Lafayette
Henfield John jr. shoemaker, house 19 Warren
Henfield Joseph H. clothing and furnishing goods, 10 Front, house Bott's court
Henman Hannah K. Mrs. house 13 Curtis
Hennessey John, tanner, house rear Oak, near Beach
Hennessey John, currier, boards 14 Oak
Hennessey Margaret, widow, house 81 Mason
Hennessey Mary, widow, house 25 Albion
Hennessey Michael, laborer, house 43 Union
Hennessey Patrick, currier, house 168 Federal
Hennessey William, laborer, house 81½ Mason
Henry Elizabeth Mrs. house Ives court, cor. St. Peter
Henry John, currier, house Mason Hill
Hensmun George, shoemaker, house 22 Cedar
Hensman John, mariner, house 20 Salem
Henville William W. hatter (B.), house 18 Cambridge
Herlihy Mary, widow, house 28 Congress
Herrick Austin F. Rev. house 80 Summer
Herrick Israel, shoemaker, house 20 Winthrop
Herrick Mary, house 70 North
Hersey Benjamin, mariner, house 7 English
Hersey William H. currier, house 25 Beckford
Hetherington William, clerk 16 Mill, boards 8 do.
Hicock William B. cigar maker, boards 20 Norman
Hickey Julia, house Putnam
Hickey Patrick, coachman, 136 Essex, house 5 Church
Hifield John, laborer, house 8 English
Higbee Benjamin L. Mrs. house 64 Broad
Higbee Betsey Mrs. house 64 Broad
Higbee Lemuel, leather, 76 North (B.), house 387 Essex
Higbee Charles, leather, 6 Blackstone (B.), house 155 Federal
Higgins Philip, currier, house 383 Essex
Higgins Yates, currier, house Aborn
Hill Alexander A. boatbuilder, house 48 Essex
Hill Anstiss P. widow, house 61 Derby
Hill Abner E. house 32 Derby
Hill Edwin R. shoemaker and city weigher, Bridge, h use 23 Oliver
Hill Elizabeth Mrs. house 4 Palfrey court
Hill Henry, shoemaker, house 23 Salem
Hill Horace L. cooper, house 61 Derby
Hill Ira, carpenter, house 4 Winthrop
Hill John, house 121 Lafayette
Hill J. Archer, currier, house 48 Essex
Hill Moses, trader, house 175 Bridge

Hill Richard, cooper, house 8 Bentley
Hill Robert *(W. & R. Hill)*, house 8 Bentley
Hill Samuel, captain, house 4 Lagrange
Hill Sarah E. widow, house 11 Salem
Hill Thomas, painter, 7 Walnut
Hill Ursula, house 9 May
Hill William Mrs. house 22 Beckford, cor. Federal
Hill William A. clerk (B), boards 10 Walter
Hill William & R, dry goods, 277 Essex, house 10 Walter
Hill William M. currier, house 48 Essex
Hiltz Deborah, widow, house 45 Endicott
Hinchion Mary, widow, house 4 High street court
Hinchion Nancy, widow, house 1 High street court
Hinchion Patrick, stonemason, house 13 Upham
Hinchion Patrick, mason, house 3 Church
Hines George, carpenter, house 128 North
Hinkley Ezekiel F. trader, house 144 North
Hinkley George O. trader, boards 144 North
Hinds Edward, laborer, house 13 Gedney court
Hinds Richard, laborer, house High street court
Hitchens Abijah, carpenter, house 12 Allen
Hitchens Abijah jr. copal varnish maker, house 9 Allen
Hitchens Mary Mrs. house 16 Becket
Hitchens Nathaniel, carpenter, house 7 Becket
Hitchens Richard, ropemaker, house 8 English
Hobart Charles, teacher, house Bott's court
Hobart Charles Mrs. house 18 Walnut
Hobart Elcey J. widow, house Bott's court
Hobart Hannah Miss, house 18 Walnut
Hobart Matthew, shipwright, house 8 Allen
Hobart Sarah, teacher, house 8 Allen
Hobbs Edward, clerk, 206 Essex, house 9 Norman
Hobbs Horatio D. shoemaker, house 9 Norman
Hobbs James S. currier, house 5 North court
Hobbs John E. carver, boards 21 Lafayette
Hobbs William H. teamster, house 23 Cedar
Hodgdon Betsey Mrs. house 14 Hardy
Hodgdon David, captain, boards 199 Bridge
Hodgdon Robert H. tailor, house 14 Hardy
Hodges Edward, clerk of register of deeds, house 345 Essex
Hodges Gamaliel, captain, house 14 Church
Hodges George A. house 2 Briggs
Hodges Hannah, house 5½ Brown
Hodges John, merchant, house 266 Essex
Hodges Joseph, merchant, house 95 Essex
Hodges Samuel R. distiller, 17 Elm, house 4 Chestnut
Hodges Thorndike D. house 266 Essex

Hodgkins George L. house 91 Bridge
Hodgkins Lucy M. house 9 Mount Vernon
Hodskinson Jabez, machinist, house 2 Curtis
Hoffman Charles, merchant, 12 Derby wf. house 26 Chestnut
Hogan James H. blacksmith, house rear 28 North
Hogan John, currier, house Grove
Holbrook Joseph, oysters, &c. 5 Derby sq. h. 20 Charter
Holbrook Samuel, house Neck
Holbrook Solomon H. 5 Derby sq. house 16 St. Peter
Holbrook Sylvia Mrs. fortune teller, house Neck
Holden Nathaniel Mrs. house 17 Briggs
Holden Thomas B. New Hampton Theo. Inst. house 17 Briggs
Holland David, carpenter, house 4 Albion
Holland John, laborer, house 4 Gerrish place
Holland William W. shoemaker, house 45 Broad
Holman Jonathan Mrs. house 337 Essex
Holman Lyman, building mover, house 175 Boston
Holman Sarah, house 25 Lynde
Holmes Gervenius, carpenter, boards 218 Essex
Holmes James H. house 365 Essex
Holmes Mary M. Mrs. h. 218 Essex
Holmes Thomas, captain, house 335 Essex
Holmes Thomas O. captain, house 335 Essex
Holroyd Benjamin, gasfitter, 273 Essex, boards 9 Norman
Holt Lucy J. Mrs house 6 Winthrop
Holt Sophia C. upholsteress, house 9 Rust
Holt William, house 1 Sewall
Homan Abigail, nurse, house 368 Essex
Honeycomb Samuel R carpenter, 16 Endicott, house 5 Saunders
Honeycomb Sarah E. music teacher, house 7 Lemon
Honeycomb Thomas P. carpenter, 31 North, house 100 do.
Honeycomb William H. carpenter, 14 Cross, house 7 Lemon
Hood Abraham, gardener, house 9 Webb
Hood Asa, house 12 Daniels
Hood David B. carpenter, Turner, near Essex, house 9 Allen
Hood Hiram D. shoemaker, house foot of Northey
Hood Jacob, agent Am. Bible Society, house 15 Lynde
Hood Nathaniel S. cooper, house 12 Daniels
Hooper Hannah & Lydia Misses, house 12 Beckford
Hooper John, laborer, house 24 Ward
Hooper Nathaniel, shoemaker, 276 Essex, house 96 do.
Hooper Nathaniel M. shoemaker, house 6 High
Hopkins John, currier, house 1 Beaver court
Hopkinson Lyman, shoemaker, boards 6 River
Hoppin James M. Rev. house 364 Essex
Horne Moses P. music teacher, house 15 Dean
Horton David W. Mrs. house 10 Mall

Horton Nathaniel, currier, Buffum, house 22 do.
Horton Nathaniel A. *(Foote & Horton)*, publishers " Salem Gazette," 191 Essex, house 22 Buffum
Hovey Charles F. coach and chaise painter, Spring, cor. Webb, boards 25 Cedar
Hovey Geo. H. hairdresser, 157 Essex, h. Barton, c. Barton ct.
Hovey Hannah B. widow, house 9 Creek
Hovey John Mrs. house Barton, cor. Barton ct.
Hovey Thomas, mason, house 12 Winter
Howard David R. shoemaker, house 8 Walter
Howard John Mrs. house 2 Winter
Howard John C. house 17 Cedar
Howard John D. clerk, house 159 Boston
Howard John S. carpenter, house 5 Gardner ct.
Howard Otis J. clerk (B.), house 147 Bridge
Howard William R. house 2 Winter
Howarth John, oil manuf. house 14 Lynde
Howe Edward, laborer, house 28 Peabody
Howe Israel T. captain, house 4 Hardy
Hoyer Edward P. mariner, house 7 Carlton
Hoyt Charles C. 24 Front, boards 90 Federal
Hoyt Edwin A. teamster, house 30 Winthrop
Hoyt Erastus, teamster, Central, cor. Front, h. 34 Essex
Hoyt George R. carpenter, house 28 Harbor
Hoyt Ichabod R. shipcarpenter, house 28 Harbor
Hoyt Oliver R. clerk, 5 Boston, house Grove
Hubbard J. Geo. shoe manuf. 246 Essex, house 246½ do.
Hubbard Mary, house 369 Essex
Hubon Henry & H. G. coffin warehouse, 48 Wash. h. 2 Jeffrey ct
Hubon Henry G. *(H. & H. D. Hubon)*, house 1 Jeffrey ct.
Hubon S. Frederick, carpenter, house 3 Jeffrey court
Huddell William, laborer, house 14 Conant
Huff John T. shoemaker, boards at Jonathan Gardner's
Hughes Timothy, stonecutter, house 1 Sewall
Hull A. B. & Co. tanners and curriers, rear 11 Mason
Hunt Alice, widow, house 48 Forrester
Hunt Frederick H. at gum copal works, house 12 Becket
Hunt John, tinsmith, boards 168 Federal
Hunt Joseph Mrs. house 19 Church
Hunt Mary Mrs. house 54 Charter
Hunt Thomas, merchant, house 64 Bridge, cor. Pearl
Hunt William, merchant, 16 Asiatic building and Phillips whf. house 1 Brown [Chestnut
Huntington Asahel, clerk of the courts, Court House, house 35
Huntington Kimball C. currier, house 148 Federal
Huntoon F. W. L. *(Francis Choate & Co.)*, dry goods, 222 Essex, house 28 Pleasant

Huntress Darling, teamster, at J. Dike & Co.'s, h. 23 Hardy
Hurd Thomas, stonemason, house 24 Hathorne
Hurd William H. mason, boards 17 Creek
Hurd William W. dentist, 251 Essex, boards 5 Barton sq.
Hurd, see Heard
Hurley Catharine, house Naumkeag wharf
Hurley Charles, calico printer, house 16 Ward
Hurley Cornelius, blacksmith, house 41 Union
Hurley David, laborer, house Tucker's wharf
Hurley Elizabeth, widow, house foot Pingree
Hurley James, laborer, house 4 Elm
Hurley Jeremiah, tanner, boards 123 Boston
Hurley John, currier, house 10 Beaver court
Hurley John, currier, house 12 Beach
Hurley John, laborer, house 25 Ward
Hurley Margaret, widow, house 42 Union
Hurley Patrick, currier, boards 53 Warren
Hurley Thomas, laborer, house 142 Derby
Hurst George, mariner, house 29 Mill
Huse John, currier, 59 Boston, house 171 Federal
Hussey Albert, tinplate worker, house 122 Bridge
Hussey George B. coachman at Mansion House, h. 24 Harbor
Hussey Robert, captain, house 7 Orange
Hutchings Augustus *(Harris & H.)*, house 89½ North
Hutchings Charles W. mariner, house r. 59 North
Hutchings George S. carpenter, boards 62 North
Hutchinson Benjamin, mariner, house 96 Bridge
Hutchinson Charles E. house 83 Summer
Hutchinson Daniel H. mariner, house 22 Norman
Hutchinson George, captain, house 30 Turner
Hutchinson George C. (Cal.), house 30 Turner
Hutchinson Hannah Mrs. house Putnam
Hutchinson John I. bookkeeper Mercantile Bank, h. 96 Bridge
Hutchinson Mary Mrs. house 22 Norman
Hutchinson Samuel, captain, house 96 Bridge
Hutchinson Samuel jr. captain, house 52 Bridge
Hutchinson Sarah Miss, house 17 Conant
Hutchinson Thomas, cabinet maker, house 13 Federal
Hutchinson Thomas J. job printer, 175½ Essex, h. 60 Federal
Hutchinson William, teamster, house 6 Whittemore
Hynes Patrick J. furniture, 25 Front, house 25 High

IDE EDWIN R. carpetings and dry goods, 223 Essex, house 12 Mason
Imperial Harriet Mrs. house Orange, cor. Derby
Ingalls Charles H. currier, boards 29 Buffum
Ingalls Collins Mrs. house 14 Prescott

Ingalls Elizabeth, widow, house 68 Essex
Ingalls Ira Mrs. house 29 Buffum
Ingalls Ira F. currier, 13 Beach, h. Tremont, n. S. Danvers line
Ingalls Mary Mrs. house 7 Pratt
Ingalls Mary Mrs. house 66 Mill
Ingalls Wilson H. carpenter, house 4 Cabot
Ingersoll Elizabeth Mrs. house 57 Charter
Ingersoll Nathaniel, captain, house 77½ Bridge
Ingersoll Nathaniel Mrs. house 77½ Bridge
Ingersoll Horace, counsellor, 150 Essex, h. 34 Turner
Innis John, shoemaker, house 32 Derby
Innis John A. newspaper and book agent, house 18 Beckford
Innis Sarah A. widow, house 18 Beckford
Ireland Eliza S. Mrs. house 90 Mill
Ireland Mary Mrs. house 14 Odell square
Ireland William A. clerk, 214 Essex, house 14 Odell square
Irish Joseph, shoemaker, house S. Prospect, near Congress
Irving Henry H. 173 Essex, boards 196 Derby
Isaackson Sarah A. Mrs. nurse, house 29 Norman
Ives David P. fancy goods (83 Milk, B.), house 1 Lynde
Ives *(Henry P.)* & Smith *(A. A.)*, bookstore and bindery, 232 Essex and 36 Washington, h. 102 Federal
Ives John M. house 17 Pickman
Ives John S. books, stationery, and fancy goods, 281 Essex, house 7 Cherry
Ives Lydia A. Mrs. house 19 Washington
Ives Mary Miss, house 368 Essex
Ives Stephen B. merchant (83 Milk, B.), house 26 Brown
Ives *(Stephen B. jr.)* & Peabody *(J. B.)*, counsellors, 226½ Essex, house r. 26 Brown
Ives William & Co. *(George W. Pease)*, printers, and publishers "Salem Observer," 226½ Essex, house 390 do.

JACKMAN NATHANIEL C. house 22 Andrew
Jackman Nathaniel M. printer (B.), house 29 Norman
Jackson Andrew, mariner, house 47 Federal
Jackson Nancy and Elizabeth, house 20 Oliver
Jackson Thomas, lastmaker, house 16 Nursery
Jackson William H. merchant (17 Doane, B.), h. 93 Lafayette
Jaques Bridget, widow, house 28 Ward
Jameson Mary Mrs. house 55 North
Jamin A. boards Mansion House
Janes Abraham, tanner, house rubber factory, Ward
Janes Edwin, shoemaker, house 3 Pond
Janes Joshua B. carpenter, house 19 Winthrop
Janes Lydia, house rubber factory, Ward
Janes Sarah Mrs. house 86 Mill

SALEM [J] DIRECTORY. 117

Jarvis William, mariner, house 15 Briggs
Jeffs A. Perry, shoemaker, house 3 Laboratory
Jeffs James M. shoemaker, house 18 Conant
Jefferds George, laborer, house 182 Federal
Jeffrey John, teamster, house 138 North
Jelly Charles, hackman, house 22 Crombie
Jelly Charles H. baker, 10 Cedar, house do.
Jelly John A. captain, house 18 Endicott
Jelly Lizzie A. teacher, boards 10 Beckford
Jelly Samuel S. laborer, house 3 Winter   [10 Beckford
Jelly William, agent and collector Aqueduct Co. 2 Sewall, h
Jelly William H. house 73 Essex
Jelly William F. mariner, house 18 Endicott
Jenkins Aaron, musician, house 84 North
Jenks Charles A. *(H. E. Jenks & Co.)*, merchant, 226½ Essex, house at Somerville
Jenks Elias Mrs. house 30 Harbor
Jenks Henry E. & Co. *(C. A. Jenks & J. E. Berry)*, merchants. 226½ Essex, house 94 Essex
Jenness Susan F. house 13 River
Jennings Bridget, widow, house Odell square
Jerome N. H. teacher of French, 243½ Essex, h. 81 Lafayette
Jewell Benjamin, laborer, house 15 Mall
Jewett Daniel H. wood agent E. R. R. house 61 Charter
Jewett George B. Rev. house 5 River
Jewett John *(Prime, Kenny & Co.)*, mahogany, &c., City Mills, house 24 Winter
Jewett Thomas E. machinist, boards 45 St. Peter
Jewett Thomas S. assessor, City Hall, h. 45 St. Peter
Jocelyn Henry E. *(Adams, Richardson & Co.)*, hardware, 207 Essex, boards 9 Washington
Jocelyn Mary E. teacher, house 22 Norman
Johns Shadrach, blacksmith, boards 5 Oak
Johnson Caleb C. clerk, 23 Front, house 3 Spring
Johnson Daniel H. shipbroker, house 10 North
Johnson Daniel H. jr. clerk (B.), house 10 North
Johnson Emery Mrs. house 362 Essex
Johnson Emery S. captain, house 360 Essex
Johnson Frederick, mariner, house 59 Lafayette
Johnson Franklin, mariner, house 9 Turner
Johnson George, shoemaker, house 10 Gardner court
Johnson Henry D. salesman (B.), house 10 North
Johnson Henry L. captain, house 3 Spring
Johnson Lydia Mrs. house 31 Boston
Johnson Nicholas, captain, house 31 Harbor
Johnson Peter, mariner, house 17 Pond
Johnson Samuel, physician, house 2 Chestnut

Johnson Samuel jr. Rev. house 2 Chestnut
Johnson Thomas H. clerk, 27 Washington, h. 102 North
Johnson William Mrs. house 84 Bridge
Johnson William B. F. *(Sumner & J.)*, teamster, 132 Derby, house 84 Bridge
Johnson William Henry, bookkeeper (B.), house 98 Essex
Jones Abby B. millinery and dressmaking, 169 Essex, house 20 Norman
Jones Celeste, mariner, house Neck
Jones George W. (Cal.), house 26 Liberty
Jones George W. cardbox maker, house foot Leach
Jones John S. *(Dodge & J.)*, flour, &c., Pierce's wharf, house 29 Broad
Jones Owen, shoe manuf. 4 Norman, h. 18 Chestnut
Jones Reuben, engineer, E. R. R. house 20 Norman
Jones Samuel G. merchant tailor, 177 Essex, house 16 Howard
Jones Sarah V. house 3 Salem
Jones Wm. house & ship carpenter, 171 Derby, h. 26 Liberty
Jones Wm. F. sawyer, City Mills, house 49 Endicott
Joplin Elizabeth, widow, house 61 Summer
Joplin Wm. shoemaker, house 61 Summer
Jordan Allen Mrs. boarding house, 20 Crombie
Jordan George W. shoemaker, boards 17 Dearborn
Jordan Hannah Mrs. house 17 Dearborn
Jordan James, shoemaker, house 93 Derby
Jordan Michael, shoemaker, house 4 Elm
Joseph Thomas, mariner, house 4 Palfrey court
Joye Joseph, shoemaker, house 129 North
Julio William T. captain, boards 4 Prince
Juniford John, mariner, house rear 13 Daniels
Just Philibert, carver, house 7 Mall

KALORAN LUKE, currier, house Putnam, near Hanson
Kaloran Marcus, currier, boards rear 67 Mason
Kane John, laborer, house Grove, near Cemetery
Keating James, printer, 185 Essex, boards 10 Lagrange
Keating Mary, widow, house Grove
Keefe Dennis, tanner, house Hanson, corner Varney
Keefe Jeremiah, currier, Putnam, near Hanson
Keefe John, currier, house 95 Mason
Keefe Patrick, laborer, house 10 Herbert
Keever William, blacksmith, house 7 Ward
Kehew Aaron, house 24 North
Kehew Aaron Augustus, carpenter, house 114 Bridge
Kehew Aaron jr. Mrs. house 114 Bridge
Kehew Charles, laborer, house rear 14 Central
Kehew Frank, cooper, house 17 Derby

SALEM [K] DIRECTORY.

Kehew George L. painter, house 16 Lemon
Kehew John, brassfounder, house 19 Becket
Kekew John H. cooper, house 108 Derby
Kehew Joseph C. carpenter, house 114 Bridge
Kehew Samuel cooper, 47 Union, house 11 Herbert
Kehew William B. mason, house 24 North.
Kehew William H. watchmaker, 230 Essex, h. 15 Beckford
Kehrhahn Henry, musician, house Ives court
Kelley Andrew, currier, house rear Adams
Kelley Ann Mrs. house 170 Federal
Kelley Charles, gardener, house 58 Mill
Kelley Charles R. dentist, house 3 Central
Kelley James (Quinn & K.), tailor, 184 Essex, h. 4 Main
Kelley James, currier, house 148 Boston
Kelley James, tanner, house 12 Beach
Kelley James, blacksmith, boards 14 Oak
Kelley James H. mariner, house 15 Brown
Kelley John, currier, house rear Adams
Kelley John, laborer, house 26 Mill
Kelley John, boarding house, 64 Harbor
Kelley John, currier, house North, near Catholic Cemetery
Kelley Jonathan D. farmer, house Lynn road, near Lafayette
Kelley Mary, millinery, 15 Lafayette, house 3 Ward
Kelley Michael, laborer, house 101 Derby
Kelley Michael, laborer, house 13 Upham
Kelley Nathaniel, farmer, house Lynn road, near Lafayette
Kelley Nathaniel jr. laborer, house 60 Broad
Kelley Patrick, harness maker, boards 184 Federal
Kelley Peter, stonemason, house 22 Congress
Kelley Simon, 1 Market House, house 3 Ward
Kelley Stephen, gardener at the Derby farm, Lafayette
Kelley Thomas, shoemaker, house 156 Bridge
Kelley William, laborer, house 26 Peabody
Kelman John, mariner, house 28 Essex
Kelman John Mrs. house 28 Essex
Kelman William W. livery stable, Church, cor. Washington, house 181 Bridge
Kelsey Isaac, mariner, house 3 Pratt
Kemp Samuel, sailmaker, head Peabody's wharf, h. 102 Bridge
Kendall Alvah, stairbuilder, house 11 Hathorne
Kendall Daniel, morocco dresser, boards 4 N. Pine
Kennedy Cornelius, laborer, house 123 Boston
Kennedy Elbridge, tanner, house Grove
Kennedy Martin, shoemaker, house 36 Mill
Kennedy Samuel Mrs. house 18 Norman
Kennedy Samuel, captain, 18 Norman
Kenney Alanson, house 7 Orange

Kenney Bartholomew, currier, house Aborn
Kenney Benjamin M. overseer Naumkeag Mill, h. 11 Congress
Kenney Bridget, widow, house rear 28 North
Kenney Bridget, widow, house 10 River
Kenney Emily, widow, house 8 North court
Kenney Francis, 5 Derby square, house 2 North court
Kenney George, tanner, house 59 Warren
Kenney James, 5 Derby square, house 7 Elm
Kenney John, waiter at Essex House
Kenney William, tanner, Turnpike, house 421 Essex
Kenny Eliza J. house 82 Mill
Kenny George W. machinist, house 77 Mill
Kenny Jonathan A. *(Prime, Kenny & Co.)*, mahogany, &c.
   City Mills, house 8 Pond
Keyes Michael, currier, house 14 Oak
Kezaer W. Augustus, currier, house 57½ Broad
Kezar Charles H. gaiter boot maker, house Ives court
Kezar George L. clerk, 3 High, house 72 Mill
Kezar Sarah B. widow, house 4 St. Peter court
Kiely David, laborer, house 7 High st. court
Kiely Michael, laborer, house 34 Derby
Kiely Peter, scissors grinder, house 10 Herbert
Kiely Robert, 24 Derby square, boards 10 Herbert
Kilbride Daniel, peddler, house 17 Daniels
Kilby Christopher Mrs. house 20 Liberty
Kilfoil Catharine, widow, house 4 Oak
Kilham Sylvester, farmer, house 25 Pickman
Kilham William G. trader, house 11 Becket
Kilham William G. jr. clerk, house 11 Becket
Kimball Adam W. house 10 Charter
Kimball Alfred, assistant clerk, Court House, h. at Ipswich
Kimball Alfred M. shoe manufacturer, house 23 North
Kimball Augustus H. carpenter, house 80 Mill
Kimball Catharine Mrs. house 30 Beckford
Kimball Charles, office 27 Washington, house at Ipswich
Kimball Charles A. house 12 Howard
Kimball David B. counsellor, 27 Washington, h. at Manchester
Kimball David C. (93 Broad, B.), house 126 Essex
Kimball Dorcas Mrs. boarding house, 23 North
Kimball Ebenezer D. jailer, house at the jail, St. Peter
Kimball Eben W. counsellor, 214 Essex, house 13 Union
Kimball Emeline R. teacher, boards 30 Beckford
Kimball George, painter, house 30 Pleasant
Kimball George S. painter, boards 1 Harbor
Kimball Jacob, mariner, house 29 Harbor
Kimball James, chair manufacturer, 111 Essex, house 127 do.
Kimball James P. house 127 Essex

Kimball James S. captain, house 14 Pickman
Kimball John, sailmaker, house 14 Federal
Kimball John Mrs. house 45 Mill
Kimball John S. house 12 Pickman
Kimball Jonathan C. carpenter, house 29 Pleasant
Kimball Joseph, mariner, house 13 Ward
Kimball Joseph, mariner, house 5 Mechanic
Kimball Joseph A. calker, boards 45 Mill
Kimball Judith Mrs. house 1 Church
Kimball Margaret Mrs. house 82 Essex
Kimball *(Mark)* & Skerry *(Robert)*, painters, 139 Derby, house 1 Harbor
Kimball Mary Mrs. house 15 Whittemore
Kimball Mary R. teacher, house 30 Beckford
Kimball Nathaniel, carpenter, house 6 Curtis
Kimball Nathaniel A. merchant, house Pleasant, c. Andrew
Kimball Penn T. clerk, 173 Essex, boards 16 Pickman
Kimball Samuel T. *(Henderson & K.)*, furniture, 38 & 40 Wash. house 16 Pickman
Kimball Sarah F. widow, house 25 North
Kimball Sarah S. S. Mrs. house 19 Winter
Kimball Thomas, mariner, house 14 Pickman
Kimball William, hats, caps, &c. 209 Essex, house 10 Charter
Kimball William, currier, house rear 70 North
Kimball William jr. 209 Essex, house 26 Hardy
King Charles, weaver, house Perkins
King Edward, hostler, house foot Northey
King Elizabeth, house 85 Essex
King Hannah H. house 85 Essex
King Henry Mrs. house 389 Essex
King Henry F. captain, house 389 Essex
King James, wharfinger, Derby wharf, house 34 Harbor
King James, 20 Derby square, house 9 High st. court
King James B. captain, house 47 Lafayette
King James J. clerk, 79 Mason, boards 2 Beach
King John, laborer, house 18 Odell square
King John, mariner, house 8 Hardy
King John Glen Mrs. house 258 Essex
King John Gallison, counsellor (27 State, B.), h. 258 Essex
King Nancy Mrs. house Perkins
Kingman Martha, teacher in Normal School, b. 183 Bridge
Kingsley George W. baker, house 53 Summer
Kingsley John, mariner, house 8½ Turner
Kingsley Thomas P. inspector C. H. house 33 Pleasant
Kingsley George W. boards 32 Mill
Kinnily David, laborer, house 12 Ash
Kinsman John, house E. Webb

Kinsman John C. (B.), house 7 Spring
Kinsman Joseph, shoemaker, house 31 Williams
Kinsman Joshua Mrs. house 22 Brown
Kinsman Nathaniel J. captain, house 22 Brown
Kinsman Rebecca C. Mrs. house 24 Church
Kinsman *(Samuel)* & Clough *(Robert P.)*, curriers, Franklin, house 59 North
Kinsman William (B.), house 24 Church
Kirby Edward, boards rear 42 Harbor
Kirby Margaret, widow, house 156 Derby
Kirby Timothy, bowling saloon, 8 Wash. house r. 42 Harbor
Kirby Mary, widow, house 3 Church
Kirk James F. house 134 Derby
Kirvin John, currier, house 13 Rust
Kisskalt Maurice, confectioner, boards 269 Essex
Kittlewell Peter, house 365 Essex
Kittredge Jonathan, laborer, house E. Webb
Knapp Isaac N. shoemaker, house 15 Webb
Knapp J. J. Mrs. house 85 Essex
Knapp William, shoe manufacturer, house Linden
Knight Albert, baggage master E. R. R. depot, h. 13 Salem
Knight Anna Mrs. tailoress, house 7 Cross
Knight Benjamin Rev. house 6 North court
Knight Charles, mariner, house 60 North
Knight Edward H. wharfinger and freight agent, Phillips whf. house 11 Hardy
Knight Elizabeth P. nurse, house 346 Essex
Knight Foster, provisions, 48 North, house do.
Knight Jeremiah, shoemaker, house 4 Nursery
Knight John, laborer, house 31 Buffum
Knight Joseph F. currier, house 60 North
Knight Mehitable Mrs. house 40 St. Peter
Knight M. B. & M. Misses, fancy goods, 5 Pleasant, house do.
Knight Nathaniel, laborer, house 13 Whittemore
Knight Nathaniel jr. laborer, boards 13 Whittemore
Knight Richard N. clerk, boards 13 Salem
Knight Samuel, laborer, house 40 St. Peter
Knight Sally, widow, house 60 North
Knight Willard, grocer, 55 Harbor, house 53 do.
Knight William, shoemaker, 29 North, house 6 River
Knights John H. fish, house 5 Gardner court
Knowlton George, blacksmith, house 53 Charter
Knowlton W. Sargent, cabinet maker, house 10 Barton
Knowlton William Mrs. house 17 Washington
Knox Rebecca Mrs. house rear 41 Derby
Knox William, seaman, boards rear 41 Derby
Kyle Robert, shoemaker, house 9 Prince

LABDON JAMES, currier, house Adams, Mason Hill
Ladd Daniel W. house 19 Creek
Ladd Mary Mrs. house 5 Gedney court
Lagan Morris (Cal.), house 27 Daniels
Lahey Jeremiah, laborer, house 17 Harbor
Lake Calvin H. shoecutter, house Milk, corner Andrew
Lakeman Eben K. Mrs. house 12 Elm
Lakeman Horace, clerk, 232 Essex, house 12 Elm
Lakeman Lucinda, dressmaker, house 57 Washington
Lakeman Nathan, currier, house 154 Boston
Laker Elizabeth, widow, house 25 Charter
Lamb Mary Ann Mrs. house 12 Broad
Lambert Henry L. clerk, Custom House, house 110 Essex
Lambert John, captain, house 22 Hathorne
Lambert Porter, tanner, house 4 Howard
Lamont Daniel G. physician, 243½ Essex, house at Boston
Lamphor A. M. machinist, boards 62 Harbor
Lamson Asa, house 4 Northey
Lamson Charles, watchmaker, 234 Essex, house 5 Northey
Lamson Eliza, widow, house 19 Winthrop
Lamson Frederick, house 4 Northey
Lander Benjamin Mrs. house 10 Saunders
Lander Benjamin W. printer and publisher "Salem Advocate,"
  over 215 & 217 Essex, house Cross st. court
Lander Edward, merchant, house 5 Summer
Lander E. Warren, hairdresser, 9 St. Peter, b. 10 Saunders
Lander Michael, laborer, boards 11 Whittemore
Lander Sarah W. boys' clothing maker, 242½ Essex, boards 10
  Saunders
Lander William W. mariner, house 106 Essex
Lander William W. clerk, 205 Essex
Landergan Edward, currier, house 68 Mason
Landergan John, currier, house rear 347 Essex
Landergan Thomas, laborer, house rear 67 Mason
Lane Edward B. sailmaker, 57 Union, house 12 do.
Lane George N. clerk, 391 Essex, boards 46 Charter
Lane Henry J. shoemaker, house 58 Endicott
Lane Mehitabel Mrs. house 46 Charter
Lang Benj. piano dealer and tuner, 157 Essex, h. 49 Lafayette
Lang Benjamin J. house 49 Lafayette
Lang Daniel, house 8 Creek
Lang Joseph, mariner, boards 36 St. Peter
Langdell Mary, widow, house 30 Williams
Langley Jeremiah D. shoemaker, house Ropes
Langmaid Alfred A. engineer, house 1 Downing
Langmaid George W. shoemaker, boards 17 Dearborn
Langmaid John P. steamplaner, house 61 Charter

Larcom Thomas, tanner, boards 14 School
Larkin Richard, cooper, house Tucker's wharf
Larrabee Benj. F. city watchman, house 8 Peabody
Larrabee Charles W. shoemaker, house 6 North Pine
Larrabee Eben L. shoemaker, house 17 March
Larrabee Edward W. shoemaker, boards 12 Lynn
Larrabee Elias C. ice dealer, house 10 March
Larrabee George B. shoemaker, house rear 31 Bridge
Larrabee Henry A. shoemaker, boards 12 Lynn
Larrabee Joseph N. shoemaker, boards 12 Lynn
Larrabee Judith Mrs. house 5 Saunders
Larrabee Samuel F. clerk, 42 Washington, b. 15 Cambridge
Larrabee Samuel H. grocer, 13 Church, house 15 Cambridge
Larrabee Sarah, widow, house 8 Creek
Larrabee Somers N. shoe manufacturer, Beach, house 12 Lynn
Larrabee William, shoemaker, house 8 Conant
Laskey Esther Mrs. tailoress, house 57 Charter
Laskey John, tobacconist, 47 Mill, house 45 do.
Laskey Mary E. dressmaker, house 45 Mill
Lassan Peter, captain, house 7 Becket
Laughlin Lydia Ann, house 13 Curtis
Law George D. shoemaker, 12 Norman, house do.
Lawless Timothy, shoemaker, house 4 Barton
Lawrence Daniel S. boatman, house 16 Derby
Lawrence Eliza A. Mrs. house 34 Essex
Lawrence George, mason, house 42 Endicott
Lawrence John, shoemaker, house 140 Bridge
Lawrence Joseph, laborer, house 24 Derby
Lawrence Julia, widow, house 2 High st. court
Lawrence Lewis, watchman, Phillips wharf, house 35 Derby
Lawrence Lewis jr. cooper, house 20 Derby
Lawrence Michael, currier, house 18 Odell square
Lawrence Michael, currier, house 20 River
Lawson Peter, captain, house 7 Becket
Leach Sarah H. Mrs. house 78 Federal
Learock John M. shoemaker, 149 Essex, house 29 Derby
Leary Daniel, servant, house Jackson place
Leary Daniel, currier, boards 20 Fowler
Leary Dennis, laborer, house rear 8 Whittemore
Leary John, currier, house 62 Mason
Leary Margaret, widow, house rear 30 Peabody
Leary Mary, widow, house 26 Mill
Leary Timothy, currier, house 68 Mason
Leary Timothy, laborer, house Grove, near Mason
Leavitt Charles M. clerk (B.), boards at Essex House
Leavitt Eunice Mrs. house 17 Andrew
Leavitt Israel P. shoemaker, 128 Boston, house 107 do.

Leavitt Joseph H. clerk, Essex House, 176 Essex
Leavitt Joseph S. proprietor Essex House, 176 Essex
Leavitt Walter, carpenter, 39 North, house 79 do.
Leavitt William, teacher of navigation, 71 Forrester, house 6 Oliver
Lecraw Benjamin P. mariner, house 37 North
Ledgar Zachariah, currier, house 80 Boston
Lee Frances Mrs. house 83 Derby
Lee Dorcas, widow, house 48 Charter
Lee Francis H. house 14 Chestnut
Lee George, saloon, 14½ Derby square, house 89 Essex
Lee George W. boots and shoes, 291 Essex, house 3 Federal
Lee Harriet D. widow, house 5 Creek
Lee Israel S. cooper, house 18 Pickman
Lee John C. (40 State, B.), house 14 Chestnut
Lee John H. mariner, boards 23 Essex
Lee John R. merchant (B.), boards 33 Summer
Lee Joseph, currier, house 50 Mill
Lee Joseph L. foreman at Seccomb's, house 90 Mill
Lee Lois D. Mrs. house 18 Pickman
Lee Sarah R. Mrs. house 6 Prince
Leech William, dealer in boots, 205 Derby, house 25 Turner
Leeds George Rev. house 33 Summer
Leeds George W. boards Summer, cor. Chestnut
Lefavour George B. mariner, boards 91 Bridge
Lefavour John, house 15 Oliver
Lefavour John S. shoemaker, house 8 Hathorne
Lefavour John W. (Suffolk Bank, B.), house 10 Barton square
Lefavour Joseph Mrs. house 23 Pleasant
Lefavour Mary, house 18 Williams
Lefavour Mary Ann, tailoress, house 80 North
Lefavour Richard M. mariner, boards 91 Bridge
Lefavor Samuel H. mariner, house 14 Winter
Lefavour Thomas H. ship chandler and grocer, 135 Derby, house 91 Bridge
Lefavour William, captain, house 22 Williams
Legrand Charles A. Mrs. house 12 Daniels
Leighton Edwin, conductor E. R. R. house 20 Lynde
Lémasney Edward, laborer, house 22 Northey
Lemasney Thomas, laborer, house 4 Peabody
LeMaster Lydia Mrs. house rear 169 Essex
Lena John, mariner, house 9 Congress
Lendall Jacob H. tanner, house 25 Beaver
Lendall John, tanner, house 11 May
Lendholm Frederick, captain, house 18 Lafayette
Lenox Patrick, currier, house Ord
Leonard John H. morocco dresser, house 158 Boston

Lewellyn James, currier, house Grove, near Mason
Lewis Dana Mrs. house 20 Winter
Lewis Eliza A. seamstress, house 1 Turner
Lewis George A. carpenter, house 3 March
Lewis Martha Ann W. widow, house 319 Essex
Lewis Peter, mariner, house 32½ Endicott
Lewis Samuel, shipwright, house 14 Ward
Lewis Thomas D. hairdresser, house 12 Cedar
Lewis William, laborer, house 4½ Turner
Libby Henry, currier, house 185 Federal
Libby John F. clerk, house 185 Federal
Lillis Owen, laborer, house 7 High street court
Lindegaard James C. house 8½ Carpenter
Lindsey Richard, agent M. P. Union Store, 25 Lafayette, house 4 Broad
Linehan Daniel, laborer, house 49 Harbor
Linehan Daniel, wines and liquors, 6 Derby sq. h. Harbor
Linehan Jeremiah, laborer, house 13 Park
Linehan John, laborer, house 5 Charter
Linehan William, laborer, house 7 Ward
Linsky Margaret, widow, house near foot of Pingree
Little Joshua B. Mrs. house 344 Essex
Little John, laborer, house 36 Mill
Little Michael, laborer, house 18 River
Littlefield Daniel, fish, house 26 Essex
Littlefield Dependence, shoemaker, 5 North, house 310 Essex
Littlefield Hannah Mrs. nurse, house 14 Odell square
Littlefield Moses H. carpenter, house 22 Mechanic
Littlefield Peletiah, teamster, house 7 Albion
Livingston Macolm, captain, house 18 Pickman
Lloyd William H. pilot, house 49 St. Peter
Locke Ira D. Naumkeag Mill, house 42 Harbor
Locke Milton P. *(Bousley & L.)*, carpenter, 16 Mill, house 10 Church
Lockwood Charles M. shoemaker, house 6 English
Logue Joseph, trader, house 98 Derby
Lombard Joanna C. widow, house 68 Essex
Looby Ellen, widow, house rear 8 Whittemore
Looby Jeremiah, laborer, house 22 Beaver
Looby Patrick, house Irving, near Harrod
Looby Thomas, tanner and currier, Grove, near Milldam, house 105 Mason
Looney William, currier, house 56 Broad
Lord Andrew & D. marble and grave stone manufacturers, Market wharf, house 12 Odell square
Lord Calvin, 1 & 2 Market House, house at South Danvers
Lord Charles A. captain, house 60 North

Lord Charles H. clerk, 37 Endicott, house 52 do.
Lord Charles L. mariner, house 195 Bridge
Lord Daniel *(A. & D. Lord)*, house 195 Bridge
Lord Daniel A. tanner, house 51 Warren
Lord Daniel B. inspector Custom House, house 24 Howard
Lord Daniel B. jr. gasfitter, 151 Essex, house 9 Curtis
Lord Daniel W. stonecutter, boards 15 Whittemore
Lord David A. blacksmith, house 29 Endicott
Lord David Mrs. house 27 Pleasant
Lord Enoch, house 180 Federal
Lord Emeline, teacher private school, house 94 Bridge
Lord Ephraim, tailor, 249 Essex, house 89½ North
Lord Francis, tanner, house Phelps court
Lord George C. architect, boards 12 Odell square
Lord George E. mariner, house 27 Pleasant
Lord George F. salesman (B.), boards 195 Bridge
Lord Harriet N. teacher, house 27 Pleasant
Lord Henry, currier, boards 5 May
Lord John B carpenter, house 7 Lagrange
Lord James, tanner, rear 180 Federal, house 180 do:
Lord James A. tanner, Pope's court, house 188 Federal
Lord Joseph B. mariner, house 27 Pleasant
Lord Louisa Miss, house 6 Lynde
Lord Michael, captain, house 173 Federal
Lord Nancy D. Mrs. house 9 Curtis
Lord Nathaniel J. counsellor, 194 Essex, house 312 do.
Lord Otis P. counsellor, 27 Washington, house 312 Essex
Lord Samuel A. mariner, house 9 Curtis
Lorgan John, laborer, house 5 Gerrish place
Lorigan Ellen, widow, house 13 Lynn
Lorigan Thomas, laborer, house 13 Lynn
Loring Edward D. coach and chaise maker, West place, house 80 Summer
Loring George B. house 328 Essex
Loring Joshua, coachmaker, house 55 Federal
Loud Noah, sparmaker (B.), house 2 Mason   [325 do.
Lougee Joseph *(Haskell & L.)*, cabinet maker, 296 Essex, bds.
Lovejoy John, carpenter, 108 Essex, house 40 do.
Lovering Lydia Mrs. carpet maker, house 14 Federal
Loves Nancy Mrs. house 44 Forrester
Lovett Josiah, shoemaker, house 67 Mill
Low Aaron T. *(Averell & L.)*, house 79 Boston
Low Anna M. Miss, boards 6 Federal court
Low Charles, teamster, boards 30 Winthrop
Low Edward A. ropemaker, house 26 Endicott
Low Edward A. jr. clerk, 225 Essex, boards 26 Endicott
Low Elijah, laborer, house 17 Becket

Low Francis A. clerk (B.), house 79 Boston
Low Gideon (Cal.), house Phelps court
Low Hannah, house 9 Gedney court
Low Richard, cooper, house 9 Gedney court
Lowd David, tanner, house 12 Hathorne
Lowd Joseph G. currier, boards 12 Hathorne
Lowd Mark, painter, 8 North, house 9 Buffum.
Lowe Charles Rev. house Lafayette, near R. R. crossing
Lowe Daniel, clerk, 201 Essex, boards 9 Gedney court
Lucas Sarah H. Mrs. house 2 Winthrop
Lucey Bartholomew, teamster, house rear 8 Pratt
Lucy Bartholomew, laborer, house rear 3 Church
Lull John E. laborer, house 140 Bridge
Lummus Abram, carpenter, boards 13 Aborn
Lummus William, morocco dresser, house 13 Aborn
Lundagan Patrick, laborer, house 153 Bridge
Lundergan James, laborer, house 54 Charter
Lundergan William, laborer, house 53 St. Peter
Lundgreen Dennis, peddler, boards 176 Derby
Lundgreen Samuel, peddler, boards 176 Derby
Lundgren Peter, laborer, house 23 Essex
Lunt Alice W. widow, house 5 Margin
Lunt Edward, Naumkeag Mill, boards 38 Harbor
Luscomb Augustus F. mariner, boards 39 Lafayette
Luscomb Caroline, teacher, boards 41 Lafayette
Luscomb Charles B. clerk (B.), house 30 Winthrop
Luscomb George, shoemaker, house 3 Dow
Luscomb George, cooper, house 41 Lafayette
Luscomb Hannah Mrs. house 2 Endicott
Luscomb Harriet A. teacher, boards 41 Lafayette
Luscomb Henry, mariner, house 39 Lafayette
Luscomb Henry jr. shoemaker, house rear 23 Cedar
Luscomb Henry R. carpenter, boards rear 23 Cedar
Luscomb John C. captain, house 8 Northey
Luscomb *(John G.)* & Pratt *(C. W.)*, jewellers, 162 Essex, house 24 Lafayette
Luscomb Joseph W captain, house 4 Conant
Luscomb Mary Mrs. house 72 Mill
Luscomb William, shoemaker, house 78 North
Luscomb William F. carpenter, boards 8 Northey
Luscomb William H. sign and fancy painting, 341 Essex, b. 41 Lafayette
Lyford Francis W. cooper, house 30 Turner
Lynch Anthony, currier, house Hanson
Lynch Dennis, dry goods, 94 Derby, house 91 do.
Lynch Ellen, widow, house 10 Herbert
Lynch John, teamster, house 2 High street court

Lynch Joseph, currier, house 148 Boston
Lynch Michael, house 11 Charter
Ly ch Patrick, umbrella maker, house 92 Derby
Lynch Patrick, currier, house Green place
Lynch William, peddler, house 91 Derby
Lyons Humphrey, gum copal works, boards 14 Daniels
Lyons Jeremiah, laborer, house 14 Daniels
Lyons John, gum copal worker, boards 14 Daniels

MACK THOMAS, mason, house rear Adams
Mack William, physician, house 21 Chestnut
Mackie John, upholsterer, 131 Essex, house do.
Mackintire John, jeweller, 10 Central, house 22 Crombie
Mackintire Samuel, secretary Working Men's Loan and Fund
 Corporation, 18 Asiatic block, house Federal, cor. Dean
Mackintire Samuel A. insurance agent, 27 Washington, house
 5 Dodge, near Dearborn
Mackintosh Laura A. house 11 Ash
Madden Patrick, laborer, house 14 Congress
Madigan John, currier, boards 14 Oak
Magner Timothy, laborer, house Aborn, near Boston
Magoun Thomas, shipwright and calker, house 28 Derby
Magoun Warren, mariner, house 1 Allen
Maguire Andrew, at Gas House, house 25 Northey
Maguire Peter, shoemaker, boards 21 Fowler
Mahoney Daniel, laborer, boards 7 Upham
Mahoney Dennis, currier, house 56 Broad
Mahoney James, laborer, house 28 Congress
Mahoney Jeremiah, currier, 55 Boston, house 12 do.
Mahoney John, laborer, house Becket avenue
Mahoney John, laborer, house Tucker's wharf
Mahoney John, currier, boards 184 Federal
Mahoney Mary, widow, house 7 Upham
Mahoney Michael, tailor, house 19 Daniels
Mahoney Patrick, laborer, house 3 Parker's court
Mahony Matthew, laborer, house Tucker's wharf
Mahony Patrick, laborer, house Tucker's wharf
Mahony Patrick, gardener, house 200 Derby
Mahony Thomas, waiter at 21 Federal
Mahony Timothy, laborer, house 170 Derby
Main P. J. Miss, boards 5 Upham
Mallan Andrew, farmer, house rear Adams
Mallan Ellen, widow, house 87 Beaver
Maloney Samuel, currier, boards 2 Mason
Malony James, Naumkeag Mill, boards 10 Prince
Malony Martin, currier, house 13 Rust
Malony Patrick, Naumkeag Mill, boards 10 Prince

Maloon Abigail Mrs. house 81 Boston
Maloon John W. tanner, house 81 Boston
Maloon Nicholas, laborer, house 8 Turner
Maloon *(William)* & Harrington *(Wm. H.)*, tanners, Goodhue, house School, corner Tremont
Maly James, laborer, house rear 35 Harbor
Mann Elizabeth N. private school, 190 Federal, boards 180 do.
Mann James B. grocer, 40 Boston, house 42 do.
Manning Charles H. weigher and gauger, Custom House, h. Phelps court, opposite Green place
Manning Daniel, currier, house 6 Aborn
Manning Daniel A. cabinet maker, house 14 Albion
Manning Daniel C. *(Smith & M.)*, livery stables, h. 62 Forrester
Manning James, proprietor Merchants' News Room, Asiatic building, house 4 Daniels
Manning Joseph, bootmaker, house 20 Mall
Manning Michael, stonemason, house 76 North
Manning Otis T. mason, house Flint, corner Warren
Manning Catharine, house 68 Mason
Manning Rebecca D. widow, house 33 Dearborn
Manning Richard, tailor, house 8 Aborn
Manning Richard C. *(John Dike & Co.)*, coal, wood, &c., 183 Derby, house 33 Dearborn
Manning Robert, nursery of fruit trees, house 33 Dearborn
Manning Robert, captain, house 4 Daniels
Manning Thomas, laborer, house 5 Church
Manning William, boards Mansion House
Manning William S. morocco dresser, boards 8 Aborn
Mannigan Patrick, laborer, house 25 Albion
Mansfield Benjamin S. painter, 8 Endicott, house 55 Mill
Mansfield Charles, captain, house 62 Washington
Mansfield Charles A. mariner, boards 62 Washington
Mansfield Charles H. mason, boards 55 Mill
Mansfield Daniel A. provisions, 33 Endicott, house 50 Mill
Mansfield Daniel H. merch. and consul at Zanzibar, h. 2 Broad
Mansfield George S. upholsterer, 50 Washington, h. 19 Harbor
Mansfield Henry, shoemaker, house Milk
Mansfield Henry T. clerk, house 4 Rust
Mansfield Henry T. jr. clerk (Suffolk Bank, B.), b. 76 Essex
Mansfield Ira, mason, Congress, house 3 Lagrange
Mansfield Ira K. clerk, 141 Essex, boards 3 Lagrange
Mansfield John, house 50 Mill
Mansfield John R. shoemaker, house Nursery
Mansfield Joseph, painter, 9 Lafayette, house 21 Harbor
Mansfield Lois Mrs. house 177 Bridge
Mansfield Micajah B. machine sewing, 230½ Derby, h. 55 Mill
Mansfield Nancy & Freelove, dressmakers, house 13 Crombie

SALEM [M] DIRECTORY.

Mansfield Nathaniel B. merchant, house 27 Broad
Mansfield Stephen W. bookkeeper (B.), house 76 Essex
Mansfield William, constable and city messenger, house 55 Mill
Mansfield William, candle maker, house 88 Mill
Mansfield William D. clerk, boards 62 Washington
Mansfield William R. D. mariner, house 55 Mill
March George H. currier, boards 4 N. Pine
Marden Aaron, carpenter, house 97 Bridge
Marden Joseph, carpenter, house 20 Endicott
Marden Lemuel, carpenter, 9 Beckford, house 22 North
Markoe George F. H. clerk, 123 Essex, boards 39 Derby
Markoe Nancy, seamstress, house 39 Derby
Markoe Philip Mrs. house 39 Derby
Marks Benjamin N. clerk (B.), boards 9 Cambridge
Marks John, house 9 Cambridge
Marks John L. clerk, 165 Derby, house 10 Winter
Maroney Jeremiah, currier, house rear 67 Mason
Maroney Maurice, shoemaker, house Adams
Maroney Thomas, laborer, house foot of Ropes
Marritt Joseph, tanner, house 19 Albion
Marrs Daniel, shoemaker, house rear Shillaber
Marrs James, shoemaker, house rear Shillaber
Marrs James jr. shoemaker, house rear Shillaber
Marrs Michael, shoemaker, house Parker's court
Marrs William, shoemaker, house Shillaber
Marshall Daniel, captain, house 4 North Pine
Marshall E. H. trader, boards 63 Harbor
Marshall Hannah Mrs. upholsteress, house 101 Federal
Marshall Joseph, mason, house 13 Mount Vernon
Marshall Samuel, shoemaker, house 64 Boston
Marshall Samuel K. cabinet maker, house 19 Andrew
Marsins Dominick, mariner, house 74 Essex
Marston Asa, boards Mansion House
Marston Daniel, house 7 Ash
Marston George M. seaman, boards 218 Essex
Marston Henry, coachman, house 220 Essex
Marston Isabella T. house 15 Washington
Marston Simon, watchman, house 218 Essex
Martin Christopher, bootmaker, 23 Washington, h. 8 Ward
Martin Henry carpenter, house 9 Turner
Martin John N. fishmarket, 14 Front, house 54 Bridge
Martin Lucy, house 100 Federal
Martin William, restorator, basement 6 Washington
Martin William P. currier, foot of Beach, house 159 Federal
Mason Abigail Miss, house 2 Monroe
Mason Ann M. house 2 Monroe
Mason Henry, mariner, house 6 Becket

Massey Sally, widow, house 62 Forrester
Masterson James, shoemaker, house 77 Derby
Masury John, shipwright, house 9 Becket
Mathews John, mariner, house 7 Federal
Mathews Richard, captain, house 1 Summer
Matthews James, teamster, house 17 Flint
Matthews James, teamster, house 89 North
Matthews Sarah N. Mrs. nurse, house 7 Federal
Matthews Patrick, tanner, house Adams
Matthews ———, hairdresser, boards 9 Norman
Matteson Daniel, machinist, Naumkeag Mill, house 9 Curtis
Matteson James A. machinist, house 25 Salem
Maxey Sarah, house 2 Turner
Maxfield Benjamin, laborer, house 84 Mill
Maxfield James, tanner, house May, near Boston
Maxfield James jr. currier, boards May, near Boston
Maxfield Joseph H. shoemaker, house 75 Mill
Maxfield Josiah, fireman, house 57 Derby
Maxfield Martha Mrs. house 28 Chestnut
Maxfield Thomas, Naumkeag Mill, house 16 Salem
Maxwell Silas, shoemaker, house 38 Federal
May Calvin W. furniture, 274 Essex, house 28 Lynde
May Charles H. shoemaker, house 5½ Gedney court
May George T. shoemaker, house 18 Conant
May James, farmer, house 5½ Gedney court
Mayer Joseph, laces, hosiery, &c. 171 Essex, house 27 St. Peter
Maynes William, hats, caps, and furs, 35 Wash. h. 88 North
McAuliff Timothy, currier, house Hanson
McBride Mary, widow, house 22 Congress
McCabe John, tanner, house 41 North
McCabe Patrick, laborer, house 21 Ward
McCalley Andrew, currier, rear 180 Federal, h. 184 Federal
McCallum David, Naumkeag Mill, house 2 Dow
McCannon Susan Mrs. house 53 Warren
McCannon Thomas, currier, boards 53 Warren
McCarron Patrick, laborer, house 22 Congress
McCarten George, currier, boards 184 Federal
McCartney James Mrs. house 71 Federal
McCarty Charles, laborer, house 24 River
McCarty Daniel, laborer, house 28 Peabody
McCarty Ellen, widow, house rear 20 Congress
McCarty Ellen, house 4 Albion
McCarty Florence, currier, house rear Adams
McCarty Florence, currier, house 411 Essex
McCarty Jeremiah, house 32 North
McCarty John, tanner, house 27 Beaver
McCarty John, currier, house 37 Beaver

SALEM [M] DIRECTORY.

McCarty John, laborer, house 91 Derby
McCarty John, shoemaker, house 148 Derby
McCarty John, laborer, house 405 Essex
McCarty Mary, widow, house rubber factory, Ward
McCarty Mary, widow, house 10 Ward
McCarty Mary, widow, house 6 Pratt
McCarty Mary, widow, house 9 Charter
McCarty Mary, widow, house 36 Peabody
McCarty Michael, currier, house Ives
McCarty Michael, shoemaker, house 43 Union
McCarty Michael, currier, house 24 River
McCarty Patrick, laborer, house 158 Boston
McCarty Timothy, blacksmith, house 6 Pratt
McCarty Sarah, widow, house 7 Charter
McCauley Thomas, laborer, house 2 High street court
McClennan John, laborer, house Odell square
McCloy Alexander, blacksmith, house 17 Union
McCloy Alexander jr. carpenter, house 4 Walnut
McCloy Henry, tailor, 177 Essex, house 6 Walnut
McCloy John, house 17 Union
McCloy Robert Mrs. house 14 Union
McCloy Robert, salesman, house 14 Union
McConnell Eliza A. Mrs. house 14 Federal
McCord Thomas, clothing and boarding, house 146 Derby
McCormick John, laborer, house 26 Mill
McCormick John, laborer, boards at William Cronan's
McCormick Patrick, laborer, house 77 Derby
McCormick Peter, morocco dresser, house 12 Goodhue
McCue Michael, farmer, house foot of Dearborn
McCullen Michael, seaman, house 7 Charter
McCurdy Thomas, laborer, house rear 19 Daniels
McCurdy Thomas G. currier, 67 Mason, house do.
McDermott Patrick, laborer, house 18 Odell square
McDonald John, currier, house 4 Beaver
McDonald Michael (Cal.), house rear 31 Derby
McDonald Michael, laborer, house 10 Herbert
McDonnell Alexander, ship carpenter, boards 16 Dow
McDonnell Catherine, widow, house 15 Turner
McDonnell David, laborer, house 77 Derby
McDonnell John, laborer, house 7 Charter
McDonnell Michael (Cal.), house 34 Derby
McDonnell Philip, shoemaker, boards 15 Turner
McDonough Edward, currier, house Warren court
McDonough Patrick, shoemaker, boards 21 Fowler
McDonough William, currier, house 16 Congress
McDuffee Charles D. dresser, house 65 Harbor
McDuffee Elizabeth Mrs. house 26 Harbor

McDuffie Augustus P. trader, house 113 North
McDuffie George, tanner, boards at Henry Clark's
McFadden Daniel, fisherman, house 29 Derby
McFaden Charles A. cigar maker, boards 55 Derby
McFarland Catherine, widow, house East Gardner, n. Harbor
McFarland Charles, carpenter, boards E. Gardner, n. Harbor
McFarland James, moulder, boards East Gardner, n. Harbor
McFarland William, captain, house 7 Harbor
McGeary Bernard, house rear Adams
McGeary James, leather (North, B.), house 65 Mason
McGee Cormick, currier, house 13 Gedney court
McGee Thomas, currier, boards Hugh M. Scott's, Adams
McGinnis John, currier, house rear 56 Broad
McGinnis Michael, Naumkeag Mill, house Pingree
McGlue Rosanna, widow, house 19 Salem
McGlue Thomas, blacksmith, boards 19 Salem
McGrain John, teamster, house 8 Pratt
McGrain Nicholas, laborer, house 89 Derby
McGrain William, laborer, house 140 Derby
McGrath James, tanner, house Adams
McGrath James, tanner, house 142 Bridge
McGrath John, tanner, house 168 Federal
McGrath John, currier, house Phelps court, near Jackson place
McGrath John, laborer, house Tucker's wharf
McGrath Michael, laborer, house rear Adams
McGrath Patrick, currier, house Adams
McGrath Peter, laborer, house 4 Pingree
McGrath William, laborer, house rear Adams
McGrath William, house rear Adams
McGuire Andrew, laborer, house rear 40 St. Peter
McGuire Bernard, ag't, N. E. P. Union, 12 Front, h. 19 Fowler
McGuire Bridget, widow, house 65 Mason
McGuire Ellen, house Adams
McGuire *(John)* & O'Leary *(T.)*, tailors, 41 Charter, h. 25 do.
McGuire Patrick, currier, house Hanson, near Varney
McGuire Thomas, laborer, house 11 Flint
McGuire John, laborer, house 3 Gerrish place
McGuire William, laborer, house 142 Bridge
McIntire Ann, widow, house 2 Dow
McIntire Hannah, widow, house 12 Carpenter
McIntire Henry, coachmaker, 12 Sewall, house 27 Liberty
McIntire Mary, washer woman, house 25 Liberty [Whittemore
McIntire Samuel J. livery stable and teaming, Mechanic, h. 4
McIntire William E. carpenter, 39 North, house 4 Whittemore
McIntyre Hannah & Mary, tailoresses, house 36 Norman
McIntyre Mary E. D. dressmaker, house 12 Carpenter
McIntyre Nathaniel, laborer, house 72 Mill

McKean William, currier, house 20 Fowler
McKearing Timothy, laborer, house foot of Park
McKeever Hugh, laborer, house 21 High
McKeon William, farmer, house North, near boundary line
McKenney Cornelius, tailor, house 11 Gedney court
McKenzie John W. tailor, 249 Essex, boards 114 Derby
McKenzie Joseph (Cal.), house Gedney court
McKenzie Margaret Mrs. house 4 Andover
McKenzie Reuben Mrs. house 7 Williams
McKenzie Roderick A. *(Chamberlain & McK.)*, tailor, 29 Washington, house 4 Andover [Gardner
McKey John, clothing and furnishing goods, 189 Essex, house
McLaughlin Daniel, currier, boards 29 Beaver
McLaughlin Edward, currier, boards 29 Beaver
McLaughlin John, currier, boards 29 Beaver
McLaughlin Mary Miss, boards 34 Peabody
McLaughlin Michael, laborer, house Odell square
McLellan Ann, widow, house 111 Boston
McMahan Philip, weaver, boards 64 Harbor
McMahan Susan, widow, house 32 Union
McMaher John, salesman, 12 Front, boards 19 Fowler
McManners Thomas, laborer, house 3 Pratt street court
McMullan William, merchant, Central wf. house 8 St. Peter
McMurphy Benjamin F. gasfitter, 273 Essex, h. 23 Andover
McMurphy James D. baggage master South Reading Branch R. R. house 9 Lemon
McNiff James, stonelayer, house Green place
McNulty Catharine, house 7 Charter
McNulty James, laborer, house 200 Derby
McNulty Michael, laborer, house 15 Turner
McShane Bernard, 34 Front, house 69 Summer
Mead William E. mariner, boards rear 89 North
Mead William J. shoemaker, house rear 89 North
Meady Daniel F. confectioner, house 10 Carlton
Meady Louisa, widow, house 10 Carlton
Meek Henry, boatman, Custom House, house 2 Curtis
Meeker William, cigar maker, house 7 Becket
Melcher Edward, carpenter, 83 North, house 32 Buffum
Melcher George B. painter, boards Melcher court
Melcher John, carpenter, house 1 Mechanic
Melcher John E. carpenter, boards 32 Buffum
Melcher Levi L. mason, house Melcher court
Meldon George, laborer, house 4 Essex
Mellody Martin, peddler, house foot Pingree
Meloney Henry E. currier, rear 97 Mason, house 101 do.
Melzeard Thomas Mrs. house 16 St. Peter
Melzeard Thomas, house 16 St. Peter

SALEM [M] DIRECTORY.

Melzeard Thomas B. shoemaker, boards 15 Lemon
Merrill Elizabeth K. Mrs. house 42 Broad
Merrill Henry, stonecutter, house 102 Lafayette
Merrill Isabella, widow, house 171 Boston
Merrill Jonathan, cooper, house 12 Liberty
Merrill Moses H. currier, house 171 Boston
Merrill Samuel A. farmer, house rear 118 Lafayette
Merrill William H. cooper, house 12 Liberty
Merritt Alfred S. 14 Washington, house 11 Upham
Merritt David & Co. *(David jr.)*, merchants and express line, 14 Washington, house 94 Federal
Merritt David jr. *(Merritt & Co.)*, 14 Washington, h. Mason, corner Barr
Merritt Henry (5 Mer. Row, B.), house 14 Lynde
Merritt William, sup't B. & M. R. R. house 35 Pleasant
Messervy Eliza A. K. Miss, house 91 Lafayette
Messervy John, painter, 34 Lafayette, house 2 Lagrange
Messervy Thomas K. mariner, house 91 Lafayette
Messervy William S. house 91 Lafayette
Metcalf Benjamin G. farmer, house Lafayette, near the F. R. Lead works
Metcalf David D. fruit and vegetables, 20 Lafayette, h. 25 Harb.
Micklefield Rebecca B. house 20 Central
Miller Andrew, bootmaker, boards Mansion House
Miller Charles H. merchant, house 12 Pickman
Miller Edward, mariner, house 26 Derby
Miller Edward, mariner, house 3 Dow
Miller Edward F. shipbuilder, E. Gardner, house 41 Harbor
Miller Ephraim F. British consular agent, 112 Derby, house 66 Bridge
Miller Joseph, mariner, house 83 Derby
Miller Lewis F. captain, house 31 Salem
Millett Andrew J. currier, boards 12 Prescott
Millett Benjamin F. cooper, house 19 Becket
Millett Benjamin R. *(Currier & M.)*, furniture, 261 Essex, h. 22 Lynde
Millett Charles, captain, house 24 Pleasant
Millett Charles 2d, captain, house 9 Hardy
Millett Dan. groceries and western produce, 67 Derby, h. 69 do.
Millett Edward A. clerk, Webb's wharf, house 4½ Northey
Millett Eliza, house 9 Hardy
Millett George, mariner, boards 9 Hardy
Millett Joseph H. captain, house 4½ Northey
Millett Joseph Henry, clerk, 67 Derby, house 69 do.
Millett Joseph H. jr. (B.), house 7 Williams
Millett Louisa Mrs. house 14 Allen
Millett Martha H. widow, house 61 Summer

Millett Nathan, house 9 Hardy
Millett Nathan H. captain, house 8 Curtis
Millett Needham C. apothecary, 39 North, house 8 Buffum
Millett Sarah L. Mrs. house 12 Prescott
Millett William, cooper, house 13 Becket
Millett William H. boards 9 Hardy
Mills Robert C. Rev. house 119 Federal
Mills Sarah Mrs. house 1 Peabody
Minehan Daniel, laborer, house 86 Derby
Minor Albert H. expressman, 10 Washington, h. 10 Cambridge
Minor Mary Mrs. house 12 Daniels
Minor ———, Naumkeag Mill, boards 38 Harbor
Mitchell Edward, tinsmith, house 18 Carlton
Mitchell James, laborer, house rear 28 Beaver
Mitchell John, laborer, house near foot Thorndike
Mitchell John, shoemaker, house 91 North
Mitchell John, variety store, 44 Peabody, house do.
Mitchell Patrick, Naumkeag Mill, house 15 Park
Mitchell Robert, 165 Derby, h. E. Gardner, cor. S. Prospect
Mitchell Winnifred, widow, house rear 28 North
Monahan Catharine, widow, house 1 Pratt
Monahan John, shoemaker, house 1 Pratt
Monahan Joseph, painter, house 1 Pratt
Monarch Ebenezer, stevedore, house near foot of Pingree
Monies Michael D. laborer, house 86 Boston
Monies William, butcher, house 8 Whittemore
Monies William A. laborer, house 66 Mill
Monies William H. shoemaker, boards 66 Mill
Monroe George, tanner, house 14 Flint
Monroe Olive Mrs. house 2 Turner
Montague John, mariner, house 156 Derby
Moody Lewis B. newspaper and periodical depot, basement Asiatic building, house 2 Mill
Moody Mary, house 6 Gardner court
Moody William H. Mrs. house 2 Mill
Mooney Andrew, laborer, house 153 Boston
Mooney John, gum copal worker, boards rear 41 Derby
Mooney John T. trader, boards 113 North
Mooney Matthew, shoemaker, house 170 Derby
Mooney Patrick, teamster, house rear Adams
Moore Charles E. clerk, 222 Essex, bds. at S. Danvers
Moore David, merchant, 21 Derby wharf, house 226 Derby
Moore Elizabeth, widow, house 17 Whittemore
Moore Harriet, widow, house 68 North
Moore James, carpenter, house 14 Whittemore
Moore John, morocco dresser, boards 8 Aborn
Moore Patrick, currier, house 14 Friend

Moore William, currier, house 7 Dean
Moore William H. morocco dresser, house 8 Aborn
Moran Edward, laborer, house Grove
Moran John, tanner, house 47 Beaver
Morant Philip, mariner, house 50 Mill
Moreland Augusta M. fancy goods, 241 Essex, h. 4 Becket
Moreland George W. carpenter, house 19 Carlton
Moreland John H. job printer, 235 Essex, and periodicals, 241 Essex, house 8 Cambridge
Moreland John S. house 4 Becket
Morgan Beckford, foreman at Stow & Tibbett's, bds. 21 Essex
Morgan George S. laborer, house 18 Park
Morgan Henry B. tanner, boards 2 Goodhue
Morgan John, soapboiler, house 2 Goodhue
Morgan John, laborer, house 15 River
Morgan John A. rigger, house 10 Ash
Morgan John P. shoemaker, house Odell square
Morgan Lucy Mrs. house 16 Summer
Morgan Martin Mrs. house rear 13 Lynn
Morgan Patrick, laborer, house 11 English
Morgan Richard, laborer, house Dodge
Morgan Theodore Mrs house 358 Essex
Morgan Thomas, marble worker, 14 Central, house 16 do.
Morrill *(Phebe)* & Walker *(Mary M.)*, millinery, 217 Essex, house 15 Church
Morris George, currier, house Aborn, near Boston
Morris James, mariner, house 64 Mill
Morris Joseph B. restaurant, 18 and 20 Derby sq. h. 17 Mall
Morris Mercy, widow, house 5 Creek
Morris William R. house 1 Ropes
Morse Charles H. tanner, boards 28 Broad
Morse Ebenezer, carpenter, rear 123 Lafayette, house 123 do.
Morse Edward A. currier, house 28 High
Morse E. Henry, carpenter, house 19 Dean
Morse Francis Y. carpenter, boards 123 Lafayette
Morse George W. clerk, 174 Essex, boards 91 Federal
Morse Joanna C. house 31 Church
Morse John Mrs. house 28 Broad
Morse Lucius B. tanner, 71 Mason, house 162 Federal
Morse Mary E. Mrs. house 91 Federal
Morse Payne, shoemaker, house 133 North
Morton Henry, salesman, 245 Essex, boards 25 Buffum
Moseley Joseph, captain, house 11 Barr
Moseley Martha Mrs. house 156 Federal
Moseley Martha P. Mrs. house 97 Essex
Moses Aaron, mariner, house 19 Webb
Mottey John, house 46 Charter

SALEM [M] DIRECTORY. 139

Moulton Benjamin M. currier, boards 6 N. Pine
Moulton Frederick, mason, house 105 Federal
Moulton George F. currier, boards 4 N. Pine
Moulton *(Jay H.)* & Davis *(Jacob)*, expressmen, 10 Washington, house Everett, cor. Salem
Moulton John G. teamster, 1 Front, house 35 Salem
Moulton Joseph C. carpenter, boards 5 Mechanic
Moulton Joshua W. daguerreotype artist, 214 Essex, h. 4 Margin
Moulton Mary Mrs. house 17 Whittemore
Moulton Mary Mrs. house at Oliver Wilson's
Moulton Nathaniel P carpenter, house 5 Mechanic
Moulton Newell, cooper, boards 55 Derby
Moulton William, trader, house 20 High
Moulton William, laborer, house rear 53 Warren
Muchmore George H. cabman, house 8 Church
Muchmore Richard, city express office, rear Essex House, h. 8 Church
Mudgett Daniel, teamster at the F.R. lead mills, h. 3 Lagrange
Mudgett Daniel A. teamster, house 14 Curtis
Mudgett Samuel A. clerk, 10 Derby square, h. 17 Winthrop
Mugford Charles D. merchant, house 339 Essex
Mugford George Mrs. house 88 Federal
Mugford Henry F. shoemaker, house 150 Federal
Mugford Sarah S. house 150 Federal
Mugford Thomas S. mariner, house 150 Federal
Muhlig James J. boards 2 Mason
Muhlig Robert, tanner, foot Buffum, house 8 Barr
Mulcahey Edward, carpenter, house 25 Albion
Mulcahey James, wheelwright, house 121 Boston
Mulcahey Morris, laborer, house 21 Becket
Mullally John, carpenter, house Ord
Mullen David, laborer, house 148 Derby
Mullen Edward, tailor, house 11 Lynn
Mullen James, laborer, house 204 Derby
Mullen John, Mrs. boards 36 Charter
Mullen Matthew, laborer, house 142 Derby
Mullen Patrick, currier, house 22 Congress
Mullen Patrick, currier, house 7 Prospect
Mullett George W. inspector Custom House, h. 62 Summer
Mulliken Rebecca, widow, house 15 Friend
Munday John, laborer, house 4 Daniels
Munroe Jeannette Mrs. house 24 Beckford
Munsey Alfred T. shoemaker, house 12 Ward
Murphy Christopher, shoemaker, house Adams
Murphy Daniel, boiler maker, house 4 Pingree
Murphy David, currier, house 143 North
Murphy Eliza M. Mrs. house 25 Summer

Murphy James, laborer, house 172 Derby
Murphy James, currier, house Grove
Murphy James, laborer, house Odell square
Murphy Jeremiah, currier, house 76 North
Murphy John, currier, house 14 Oak
Murphy John, laborer, house 4 Gerrish place
Murphy John, laborer, house Grove
Murphy John, currier, house rear 8 Whittemore
Murphy John, laborer, house Tucker's wharf
Murphy John, laborer, house 26 Peabody
Murphy John, currier, house rear Shillaber
Murphy Margaret, widow, house Grove, near the Cemetery
Murphy Mary, house Congress, west side
Murphy Matthew, laborer, house 23 Charter
Murphy Michael, laborer, house Adams
Murphy Nicholas, laborer, house Grove, near the Cemetery
Murphy Patrick, currier, house Salem Turnpike
Murphy Patrick, waiter, 204 Essex
Murphy Patrick, house 153 Boston
Murphy Peter, house Grove, above Mason
Murphy Richard, currier, boards 80 Boston
Murphy Thomas, blacksmith, house 26 Daniels
Murphy William C. currier, foot Buffum, house 4 Orne
Murray Hugh, laborer, house Pingree
Murray Margaret, widow, house 18 High
Murray ——, shoemaker, house 34 Buffum
Musgrove Peter, currier, boards 2 Mason
Myers Daniel, laborer, house near foot Dearborn
Myers David, laborer, house 24 Ward
Myers Ellen, widow, house Adams
Myers John, laborer, house 53 St. Peter
Myers Patrick, laborer, house 8 Ropes
Myers Thomas, Naumkeag Mill, house Pingree, near Harbor
Myers Thomas, laborer, house 26 Peabody
Mynahan Thomas, laborer, house rear 36 Peabody

NAGEEL JACOB, tailor, house 11 Church
Naos Henry, laborer, house 58 Broad
Naos Henry E. tanner, boards 58 Broad
Narbonne Nathaniel A. mariner, house 71 Essex
Narbonne Sarah Mrs. house 71 Essex
Nason David, E. R. R. depot, house 4 Downing
Nason Samuel, farmer, house 8 Gardner court
Nay Joshua, engineer, house 10 Park
Naylon John, tanner, boards at Michael Gallivan's
Neagle Ellen, widow, house 6 High st. court
Neal Benjamin B. captain, house 9 Cambridge

Neal David A. house 10 Chestnut, cor. Cambridge
Neal Edward, shoemaker, boards 4 Barton
Neal George L. carpenter, boards 19 Hathorne
Neal Henry, coachdriver, 212 Essex, house 12 Broad
Neal James, shoemaker, house n. foot of Pingree
Neal John H. sexton, house 66 Federal
Neal Jonathan, mason, house 12 Broad
Neal Joseph, mason, house 19 Hathorne
Neal Mary Mrs. house 9 Cambridge
Neal Michael, laborer, house Fowler
Neal Michael, laborer, house 10 Peabody
Neal Theodore A. merchant (B.), house 4 Barton square
Neal William H. Mrs. house 13 Chestnut
Needham Elizabeth, house 57 Washington
Needham James, shoemaker, house 7 Pleasant
Needham John, currier, house 127 Boston
Needham (J. S.) & Hawkes (T.), fruit & confectionary, 144 & 272 Essex, house Locust Dale, W. Danvers
Nelson Charles H. captain, boards 21 Beckford
Nelson James F. 138 Derby, boards 21 Beckford
Nelson John F. captain, house 48 Charter
Nelson Marques, stevedore, house 7 Cedar
Nelson Mary H. Mrs. house 9 Federal
Nelson Samuel F. shoemaker, house 21 Beckford
Nelson William H. captain, boards 48 Charter
Nevers Ellen, widow, house rear 21 Becket
Nevers William, laborer, house 21 Becket
Neville Julia, widow, house Phillips, near Grove
Neville Maurice, laborer, house Phillips, near Grove
Neville Phillip J. currier, boards 14 School
Neville Thomas, laborer, house 27 Beaver
Newcomb Bryant, house 26 Lafayette
Newcomb Caleb, 186 Essex, house 2 Milk
Newcomb Caleb H. provisions, 14 Newbury, house at Beverly
Newcomb Charles B. engineer, house 22 Salem
Newcomb Charles B. jr. turner, house rear 18 Becket
Newcomb David, oysters, 24 & 26 Derby sq. house 5 Dean
Newcomb David B. 24 Derby sq. boards 5 Dean
Newcomb George L. machinist, 18 Peabody, house 1 Cedar
Newcomb James Alfred, machinist, house 40 Lafayette
Newcomb John, 24 Derby square, boards 5 Dean
Newcomb Olivia Mrs. house rear 68 Washington
Newell Joseph, sash, blind, and door manufacturer, 7 Front, house 38 Lafayette
Newell Thomas P. billiard hall, 157 Essex, house 108 Derby
Newhall Ezra F. clerk (B.), house 9 Pleasant
Newhall Francis, farmer, boards at John Stanton's

Newhall Frederick A. watchmaker, 24 Wash. house at Lynn
Newhall Gilbert, 56 Washington, house 38 Church
Newhall Gilbert G. gunpowder (17 Doane B.), house 9 Pleasant
Newhall John, farmer, house 6 Webb
Newhall John F. printer, 191 Essex, house 57 Lafayette
Newhall Joseph M. clerk, 29 Front, house 47 St. Peter
Newhall Rebecca, widow, house 39 St. Peter
Newhall Sarah Mrs. house 47 St. Peter
Newhall William, city crier, house 3 Jeffrey court
Newman Stephen J. cigar maker, house 17 Daniels
Newport Sarah A. Mrs. nurse, house Cedar court
Newton Albert, baker, boards 1 Mount Vernon
Newton John H. constable, house 1 Whittemore
Nichols Abby, house 105 Boston
Nichols Abigail, widow, house 10 Northey
Nichols Abigail, house 68 Boston
Nichols Abigail A. house 16 School
Nichols Andrew Mrs. house 8 Central
Nichols Andrew, house 8 Central
Nichols Charles S. secretary Salem M. F. I. Co. 42 Washington, house 6 Chestnut
Nichols Daniel A. tanner, boards 186 Federal
Nichols Daniel F. tanner, rear 186 Federal, house 186 do.
Nichols David, tanner, Pope's court, house 8 Proctor court
Nichols George, auctioneer, 42 Wash. house 80 Federal
Nichols George, house 41 Warren
Nichols George jr. house 403 Essex
Nichols George S. tanner, boards 186 Federal
Nichols Hervey, tanner, house 37 Boston
Nichols Isaiah, merchant, house 104 Boston
Nichols James, shoemaker, house Tremont, above Grove
Nichols James B. tanner, Nichols, n. Prospect, h. 115 Boston
Nichols Jane, house 105 Boston
Nichols J. Henry, shipsmith, 45 Union, house 10 Elm
Nichols John, shipsmith, 45 Union, house 10 Elm
Nichols John *(W. H. Nichols & Brother)*, boards 12 Essex
Nichols John, wheelwright, 29 North, house 16 Cambridge
Nichols John H. auctioneer and insurance agent, 42 Washington, house 37 Chestnut
Nichols John R. watchman E. R. R. depot, house 14 Webb
Nichols Jonathan Mrs. house 104 Boston
Nichols Mary, house 105 Boston
Nichols Mary B. widow of Stephen, house 68 Boston
Nichols Nancy, widow, house 14 Becket
Nichols Nathan (19 Portland B.), house 172 Federal
Nichols Samuel B. shoemaker, house 4 Botts court
Nichols Sarah, widow, house 131 North

Nichols Stephen F. painter, 113 Derby, house 44 Forrester
Nichols Thomas, currier, Goodhue, house 3 Boston
Nichols *(Thomas jr.)* & Shepard *(Samuel)*, tanners and curriers, Nichols near Prospect, house 400 Essex
Nichols Thomas B. clerk, 288 Essex, boards 3 Boston
Nichols William C. musician, house 6 Buffum
Nichols William D. shoemaker, house 6 Allen
Nichols William F. grocer, 107 Boston, house 115 do.
Nichols William H. & Brother *(John Nichols)*, coopers, Brookhouse wharf, house 12 Essex
Nichols William H. painter, house 6 Northey
Nicholson Thomas jr. boots and shoes, 164 Essex
Nickerson Asa W. thread store, 174 Essex, b. Essex House
Niles Amos (Cal.), house 35 Derby
Nimblet Benjamin, tanner, house Hanson
Nimblet Benjamin jr. currier, house Summit
Nimblet Eliza, house 22½ Beckford
Nimblet Sarah, house 22½ Beckford
Noah Charles S. house 103 Boston
Noah George G. currier, house 53 Boston
Noah Henry C. tanner, house 93 Boston
Noah John G. wheelwright, house 103 Boston
Noah Samuel, wheelwright & blacksmith, 101 Boston, h. 103 do.
Noah Samuel jr. currier, 34 Boston, house 420 Essex
Noble Joseph, house 92 Essex
Noble Richard S. Mrs. house 67 Essex
Nolan Dennis, laborer, house 9 Herbert
Nolan Henry, at F. R. Mills, house 10 Lagrange
Nolan James, currier, house 129 Boston
Nolan Mary, widow, house 17 Harbor
Noonan James, laborer, house Pratt
Noonan John, laborer, house 2 Tucker's wharf
Norcross Horatio N. carpenter, house 43 Bridge
Norcross James A. carpenter, house Phelp's court
Norcross Margaret A. house 23 Ward
Norcross Martha, widow, house Beaver
Norcross Orlando W. carpenter, boards 26 Ward
Norfolk Edward L. portable grain mill manuf. 13 Front, house 15 Curtis
Norfolk John R. machinist, house 13 Briggs
Norfolk Joseph, sailmaker, house 72 Derby
Norfolk Joseph G. mariner, house 72 Derby
Norris Charles H. merchant tailor, 188½ Essex, h. 6 Lagrange
Norris Elizabeth & Mary, house 5 River
Norris John, boards 156 Federal
Northend *(William D.)* & Choate *(George F.)*, counsellors, 20 Asiatic Building, house 24 School

Northey Ezra Mrs. house 395 Essex
Northey William, secretary Salem Marine Insurance Co. house 395 Essex
Norton Patrick, farmer, house Adams
Norton Thomas, currier, house Beach
Norwood Alexander, captain, house 25 Daniels
Nourse Aaron, hats, caps, & furs, 37 Wash, house 35 Andrew
Nourse Abigail, house 375 Essex
Nourse Ebenezer, fruit & confectionery, 41 Washington, house 135 Nor h
Nourse Samuel, shoe tool manuf., English, house 74 Essex
Nourse William, 41 Washington, house 135 North
Nowell Moses, laborer, house 163 Boston
Nowell Phœbe A. nurse, house 8 Norman
Noyes Enoch K. & Co. *(E. F. Baker)*, grocers, 6 & 8 Front, house Lafayette, cor. Holly
Noyes Isaac S. *(Brooks & N.)*, grocer, 121 Essex, h. 21 Andrew
Noyes Jane S. W. Mrs. tailoress, house 34 Church
Noyes J. Plumer, Naumkeag Mill, house 69 Harbor
Nutter Horace, trader, house 8 Hathorne
Nutter John, shoemaker, house 4 Friend
Nutting Joseph G. cabinet maker, house 30 Williams
Nutting Rachel, house 12 Beckford
Nutting William G. captain, boards 98 Lafayette

OAKES THOMAS, sailmaker, 7 Derby wf. boards Essex House
Ober Andrew, carpenter, 42 Charter, house 8 Winthrop
Ober Samuel, provisions, 2 Norman, house 57 Charter
O'Brien Christopher, laborer, house 17 Harbor
O'Brien James, laborer, house 21 High
O'Brien James, laborer, house 27 Daniels
O'Brien John, laborer, house 10 Odell square
O'Brien John, laborer, house rear 89 Derby
O'Brien John, laborer, house 26 Union
O'Brien John, laborer, house 3 Tucker's wharf
O'Brien J. bootmaker, boards Mansion House
O'Brien Stephen, laborer, house Tucker's wharf
O'Brien Thomas, currier, house Jackson place
O'Brien Timothy, currier, house Putnam, near Hanson
O'Brien William, clerk, 27 Summer, house 21 High
O'Connell Dennis, coachman, house 16 Park
O'Connell John, grocer (S. Danvers), house 106 Boston
O'Connel Timothy, boots and shoes, 5 Central, house rear 76 Federal
O'Connor Thomas, trader, house 9 Prince
O'Day Bartholomew, laborer, house 10 Odell square
Odell Charles, clerk, 282 Essex, boards 16 Odell square

Odell David, cabinet maker, house 43 Bridge
Odell Eliza Mrs. house 48 Essex
Odell Henry W. house 16 Odell square
Odell James Mrs. house 16 Odell square
Odell James A. wines, &c. 23 Front, house 4 Winthrop
Odell Lydia J. Mrs. house 16 High
Odell Thomas F. house 28 North
Odell William H. city watchman, house 48 Essex
Odlin Mary, widow, nurse, house 25 Hardy
O'Donnell Daniel, agent for "Boston Pilot," house 58 Mill
O'Donnell James, house 23 Ward
O'Donnell James, clerk, 20 Front, house 31 Forrester
O'Donnell Malachi, currier, house 170 Derby
O'Donnell Mary, widow, house 73 Mason
O'Donnell Michael, laborer, house 10 Herbert
O'Donnell Patrick, weaver, boards 64 Harbor
O'Donnell William, laborer, house foot Ropes
O'Flaherty Catharine, Jane M. and Polly, house 131 Bridge
Ogden Amos, boiler maker, house foot of East Gardner
Ogden Benjamin, Naumkeag Mill, house 11 Park
O'Hara James, currier, house Adams. Mason Hill
O'Hara Patrick, currier, house rear 67 Mason
O'Hare Stephen, gardener, house 32 Williams
O'Hern Michael, laborer, house 2 Tucker's wharf
O'Keefe Mary Mrs. house 30 Union
O'Keefe Patrick (Cal.), house 79 Mason
O'Keefe Simon, moulder, house 130 Derby
O'Keefe Timothy, tanner, house Ab rn
Oldson Francis, mariner, house 11 Carlton
Oldson Joseph Mrs. house 56 Derby
O'Leary Jeremiah, mason, house 21 High
O'Leary John, laborer, house 24 Ward
O'Leary Timothy (*McGuire & O'Leary*), tailor, 41 Charter, house 174 Derby
Oliver Frederick, engineer, house 49 Warren
Oliver Henry, laborer, house 7 Herbert
Oliver John E. farmer, house Salem turnpike
Oliver Robert, mariner, house 16 Peabody
Oliver Sarah S. house 33 Broad
Oliver Sarah S. widow of Francis, boards 59 Harbor
Oliver William W. house 36 Broad
O'Mara Durgin, laborer, house 22 Daniels
O'Neal Bridget, house Peabody
O'Neal Daniel, teamster, house 93 Derby
O'Neal James, currier, house Warren
O'Neal James, tanner, house rear 56 Broad
O'Neal Thomas, tanner, house rear 56 Broad

O'Neil Cornelius, laborer, house 3 Tucker's wharf
O'Neil Thomas, laborer, house 27 Daniels
O'Neil William, laborer, house 92 Derby
Orne Annis, house 24 Northey
Orne Jonathan H. weigher and gauger, C. H., h. at Marblehead
Orne Sarah F. Mrs. house 318 Essex
Osborn Charles P. tinsmith, house 7 Winter
Osborn David S. fireman, house 128 North
Osborn Jane F. dressmaker, 5 Winter
Osborn John, farmer, house Orne, near Upham
Osborn Jonathan, sailmaker, house 21 Pickman
Osborn Jonathan, 173 Essex, boards 17 Turner
Osborn Joseph, cooper, house 17 Turner
Osborn Josiah B. hairdresser, 60 Derby, house 10 Hardy
Osborn Lydia Mrs. house 17 Turner
Osborn Richard S. tanner, at S. Danvers, house 17 Boston
Osborn Samuel B. horticulturist, house Orne, near Upham
Osborn Sarah Mrs. house 65 Mill
Osborne Aaron, clerk, E. R. R. house 88 Mill
Osborne David S. house rear Nursery, near Liberty Hill
Osborne Ezra, constable, house 88 Mill
Osborne Henry, 183 Essex, house 24 Mechanic
Osborne Horace *(W. A. & H. Osborne)*, tanner, 35 Boston, boards 5 May
Osborne Nathan W. N. clerk, boards 17 Oliver
Osborne Stephen H. 183 Essex, house 17 Oliver   [Oliver
Osborne Stephen, hat, cap, and fur store, 183 Essex, house 17
Osborne William A. & Horace, tanners and curriers, 35 Boston, house 5 May
Osgood Benjamin H. harness maker, 9 Church, house 31 do
Osgood Carlton, house 15 Mall
Osgood Charles, artist, 7 Central, house 78 Bridge
Osgood Charles C. captain, house 3 Daniels
Osgood Chas. S. clerk, Register of Probate's office, b. 78 Bridge
Osgood Edward A. house 401 Essex
Osgood Elizabeth, house 15 Norman
Osgood Elizabeth C. Mrs. house 314 Essex
Osgood John B. Mrs. house 45 Lafayette
Osgood John C. merchant, 63 Union, house 3 Barton square
Osgood John F. house 314 Essex
Osgood John W. house 29 Charter
Osgood Joseph, captain, house 10 Crombie
Osgood Joseph B. F. counsellor, 235 Essex, house 17 Norman
Osgood Nathaniel Mrs house 401 Essex
Osgood Nathaniel W. tanner, Goodhue, house 175 Federal
Osgood Nathaniel W. jr. tanner, Goodhue, house 404 Essex
Osgood Sarah M. Mrs. house 4 River

Osgood Susan, house Osgood farm, 126 Lafayette
Osgood Susan W. house 15 Norman
Osgood Thaddeus Mrs. house 97 Essex
Osgood William H. captain, house 314 Essex
O'Shea Timothy, currier, house 36 Beaver
Ottignon Firmin, umbrella maker, house 53 Wash. cor. Lynde
Owen Edward, hairdresser, boards 19 Webb
Owen James, shoemaker, house 10 Carlton

PACK WILLIAM, shoemaker, house Irving, near Harrod
Page Benjamin, shoemaker, house 142 Bridge
Page Elizabeth D. Mrs. house 9 Cedar
Page Isaac M. baggage master, E. R. R. boards 80 Mill
Page Jeremiah, president Salem Marine Insurance Co., Asiatic building, house 140 Federal
Page Josiah, currier, house 10 May
Page J. Henry, captain, house 47 Federal
Page Mary Mrs. house 8 Federal
Page Sarah L. Mrs. house 84 Derby
Page Timothy E. carpenter, house 8 Broad
Paine John L. truckman, house 8 Saunders
Paine Jos. A. bonnets and dry goods, 153 Essex, h. 11 Liberty
Palfray Charles W. *(Chapman & P.)*, publisher "Salem Register," 185 Essex, house 116 Federal
Palfray Edward, dry goods, 2 St. Peter, house 15 Dean
Palfray Elizabeth Mrs. house 113 Federal
Palmer Charles Mrs. house 10 Oak
Palmer Charles W. carpenter, boards 10 Oak
Palmer Margaret P. widow, house rear 218 Essex
Palmer Richard, house Phelps court
Palmer Theron, boots, shoes, and rubbers, 216 Essex, house 13 Buffum
Palmer William, laborer, house Phelps court
Palmer William H. carpenter, boards 10 Oak
Palmer William W. & Co. dry goods, 175 Essex, h. 11 North
Parker Charles, house 107 Essex
Parker Eldred S. expressman, 14 Wash. house 18 Lynde
Parker Emeline A. teacher, house 6 Federal
Parker George A. auctioneer, 30 Front, house 107 Essex
Parker Harriet M. Mrs. house 6 Federal
Parker Isaac, machinist, house Lynde, corner North
Parker John B. treas. Eastern Railroad (B.), house 6 Federal
Parker Josiah W. musician and carpenter, house 8 Park
Parker Sophia, widow, house 155 Bridge
Parker William B. merchant, house 22 Pleasant
Parker William B. Mrs. house 107 Essex
Parker William H. shoemaker, house 13 Pond

Parks *(Thomas C.)* & Harris *(Israel P.)*, grocers, 4 St. Peter, boards 14 do.
Parnell Mary B. Mrs. house 20 High
Parris J. Joseph, cook, Front, cor. Derby sq. house 27 Salem
Parshley Calvin H. house 5 at the F. R. Lead Mills
Parshley Charles, Lynn express, 15½ Central, house 22 Ward
Parshley David T. currier, house 9 Fowler
Parshley Joseph, currier, boards 6 North Pine
Parshley Nathaniel H. shoemaker, house 72 Mill
Parson Frederick, aqueduct office, Sewall, house 19 Creek
Parsons George W. printer, "Observer" office, h. 210 Derby
Parsons John, tanner, house 6 Oak
Parsons John H. musician, boards 3 Pleasant
Parsons *(John M.)* & Shackelford *(Wm.)*, fish and water for shipping, 64 Union, house at Gloucester
Parsons Joseph, mason, boards 11 Prescott
Parsons Oliver Mrs. house 27 Summer
Parsons William, teamster, boards 101 North
Parsons William D. mason, boards 39 St. Peter
Partland Owen, laborer, house foot of Pingree
Patch Ephraim, tailor, 247 Essex, house 16 Church
Patch Ira H. wheelwright, 7 Sewall, house do.
Patch Ira J. clerk's office, Court House, house 7 Sewall
Patten John R. physician, house 25 Harbor
Patterson Nancy, widow, house 6 Andrew
Patterson William, stairbuilder, house 15 Oliver
Paul Jeremiah, shoemaker, house 55 Broad
Payne Phebe, widow, house 59 Summer
Payson Edward H. cashier Commercial Bank, 7 Central, house at Swampscott
Payson Joanna Mrs. house 27 Forrester
Peabody Alfred, merchant (134 State street, B.), h. 45 Summer
Peabody Brackley R. captain, house 391½ Essex
Peabody Brackley R. 2d, mariner, boards 14 Ward
Peabody Charles E. shoemaker, boards 10 Andrew
Peabody David R. shoemaker, house 12 Prescott
Peabody Edward Augustus, chair painter, 111 Essex, house 13 Pickman
Peabody Edward C. inspector Custom House, house 10 Andrew
Peabody Eliza H. widow, house 119 Boston
Peabody Francis, house 136 Essex
Peabody Francis jr. merchant (B.), house 136 Essex
Peabody George, merchant, house 7 Brown
Peabody George A. (B.), house 7 Brown
Peabody George W. cabinet maker, house 6 Howard
Peabody George W. mariner, boards 16 Flint
Peabody Henry W. clerk (B.), house 45 Summer

Peabody James M. carpenter, house 10 Mason
Peabody John B. *(Ives & P.)*, counsellor, 226½ Essex, house Chestnut street, South Danvers
Peabody John F. machinist, house 14 High
Peabody John P. embroideries and trimmings, 238 Essex, boards F. Porter's
Peabody Joseph, house 136 Essex
Peabody Oliver, carpenter, house 16 Flint
Peabody Ruth and Mary Misses, house 7 Aborn
Peabody Sally Mrs. nurse, house 6 Howard
Peabody Samuel E. *(Curtis & Peabody)*, merchant *(B.)*, house 31 Warren
Peabody Silas, principal Phillips School, boards 114 Essex
Peabody William G. currier, house 173 Boston
Peace William H. mariner, boards 45 Essex
Peach Augustus L. (Cal.), house 84 Mill
Peach Benjamin, house 27 Harbor
Peach Franklin, shoemaker, house 4 Leach
Peach George, shoemaker, house 4 Leach
Peach Thomas S. stonecutter, boards 4 Leach
Peach William, fish dealer, house 4 Leach
Peach William jr. painter, boards 103 Lafayette
Pearson David, salesman, boards 7 Herbert
Pearson Nathan, farmer, house 130 Boston
Pearson Mary, widow, house 7 Herbert
Pearson William, house 16 English
Pease Benj. salesman, 25 Lafayette, house 5 Pond
Pease Geo. W. *(Wm. Ives & Co.)*, publishers "Salem Observer," 226½ Essex, house 45 Federal
Pease Mary, widow, house 11 High
Pease *(Richard)* & Price *(Charles)*, bakers, 13 High, h. 11 do.
Pease Samuel W. stoves and tinware, 128 Derby, h. 75 Bridge
Pease William, currier, house 10 Aborn
Peck E. S. clerk, 240 Essex, boards 99 do.
Peck F. S. clothing and furnishing store, 240 Essex, h. 99 do.
Peckham Charles, mariner, house 22 Becket
Peckham George W. 60 Charter, house 26 Essex
Peckham Sarah B. Mrs. house rear 14 Hathorne
Peele J. Willard, merchant, house 12 Chestnut
Peele Robert, hardware and crockery, 282 Essex, h. 86 Federal
Peele Susan Miss, house 77 Bridge
Peele William Mrs. house 77 Bridge
Peirce Henry (State Bank, B.), house 33 Summer
Peirce Jonathan (13 Central, B.), house 10 Summer
Peirce Mary A. widow, house 12½ Hathorne
Peirce Nathan, stock and loan office, 163 Essex, h. 139 do.
Peirce William P. merchant, house 29 Chestnut

Peirson Abel L. Mrs. house 11 Barton square
Peirson Edward B. physician, house 13 Barton square
Peirson George H. blacksmith, West place, h. 34 Pleasant
Pendar Simon, house 60 Endicott
Pender John, currier, house 12 Friend
Pendergast Michael, currier, house 1 Friend
Pendergrass Edward, currier, house Hanson, cor. Varney
Pendergrass Thomas, laborer, house 24 Congress
Pennell Mary Mrs. house 7 Cross
Pepper Charles H. confectioner, house 32 Dearborn
Pepper Eliza Mrs. nurse, house 1 English
Pepper George W. confectioner, house 42 Buffum
Pepper John S. shoemaker, house 19 St. Peter
Pepper John W. Mrs. confectioner, 44 Buffum, house do.
Pepper Philadelphia, widow, house 10 Whittemore
Pepper Thomas S. confectionery, 48 Harbor, house 58 do.
Perkins (*Aaron*) & Brown (*Wm. B.*), clothing and furnishing
 store, 137 Derby and 36 Union, house 34 Lafayette
Perkins Augustine S. merchant, house 82 Lafayette
Perkins A. W. clerk, 165 Derby, boards 34 Lafayette
Perkins Benjamin M. tailor, 181 Essex, house 11 Turner
Perkins Betsey, widow, house 84 Mill
Perkins Charles T. operative, house 61 Harbor   [Church
Perkins Daniel, merchant tailor, 181 Essex, cor. Central, h. 15
Perkins Daniel, house 11 Williams
Perkins David, house 18 Lynde
Perkins Ebenezer S. mariner, boards 14 Saunders
Perkins Edward B. carpenter, 11 Cherry, house 9 do.
Perkins Edward F. engineer, house 1 Mechanic
Perkins Elijah R. ambrotype artist, 241 Essex, h. 27 Endicott
Perkins Emery J. house 18 Northey
Perkins George, clerk, Mercantile Bank, b. 34 Lafayette
Perkins Geo. A. physician, 5 Newbury, house 129 Essex
Perkins Henry C. mariner, boards 34 Lafayette
Perkins Henry S. machinist, boards 1 Mechanic
Perkins Henry W. weigher and gauger Custom H., h. 21 Hardy
Perkins Henry W. jr. bookkeeper (National Bank, B.), house
 21 Hardy
Perkins Isaac, carpenter, house 26 Cedar
Perkins James, blacksmith, house 7 Daniels
Perkins Jeremiah S. superintendent burials, City Hall, house 2
 Pleasant street avenue
Perkins John, house 18 Winthrop   [Essex, h. 130 Federal
Perkins Jonathan C. judge Court Common Pleas, office 243½
Perkins Jonathan W. captain, house 14 Saunders
Perkins Joseph, pilot, house 17 Derby
Perkins Joseph S. postmaster, house 171 Federal

Perkins J. Warren, captain, house 21 North
Perkins Nathaniel B. cashier Merchants' Bank, h. 5 Oliver
Perkins Rebecca D. Mrs. house 23 Dearborn
Perkins Samuel W. clerk (B.), boards 21 Hardy
Perkins Sarah Mrs. house 15 Church
Perkins Thomas, merchant, house 124 Federal
Perkins Thomas jr. merchant, house 298½ Essex
Perkins Thomas B. city marshal, City Hall, h. 14 Winthrop
Perkins William A. carpenter, house 17 Briggs
Perkins William E. carpenter, 153 Derby, h. 122 Bridge
Perley Jacob, morocco dresser *(*Danvers*)*, house 179 Boston
Perley John, boots, shoes, and rubbers, 252 Essex, h. 254 do.
Perley John E. mariner, house 15 Federal
Perley Jonathan, house 29 Beckford   [h. 29 Beckford
Perley Jonathan jr. & Co. *(J. Carter)*, bookbinders, 191 Essex.
Perrigen David, mariner, house 5½ English
Perry Abigail, house 21 Carlton
Perry Albert H. gunsmith, house 21 Carlton
Perry Augusta, house 45 Derby
Perry Augustus, merchant, house 29 Warren
Perry Augustus H. gunsmith, boards 7 Curtis
Perry Benjamin, refreshments, 60 Boston, house do.
Perry Francis L. blacksmith, Phillips wharf, house 33 Derby
Perry Henry W. shoemaker, 61 North, house do.
Perry Horatio Mrs. house 45 Derby
Perry Horatio B. gunsmith, Blaney, house 7 Curtis
Perry Ittai, pilot, house 12 English   [h. 13 Hardy
Perry *(J. W.)* & Endicott *(W. C.)*, counsellors, 182 Essex,
Perry Margaret B. widow of John, h. 80 Bridge
Perry William F. provisions, 319 Essex, h. at S. Danvers
Pervier Jeremiah J. shoemaker, h. 20 Conant
Peters Frances Mrs. house 7 Orange
Peterson John, mariner, h. 38 Derby, cor. Becket avenue
Peterson Joseph, police, house 163 Bridge
Peterson Priscilla Mrs. nurse, house 5½ Gedney court
Peterson Thomas S. mariner, house 10 Creek
Pethick James, mariner, house 9 Webb
Petrey John, mariner, house 98 Derby
Pettengill Samuel W. carpenter, house 4 Woodbury's court
Pettey Caroline, widow, house 1 Turner
Pettingill George, farmer, h. Ledge Hill, n. Harmony Grove
Pettingill Eliza E. house 4 Woodbury's court
Pettingill Sarah Mrs. house 108 North, corner Orne
Pew George W., Naumkeag Mill, house 26 Lafayette
Phelps Abigail M. widow, house 130 Boston
Phelps Charles, bellhanger, 84 Federal, house 1 do.
Phelps Hannah, house 160 Boston

Phelps Israel R. *(W. Phelps jr. & Co.)*, house 6 Whittemore
Phelps James R. musician, house 6 Whittemore
Phelps John P. (*W. Phelps jr. & Co.*), house 8 Monroe
Phelps William jr. & Co. *(John P. & Israel R.)*, sash and blind makers, 84 Federal, house 16 River
Phelps William, house 1 Federal
Philbrick John, mariner, house 170 Derby
Philbrick Mary, widow, house 4 Orne
Phillips Edward B. tailor, 211 Essex, house 9 Salem
Phillips Eliza A. Mrs. dressmaker, house 10 Lafayette
Phillips Elizabeth Mrs. house 17 Chestnut
Phillips George Mrs. variety store, 38 St. Peter, h. do.
Phillips Henry B. machinist, house 28 Lafayette
Phillips John, at Laboratory, house 64 North
Phillips John, captain, house 28 Charter
Phillips Lemuel, shipwright, house 19 Turner
Phillips Samuel jr. (cashier Maverick Bank, B.), h. 85 Lafayette
Phillips Stephen C. Mrs. house 17 Chestnut
Phillips *(Stephen H.)* & Gillis *(James A.)*, counsellors, 22 Asiatic Building, house 17 Chestnut
Phillips Willard P. merchant, Phillips whf. house 7 Chestnut
Phillips William A. inspector, C. H. house at Swampscott
Phippen Abraham W. currier, house 24 Northey
Phippen Ann, house 18 Norman
Phippen Benjamin, cooper, house 25 Hardy
Phippen Benjamin H. Mrs. house 15 Cambridge
Phippen Benjamin C. baker, house 188 Derby
Phippen Benjamin F. cooper, house 25 Hardy
Phippen Charles F. tanner, house Laboratory
Phippen David, seaman, boards 188 Derby
Phippen Edward A. laborer, house 66 North
Phippen George B. clerk, Salem Bank, boards 92 Bridge
Phippen George D. cashier Salem Bank, h. 92 Bridge
Phippen Hardy, house 38 Pleasant
Phippen Israel, captain, house 6 Becket
Phippen Joseph E. cooper, house 12 English
Phippen Joseph H. shoemaker, house 14 Hathorne
Phippen Joshua, gasfitter, 151 Essex, house 25 Hardy
Phippen J. Hardy, cashier Mercantile Bank, h. 94 Bridge
Phippen *(Joshua)* & Endicott *(Charles)*, merchants, 61 Union, house 330 Essex
Phippen Mary J. laundress, house 10 Ash
Phippen Nathaniel, cooper, house 25 Hardy
Phippen Nathaniel 2d, shoemaker, boards 25 Hardy
Phippen Rebecca, grocer, 85 Bridge, house do.
Phippen Robert A. at Laboratory, house 72 North
Phippen Robert C. tanner, house Laboratory

SALEM [P] DIRECTORY. 153

Phippen William H. at Laboratory, house Laboratory
Phipps Eliza, widow, boards 29 Williams
Phipps Harriet, widow, house rear 72 Mill
Phipps Henry B. clerk, Registry of Deeds office, b. 25 Becket
Phipps John A. captain, house 25 Becket
Phipps John A. jr. mariner, house 25 Becket
Phipps Joseph, currier, Franklin, n. North, h. 59 Endicott
Phipps Mehitable, widow, house 40 St. Peter
Phipps Samuel, laborer, house 59 Broad
Phipps Thomas P. tanner, house Phelps court, c. Green place
Pickering Benjamin F. shoemaker, house 25 Summer
Pickering Jackson H. provisions, South Market, 37 Lafayette, house do.
Pickering James, teamster, 194 Derby, h. Prescott, n. Summer
Pickering John, broker (40 State, B.), house 18 Broad
Pickering John jr. clerk, 153 Essex, house 78 Summer
Pickering William, house 27 Harbor
Pickering William jr. boards 27 Harbor
Pickett John A. hostler, house 13 Ash
Pickman Francis W. house 19 Broad
Pickman L. Rawlins Miss, house 328 Essex
Pickman Sophia Mrs. house 328 Essex
Pickman Wm. D. merchant, 14 Asiatic build. h. 27 Chestnut
Pierce Anstiss D. Mrs. house 12 Summer
Pierce Charles H. shoemaker, house 14 Flint
Pierce Charles H. mariner, boards 8 River
Pierce John, shoemaker, house foot of Leach
Pierce Leonard, provisions, Pleasant, c. Bridge, h. 77 Bridge
Pierce Mark, at Laboratory, house Walter
Pike William B. collector, Custom House, house 18 Crombie
Pillsbury Lucy A. fancy goods, 284 Essex, house 310 do.
Pillsbury Lucy Mrs. house 310 Essex
Pinel Philip P. captain, house 44 Federal
Pingree Annar, house 2 Ash
Pingree David, merchant, 172 Essex, house 128 do.
Pingree Rufus D. hairdresser, 16 Derby square, h. 21 Church
Pingree Thomas P. merchant, 61 Union, house 6 Broad
Pingree Thomas P. 3d, merchant, house 128 Essex
Pingree T. Perkins jr. counsellor, 243½ Essex, b. Essex House
Pingree William G. grocer, 8 Brown, house at Wenham
Pinkham Charles H. apothecary, 288 Essex, house 12 North
Pinkham Lydia, widow, house 29 Forrester
Pinkham William A. baker, boards 24 Turner
Pinnock Thomas, slater, 6 Peabody, house do.
Pitcher Joseph W. mariner, boards 40 Harbor
Pitcher Washington, captain, house 40 Harbor
Pitman Augustus P. clerk, 110 Derby, house 23 Oliver

Pitman Benjamin, currier, boards 418 Essex
Pitman Benjamin, house 11 Andover
Pitman Harriet Mrs. nurse, house 14 Norman
Pitman Henry, currier, boards 4 Boston
Pitman John C. currier, 5 Pope's court, house 13 Boston
Pitman John H. currier, house 57 Warren
Pitman Michael Mrs. house 178 Federal
Pitman Nathaniel, currier, 24 Boston, house 418 Essex
Pitman Nathaniel jr. currier, house Salem Turnpike
Pitman Samuel, house 4 Boston
Pitman Samuel jr. currier, Goodhue, house 4 Boston
Pitman Sophia, widow, house 327 Essex
Pitman William, tanner, house 12 Beach
Pitman William H. painter, house 16 Norman
Pitts Darling, teamster, 2 Lafayette, house 30 Winthrop
Pitts Henry Mrs. house 7 Park
Pitts Nathaniel, teamster, 5 Front, house 14 Ward
Pitts Otis, teamster, house 58 Endicott
Pitts Thomas, teamster, house 15 Briggs
Plander John G. provisions, 116 Derby, house 16 Curtis
Plum Eliza P. Mrs. variety store, 117 Essex, house do.
Plummer Abigail, house 22 High
Plummer Albert, shoemaker, 161 Essex, house 21 Northey
Plummer Elvira Mrs. house 17 Webb
Plummer James, mariner, house 21 Northey
Plummer Moses Mrs. house 21 Northey
Plummer Moses J. boots and shoes, 161 Essex, h. 21 Northey
Plummer Rhoda Mrs. variety store, 248 Essex, house do.
Plummer William, tanner, house 101 North
Plummer William H. ropemaker, house Barton court
Plummer William H. teamster, boards 101 North
Pollen James T. ship carpenter, boards 23 Cedar
Pollock James, laborer, house 21 High
Pollock Samuel, laborer, house 11 Prince
Pollock Thomas, laborer, house 12 Prince
Pomeroy Arad Mrs. house 14 Dow
Pond James S. dry goods, 29 Lafayette, house 2 Ward
Pond Joseph P. house 3 Dean
Poole Nathan, machine sewing, 1 Holly, house do.
Poor James, currier, house 60 Broad
Poor James, house 13 Prince
Poor William, tanner, house 156 Boston
Pope Eleazer, tanner, rear 37 Boston, house 98 do.
Pope Hannah, widow, house 171 Boston   [versport
Pope Horatio J. clerk, Register of Deeds office, house at Dan-
Pope John R. tanner, house 2 Goodhue
Pope Maria, tailoress, house 1 Hardy

Pope Miss, house 54 Federal
Pope Rebecca S. Mrs. nurse, house 14 Peabody
Pope Thomas S. mariner, house 155 Bridge
Pope William A. tanner, house 93 Boston
Porter Ann B. tailoress, house 6 Ash
Porter Benjamin P. tanner and currier, house rear 59 Warren
Porter Frederick, provisions, 17 St. Peter, h. North, c. Nursery
Porter Hathorne Mrs. house 58 Federal
Porter John D. shipwright, house 51 St. Peter
Porter Joseph G. carpenter, house 10 Sewall
Porter Martha A. copyist, house 58 Federal
Porter Mary Mrs. house 6 Ash
Porter William (Cal.), house 49 Derby
Porter William R. tanner, house 4 School
Potter Daniel, deputy sheriff, 210 Essex, house 343 Essex
Potter Francis A. Mrs. house 3 Palfrey court   [Fowler
Potter James F. *(Elwell & P.)*, carpenter, 38 Peabody, house 9
Potter Jesse F. captain, house 82 Essex
Potter Joseph, Boston express, 34 Front, house 23 Union
Potter Joseph A. clerk, 18 Asiatic building, house 47 Federal
Potter William O. captain, house 9 Becket
Poulson Lucifer N. mariner, house 9 Charter
Pousland Edward, captain, house 17 Dearborn   [103 Lafayette
Pousland George A. *(Rhodes & P.)*, painter, 20 Peabody, house
Pousland George W. captain, house 100 Lafayette
Pousland Joseph, carpenter, house 133 North
Pousland Thomas D. cigar maker, house 58 Charter
Pousland William, captain, house 102 Lafayette
Powell Nathaniel, mariner, house 67 Mill
Power Nathaniel, mariner, house 67 Mill
Power Wm. A. marble worker, 11 St. Peter, b. Mansion House
Powers Catharine, widow, house rear 30 Peabody
Powers Edmund, laborer, house 3 Tucker's wharf
Powers Edward, currier, boards 11 Whittemore
Powers Edward, currier, house 93 Mason
Powers Eliza, widow, house 14 English
Powers James, laborer, house Grove, above Mason
Powers James, laborer, house foot Phelps court
Powers John, currier, house Warren court
Powers John, currier, house 130 North
Powers Michael, currier, house 130 North
Powers Stephen, pilot, house 9 Webb
Pratt Benjamin, house 98 Lafayette
Pratt Caleb, tanner, house 7 Beach   [16½ Lemon court
Pratt Charles W. *(Luscomb & P.)*, jeweller, 162 Essex, house
Pratt Elisha (B.), house 12 Oak
Pratt George W. currier, house rear 12 Oak

SALEM [P] DIRECTORY.

Pratt Henry J. druggist, 141 Essex, house 4 Liberty
Pratt John, house 60 Lafayette
Pratt John W. farmer, house rear 130 Lafayette
Pratt Relief Mrs. house 12 Union
Pratt Samuel, farmer, house rear 130 Lafayette
Pratt William, toll gatherer, house Salem turnpike
Pray Isaac C. shoebinder, 16 Lafayette, and *(Pray & Boynton)*, eating house, 25 Front, house 2 Leach
Presby Frederick A. clerk, 228 Essex, boards 17 Mason
Presby *(William A.)* & Fearing *(E. P.)*, dry goods, 228 Essex, house 17 Mason
Prescott David, mason, house 12 Beaver court
Prescott John, teamster, boards 12 Beaver court
Prescott William (Cal.), house 10 English
Prescott William C. counsellor, 27 Washington, h, 15 Winter
Preston John, baker, 53 Summer, house 1 Mount Vernon
Preston Jonathan, tinplate worker, 12 Central, h. 55 Summer
Preston Jonathan jr. tinplate worker, 12 Central, h. 62 Summer
Preston Joseph Mrs. house 67 Essex
Preston Richard, ropemaker, house 20 Osgood
Preston Sarah, widow, house 53 Summer
Preston William B. mason, boards 20 Osgood
Price Augustus E. millinery, trimmings, and dry goods, 220 Essex, house 81 Summer
Price Benjamin (B.), house 81 Summer
Price Charles *(Pease & P.)*, house 11 High
Price Charles H. *(Browne & P.)*, druggist, 226 Essex, h. 364 do.
Price Eben. N. trunk & harness maker, 237 Essex, h. 81 Summer
Price Henry A. baker, house 30 Endicott
Price John, livery stable, 8 Norman, house 10 do.
Price Joseph, 226 Essex, house 81 Summer
Price William, ropemaker, house 30 Endicott
Pride Elisha, ship carpenter, boards 23½ Harbor
Prime B. Franklin, tanner, boards Melcher court
Prime D. Nelson, mariner, house 21 Beckford
Prime David N. Mrs. house Melcher court
Prime Hiram, brickmaker, house 3 Mechanic
Prime James M. grocer, 115 North, house 113½ do.
Prime *(Thomas H)*, Kenny *(J. A.)*, & Co. *(John Jewett)*, dealers in mahogany, fancy wood, furniture, and veneers, City Mills, 35 to 43 Mill, house 10 Margin
Prince Elizabeth, widow, house Pickman
Prince George, shoemaker, house 16 Flint
Prince John, baker, 2 Front, house 27 Williams
Prince John jr. Mrs. house 26 Howard
Prince Nathaniel W. currier, house 6 Albion
Prince Susan. S. house 27 Williams

SALEM [P] DIRECTORY.

Prior Lawrence, currier, house 29 Boston
Proctor Benjamin, house 51 Warren
Proctor Elizabeth M. Mrs. house 404 Essex
Proctor Eliza Mrs. house 63 Harbor
Proctor John W. shoemaker, house 11 English
Proctor Mary A. Miss, house 136 Boston
Proctor Nicholas, engineer, house 12 Walter
Proctor William, shoemaker, house 6 Cabot, near Cedar
Pulsifer Charles H. painter, 51 Boston, house rear 95 do.
Pulsifer David & Co. *(E. B. Pulsifer)*, painters, 25 Front, house 20 Lynde
Pulsifer Ebenezer, carpenter, house 23 Oliver
Pulsifer Edward B. *(D. Pulsifer & Co.)*, boards 20 Lynde
Pulsifer Elizabeth F. dressmaker, house 63 Essex
Pulsifer Joseph, painter, 230 Derby, h. 75 Summer
Pulsifer Lydia P. Mrs. house 40 Federal
Pulsifer Sarah E. dressmaker, house 63 Essex
Pulsifer Nath'l, painter and carpet manuf. 11 Spring, h. 9 do.
Pulsifer Nath'l F. painter, boards 9 Spring
Punchard Jesse S. painter, house 15 Winthrop
Punchard Keziah, house 116 Federal
Punchard Jonathan P. gaiter boot manuf. 24 Winthrop, h. do.
Purbeck Aaron Mrs. house rear 89 North
Purbeck William, fruit, &c. 15½ Central, house r. 10 Church
Purbeck William A. merchant tailor, 267 Essex, h. 5 Harbor
Putnam Allen, house 35 Warren
Putnam Amos P. carpenter, 3 Beach, house 1 Oak
Putnam Caroline E. hair work manuf. 175½ Essex
Putnam Charles A. engineer and surveyor, 251 Essex. h. 59 do.
Putnam Charles F. horticulturalist, house Orne
Putnam David, house 242 Essex
Putnam Eben, boards 33 Summer
Putnam Francis, florist, house 59 Essex
Putnam George, druggist, 275 Essex, house Orne
Putnam George F. *(J. Putnam & Co.)*, boards 94 Boston
Putnam Hannah P. millinery, 293 Essex, house do.
Putnam Israel, house 69 Mill
Putnam Jacob & Co. *(G. F. Putnam)*, tanners and curriers, 65 Boston, house 94 do.
Putnam James H. brickmaker, house 149 North
Putnam James S. house 94 Boston
Putnam John P. painter, house 13 Walnut
Putnam Joseph, brick manuf. 10 Franklin, house 14 Sewall
Putnam Joseph H. house 9 Oak
Putnam Joseph P. clerk, 173 Essex, b. 1 Rust
Putnam Mary, house 50 Broad
Putnam Nathan, wood and lumber, 157 Derby, h. 2 Winthrop

Putnam Perley, commissioner of streets, house 10 Andrew
Putnam Perley Z. M. P. Mrs. house 16 Lemon
Putnam William S. mariner, house Orne

QUARLES SAMUEL, merchant (Cal.), h. 4 Church
Quarles Wm. A. (Cal.), boards 4 Church
Quimby Ann Maria, music teacher, house 48 Federal
Quimby E. Hervey, physician, house 48 Federal
Quimby Elisha, physician, house 48 Federal
Quimby Moses Y. house 4 at the F. R. Lead Mills
Quinlan Thomas, laborer, house 16 Turner
Quinlan Timothy, currier, house 18 Beaver court
Quinn Charles, house 47 Harbor
Quinn Daniel, Naumkeag Mill, house 47 Harbor
Quinn Patrick, currier, house 82 Mason
Quinn Patrick, tanner, house Oak, near Beach
Quinn Patrick, laborer, house 56 Charter
Quinn Patrick, shoemaker, boards 16 Ward
Quinn *(Thomas)* & Kelley *(James)*, tailors, 184 Essex, house 22 Charter
Quint Lorenzo A. shoemaker, house Grove

RABORDY JULIUS, mariner, boards Orange, cor. Derby
Radford Benjamin F. shoemaker, house 25 Winthrop
Radford Charles F. shoemaker, house 10 Peabody
Radford John, shoemaker, house 56 Endicott
Radford Martha Mrs. house 13 Pond
Ragan William, laborer, house rear 4 Pratt
Ralihan Patrick, currier, house 141 Boston
Ralihan Thomas, currier, house 143 Boston
Ramsdell Alexander, ropemaker, house E. Webb
Ramsdell Arthur W. captain, house 20 Cedar
Ramsdell Joseph R. ropemaker, boards E. Webb
Ramsdell Peter A. shoemaker, boards E. Webb
Ramsdell Wm. sawyer, City Mills, house 82 Mill
Ramsdell Wm. G. Mrs house 10 Cedar
Rand Augustus, stonecutter, house 55 Lafayette
Rand Charles F. contractor, house 55 Lafayette
Randall Edward H. tinsmith, house 8 Andrew
Randall Frank (Cal.), house Melcher's court
Randall Moses D. inspector, C. H. house 8 Andrew
Randall Samuel Mrs. house 28 Buffum
Randolph Nancy, widow, house 15 Pond
Rantoul Robert S. counsellor, 22 Asiatic building, h. 47 Summer
Rawson Charles E. shoemaker, house 28 High
Raymond Alfred A. blacksmith, 33 North, h. rear 27 Buffum
Raynes Willey, currier, boards 1 Sewall

Rea Bridget, widow, house 42 Union
Rea Edward H. house 46 Broad
Rea Samuel G. merchant, house 45 Washington
Rea Sarah Mrs. house 45 Washington
Read Andrew, laborer, house rear E. Webb
Read George F. teacher, house 42 Buffum
Read John, house 87 Federal   [house 11 North
Read John F. fruit and vegetables, 7, 8, and 9 Market House,
Read Warren A. butter and cheese, 10 and 11 Market House,
    house 12 Mason
Readey Wm. mariner, house 140 North
Real Frederick E. laborer, house 31 Hardy
Reardon John, laborer, house rear 30 Peabody
Reardon John, laborer, house 21 High
Reardon Judith, widow, house 16 Turner
Reardon Patrick, laborer, house Philipps
Reaves Abigail, house 70 North
Reaves Edward, painter, house 37 Pleasant
Reaves George, house 70 North
Reaves Robert, ropemaker, house 37 Pleasant
Redding Elizabeth Mrs. house 17 Whittemore
Redmond Bridget, widow, house 100 Mason
Redmond John, currier, house 95 Mason
Redmond John, currier, Goodhue, house 6 Beach
Redmond Lucy J. widow, h. Phelps ct. cor. Green pl.
Redmond Miles, grocer, 12 Derby, house do.
Reed Henry L. carpenter, house 23 Warren
Reed John, Washington House, 9 Higginson square
Reed Joseph, house 11 Endicott
Reed Lydia, house 354 Essex
Reed Mary Mrs. nurse, house 13 Warren
Reed Nathan J. shoemaker, house 66 Mill
Reed Nathaniel Mrs. house 90 Federal
Reed Richard B. postman, house 13 Warren
Reed Samuel, carpenter, house 9 Barr
Reed Sarah, house 354 Essex
Reed Sarah Mrs. house 1 Daniels
Reed Sarah W. nurse, house 43 Bridge
Reed Thomas, candle maker, house 35 Harbor
Reed Thomas, shoemaker, house 160 Bridge
Reed William, laborer, house 48 Buffum
Reeves John, cooper, house Skerry
Reeves William, grocer, 20 Essex, house 1 Forrester
Reith Ann Mrs. house 16 Federal
Reith Wm. jr. clerk, 153 Essex, house 16 Federal
Remon Simon L. house 5 Gedney court

Remon Elizabeth, widow, house 5 Gedney court
Remon John C. cooper, house 4 High
Remond Charles L. house 9 Dean
Remond John, old wines, cordials, &c. 5 Higginson sq. h. do.
Remond *(M. J.)* & Babcock *(C.)*, hair work, 188½ Essex, h. 5 Higginson square
Rennard Frederick W. laborer, house 130 North
Restell John, saloon, 96 Derby, house 5 North court
Reynolds John P. mason, house 13 Northey
Reynolds John P. jr. clerk, 167 Essex, boards 13 Northey
Reynolds Moses C. & Co. *(D. B. Gardner, jr.)*, grocers, 20 Front, house 65 Lafayette
Reynolds Thomas, tanner, house 170 Federal
Reynolds Thomas, currier, house Varney
Rhodes Amos H. engineer, Naumkeag Mill, h. 58 Harbor
Rhodes Crispus, shoemaker, house 20 Cedar
Rhodes *(John W.)* & Pousland *(G. A.)*, painters, 20 Peabody, house 30 Andrew
Rial John F. rigger, house 4 Herbert
Rice Abner, currier, boards 4 N. Pine
Rice James B. currier, boards 4 N. Pine
Rice John, tailor, house 13 Lynn
Rice Sylvester, shoemaker, house Adams
Rich Joshua, mariner, house 60 Essex
Rich N. A. dressmaker, 238½ Essex, house do.
Richards George S. Mrs. house 3 N. Pine
Richards John H. printer, boards 3 N. Pine
Richards Lewis D. clerk, S. I. P. h. Green pl. cor. Phelps ct.
Richards Lydia Mrs. house 25 High
Richardson Alfred, currier, boards 29 Beaver
Richardson Bodwell, house 12 School
Richardson Charles, house 2 North Pine
Richardson Chas. M. *(Adams, Richardson & Co.)*, hardware, 207 Essex, house 31 Broad
Richardson Elizabeth, widow, house 24 Dearborn   [2 River
Richardson Jeremiah, boots, shoes, and rubbers, 213 Essex, h.
Richardson Jeremiah J. house 55½ Broad
Richardson Lydia Mrs. nurse, house 108 Bridge
Richardson Wm. H. teamster, house 37 Beaver
Richers Henry, captain, house 50 Harbor
Ricker Morrill, mason, house 56 Endicott
Ricker Oliver P. house 22 Winter
Ricker Richard, laborer, house Putnam
Rideout Justin, clerk, 16 Asiatic building, house 4 Bentley
Rideout Ellen, teacher, Phillips School, boards 4 Bentley
Rideout Nathaniel, carpenter, house 4 Bentley
Rideout Ruth, widow, house Ord

SALEM [R] DIRECTORY.

Rider Geo. W. clerk, 242 Essex, boards 152 Federal
Rider Henry, captain, house 152 Federal
Rider Joseph Mrs. house 152 Federal
Rider Joseph J. watches and jewelry, 242 Essex
Rider Joshua O. mariner, house 152 Federal
Riley David M. newspaper and periodical depot, 7 Washington, house 3 Elm
Riley James, laborer, house 21 Daniels
Riley James, currier, 91 Mason, house Phillips
Riley John, laborer, house Dodge, n. Walter
Riley Matthew, laborer, house 21 Daniels
Riley Patrick, laborer, house 20 Carlton
Riley Philip, servant at 122 Lafayette
Ring David, laborer, house 26 Ward
Ring Mary, tailoress, house 46 Charter
Rinks John, shipkeeper, house rear 7 Turner
Roach John, hostler, 212 Essex, h. 10 High street court
Roach Julia, widow, house 10 Odell square
Robbins Charles F. clerk, 165 Derby, house 2 Pickman
Robbins Henry P. mariner, house 20 School
Robbins Nathaniel C. merchant, house 2 Pickman
Robbins N. O. Mrs. house 167 Boston
Robbins Thomas A. house 167 Boston
Robbins William S. mariner, house 20 School
Roberts Charles, porkdealer, house Prospect, n. Summer
Roberts David, counsellor, 118 Essex, Franklin building, h. 21 Winter
Roberts David A. mariner, house 24 Mechanic
Roberts Edward F. & J. W. fruit and confectionery, 203 Essex, boards 10 Sewall
Roberts Ezekiel, house 13 Cedar
Roberts George, teamster, house 4 Becket
Roberts Hannah Mrs. house 24 Mechanic
Roberts Hannah J. Miss, dressmaker, 52 Harbor, b. 16 High
Roberts Henry O. clerk, house 24 Mechanic
Roberts John, 12, 13, & 14 Market House, h. Prospect, cor. Summit
Roberts John jr. butcher, house Summit, n. Prospect
Roberts John W. *(E. F. & J. W. Roberts)*, boards 10 Sewall
Roberts Joseph W. housewright, house 12 Herbert
Roberts Mary W. widow, house Prospect, near Summit
Roberts Stephen H. teamster, house 3 Hardy
Roberts William, house 91 Federal
Roberts William S mason, house 12 St. Peter
Robertson Stratton W. soap and candle manuf. r. 44 Boston, house 44 do.
Robinson Catharine, dressmaker, house 107 Derby

Robinson Henry, mariner, house 59 Derby
Robinson John G. clerk, 175 Essex, b. Mrs. Robinson's, Hancock
Robinson Lucy Ann Mrs. house foot Hancock
Robinson Martha C. Mrs. house 23 Church
Robinson Peter A. mariner, house 9 High street court
Robinson Sylvester C. house 138 Federal
Robinson Uriah, farmer, house foot of Orne
Robinson William W. fireman, E. R. R. house 6 Ash
Rock John, saloon, West place, house 188 Derby
Rocko Matthew, mariner, house 11 Becket
Rodigrass John, painter, house 15 Osgood
Rogers Albert, laborer, house 57 Broad
Rogers Augustus D. counsellor, house 376 Essex
Rogers Benjamin F. provisions, house 3 Daniels
Rogers Charles D. mariner, house 13 Carlton
Rogers Edward S. clerk, Register Deeds office, h. 376 Essex
Rogers Jacob C. house 136 Essex
Rogers Joseph, shoemaker, house 8 Peabody
Rogers Joseph P saloon, 41 Derby, house 90 Essex
Rogers Lucinda Mrs. house 27 Turner
Rogers Martha Mrs. house 27 Turner
Rogers Mary Mrs. house 114 Bridge
Rogers Nathaniel L. Mrs. house 376 Essex
Rogers Richard D. merchant, house 136 Essex
Rogers Richard E. merchant (B.), house 136 Essex
Rogers Richard S. merchant, house 204 Essex
Rogers Russell, laborer, house 7 Fowler
Rogers Samuel, captain, house 57 Harbor
Rogers Seabury F. confectionery, 170 Essex, house 6 Cross
Rogers Thomas, laborer, house 77 Derby
Rogers William C. merchant, house 204 Essex
Roles Samuel, shoemaker, house 24 Mechanic
Roles Samuel jr. dyer, 7 Franklin, house 12 Mechanic
Rollins Abijah, stonecutter, boards 12 Harbor
Rollins George W. S. carver, boards 21 Lafayette
Rollins John B. machinist, house 21 Lafayette
Rollins Sarah J. Mrs. boarding house, 21 Lafayette
Ronan James, laborer, house 7 Ropes
Ronan Michael, laborer, house 36 Peabody
Ropes Andrew, mariner, house 4 Palfrey court
Ropes Benjamin A. mess. Salem Savings Bank, h. 106 Derby
Ropes Benjamin M. house 106 Derby
Ropes Charles A. (R. W. Ropes & Co.), h. foot of Dearborn
Ropes Charlotte, widow, house 109 Federal
Ropes Elizabeth Mrs. house 7 Becket
Ropes Fanny, widow, house 18 Williams
Ropes George, clerk, Central wharf, h. 109 Federal

Ropes George N. captain, house 85 Essex
Ropes Hannah Mrs. house 23 Dearborn
Ropes Hannah H. house 313 Essex
Ropes Henry, treasurer Salem Savings Bank, h. 106 Derby
Ropes James, house 26 Dearborn
Ropes John C. machinist, 19 Front, boards 7 Monroe
Ropes John F. mariner, house 65 Mill
Ropes John T. & Co. *(William Ropes)*, stoves, &c. 17 and 19 Front, house 7 Monroe
Ropes Jonathan, shoemaker, house 78 Mill
Ropes Jonathan jr. shoemaker, house 126 Boston
Ropes Lucy Jane Mrs. dressmaker, house 6 Winthrop
Ropes Maria, house 43 Chestnut
Ropes Mary, widow, house 78 Mill
Ropes Mary Mrs. house 28 Williams
Ropes Reuben W. & Co. *(Charles A. & Ripley Ropes)*, flour and grain, 165 Derby, house 18 Williams
Ropes Ripley *(R. W. Ropes & Co.)*, house 106 Lafayette
Ropes Samuel Mrs. house 76 Mill
Ropes Samuel, captain, house 64 Summer
Ropes Sarah G. house 373 Essex
Ropes Timothy, crockery, glass, and hardware, 214 Essex, house 1 Pine
Ropes William *(J. T. Ropes & Co.)*, house 6 Andrew
Ropes William, shoemaker, boards 78 Mill
Rose Joseph Mrs. house 13 Harbor
Rose Martha A. dry goods, 12 Harbor, house 13 do.
Rose William S. Mrs. house 19 Washington
Ross Ann C. Mrs. house 19 Williams
Ross James D. teamster, house Phelps court
Ross Joseph, tanner, house Phelps court
Ross Nathaniel, hairdresser, 10 Boston, house 2 Beach
Ross William S. trader, house 38 Broad
Roth William Peter, stonecutter, house 32 Union
Roundey Thomas, cooper, 10 Lafayette, house 79 Summer
Roundy Charles, captain, house 47 Lafayette
Rourk Catharine, house 34 Turner
Rourke Thomas, Naumkeag Mill, house 20½ Congress
Rowe Joseph S. hairdresser, 35 Washington, corner Essex, house 5 Margin
Rowell Benjamin, painter, house 16 Upham
Rowell Edward, cooper, Webb's wharf, house 27 Carlton
Rowell Frederick, cigar maker, house 13 Carlton
Rowell Frederick jr. clerk, 175 Essex, boards 13 Carlton
Rowell Joseph, captain, house 68 Bridge
Rowell Samuel, boots and shoes (8 Central, B.), h. 7 Pratt
Rowell Sidney B. clerk, 410 Essex, boards 408 do.

Rowell Thomas P. lumber, 2 Naumkeag whf. h. 38 Harbor
Rowley Lydia L. widow, house 6 Pratt
Rowley Mary, dressmaker, house Melcher's court
Rowley Robert, currier, house Melcher's court
Rubashoe Paul, ship carpenter, house S. Prospect, n. Congress
Ruee Benjamin, cooper, house 9 Walnut
Ruee Helen Mrs. house 48 Essex
Ruee Henry A. carpenter, house 10 Howard
Ruee Philip B. 196 Essex, house 10 Howard
Ruee Sarah, widow, house 9 Walnut
Ruee Thomas, kegmaker, boards 9 Walnut
Ruff Caroline A. Mrs. house 65 Essex
Ruliff James B. mariner, house rear 131 North
Rupp Andrew, currier, rear 31 Boston, house 164 Federal
Rupp Frederick, currier, house 17 Hathorne
Rush Francis, currier, house 17 Beaver court
Russ John V. W. mariner, house 7 Turner
Russell Benjamin Mrs. house 11 Pickman
Russell Benjamin W. bookkeeper, Salem Bank, b. 11 Pickman
Russell Ephraim, baker, house 61 Charter
Russell Elizabeth C. teacher, house 11 Pickman
Russell Francis, carpenter, house Pingree
Russell George, clerk, E. R. R. depot (B.), house 126 Essex
Russell Henry Mrs. house 18 Brown
Russell John, pump and block maker, 48 Union, h. 43 Broad
Russell John B. Mrs. house Summit, Prospect Hill
Russell John Mrs. house 22 Lafayette
Russell John H. mariner, house E. Gardner, n. S. Prospect
Russell John H. jr. lamplighter, house 72 Mill
Russell John L. Rev. house 22 Lafayette
Russell John W. carpenter, house 53 Essex
Russell Joseph W. mariner, house 26 Endicott
Russell Mary Mrs. house 97 Essex
Russell Samuel H. house 11 Hardy
Russell Susan Mrs. nurse, house 26 Endicott
Russell Thomas B. model maker (B.), house 354 Esssx
Russell Wm. job wagon, 21 Front, house 29 Norman
Russell William, laborer, house 152 Derby
Russell Wm. shoemaker, boards 59 Harbor
Russell Winslow, shoemaker, boards 59 Harbor
Rust Francis A. P. house 59 Lafayette
Rust Horace, bath house, 148 Bridge, and keeper Lyceum Hall,
  house 4 North court
Rust Lydia J. house 2 Rust
Rust N. P. Mrs. variety store, 59½ Lafayette, house 59 do.
Rust Susan, widow, house 72 Essex
Ruth James, painter, house 10 Herbert

Ruth Richard, carpenter, house 26 Congress
Ryan David, currier, house Salem Turnpike
Ryan Ellen, widow, house 28 Peabody
Ryan Hannah, widow, house 13 Charter
Ryan James, currier, house Phillips, near Grove
Ryan James, tanner, house 129 Boston
Ryan James, currier, house rear 347 Essex
Ryan James, currier, boards 4 N. Pine
Ryan James, gardener, house 95 Lafayette
Ryan John, naval officer, Custom House, house 27 Buffum
Ryan John, clothescleaner, 13 St. Peter, house do.
Ryan Joseph, currier, house Varney
Ryan Kenneday, currier, house 21 Warren
Ryan Mary, widow, house 4 Pratt
Ryan Michael, laborer, house 123 Boston
Ryan Michael, laborer, house 12 River
Ryan Patrick, laborer, house 11 Whittemore
Ryan Patrick, tanner, house May street court
Ryan Richard, tanner, boards 81 Mason
Ryan Robert, currier, house 10 Aborn
Ryan Simon, gardener, boards 4 N. Pine
Ryan Timothy, house Adams
Ryan Winnifred, widow, house 27 Buffum
Ryell William, boarding house, 156 Derby

SADLER GEORGE G. boiler maker, house 16 Salem
Sadler Harriet M. dressmaker, house 13 Church
Sadler Joseph D. painter, house 13 Church
Safford D. E. counsellor, 24 Asiatic building, h. at Hamilton
Safford Elizabeth E. teacher, house 33 Essex
Safford Henry F. surveyor, house 12 Laboratory
Safford James O. hides, &c. (17 Blackstone, B.), h. 19 Brown
Safford Joshua, house 21 Mall
Safford Joshua F. captain, house 12 Laboratory
Safford Samuel A. house 24 Chestnut
Sage John, mariner, house 1 Daniels
Saltonstall Annie E. & Caroline, house 39 Chestnut
Saltonstall Nathaniel Mrs. house 43 Chestnut
Saltonstall William G. house 43 Chestnut
Sanborn Benjamin B. carpenter, house 6 Bentley
Sanborn Eliza M. seamstress, house 7½ St. Peter
Sanborn Franklin T. *(G. & F. T. Sanborn)*, house 14 Walnut
Sanborn George & F. T. coal and wood, 115 Derby, h. 3 Turner
Sanborn George, carpenter, boards 6 Bentley
Sanborn Hiram, cooper, house 4 Allen   [near Upham
Sanborn James, tanner and currier, rear 11 Mason, house Orne,
Sanborn Joseph W. tanner, house 17 School

Sanborn Mark, hair dealer, house 15 Buffum
Sanborn Mary Ann, widow, house 5 Allen
Sanborn Theophilus, house 5 Becket
Sanborn Washington T. carpenter, house 15 Buffum
Sanders George T. Mrs. house 292 Essex
Sanderson John Mrs. cabinet maker, 122 Federal, house do.
Sanderson John A. carpenter, boards 122 Federal
Sanderson John W. machine sewing, 25 Daniels, house do.
Sanger Edward H. baker and caterer, 416 Essex, house do.
Sargent Octavius, carpenter, boards 14 Harbor
Saul John, watchman, house 7 Gedney court
Saul John S. carpenter, house Green place
Saul Joseph, tailor (B.), house 1 Lagrange
Saul Thomas, mariner, house 7 Mount Vernon
Saul Thomas, provisions, 79 Mason, house 2 Beach
Saunders Charles H. mariner, house 5 Cedar
Saunders Charles R. P. carpenter, house Ord
Saunders David E. (B.), house 8 Winter
Saunders David E. clerk, Asiatic Bank, boards 8 Winter
Saunders Elizabeth, widow, house 5 Buffum
Saunders George M. mariner, house rear 63 Essex
Saunders Henry T. house 5 Cedar
Saunders Jeremiah, currier, house Beaver lane
Saunders John, house 14 Margin
Saunders Lewis, Salem and Lawrence express, 10 Washington
Saunders Lydia, dressmaker, house 6 Norman
Saunders Margaret, nurse, house 343 Essex
Saunders Mary A. M s. house 5 Cedar
Saunders Oliver H. captain, house 5 Cedar
Saunders Philip H. carpenter, house Prospect, near Summit
Saunders Robert J. veterinary surgeon, house 16 Buffum
Saunders Robert S. Mrs. house 38 Summer
Saunders Thomas M. captain, house 14 Andrew
Saunders William, veterinary surgeon, house 5 Buffum
Savage Margaret, house 35 Broad
Savage Thomas, boarding house, 89 Derby
Savory & Co. *(B. Savory & J. A. Goldthwait)*, Salem and Boston Express, 7 Washington
Savory Augustus, mariner, house 9 Creek
Savory Benjamin *(Savory & Co.)*, house 17 Williams
Savory Benjamin jr. clerk (B.), house 15 Winthrop
Savory James, shoemaker, boards 21 Lafayette
Savory Mary, dressmaker, house 21 Beckford
Savory Mary, widow, house 9 Creek
Savory Richard Mrs. house 120 Derby
Savory Tristram T. clerk, 7 Washington, boards 17 Williams
Savory William, captain, house 120 Derby

SALEM [S] DIRECTORY. 167

Sawyer Asa, provisions, 17 & 18 Market House, house at South Danvers
Sawyer Hannah, widow, house 6 Winthrop
Sawyer Martha A. Mrs. house 15 Chestnut
Sawyer Norris, foreman, 15½ St. Peter, boards 8 Federal
Sawyer Nathaniel Mrs. house 5 Woodbury's court
Sawyer Thomas H. clerk, 17 Market Ho. h. at South Danvers
Saxby W. L. mastic roofing, 153 Derby
Scanlan David, laborer, house 24 Peabody
Scanlan John, currier, house 19 Fowler
Scanlan Michael, currier, house rear 28 Beaver
Scanlan Patrick, currier, house 18 River
Scanlan Thomas, currier, house 11 Lynn
Scholfield Rebecca, house 369 Essex
Scobie Catharine, house 6 Oliver
Scotchburn George A. Mrs. dressmaker, house 3 Central
Scott Benjamin, farmer, house 14 Curtis
Scott Benjamin jr. machinist, 159½ Essex, boards 14 Curtis
Scott Hugh M. tanner, house Adams
Scribner R. E. clerk, 20 Front, boards 20 Crombie
Scriggins Joshua C. sawyer, house 16 Williams
Sculley Mary, widow, house 4 Pingree
Sculley Thomas, laborer, house Tucker's wharf
Searl Augustus (18 Blackstone, B.), boards 144 Boston
Searl Curtis, tanner, boards 144 Boston
Searl George, painter, house 140 Boston
Searl Joseph, tanner, house 144 Boston
Searl Joseph jr. tanner, boards 144 Boston
Searl Mary, widow, house 144 Boston
Seaver Daniel A. Naumkeag Mill, house 60 Harbor
Seaver Rachel Mrs. house 70 Harbor
Seccomb Ebenezer, adamantine candles, lard and oils, foot of Harbor (and 89 Commercial, B.), house 21 Andrew
Segee Mary M. widow, house 11 Pond
Selby William, mariner, house 14 Harbor
Seley George, fisherman, house 48 Derby
Severence Joshua, painter, house 16 Upham
Sevour James, shoemaker, boards 63 Harbor
Sewall Charles, student at law, 226½ Essex, boards 25 Buffum
Sexton Michael, shoemaker, boards 12 Beach
Shackelford William *(Parsons & Shackelford)*, fish, 64 Union
Shackley Moses A. stage proprietor, 13 Central
Shahan Thomas H. Rev. house 14 Mall
Shanly Ellen, widow, house 170 Federal
Sharkey Charles, laborer, house 13 Daniels
Sharp Richard, shoemaker, boards 59 Harbor
Shatswell James, clerk, Register of Deeds, boards 28 Andrew

Shatswell Joseph, merchant, 23 Front, house 80 Lafayette
Shatswell J. Augustus, clerk, 12 Derby wharf, b. 80 Lafayette
Shatswell Moses, shoemaker, 26 Andrew, house 28 do.
Shaw Aaron, shoemaker, house 14 Park
Shaw Alpheus, captain, boards 40 Harbor
Shaw Ann, widow, house 14 Park
Shaw Bartholomew, at gas works, house 17 Lemon
Shaw Collin W. cabinet maker, house 13 Saunders
Shaw Jacob N. grocer, house 4 North Pine
Shaw Jacob N. jr. boards 4 North Pine
Shaw John H. (Cal.), house 54 Endicott
Shaw Jonathan A. shoemaker, house Perkins
Shaw Robert C. carriage maker, house 66 North
Shaw Timothy R. gardener, house 28 Union
Shaw Xenophon H. gilder, 291 Essex, house 144 Federal
Shay Bartholomew, laborer, house foot of Ropes
Shay Patrick, currier, house 83 Mason
Shea Daniel, laborer, house Phelps court
Shea Daniel, currier, house Grove, above Mason
Shea Michael, laborer, house 8 Turner
Shea Nicholas, tanner, house Oak, near Beach
Shea Owen, laborer, house 12 River
Shea Patrick, laborer, house 27 Daniels
Shea Thomas, currier, house Phelps court, near Jackson place
Shea Thomas, tanner, house Phelps court
Shea William, shoemaker, house East Webb
Shearman Charles, boards 9 Dean
Shearman James L. oysters, West place, house 9 Dean
Shedd John, butcher, house North, near Nursery
Sheehan Bridget, house 32 Union
Sheehan Daniel, tanner, house Putnam, near Hanson
Sheehan Ellen, widow, house Aborn
Sheehan James, currier, house 1 High street court
Sheehan Morris, laborer, house 9 Congress
Sheehan William, laborer, house South Prospect, cor. Pingree
Shelden Gertrude, teacher Normal School, house at Lowell
Sheldon Eliab, laborer, house 11 River
Shepard Elizabeth, house 33 Summer
Shepard Elizabeth, house 61 Charter
Shepard Henry F. merchant, Central wharf, house 302 Essex
Shepard Isaac B. paper hanger, h. 40 Federal [h. 63 Lafayette
Shepard John B. & S.D. dry goods, 171 Essex (Pickman place),
Shepard Martha Mrs. house 26 Harbor
Shepard Mary Ann Mrs. seamstress, house 8 Williams
Shepard Mary L. teacher Higginson School, house 40 Federal
Shepard Michael W. house 300 Essex
Shepard Saml. *(Nichols & S.)*, tanners, Nichols, h. 173 Federal

Shepard Samuel, upholsterer, 298 Essex, house 9 Lynn
Shepard Samuel D. *(J. B. & S. D. Shepard)*, house 61 Lafayette
Shepard Stephen W. Mrs. house 25 Brown
Sheridan Elizabeth Mrs. house 3 Gerrish place
Sheridan Francis, salesman, 12 Front, house 19 Fowler
Sheridan James, laborer, house 21 Fowler
Sheridan John, shoemaker, 14 Lafayette, house 21 Fowler
Sheridan Philip, laborer, house 21 Fowler
Sherman Charles F. tanner, house Beach, near Oak
Sherwin Christopher, seaman, boards 39 Essex
Sherwin William, tobacconist, house 39 Essex
Shillaber Sally, thread and hosiery, 253 Essex, house 19 Lynde
Shinkwin William, currier, house 148 Boston
Shirley Caroline Mrs. house 15 Salem
Shirley Jonathan, mariner, house 32 Salem
Shirley William, shoemaker, boards 27 Norman
Short Charles, patent door fenders, house 22 High
Short James, cooper, house 6 Northey
Short Lydia A. Mrs. house 6 Northey
Shortell James, shoemaker, house 17 River
Shortell Michael, shoemaker, house 4 Barton
Shorter Royal M. stovesetter, house 11 Osgood
Shortwell William, shoemaker, boards East Gardner, n. Harbor
Shreve Benjamin *(Jones, Shreve, Ball & Co.)*, (B.), house 128 Federal
Shreve Isaac Mrs. house 22 Dearborn
Shreve Samuel V. merchant, house 224 Derby
Sibley George, shoecutter, 17 Central, boards 4 Park
Sibley George V. shoe manufacturer, 17 Central, house 4 Park
Sibley John S. shoe manuf. 42 Lafayette, house Hancock
Sibley Joseph, house 54 Mill
Sibley Moses H. tailor, 10 Front, house 6 Pond
Sibley William H. carpenter, house 20 Pickman
Silsbee Benjamin H. president Merchants' Bank, 32 Washington, house 2 Oliver
Silsbee Edward A. captain, house 11 Pleasant
Silsbee George Z. merchant (B.), h. Warren, corner Flint
Silsbee John B. merchant, Central wharf, house 6 North
Silsbee John H. merchant, 14 Asiatic building, h. 380 Essex
Silsbee Nathaniel, mayor, house 16 Pleasant
Silsbee Nath'l D. com. mer. (25 Doane, B.), house 23 Briggs
Silsbee Zachariah F. merchant, house 11 Pleasant
Silver Augustus, tanner, house 25 Beckford
Silver Eliza, widow, house 8 High
Silver James Mrs. house 384 Essex
Silver Joseph M. hairdresser, boards 8 High
Silver Thomas H. hairdresser, house 8 High

Silver William, captain, house 146 Federal
Simmons Franklin, painter, boards 1 Turner
Simmons Martha, widow, house 10 Winthrop
Simmons Sarah Mrs. house 1 Turner
Simmons William, cigar maker, boards 1 Turner
Simon Francis B., Boston Express, 27 Front, h. 32 Charter
Simon John, confectioner, 160 Essex, house do.
Simon Stephen Augustus, confectioner, house 160 Essex
Simons William, laborer, house South Prospect, c. Pingree
Simonds Edward A. *(S. C. & E. A. Simonds)*, h. 101 Bridge
Simonds George W. clerk (60 State, B.), boards 101 Bridge
Simonds Samuel, grocer, 76 Derby, house 101 Bridge
Simonds Samuel C. & E. A. crockery, hardware, and paper hangings, 32 Front, house 4 Winter
Simonds Wm. H. painter, 76 Derby, house 17 Hardy
Sims Caroline, widow, house 17 Conant
Sims Richard T. captain, house 46 Lafayette
Sinclair David, carpenter, house 11 Gedney court
Sinclair John Gasper, laborer, house 36 St. Peter
Sisty Benjamin F. marble cutter, boards 21 Lafayette
Skerrett George, clerk, boards 9 Norman
Skerry Edward S. painter, house 18 English
Skerry Henry F. *(F. Skerry & Son)*, 180 Essex, house 19 Oliver
Skerry Francis, carpenter, house 56 North
Skerry Francis jr. & Son *(H. F. Skerry)*, fancy goods, 180 Essex, house 3 Lynn
Skerry Robert *(Kimball & S.)*, painter, 139 Derby, h. 17 Federal
Skinner James N. painter, boards 62 Federal
Skinner Jane Mrs. house rear 14 Central
Skinner John B. printer, boards 62 Federal
Skinner John D. conductor E. R. R. house 29 Endicott
Skinner Philip G. cigar maker, house 95 North
Skinner Richard & Son *(Richard Skinner jr.)*, tobacconists, 64 Federal, house 62 do.
Skinner Richard jr. *(R. Skinner & Son)*, house 14½ Andrew
Skinner Samuel S. proprietor of Mansion House, 188 Essex
Skinner Stephen S. cigar manuf. 104 Derby, h. 2 North court
Slattery Ellen, widow, house 1 Pratt
Slattery James, tanner, house Grove
Slattery Joseph, currier, house 24 High
Slee Samuel J. mariner, house 19 Carlton
Sleeper Hezekiah, shoemaker, house 17 Creek
Sleeper Maria M. Mrs. house 6 Norman
Slocum Ebenezer, mason, house 4 Hardy
Slocum Sarah Miss, house 19 Andrew
Sloper William, currier, boards 6 North Pine
Sleuman Andrew, tailor (B.), house 2 Harrison avenue

Sluman Benjamin H. expressman, house 8 Winthrop
Sluman Sarah, widow, house 2 Lagrange
Small Dennis, shoemaker, house 20 Congress
Small William, billiards, boards 166 Essex
Small Wm. F. gas and steam fixtures, 273 Essex, h. 17 Andrew
Smally Rolland, stevedore, house 8 Daniels
Smiley Samuel P. carpenter, boards Summit, near Prospect
Smith Aaron, house Orne, near Upham
Smith Aaron jr. carpenter, 3 Howard, house do.
Smith A. Augustus *(H. P. Ives & A. A. Smith)*, bookstore and bindery, 232 Essex, house 12 Church
Smith Addison, carpenter, house 10 Whittemore
Smith Agnes, house 36 Summer
Smith Amos F. carpenter, house 54 Bridge
Smith Benjamin H. student at law, 20 Asiatic building, boards 25 Buffum
Smith Caleb, house 12 Lynde
Smith Caleb A. house 143 North
Smith Catharine Mrs. nurse, house 18 Derby
Smith Dana Z., Eastern R. R. house 3 Margin
Smith Daniel T. watchmaker, 262 Essex, house 48 Endicott
Smith Edmund, treasurer Naumkeag S. C. Co. h. 17 Winter
Smith Edward, tailor, boards 22½ Beckford
Smith Edward A. watchmaker, 262 Essex, h. 16 Winthrop
Smith Francis E. grain dealer, house 13 Barr
Smith George, tanner, boards 241 Essex
Smith George, in oil factory, boards 62 North
Smith George C. carpenter, house 14 Mechanic
Smith George H. house 2 Federal
Smith George P. Mrs. house 45 Lafayette
Smith Georgiana and Adelaide Misses, h. 34 Buffum [R. depot
Smith Gorham, supt. Essex R. R. in Salem, h. over Essex R.
Smith Hannah, widow, house 11 Charter
Smith Hannah S. widow, house 100 North
Smith Henry B. collector and treasurer, City Hall, h. 12 Winter
Smith Henry W. Mrs. house 22 School
Smith James Mrs. house 15 Barr
Smith James, Naumkeag Mill, boards 62 Harbor
Smith James A. carpenter, 10 Walnut, house 11 Elm
Smith *(J. Ford)* & Chamberlain *(B. M.)*, manufacturing jewellers, 201 Essex, house 20 Mason
Smith Jesse Mrs. house 15 Norman
Smith Jesse, watchmaker, 262 Essex, house 36 Summer
Smith Jesse R. watchmaker, 262 Essex, house 36 Summer
Smith J. Jewett, house 3 Federal
Smith Joanna, widow, house 19 Beaver court
Smith John, shoemaker, house Dodge

Smith John, currier, house 12 Friend
Smith John Mrs. house 21 Beckford
Smith John E. house 6 F. R. L. Mills
Smith John H. baker, house 8 Cambridge
Smith John H. brass finisher (B.), house 52 Bridge
Smith John H. baker, boards 11 High
Smith John R. & S. iron founders and machinists, S. Prospect, cor. E. Gardner, house 29 Harbor
Smith Jonathan C. cigar maker, boards 9 Norman
Smith Joseph, shoemaker, house 10 Dearborn
Smith *(Joseph)* & Manning *(D C.)*, livery stable, 212 Essex, 9 Hamilton, and 47 Wash. house 3 Hamilton
Smith Joseph C. clerk (B.), house 3 Hamilton
Smith Joseph A. cabinet maker, house 26 Winthrop
Smith Lorenzo A. foreman, Oil Co. house 50 North
Smith Mary Mrs. house 29 Mill
Smith Mary A. Mrs. house 9 Pond
Smith Mary F. Mrs. house 8 Saunders
Smith Mehitable, tailoress, house 17 Lynde
Smith Nathan Mrs. house 14 Pickman
Smith Oliver C. machinist, Naumkeag Co's wf. h. 110 Essex
Smith Patrick, laborer, house foot of Pingree
Smith Peter M. cooper, house 13 Union
Smith Robert B. Mrs. house 34 Buffum
Smith Samuel H. jeweller, 201 Essex, boards 20 Mason
Smith Sarah, teacher, house 16 Summer
Smith Sarah J. widow, house 6 Prince
Smith Sarah L. widow, house 9 Oak
Smith Sarah R. teacher Normal School, house at Beverly
Smith Sterry *(J. R. & S. Smith)*, house 14 Harbor
Smith Thomas, teamster, 198 Derby, house 12 Congress
Smith Thomas, currier, house 73 Mason
Smith Walter, tanner, house 73 Mason
Smith William, laborer, house 22½ Beckford
Smith William, gum copal worker, house 18 Derby
Smith William A. shoemaker, boards 10 Dearborn
Smith William B. merchant, house 52 Bridge [h. 27 Norman
Smith *(Wm. R.)* & Bartlett *(F. B.)*, cigar makers, 132 Derby,
Smothers Benjamin, ropemaker, house 6 Pearl
Smothers Olive, seamstress, house 14 Norman
Snell Nicholas T. captain, house 17 Brown
Snell Wm. photograph artist, 208 Essex, house 11 Central
Snelling John Mrs. nurse, house Porter court
Snow Elbridge, provisions, 44 North, house 14 School
Snow Henderson I. stonecutter, house 7 Elm
Snow Nathaniel, currier, foot of Beach, house 60 Mason
Snow Nathaniel, house 396 Essex

SALEM [S] DIRECTORY. 173

Solaris George A. shoemaker, boards rear 89 North
Soley George Mrs. house 26 Derby
Soley Nathaniel, laborer, house 33 Derby
Southward Geo. portrait painter, 7 Central, h. 113 Essex
Southward Jonathan R. house 24 Lemon
Southward Richard Mrs. h. 51 Summer [33 Brown
Southward Samuel S. carriage maker, r. Essex House, boards
Southwick Daniel, tanner, house 16 Boston
Southwick Edward, tanner, house 6 Fowler
Southwick Eliza Mrs. nurse, house 52 Endicott
Southwick John jr. shoemaker, 48 Derby, house do.
Southwick Mary, widow, house 23 Warren
Southwick Samuel F. shoemaker, house 16 Boston
Spalding Josiah, merchant, house 106 Bridge
Sparks Samuel, captain, house 105 North
Spiller John P. wheelwright, West place, house 59 Harbor
Sprague Priscilla G. house 92 Federal
Stacy Joseph, currier, house 20 Boston
Stacy Mary Mrs. house High, corner Summer
Stacy Rebecca H. teacher, house 57 Summer
Stacy Samuel E. 175 Essex, b. Mrs. Robinson's, Hancock
Stacy Varnum, shoemaker, house 57 Summer
Stafford Helen Miss, house 29 Salem
Stafford J. Warren, shoemaker, house 14 River
Stafford William, house 14 River
Stamper Frederick W. shoemaker, house 8 Prince
Standley Benjamin F. shoemaker, house 24 Barr
Staniford Chas. assistant superintendent of burials, 275 Essex, house 26 North
Staniford Daniel, printer, 175½ Essex, boards 26 North
Staniford David P. mariner, house 142 North
Staniford John F. carpenter, house 108 Bridge
Staniford Sarah C. Mrs. house 42 Broad
Staniford, see Stentiford
Stanley Abraham J. house 3 Pleasant
Stanley Edward Mrs. house 5 Daniels
Stanley Elizabeth Mrs. house 18 Andrew
Stanley John, carpenter, house 5 Spring
Stanley John W. tailor, 39 Washington, house 18 Andrew
Stanley Mary, widow, house Aborn
Stanley Nancy, house 1 Federal
Stanley Thankful Mrs. boarding, house 3 Pleasant
Stanley Thomas, tanner, house 148 Boston
Stanton Charles, painter, house 14 Winter
Stanton John, farmer, house Orne
Stanton John, laborer, house rear 36 Peabody
Stanton Mary Mrs. nurse, house 16 Norman

12

Stanton Michael, currier, house 24 High
Stanton Patrick, laborer, house 18 High
Stanton Thomas, laborer, house 2 Pratt
Stanwood Frank, Naumkeag Mill, boards 38 Mill
Stanwood George S. boards Dodge, opposite Southwick
Stanwood Louisa M. Mrs. millinery, 148 Essex, h. 33 Brown
Stanwood Samuel D. cigar maker, h. Dodge, opp. Southwick
Stanwood Wm. Henry, shoemaker, house 62 Mill
Staples Elias C. mariner, house 13 Curtis
Staples George, teamster, house 23 Hardy
Staples Mary Mrs. house 28 Norman
Stapleton Paul, currier, house 14 Congress
Staten Daniel F. gasfitter, 151 Essex, boards 1 Rust
Staten George, blacksmith, house 14 Federal
Staten Edward H. gas and steam fixtures, 151 Essex, boards Essex House
Stearns Moses M. mariner, house 35 Essex
Stearns Sarah E. boards 384 Essex
Stearns William, house 384 Essex
Stearns William, mariner, house 42 Bridge
Stedman George B. car trimmer (B.), house 3 Howard
Stedman Joseph T. painter, house 165 Federal
Stedman Martha, widow, house 2 Goodhue
Stedman Samuel L. tailor, house 165 Federal
Steele Ann, widow, house 30 Union
Steele *(Elizur)*, Blodgett *(P. D.)* & Co. flour and produce, 26 Front, house 14 Elm
Steele Walter S. clerk, 26 Front, boards 14 Elm
Stentiford Charles H. painter, house 33 Barr, near School
Stephenson Elizabeth Mrs. variety store, 34 Peabody, house 214 Derby
Stetson James, shoemaker, 31 North, house 42 Buffum
Stetson Lincoln, shipwright, house 3 Salem
Steteson Silas M. house 90 Essex
Stevens Alden, house 57 Endicott
Stevens Ann P. teacher, Hamilton Hall, house 14 Broad
Stevens Caroline, teacher, house 20 Winthrop
Stevens Daniel Webster, currier, boards 14 Broad
Stevens Eunice, house 25 Turner
Stevens Edward P. baker, house 4 Andover
Stevens Geo. O. currier, boards Pope's court
Stevens Henry J. cigar maker, house 22 Forrester
Stevens Horace H. enamel and patent leather manufacturer, Mason Hill, house 8 Buffum
Stevens Israel, tanner, house 20 Winthrop
Stevens Martha Mrs. house 2 Hamilton
Stevens Sarah B. Mrs. house 10 Pleasant

Stevens Solomon, tanner, house Pope's court
Stevens Timothy J. measurer of leather, house 20 Winthrop
Stevens William, grocer, 13 Derby square, house 14 Broad
Stevens William A. grocer, 13 Derby square, h. 11 Hathorne
Stevenson Robert, mariner, boards 7 Turner
Stewart James, peddler, house Rubber Factory, Ward
Stewart Latt, hairdresser, 8 Washington
Stickney Charles T. carpenter, house 29 Forrester
Stickney Franklin, captain, house 32 Mill
Stickney Harriet Miss, music teacher, house 32 Mill
Stickney Joseph, calker and graver, house 8 Turner
Stickney Joseph, mariner, house 8 Webb
Stickney Matthew A. house 119 Boston
Stickney Richard, carpenter, house rear 22 Hardy
Stickney William Mrs. house 32 Mill
Stiles Charles D. carpenter, boards 53 Endicott
Stiles Dean, carpenter, 23 Harbor, house 53 Endicott
Stiles Joseph P. stonemason, house 86 North
Still Thomas, bootmaker, house 6 Park
Stillman Samuel, shoemaker, house 14 Ward
Stillman Samuel jr. clerk, boards 14 Ward
Stimpson Edward, carriage depot, Spring, h. r. 218 Essex
Stimpson Edward jr. mariner, boards rear 218 Essex
Stimpson James C. tanner and currier, rear 39 Boston, h. 39 do.
Stimpson James B. currier, rear 39 Boston, house 192 Federal
Stimpson Thomas M. counsellor, 194 Essex, h. at S. Danvers
Stocker John W. coach and chaise maker, 23 Endicott, house 16 Federal
Stoddard Benjamin, blacksmith, house 39 Harbor
Stoddard Daniel, blacksmith, house 51 Lafayette
Stoddard Hannah, house Prospect
Stoddard Mary, widow, house 120 Federal
Stodder Simon, captain, house 104 North
Stone Alfred, architect (B.), house 21 Chestnut
Stone Benjamin, mason, house 21 Williams
Stone Benj. W. merchant, 14 Asiatic building, h. 23 Chestnut
Stone Ebenezer, brickmaker, house Liberty Hill road, n. North
Stone Ebenezer jr. currier, house 7 May
Stone Esther P. Miss, house 8 Ash
Stone H. Osgood, physician, house $314\frac{1}{2}$ Essex
Stone Irving *(L. Chandler & Co.)*, periodicals, &c. 4 Wash. house 17 Crombie
Stone Isaac, carpenter, house 107 North
Stone James, mason, house Flint, corner Warren
Stone James jr. M. D. house 40 Broad
Stone John, laborer, house Ord
Stone John, tailor, boards 166 Essex

Stone John H. house 18 Summer
Stone Joseph W. house 23 Chestnut
Stone Lincoln R. physician, over 174 Essex
Stone Lucinda, house 385 Essex
Stone Maria Mrs. house rear 68 Washington
Stone Mary, widow, house 109 Boston
Stone Mary H. widow, house 345 Essex
Stone Priscilla, widow, house 22 High
Stone Robert, house 23 Chestnut
Stone Sally Mrs. house 30 St. Peter
Stone Sarah E. dressmaker, house 7 Pleasant
Stone Sarah M. widow, house 7 Pleasant
Stone Stephen H. blacksmith, house 11 Creek
Stone William, house 163 Boston (Cal.)
Stone William, merchant, 14 Asiatic building, h. 23 Chestnut
Stone William R. tanner, house 163 Boston
Story Augustus, counsellor, 27 Washington, house 98 Bridge
Story Daniel, cooper, 4 Cambridge, house 6 do.
Story William, captain, house 98 Bridge
Story Isaac, counsellor (B.), house 5 Carpenter
Stout Job, mariner, house Rubber Factory, Ward
Stover Charles B. clerk, E. R. R. depot, house 12 Mill
Stover Nathaniel, machinist, house 13 English
Stow *(Volney C.)* & Tibbetts *(A. J.)*, bakers, head of Phillips wharf, house 21 Essex, corner Becket
Stowell Hannah, widow, house 158 Boston
Stowers Joseph Mrs. house 315 Essex
Stowers Nathaniel, chairpainter, house 3 Cambridge
Stowers Nathaniel H. house 3 Cambridge
Strafford James M. gum copal worker, house 22 Becket
Straw Benjamin, wood mouldings, 5 Front, house at Lynn
Straw Isaiah, house 13 Barr
Streeter Gilbert L. teller Commercial Bank, house 17 Pickman
Streeter Sarah Mrs. house 17 Pickman
Strout J. W. captain, house 19 North
Strout Samuel, mariner, house 5 Gedney court
Striley Jacob, fisherman, house rear 13 Osgood
Striley Jacob jr. shoemaker, house 13 Osgood
Sullivan Bridget, widow, house 26 Peabody
Sullivan Cornelius, laborer, house 4 Gerrish place
Sullivan Daniel, laborer, house 19 Daniels
Sullivan Daniel, laborer, house 5 Palfrey court
Sullivan Henry, laborer, house 15 Turner
Sullivan James, laborer, house Ives, near Dearborn
Sullivan Jeremiah, laborer, house East Webb
Sullivan John, laborer, house 8 Pratt

Sullivan John, teamster at J. Dike & Co.'s, house Pingree,
    near Harbor
Sullivan John, laborer, house Adams, Mason Hill
Sullivan Joseph, laborer, house 6 Tucker's wharf
Sullivan Joseph, currier, house Lummus court
Sullivan Mary, widow, house Ives
Sullivan Matthew, laborer, house 10 Webb
Sullivan Michael, laborer, house 3 Gerrish place
Sullivan Michael, laborer, house 2 High street court
Sullivan Owen, laborer, house 4 High street court
Sullivan Samuel, laborer, house 10 High street court
Sullivan Thomas, laborer, house rear 42 Harbor
Sullivan Thomas, laborer, house 28 Congress
Sullivan Timothy, laborer, house 7 Ward
Sullivan Timothy, laborer, house Congress, west side
Sullivan Timothy, laborer, house rear 8 Whittemore
Summers William Mrs. house 92 Essex
Summers William H. clerk, 222 Essex, house 92 do.
Sumner *(Harrison G.)* & Johnson *(W. B. F.)*, teamsters, 132
    Derby, house 23 Daniels
Sumner William O. cabinet maker, house 14 High
Sutton William, president Commercial Bank, 7 Central, house
    at S. Danvers
Swan Hannah Mrs. house 1 Orange
Swan Joseph W. clerk, house 16 Mechanic
Swan Nathaniel, laborer, house 69 North
Swan Rachel Mrs. house 14 Allen
Swan Samuel, laborer, house 69 North
Swaney Patrick, laborer, house 26 Beckford
Swaney William, ropemaker, house 1 English
Swasey Benjamin B. Mrs. house 57 Broad
Swasey Charles W. printer, 185 Essex, house 5 Mall
Swasey Connor B. storekeeper, Custom House, h. 47 Essex
Swasey Elizabeth, widow, house 10 Daniels
Swasey Hannah, house 8 North court
Swasey Joseph, painter, house 30 St. Peter
Swasey William M. mariner, house 57 Broad
Swasey Sarah, widow, house 61 Summer
Sweeney Daniel, laborer, house Tucker's wharf
Sweeney Dennis, currier, house 80 Boston
Sweeney James, laborer, house 13 Charter
Sweeney John, laborer, house Tucker's wharf
Sweeney William, laborer, house 20 Lemon
Sweetser Abby E. Mrs. thread and fancy goods, 165½ Essex,
    house 114 do.
Sweetser Ephraim, boots and shoes, 239 Essex, h. 15 Fowler
Sweetser Ephraim H. clerk, 239 Essex, boards 15 Fowler

Swett A. W. Miss, house 7 Summer
Sylvester Rufus, farmer, boards rear 118 Lafayette
Symonds Abigail, house 132 Boston
Symonds Benjamin, tanner and currier, house 99 North
Symonds Benjamin R. grocer, 109 North, house 95 do.
Symonds Benj. R. jr. grocer, North, cor. Bridge, house 14 Barr
Symonds Calvin, clerk, North, cor. Bridge, house 91 North
Symonds Catharine Mrs. house 46 Federal
Symonds Catharine Miss, carpet maker, house 5 Cedar
Symonds Charles B. currier, house 99 North
Symonds Charles E. assessor City Hall, house 90 North
Symonds Charles F. carpenter, 31½ Buffum, house 31 do.
Symonds Dean C. blacksmith, North, n. the bridge, h. 104 do.
Symonds Eben, shoe manufacturer, 53 North, house 51 do.
Symonds Edward, brickmaker, house 58 North
Symonds Edward jr. clerk, 74 North, house 77 do.
Symonds Edward B. house 15 Brown
Symonds Eliza G. boarding house, 98 Federal
Symonds Eliza and Pleuna, house 132 Boston
Symonds Ephraim, painter, house 18 Mechanic
Symonds Ephraim G. variety store, 107 North, house do.
Symonds Fenton, painter, house 20 Ward
Symonds George, mariner, house 5½ English
Symonds Hannah Mrs. house 47 North
Symonds Hannah, widow of Thomas, house 77 North
Symonds John D. house 47 North
Symonds J. Shove, painter, 41 North, N. Salem, h. 59 Buffum
Symonds Joseph, clerk, 109 North, house do.
Symonds Joseph P. shoe manufacturer, 55 Buffum, house do.
Symonds Joseph W. clerk, 213 Essex, house 46 Federal
Symonds Mary, widow, house 122 Federal
Symonds Nathaniel A. carpenter, boards 18 Mechanic
Symonds Nathaniel D. house 50 North   [h. 43 Buffum
Symonds Nathaniel G. treas. Salem & S.Danvers Oil Co., Mason,
Symonds Proctor, shoemaker, house 35 North
Symonds Samuel jr. grocer, 49 North, house 7 Buffum
Symonds Sarah, house 57 Washington
Symonds Stephen, house 51 North
Symonds Stephen G. painter, house 113 North
Symonds Stilman G. clerk, Exchange Bank, boards 43 Buffum
Symonds Thomas, grocer, 74 North, house 7 Dearborn
Symonds Thomas S. shoemaker, house 17 Dearborn
Symonds Timothy, shoemaker, house 91 North
Symonds T. Putman, clerk (B.), boards 43 Buffum
Symonds William A. shoemaker, house 60 Buffum
Symonds William H. shoemaker, house 147 North
Symonds William H. mason, boards 50 North

SALEM [T] DIRECTORY. 179

TABOUR WILLIAM, cigar maker, house 7 Lynn
Tafts Charles, painter, house 23 Cedar
Tait Bacon, merchant, house 29 Cedar
Talbot Charles, ship carpenter, boards 40 Harbor
Talbot Henry, boards 62 North
Tanch John, carpenter, house 41 St. Peter
Tarbox Samuel A. teamster, house 91 North
Tarbox William, shoemaker, house 89 North
Tarr Benjamin, fisherman, house 29 Derby
Taylor Catharine A. Mrs. house 6 Broad
Taylor Matilda and Margaret Misses, house 18 Chestnut
Taylor Samuel, merchant, boards 9 Lynn
Taylor Sarah N. dressmaker, house 55 Washington
Taylor Thomas, confectioner, boards 73 North
Taylor Thomas A. carpenter, house 55 Washington
Taylor Thomas W. Mrs. house 55 Washington
Taylor Warren, Naumkeag Mill, boards 62 Harbor
Teague Amos G. laborer, house 62 Mill
Teague Amos G. jr. shoemaker, house 64 Mill
Teague Robert, shoemaker, house 108 Derby
Teague Thomas A. teamster, house 77 Mason
Teague Thomas A. jr. carpenter, house 3 Congress
Tedder John, mariner, house 24 Congress
Teel Charles C. captain, house 46 Broad
Temple Jonathan S. Mrs. laundry agent, 77 Federal
Teste John B. cabinet maker, 80 Derby, house 10 Becket
Teste Mary P. nurse, house 16 High
Tetlow James, boiler maker, Naumkeag wharf, h. 27 Charter
Tetlow Thomas, machinist, boards 114 Derby
Thayer Edward S. clerk (89 Commercial, B.), boards 29 Broad
Thayer Nancy, dressmaker, boards 34 Broad
Thayer Oliver, lumber wharf, 190 and 199 Derby, h. 29 Broad
Thayer Rebecca Mrs. house 34 Broad
Thayer Rebecca, teacher, Federal court, house 34 Broad
Thayer Sarah, house 34 Broad
Thayer Stephen, clerk, 199 Derby, house 34 Broad
Thayer William O. clerk, 199 Derby, house 29 Broad
Thomas Charles S. carpenter, house 56 Harbor
Thomas Clarissa, house foot Ives
Thomas Edward A. laborer, house 13 Upham
Thomas George F. house 22 River
Thomas George H. shoemaker, house 60 Broad
Thomas Richard, fish dealer, house Phelps court
Thomas Nancy, widow, house Orne, near Upham
Thomas Samuel W. shoemaker, house Melcher court
Thomas Sarah Mrs. house Phelps court
Thompson Franklin B. seaman, house 6 Webb

Thompson George J. baker, 28 Broad, house do.
Thompson George J. clerk (B.), house 40 Chestnut
Thompson Henry, teamster, house 30 Broad
Thompson James, laborer, house 10½ Turner
Thompson James W. Rev. D. D. house 40 Chestnut
Thompson Joseph A. house 11 Salem
Thompson Rosa Mrs. house rear 8 Whittemore
Thompson Orrin F. clerk, 175 Essex, house 30 Broad
Thorndike Larkin Mrs. house 4 Brown
Thorndike William D. currier, Hanson, house Prospect
Thorner John C. shoemaker, house 5 Church
Thrasher David, farmer, house Lafayette, n. F. R. Lead Mills
Thurston Henry W. cabinet maker, house 6 Howard
Thurston Mary Mrs. house 6 Howard
Tibbets Andrew J. *(Stow & T.)*, baker, head of Phillips wharf, house 41 Essex
Tibbets Andrew R. shoemaker, house foot of Barton
Tibbets David R. agent stage office, 13 Central, h. at S. Danvers
Tibbets Eben, captain, house 7 Oliver
Tibbets George F. baker, boards 21 Essex
Tibbets Henry, house 9 Winter
Tibbets Henry H. painter, house 20 Oliver
Tierney Bridget, widow, house 29 Beaver
Tierney Dominick, currier, house 29 Beaver
Tierney James, currier, house Grove
Tierney John, laborer, house Adams
Tilton J. E. books, &c. (161 Wash., B.), house 9 North
Tilton George F. carpenter, house 4 Ash
Tilton Samuel D. carpenter, house 4 Ash
Timson Edward H. clerk, 246 Essex, house 246½ do.
Tinan James, laborer, house 22 Endicott
Tinan Ann, widow, house 22 Endicott
Tirrell Rebecca, widow, house 5 Woodbury's court
Tivnan John, shoemaker, house 10 Prince
Tivnan Margaret, widow, house 10 Prince
Tivnan Michael, peddler, house 10 Prince
Tivnan Michael, Naumkeag Mill, boards 6 Peabody
Tobin John, clerk, 7½ Boston, boards do.
Tobin Michael, laborer, house 31 Mill
Todd Charles P. hair spinner, house 9 Rust
Todd George A. clerk, boards 21 Lafayette
Todd Jeremiah, city express, house 39 Summer
Todd John E. A. captain, house 2 Cherry
Todd John H. clerk (B.), house 39 Summer
Todd Nathaniel M. boards 2 Cherry
Todd Rebecca Mrs. house 21 Creek
Todd Stephen C. clerk, 1 Boston, boards 29 Summer

SALEM [T] DIRECTORY.

Tolen Neal, laborer, house 90 Derby
Tolman S. Newell, weaver, house 67 Harbor
Tolman Sardis, shoemaker, 216 Essex, house 27 Norman
Tompkins Jesse, mariner, house 48 Buffum
Toomey Catharine, widow, house rear Adams
Toomey John F. currier, house Ord
Toomey Thomas, house 314½ Essex
Torgee George W. cigar maker, boards 21 Lafayette
Torr Joseph H. shoemaker, house 4 Becket
Torr Sally, widow, house 26 Essex
Torr Sally Mrs. house 40 Derby
Torry Francis, mariner, house 89 North
Torry Michael, laborer, house 172 Derby
Totton James, laborer, house 6 Aborn
Touret Benjamin A. soda manufacturer (B.), house 33 Bridge
Towle Abraham, carpenter, Ward, house 19 Harbor
Towle Christopher, blacksmith, house rear 95 Boston
Towne Bethia Mrs. house Phelps court
Towne Charles H. bookkeeper, Asiatic Bank, house Holly, cor. Linden
Towne Henry Mrs. house Holly, cor. Linden
Towne John C. discount clerk, Naumkeag Bank, h. 120 Bridge
Towne Joseph, bookkeeper, 10 Wash. house 17 Buffum
Towne Joseph H cashier Naumkeag Bank, house 19 Buffum
Towne Theophilus L. F., Pickman farm, Lynn road
Townes Ann Mrs. nurse, house 9 Federal
Townes William, mariner, house 9 Federal
Townsend Catharine G. house 15 Federal
Townsend Mary Ann Mrs. house 19 North
Townsend Penn Mrs. house 23 Andrew
Tozer Sally, widow, house 5 Orange
Tracy Hannah Mrs. house 31 Broad
Tracy Michael, laborer, house Grove, near Irving
Tracy Patrick, teamster, house Grove, near Irving
Traill Horace S. printer, "Observer" office, h. at Marblehead
Trainor Elizabeth, widow, house 405 Essex
Trask Abigail, widow, house 6 Lynde
Trask Amos, auctioneer, dealer in ancient and modern curiosities, house 126 Boston
Trask Benjamin, machinist, 15 Harbor, house 12 do.
Trask Benjamin, mariner, boards 135 Essex
Trask Eben P. clerk, 8 Brown, house 22 Howard
Trask Henry, miller, house 133 Boston
Trask Israel, shoemaker, house Pingree, near Harbor
Trask James, letter carrier, house 22 Howard
Trask Joseph, mariner, house 30 Hathorne
Trask Moses A. mariner, house 40 St. Peter

Trask Nancy, assistant at S. O. and C. F. Society, 7 Carpenter
Trask Thomas, house 135 Essex
Trask William, laborer, house 40 St. Peter
Tray David, currier, house Broad
Trayers Ann, widow, house rear 28 North
Trayers Patrick, currier, boards 80 Boston
Trayers William, currier, house 13 Lynn
Treadwell Nathaniel R. currier, rear 9 Mason, house 18 Barr
Treadwell Thomas, cabinet maker, house Southwick
Trefren James, shoe manufacturer, 15½ St. Peter, h. 8 Federal
Trefry John, baggage master, house 23 High
Trofatter Amos L. bookkeeper (B.), house 18 Albion
Trofatter Charles H. shoe stiffening manuf. 5 Beaver, h. 10 do.
Trofatter John H. agent, house 9 Upham
Trofatter Sarah, house 371 Essex
Trofatter Robert, tanner, house 18 Albion
Trofatter Sam'l J. shoe stiffening manuf. r. 10 Beaver, h. 10 do.
True Abraham Mrs. house 12 Brown
True Joseph, carver, 42 Mill, house 5 High
Trull Charles W. shoemaker, boards 12 Ward
Trull Frederick, shoemaker, house 12 Ward
Trull Frederick A. painter, boards 12 Ward
Trull Nathaniel W. mariner, boards 12 Ward
Trumbull Charles W. Mrs. house 6 Hardy
Trumbull Edward H. merchant, Central wf. h. 18 Winter
Tucker Gideon, house 133 Essex
Tucker Jonathan, assessor City Hall, house 29 Andrew
Tucker Lucy C. Mrs. house 25 Turner
Tucker Mary, widow, boards 10 Beaver
Tucker Samuel, fisherman, house 4 Bridge
Tuckerman J. Francis, merchant (B.), house 41 Chestnut
Tufts Charles H. coachpainter, 23 Endicott, h. 31 Norman
Tufts Horace, captain, house 5 Elm
Tufts Nathaniel, tailor, house 90 Federal
Tufts Richard Palmer, saddler, 137 Boston, house 150 do.
Tufts Rufus, clerk, 20 Front, boards 65 Lafayette
Tufts Sam'l C. provisions and groceries, 47 Derby, h. 20 Hardy
Tufts Sarah Mrs. nurse, house 15 High st. court
Tufts William, mariner, house 5 Elm
Tufts William, house 4 Cherry
Turrell Benjamin F. baker, 89 Essex, house do.
Turner Calvin, tanner, 4 Goodhue, house 66 Boston
Turner Charles W. tanner, house 69 Boston
Turner Elisha W. teamster, house Hanson
Turner George, shipwright, house 16 Ward
Turner James H. measurer of leather, house 66 Boston
Turner Margaret H. house 8 Central

Tuttle Ebenezer, currier, house 11 Boston
Tuttle Eunice E. house 11 River
Tuttle Francis W. *(Hammond & T.)*, dry goods, 167 Essex, house 6 Hathorne
Tuttle Henry A. (Cal.), house r. 14 Webb
Tuttle Henry C. physician, house 165 Federal
Tuttle Henry G. provisions, 36 Boston, h. 8 North Pine
Tuttle Hiram A. *(Whitney & T.)* carriage trimmer, West pl. h. 8 Cross
Tuttle John, livery stable, 191 Federal, house 183 do.
Tuttle John E. machinist (B), house 7 Pleasant
Tuttle John B. house 36 Derby
Tuttle Mary D. house 11 River
Tuttle Mary E. widow, house 16 Oliver
Tuttle Nathaniel, currier, 21 Boston, house 19 do.
Tuttle Wm. leather (8 Blackstone, B.), house 183 Federal
Twist Joseph C. jr. shoemaker, house 15 Lemon
Twombly E. Mrs. dressmaker, 250½ Essex
Tyler Abel H. shoemaker, h. North, n. S. Danvers line
Tyler George F. currier, house 6 Orne
Tyler Moses C. shoemaker, house 6 Nursery
Tyler Sarah A. Mrs. house 7 Cherry
Tyler Wesley, shoemaker, house foot of Northey

UPHAM ANN M. widow, house 17 Dean
Upham Benjamin N. chemist, house 70 Upham
Upham Charles W. house 52 Washington
Upham Charles W. jr. house 52 Washington
Upham Franklin, chemist, rear 70 North
Upham Joshua Mrs. house 17 Dean
Upham Joshua, chemist, laboratory, house r. 70 North
Upham Wm. P. boards 52 Washington
Upton Anna M. teacher, boards 59 Essex
Upton Benjamin Mrs. house 31 Pleasant
Upton Charles, captain, house 6 Liberty
Upton Charles H. mariner, house 39 Bridge
Upton Daniel, bookkeeper, 26 Washington, house 31 Pleasant
Upton Eben, musician, house 31 Barr
Upton Eben Mrs. house 108 North, cor. Orne
Upton Edmund, captain, house 5 Saunders
Upton Edward, tanner and currier, boards 31 Pleasant
Upton Edwin, captain, house 26 Winter
Upton Ezra, provision dealer, 2 Mill, house 4 do.
Upton Ezra W. job printer, 191 Essex, house 7 Gedney ct.
Upton Francis, music teacher, house 31 Pleasant
Upton Franklin, tinplate worker, house 8 Prescott
Upton George, captain, house 8 Liberty

SALEM [V] DIRECTORY.

Upton George L. carpenter, boards 5 Saunders
Upton George W. clerk, 2 Mill, house 4 do.
Upton Henry, boatman, Custom House, h. 9 Liberty
Upton Henry O. gasfitter, boards 108 North
Upton Henry P. merchant (B.), house 69 Essex
Upton James, merchant, 63 Union, house 100 Bridge
Upton Jesse, boards 29 Buffum
Upton Joseph, captain, house 13 Saunders
Upton Moses T. carpenter, 7 Walnut, house 67½ Essex
Upton Paul, captain, house 3 Hamilton
Upton Robert, merchant, 63 Union, house 26 Winter
Upton Samuel Mrs. house 39 Bridge
Upton Stephen, captain, house 124 Bridge
Upton Wm. B. clerk, 221 Essex, boards 4 Mill
Upton William F. captain, house 39 Bridge
Upton William M. cooper, house 10 Becket

VALENTINE B. E. MRS. house 54 Federal
Valentine Elmer, teacher at Marblehead, house 4 Ash
Vanderford Benjamin F. engineer, house 109 Boston
Vanderford Elizabeth Mrs. house 7 Lemon
Van Hagan James, tinsmith, house rear 8 Cherry
Varney Daniel *(W., D., & S. Varney)*, house 71 Boston
Varney D. Augustus, shoe dealer (B.), house 71 Boston
Varney Eliza L. Mrs. house 1 English
Varney Solomon, house 113 Boston
Varney Solomon jr. *(W., D., & S. Varney)*. house 83 Boston
Varney W., D. & S. *(William, Daniel, & Solomon jr.)*, curriers, 82 Boston
Varney Wm. *(W., D., & S. Varney)*, house 78 Boston
Varney William H. (141 Pearl, B.), house 14 Crombie
Veal Mary Mrs. house 16 English
Vent Eben, watchman, house 78 Mill
Vent Mary Mrs. vestmaker, house 10 Barton
Vent Sarah, house 86 Mill
Verrill Lydia, widow, house 28 High
Very Abraham, sexton, house 21 Summer
Very Abraham A. mariner, house 21 Summer
Very Albert, shoemaker, boards 59 North
Very Augustus, shoemaker, house 59 North
Very Edwin, musician, house 7 Dearborn
Very Ephraim P. trader, 5 Boston, b. Mansion House
Very Frances E. teacher, house 154 Federal
Very Harriet, teacher, house 1 Hardy
Very Herbert, clerk, 55 Harbor, boards 53 do.
Very Isaac, mariner, house 21 Summer
Very John F. laborer, house 1 N. Pine

Very Jones Rev. house 154 Federal
Very Joseph, trader, house 14 Fowler
Very Lydia Mrs. house 154 Federal
Very Lydia L. A. teacher, house 154 Federal
Very Martha, widow, house 91 Boston
Very Martha N. teacher private school, house 78 Federal
Very Mary, house 17 Crombie
Very Nathaniel, shipsmith, house 11 Turner
Very Nathaniel jr. cabinet maker, 274 Essex, h. 45½ North
Very Nathaniel A. clerk, 243 Essex, house 45 North
Very Nathaniel O. clerk, 113 Derby, boards 11 Turner
Very Samuel, gum copal works, house 57 Bridge
Vickery Thomas, seaman, house 22 Forrester
Victorato Constantine, bowling saloon, rear 14½ Front, house 9 Lagrange
Vincent Amos L. mast and spar maker, r. 41 Derby, h. 59 do.
Vincent Harriet F. nurse, house 59 Derby
Vincent John, house 59 Derby
Vincent Letitia Mrs. tailoress, house 12 Essex
Vincent William B. (B.), house 20 Pleasant
Vivuan Joseph, house 22 Becket
Vivuan Wilmot, carpenter, house 97 Bridge
Vollor Benj. house 3 F. R. L. Mills
Vollor Henry, tanner, house 60 Broad
Voorhees Lewis D. D. captain, house 17 Williams

WAKEFIELD ELIZA, house 12 Daniels
Wagner Daniel, currier, house 32 Buffum
Waitt Moses B. tailor, house 2 May street court
Walcott Benjamin P. house 77 Lafayette
Walcott Samuel B. Mrs. house 77 Lafayette
Walden Joseph F. currier, 48 Boston, house 176 Federal
Walden Nancy P. widow, house 148 Federal
Walden Wm. W. P. currier, boards 148 Federal
Walder Thomas, mariner, house 14 Daniels
Walker Abbott, merchant, house 301 Essex
Walker Abbott jr. boards 301 Essex
Walker George S. boards 301 Essex
Walker Mary Mrs. house 15 Church
Walker Mary Mrs. tailoress, house 15 High st. court
Walker Mary M. *(Morrill & W.)*, millinery, 217 Essex, house 15 Church
Walker Parker D. carpenter, 7 Boston, house 57 Endicott
Walker Samuel L. tanner, house rear 14 Hathorne
Walker Wm. tanner, boards 15 Friend
Wall James, currier, boards Edmund Cassin's   [Church
Wallace Thomas, physician and apothecary, 9 Wash. house 18

Wallis Eunice, house 2 Hamilton
Wallis Francis F. pilot, house 15 Essex
Wallis Jane Mrs. house 15 Park
Wallis Joseph, cabinet maker and furniture dealer, 205½ Essex, house 28 Lafayette
Wallis Patrick, coachman at the Derby farm
Wallis Wm. secretary Salem Savings Bank, h. 23 Summer
Walsh Francis, shoemaker, house rear 24 Northey
Walsh Hannah Mrs. house rear 218 Essex
Walsh Robert, painter, house 16 Flint
Walton Ebenezer, grocer, 89 Mason, house do.
Walton Eben N. 185 Essex, house 6 Herbert
Walton Edward, boards 9 Aborn
Walton George D. butcher, house 1 Aborn
Walton George M. carpenter, house r. 9 Aborn
Walton Joseph, cigarbox maker, 147 Boston, house 145 do.
Walton Joseph A. carpenter, house 16 Sewall
Walton Josiah, house 8 Beaver
Walton Josiah jr. blacksmith, 131 Boston, house 9 Aborn
Walton Naomi L. farmer, house Ord
Walton Thomas, blacksmith, boards 9 Aborn
Walton Timothy, farmer, house 161 Boston
Walton Wm. J. shoedealer (Danvers), house r. 9 Aborn
Ward Alfred A. provisions, 15 and 16 Market House, h. at S. Danvers
Ward Andrew, merchant, house 123 Federal
Ward Andrew A. mariner, house 12 Elm
Ward Charles, merchant, house 14 North
Ward Chipman, deputy collector Custom House, house rear 101 Lafayette
Ward Israel Mrs. house 4 Pickman
Ward Israel Mrs. sen. house 77 Summer
Ward James, laborer, house 21 Salem
Ward James, captain, house 9 Carlton
Ward Jonathan O. 15 Market House, house at S. Danvers
Ward Joshua Mrs. house 8 Central
Ward Louisa H. Mrs. dressmaker, house 18 Andrew
Ward Lucy Mrs. house 8 River
Ward L. Pierson, mariner, house 4 Pickman
Ward Malvina T. Mrs. house 34 Chestnut
Ward Mary Mrs. house 19 Herbert
Ward Sarah A. millinery, 278 Essex, house 54 Mill
Ward Wm. H. house 11 Pond (Cal.)
Wardwell Esther A. Mrs. h. Phelps ct. cor. Jackson place
Wardwell John, carpenter, house 40 Broad
Wardwell John S. watchman, house 20 Hathorne
Wardwell Nath'l A. shoemaker, h. Phelps ct. cor. Jackson pl.

Ware Alfred F. farmer, house Salem turnpike
Ware Erastus D. farmer, house Salem turnpike
Ware Horace, farmer, house Salem turnpike
Ware Horace C. farmer, house Salem turnpike
Ware Mary, nurse, at H. Ware's, Salem turnpike
Ware William, overseer, Naumkeag Mill, h. 67 Harbor
Warner Caleb, spectacles, 3 Central, house 92 Federal
Warner Edward L. baker, house 4 Mason
Warner Ellen, widow, house 10 Park
Warner Elizabeth G. widow, house 4 Pickman
Warner John V. cooper, boards 4 Mason
Warner Joseph A. carpenter, house 164 Boston
Warner William, clerk (Cal.), boards 4 Church
Warner William F. laborer, house 4 Endicott
Warren George H. carpenter, house 20 Northey
Warren Hannah Mrs. house 8 Hardy
Warren John, at the Laboratory, house Union place
Warren Levi S. principal Epes School, house Prescott
Warshoer Simon, embroideries and trimmings, 146 Essex, h. 33 Brown
Wasgatt Betsey M. widow, house 57 Mill
Washington John S. laborer, house 54 Forrester
Waters Andrew S. copper founder, 6 Franklin, h. 54 North
Waters Andrew S. jr. mariner, boards 54 North
Waters Arthur, umbrella maker, house 88 Derby
Waters Charles R. house 70 Derby
Waters David P. house 14 Cambridge
Waters Eben, coppersmith, house 5 Mason
Waters Edward, mariner, boards 2 Essex
Waters Henry F. G. instructor Franklin building, h. 70 Derby
Waters James D. clerk (B.), boards 6 Pleasant
Waters John, carpenter, house 2 Essex
Waters John Mrs. house 5 Mason
Waters John jr. house 5 Franklin
Waters John G. merchant, house 14 Cambridge
Waters Joseph G. judge Police Court, 150 Essex, h. 70 Derby
Waters Mary, widow, house rear 19 Daniels
Waters Richard P. merchant, 182 Essex, house Cherry Hill, Beverly
Waters Thomas S. shoe manufacturer, 31 Endicott, h. 5 Mason
Waters Lucy, widow of Wm. house Milk, cor. Andrew
Waters Wm. C. house 15 Chestnut
Waters Wm. D. merchant (B.), house 6 Pleasant
Watson Daniel P. currier, house 41 Boston
Watson Edwin P. clerk, 121 Essex, house 10 Turner
Watson Elizabeth R. milliner, house 412 Essex
Watson Fenton, saddler, 414 Essex, house 412 do.

Watson John, mariner, house 10 Turner
Watson Lucy F. teacher, house 412 Essex
Watson Mary Mrs. house 412 Essex
Watson Mary, teacher, house 412 Essex
Watson Otis, saddler, house 412 Essex
Watson Thomas R. coachman, 212 Essex, house rear do.
Watts Charles, baker, 53 Derby, house do.
Weatherdon Grace, widow, house 8 Nursery
Webb Augustine F. clerk, 154 Essex, boards 27 Brown
Webb Benjamin, merchant, Webb's wharf, house 100 Essex
Webb Benjamin jr. clerk, 54 Essex, house 52 do.
Webb Hannah, house 14 Carlton
Webb Hannah, house 8 Hardy
Webb Harriet Mrs. house 9 English
Webb Henry, mason, house rear 22 Hardy
Webb Henry jr. clerk at Mansion House
Webb John F. merchant, boards Essex House
Webb John K. merchant tailor, 197 Essex, house 22 Lynde
Webb Joseph Mrs. house 27 Brown
Webb Joseph B. merchant, Webb's wharf, house 100 Essex
Webb Joseph H. bookkeeper, Exchange Bank, h. 27 Brown
Webb Lydia, boards 98 Federal
Webb Margaret E. teacher, house 7 Curtis
Webb Mary E. teacher, Normal School, h. 27 Brown
Webb Samuel, house 11 Pickman
Webb Stephen, house 81 Essex
Webb Stephen P. counsellor, 159½ Essex, h. 7 Summer
Webb Thomas, shoecutter, house 10 Allen
Webb William, apothecary, 54 Essex, house 52 do.
Webb Wm. jr. Mrs. house 7 Curtis
Webb William jr. clerk, 54 Essex, house 52 do.
Webb Wm. T. laborer, house 8 Webb
Webber George, ropemaker, house foot of Northey
Webber Ira J. conductor on S. R. R. R. house 90 North
Webber John, shoemaker, house 31 Bridge
Webster Abigail Mrs. house 8 Ash
Webster Caleb A. house 1 Rust
Webster Catharine Mrs. house 8 Ash
Webster Edward C. hats, caps, & furs, 225 Essex, cor. Wash. h. Summer, cor. Margin
Webster Elizabeth, widow, house 51 St. Peter
Webster Gardner, tinsmith, 135 Boston, house 32 Beaver
Webster John, treasurer Newmarket Manufacturing Co. 17 Asiatic building, house 73 Lafayette
Webster John C. grocer, 4 Newbury & 116 Essex, h. 51 St. Peter
Webster Louisa S. F. Mrs. house 28 Beckford
Webster Mary Mrs. house 163 Boston

Weed Dan, counsellor, 224 Essex, house at N. Andover
Weeks Alpheus, engineer, house 99 Bridge
Weeks Betsey, widow, house 8 Dearborn
Weeks Dudley C. engineer, house 147 Bridge
Weeks Francis S. books and stationery, 188 Essex, h. 15 Hardy
Weeks Wm. gardener, house Leach
Weeks William, carpenter, house 8 Dearborn
Weeks Wm. H. carpenter, boards 8 Dearborn
Weir Alexander, japanner, house Adams
Weir Daniel P. blacksmith, house 24 Liberty
Weir Henry, house Adams, Mason Hill
Weir Kate, widow, house Adams, Mason Hill
Welch Aaron, farmer, house Neck
Welch Ann, widow, house foot of Pingree
Welch Catharine, widow, house Phillips, n. Grove
Welch Charles L. captain, house 5 Becket
Welch Edward, tanner, house rear 67 Mason
Welch Ellen Mrs. house 105 North
Welch James, laborer, house 36 Mill
Welch James, currier, house 15 Flint
Welch James, currier, house 411 Essex
Welch John, laborer, house 92 Derby
Welch John, laborer, house 86 Derby
Welch John, laborer, house 24 Peabody
Welch John, house 4 Orne
Welch Lawrence, boards rear 18 Lafayette
Welch Margaret, house Pingree
Welch Mary Mrs. house 22 Daniels
Welch Mary Mrs. house 21 Ward
Welch Michael, laborer, house 93 Derby
Welch Michael, moulder, house S. Prospect, n. Pingree
Welch Michael, laborer, house 14 Peabody
Welch Patrick, bootmaker, house 14 Ward
Welch Patrick, currier, house 7 Prospect
Welch Patrick, shoemaker, boards 59 Harbor
Welch Sarah Mrs. house 7 Cross
Welch Thomas, currier, house Green place
Welch Timothy, laborer, house 19 Daniels
Welch Walter, laborer, house 9 Congress
Welch Walter, laborer, house 28 Ward
Welch William, mariner, house 6 Turner
Welch Wm. 3 Market House, house r. 18 Lafayette
Wellman Abigail Mrs. house 82 Essex
Wellman George O. tanner, house 24 Barr
Wellman Jacob, house 20 Union
Wellman Samuel, mariner, house 14 Prescott
Wellman Timothy, shoemaker, boards 101 North

Wells George A. clerk, 54 Derby, boards 22 Hardy
Wells George W. machinist, boards 19 Saunders
Wells James, grocer, Spring, cor. Webb, h. 19 Saunders
Wells John, gum copal worker, house 22 Hardy
Wells Lucius *(S. Driver & Co.)*, shoe manuf. 16 Washington, house 22 Liberty
Wells William G. clerk (B.), boards 22 Liberty
Wentworth George G. teamster, boards 25 Cedar
Wentworth John, laborer, house 9 Park
Wentworth *(Lewis E.)* & Fifield *(C. H.)*, stoves and furnaces, 15 St. Peter, house 35 Lafayette
Wentworth Samuel, captain, house 4 Curtis
Wentworth Thomas, captain, house 57 Harbor
Wentzell David, farmer, house Orne
West Benj. A. merchant, 218 Derby, house 74 Lafayette
West Betsey, widow, house 120 Lafayette
West Elizabeth, widow, house 125 Essex
West Elizabeth, widow, house 68 Essex
West George, farmer, 120 Lafayette
West George, currier, boards 6 N. Pine
West George jr. Mrs. house 57 Forrester
West John, farmer, house 120 Lafayette
West Mary, house 23 North
West Rebecca Mrs. house 80 Lafayette
West Samuel, house 74 Lafayette
West Wm. H. farmer, house 4 Leach
Weston Charles & Sons *(Thomas F., Charles H., & John W. Weston)*, tanners and curriers, May, house 30 Boston
Weston Charles H. *(Charles Weston & Sons)*, boards 30 Boston
Weston Edward, captain, house 7 Williams
Weston Eliza Mrs. house 3 Hardy
Weston Elizabeth, teacher, Norman School, b. 6 Federal
Weston John, mariner, house 13 Allen
Weston John W. machinist, rear May, boards 30 Boston
Weston Nathaniel, merchant, house 9 Brown
Weston Nathaniel jr. clerk, 13 Front, house 9 Brown
Weston Phineas R. paper and paper stock, 164 Derby, house 46 Essex
Weston Robert (Cal.), house 9 May
Weston Thomas F. *(C. Weston & Sons)*, house 30 Boston
Whalan Michael, laborer, house 432 Essex
Whalan William, peddler, house 7 Charter
Whalen John, currier, house 432 Essex
Whartey Michael, laborer, house 89 North
Whartey Patrick, laborer, house 38 Federal
Whartey Peter, house 89 North (Cal.)
Whealton John, laborer, house 21 High

Wheatland Benjamin Mrs. house 136 Federal
Wheatland George, counsellor, 1 Market ct. house 374 Essex
Wheatland Henry, physician, house 21 Chestnut
Wheatland Richard, house 358 Essex
Wheatland Richard H. physician, house 374 Essex
Wheatland Simeon J. porter, 173 Essex, house ft. Northey
Wheatland Stephen G. counsellor, 194 Essex, house 374 do.
Wheatland William R. tanner, house 358 Essex
Wheeler Asa Mrs. house 53 Endicott
Wheeler Benjamin S. provisions, 1 and 2 Market House, house at South Danvers
Wheeler John, city watchman, house 28 Dearborn
Wheeler John H. shoemaker, boards 28 Dearborn
Wheeler Joseph, clerk, 135 Derby, house 26 Essex
Wheeler Michael S. Mrs. house 26 Essex
Wheeler Richard P. 5 & 6 Market Ho. house 53 Endicott
Wheeler Samuel B. clerk, 24 Front, boards 26 Essex
Wheeler William H. coachman, house 18 Fowler
Whiley Robert, mariner, house rear 41 Derby
Whipple Albert (S. Whipple & Brothers), house 45 Essex
Whipple Charles J. teller (Traders' Bank, B.), house 2 Andover
Whipple George M. (Henry Whipple & Son), 190 Essex, house 2 Andover
Whipple Henry & Son (George M. Whipple), books, charts, and stationery, 190 Essex, h. 2 Andover
Whipple H. G. boards 31 Turner
Whipple John, house 31 Turner
Whipple John H. sailmaker, Phillips wf. house 26 Hardy
Whipple J. Lovett (S. Whipple & Brothers), h. 47 Essex
Whipple Stephen & Brothers (Albert & J. L. Whipple), gum, copal works, 35 Turner, house 12 Hardy
Whipple Wm. H. bookkeeper, Merchants' Bank, h. 2 Andover
Whitaker Wm. carpenter, 222 Derby, boards 196 do.
Whitcomb Jared P. grocer, 22 Boston, house do.
White Benjamin R. mason, St. Peter's court, h. 62 Washington
White Christopher, laborer, house 10 River
White Daniel A. pres. Salem Savings Bank, h. 46 Washington
White Elizabeth, widow, house 111 Boston
White Franklin & Co. grocers, 56 Harbor, boards 70 do.
White George F. Mrs. house Linden, near Holly
White James, laborer, house 10 River
White John, musician and daguerreotypist, house 73 North
White Mary Ann, widow, house rear 8 Allen
White Thomas, hostler, 212 Essex, house 15 Ash
White William, laborer, house 43 Union
White William H. shoemaker, house 14 Upham
Whitford Mary, tailoress, house 8 Church

Whitmore Anna, teacher, house 73 Bridge
Whitmore Stephen, house 73 Bridge
Whitmore William W. house 73 Bridge
Whitney *(Richard S.)* & Tuttle *(H.A.)*, carriage trimmers and harness makers, West place, house 43 Lafayette
Whitney William W. teamster, 198 Derby, h. 18 Park
Whittemore Samuel, house 1 Whittemore
Whittemore Samuel 2d, shoemaker, house 15 Essex
Whittier Charles C. stonecutter, 18 Lafayette, h. 12 Harbor
Whittredge Thomas C. Mrs. house 179 Federal
Wiedeman Ado, physician, 1 Central, corner Essex
Wiessberger Leopold, cigars, 2 Phœnix building, h. 41 Lafayette
Wiggin Abigail Mrs. house 1 Federal
Wiggin Asa, teamster, at J. Dike & Co.'s, house 76 Summer
Wiggin Benj. T. shoemaker, 38 North, boards 29 Buffum
Wiggin Edward P. clerk, 152 Essex, boards 61 Lafayette
Wiggin George F. police officer, house 18 English
Wiggin Joseph W. tailor, house 28 Williams
Wiggin Levi, provisions, 12 Newbury, h. 28 Howard
Wiggin *(Nath'l)* & Clark *(Chas.S.)*, wood, coal, &c. 29 Peabody, house 48 Endicott
Wiggin Patrick, laborer, house 27 Daniels
Wiggin Peirce L. house 9 Daniels
Wiggin Sarah B. seamstress, house 1 Federal
Wiggin Thomas Mrs. house 7 Elm
Wiggin Thomas H. shoemaker, house 7 Elm
Wiggins Augustine, cabinet maker, house 5 Saunders
Wight Carrie P. milliner, 169 Essex, boards 20 Norman
Wihr Lawrence W. variety store, 52 Endicott, house do.
Wiley John G. carpenter, house 21 Cedar
Wiley Mary, widow, house 6 Prince
Wiley Moses, mariner, house 44 Harbor
Wiley William E. 14½ Front, boards 44 Harbor
Wilkins Albert, tanner, 50 Boston, house 157 Federal
Wilkins Albert jr. currier, house 2 Beaver court
Wilkins Almira, house 22 School   [15 Williams
Wilkins Charles, blacksmith and horseshoer, 28 Liberty, house
Wilkins Charles F. currier, boards 15 Williams
Wilkins Charles R. captain, house 18 Hardy
Wilkins Hezekiah, mariner, house 6 Bentley
Wilkins Hezekiah jr. varnish maker, house 12 Carlton
Wilkins Jason, carpenter, 112 Essex, house 12 Lemon
Wilkins John G. house 92 Boston
Wilkins John H. 111 Essex, house 9 Northey
Wilkins John H. tanner, house 92 Boston
Wilkins Michael, baker, house 2 Beaver court
Wilkins Rufus P. painter, house 92 Boston

SALEM [W] DIRECTORY.

Willard Josiah, watchmaker, 179 Essex, h. 27 Endicott
Willard Ora H. currier, house 14 Fowler
Willett George A. brakeman, E. R. R. house 80 Mill
Willey George E. engineer, house 47 Federal
Willey James L. cabinet maker, house 13 Gardner court
Willey Hollous, shoemaker, boards 20 Conant
Willey Mark L. shoemaker, house 31 Hardy
Willey Samuel, cabinet maker, house 14 March
Willey William, captain, house 28 Howard
Williams Abraham, laborer, house 53 Forrester   [Salem
Williams Andrew, hairdresser, 5 Arrington's building, house 38
Williams Charles F. captain, house 5 Monroe
Williams Charles H. boards 108 Federal
Williams Elizabeth C. Miss, tailoress, house 4 St. Peter court
Williams George Mrs. house rear 59 Warren
Williams Hannah Mrs. fancy cake baker, h. 4 Creek
Williams Henry L. merchant (31 Kilby, B.), h. 342 Essex
Williams Hiram F. cooper, house 4 Herbert
Williams Israel, gum copal worker, house 16 Carlton
Williams John jr. freightman, house 15 Becket
Williams John H. carpenter, head of Phillips wharf, b. 15 Becket
Williams John S. Mrs. house 3 Federal court
Williams Mary A. Mrs. cook, house 15 Pond   [Lafayette
Williams Mary E. teacher of drawing, 243½ Essex, house 126
Williams Remember, widow, house 8 High
Williams Thomas, mariner, house 15 Essex
Williams Thomas Mrs. house 36 Salem
Williams Thomas F. laborer, house 8 Porter
Williams Thos. Jefferson, shoemaker, boards 89 North
Williams Urban R. currier, Prospect, house Summit
Williams William, physician, 110 Federal, house 108 do.
Williams William, varnisher, house 14 Conant
Williams William O. boards 108 Federal
Williamson Thomas H. cooper, house 84 Derby
Willis George G. painter, house 16 Oliver
Willis John, captain, house 16 Oliver
Willis John G. clerk, house 38 Lafayette
Williston John F. mariner, house 51 Mill
Williston Samuel P. house 18½ Beckford
Williston Samuel S. sawfiler, 60 Charter, house do.
Willoughby Charles D. gaiter boot fitter, house 9 Spring
Wilson Edward, mariner, house 112 Bridge
Wilson Edward, clothier, 247 Essex, house 47 St. Peter
Wilson Edward H. clerk, 209 Essex, boards 112 Bridge
Wilson Frederick, mariner, house 16 Daniels
Wilson George W. ship carpenter, house 28 Essex
Wilson Hugh, gardener, house Hamilton, near Essex

Wilson Jabez, hosiery manuf. 7 North, house do.
Wilson Jacob, mariner, house 32 Bridge
Wilson James, laborer, house 152 Derby
Wilson John O. Mrs. house 10 Upham
Wilson Mary Mrs. house 22 Brown
Wilson Mary, widow, house 188 Derby
Wilson Mary, widow, house 17 North
Wilson Oliver, carpenter, h. Lafayette, n. F. R. Lead Mills
Wilson Priscilla, widow, boards 45 Broad
Wilson Thomas C. mariner, house 12 Cedar
Winberry Thomas, provisions, 7½ Boston, house do.
Winchester Isaac, stairbuilder, 42 Charter, h. Green place
Winchester Jacob, house 97 Boston
Winn Benjamin, brewer, Front, corner Washington
Winn Daniel D. Rev. house 179 Federal
Winn John D. currier, house 44 Buffum
Winn John K. currier, house 44 Buffum
Winn Joseph, house 121 Federal
Winn Joseph R. Mrs. house 57 Lafayette
Winn Mehitable, widow, house 8 Bentley
Winn Silas B. brewer, Front, cor. Washington, house 5 Pond
Winslow Clarissa, widow, house 120 North
Winslow Joshua, tinsmith, house 120 North
Winsor Frederick, physician, house 14 Brown
Winters Lawrence, house Perkins
Wise George H. confectioner, 271 Essex, house 269 do.
Wise Mary D. widow, house 15 Lynde
Witham Susan S. Mrs watcher, house Turner
Wogan James, coachman, 204 Essex
Wood Allen, shoemaker, house 47 Broad
Wood Andrew P. Mrs. house 13 Warren
Wood George, shoemaker, house 78 North
Wood George E. brakeman, boards 20 Norman
Wood J. G. physician, 265 Essex, house 26 Lynde
Wood Leonard S. at Laboratory, house 120 North
Wood Lydia, widow, house 107 North
Wood Marion, teacher, primary school, house 107 North
Wood William P. shoemaker, house 14 Norman
Woodberry Larkin, coffin and casketware house, 3 Sewall
Woodbury Charles, mason, house 4 Woodbury's court
Woodbury Edmund, wheelwright, house rear 95 Boston
Woodbury Ezra, carpenter, 126 Bridge, house 15 Northey
Woodbury Isaiah Mrs. house 14 Northey
Woodbury Isaiah, clerk (B.), boards 14 Northey
Woodbury James, tanner, h. 18 Whittemore, c. Dearborn
Woodbury John E. mariner, house 4 Woodbury's court
Woodbury Lydia Mrs. house 11 Northey

SALEM [Z] DIRECTORY.

Woodbury Nathaniel A. clerk (B.), boards 14 Northey
Woodbury Susan Mrs. house 19 Northey
Woodbury Misses, house 16 School
Woodford Edward, teacher, rear 161 Essex, h. at Swampscott
Woodman Mary E. Miss, millinery goods, 31 Lafayette
Woodward Eliza A. boarding house, 23 Boston
Woods Ephraim, horticulturist, house 122 North
Woods Eunice, widow, house 122 North
Woodward E. S. milliner, 252½ Essex, boards 29 Brown
Worcester Elizabeth, widow, house 19 Boston
Worcester Jonathan F. house 31 Pleasant
Worcester Samuel M. Rev. D. D. house 6 Carpenter
Works John C., L. R. Road, house 9 Mason
Worley Timothy, laborer, house 20 Carlton
Worling Edward, laborer, house 17 North court
Worling William Mrs. house 17 North court
Wormell Catharine, widow, house 49 Derby
Wright David, fish, 20 Lafayette, house Porter court
Wright David A. shoemaker, boards Porter court
Wright John, shoemaker, house 44 Broad
Wright Peter E. provisions, 50½ Derby, house 42 Essex
Wright William, coachman, 51 Washington
Wyman Charles L. shoemaker, house 14 Ward
Wyman Isaac, counsellor, house Lafayette, n. Marblehead line
Wyman Matilda F. variety store, 23 St. Peter, h. 1 Church
Wyman Theodore L. carpenter, house 29 Williams
Wyman William W. house Lafayette, near Marblehead line

YASINSKI EDMUND A. cigar maker, boards 55 Derby
York Daniel, laborer, house Rubber Factory, Ward
Young Aaron C. carpenter, house 7 Spring
Young Eunice, widow, house 7 Spring
Young Stephen, mason, house 95 Lafayette
Young William, mariner, house Salem, cor. Dow

ZIMMERMAN JOHN A. tobacconist, 35 Wash. h. 22 Lemon

BUSINESS DIRECTORY

OF THE

CITY OF SALEM,

In which the Professions and Trades are Alphabetically Arranged.

Agricultural Tools.
Adams, Richardson & Co. 207 Essex
Farless James A. 186 Essex
Hale Henry, 215 Essex

Ambrotypes & Photographs.
Fullerton J. W. 224 Essex
Moulton J. W. 214 Essex
Perkins E. R. 241 Essex
Snell William, 208 Essex

Apothecaries.
Barton Gardner, 124 Essex
Brooks W. A. 33½ Lafayette
Browne & Price, 226 Essex
Chamberlain Chas. 138 Derby
Chamberlain J. W. 1 Boston
Emerton James, 123 Essex
Farrington Geo. P. 310 Essex
Millett Needham C. 39 North
Pinkham Charles H. 288 Essex
Pratt Henry J. 141 Essex
Putnam George, 275 Essex
Stone James jr. 40 Broad
Wallace Thomas, 9 Washington
Webb William, 54 Essex

Architects and Engineers.
mmerton & Foster, 26 Asiatic bdg.
Putnam Charles A. 251 Essex

Artist.
Derby Mary, 4 Blaney

Auctioneers.
Archer William jr. 34 Front, and 18 Washington
Colman Benj. 9 Derby sq.
Glazier Ezra, Charter, c. Central
Nichols George, 42 Washington
Parker G. A. 30 Front

Bakers.
Ball William, 22 Central
Brown Daniel, 10 Mill
Byrne C. 162 Boston
Eaton N. J. 29 Brown
Fowler Edwin K. 36 St. Peter
Gardner Simon, 24 Turner
Goss Richard G. 87 North
Hathaway E. 68 Washington
Jelly Charles H. 10 Cedar
Pease & Price, 13 High
Preston John, 53 Summer
Sanger Edward H. 416 Essex
Stow & Tibbetts, head Phillips wf.
Thompson George J. 28 Broad
Turell B. F. 89 Essex
Watts Charles, 53 Derby
Williams H. Mrs. 4 Creek

Bark Mills.
Frye Joseph S., Goodhue
Hanson E. A. 13 Grove

Bathing.
Rust Horace, 148 Bridge

Blacksmiths.
Agge Jacob, 51 Harbor
Andrews Gilman, 27 Beach
Brooking Thomas, 21 Mason
Church Samuel, 5 Laboratory
Cox F. R., Bridge, corner North
Cutts Benjamin, 8 Sewall
Cutts Richard, Endicott, c. Mill
Goodell A. C. & Son, 16 Lafayette
Goodhue J. B. 3 Cambridge
Nichols John, 45 Union (*shipsmith*)
Peirson George H., West place
Perry Francis L., Phillips wharf
Raymond A. A. 35 North
Symonds Dean C. 35 North
Walton Josiah jr. 131 Boston
Wilkins Charles, 28 Liberty

Boot and Shoe Dealers.
Ashby J. J. 276 Essex
Averell & Low, 76 Boston
Bancroft James B. 108 Boston
Bancroft T. S. 108 Boston

SALEM DIRECTORY. 197

Barlow John 149 Essex
Bosson & Glover, 14 Lafayette
Bott Thomas, 46 Derby
Buswell Eben, 196 Essex
Chapman William H. 210 Essex
Driver S. & Son, 16 Washington and 34½ Front (*manuf. Ladies'*)
Ferguson T. B. 2½ Norman
Flint Harrison O. 210 Essex
Gomes Joseph, 10 Lafayette
Goodwin E 56 Derby
Henderson S. 21 St. Peter
Hubbard J. George, 246 Essex
Lee George W. 291 Essex
Nicholson T. jr. 164 Essex
O'Connell Timothy, 5 Central
Palmer Theron, 216 Essex
Perkins & Brown, 137 Derby
Perley John, 252 Essex
Plummer M. J. 161 Essex
Richardson Jeremiah, 213 Essex
Sweetser Ephraim, 239 Essex

Boot and Shoe Makers.

Ashby R. R. 21½ Salem
Barnes Joseph, Bridge, c. Williams
Beadle Josiah, 3 Lemon
Bowman James, 5 Endicott
Bryant J. Johnson, 27 Norman
Butler John S. 10 Boston
Carty J. H. on Union Bridge
Collins Thomas, 107 Derby
Dodge Wm. M. 3 Lemon
Farrell Robert, 7 Congress
Gillespie J. 34 Boston
Hay J. A. 35 Brown
Hubbard J. Geo. 246 Essex (*manuf.*)
Janes Edwin, 3 Pond
Jones Owen, 4 Norman
Knapp I. N. 15 Webb
Knight William, 25 North
Larrabee Somers, Beach
Law George D. 12 Norman
Leavitt I P. 128 Boston
Littlefield D. 5 North
Martin C. 23 Washington
Perry H. W. 61 North
Punchard J. P. 24 Winthrop (*gaiter boots*)
Shatswell Moses, 26 Andrew
Sibley G. V. 17 Central (*manuf.*)
Southwick J. jr 48 Derby
Stetson J. 31 North
Still Thomas, 6 Park
Symonds Eben, 53 North
Symonds J. P 55 Buffum (*manuf.*)
Waters T. S. 31 Endicott (*gaiters*)
Wiggin Benj. T. 38 North

Boiler Maker.

Tetlow James, Naumkeag wharf

Boarding Houses.

Baker Mrs. 9 Washington
Bowditch H. 5 Barton square
Chandler Abby B. 20 Norman
Converse A. Mrs. 196 Derby
Jordan A. Mrs. 20 Cromble
Reed John, 9 Higginson sq.
Rollins Sarah J. 21 Lafayette
Stanley T. 3 Pleasant
Woodward E. A. 23 Boston

Boat Builders & Spar Makers.

Becket & Fellows, foot of Daniels
Hart David. head Phillips whf.
Leech William, 205 Derby
Vincent A. L. rear 41 Derby

Book Binders.

Ives H. P. & Smith A. A. 232 Essex
Perley J. jr. & Co. 191 Essex

Books, Periodicals, and Stationery.

Brooks D. B. & Brother, 193 Essex
Chandler L. & Co. 4 Washington
Creamer George, 243 Essex
Ives H. P. & Smith A. A. 232 Essex
Ives J. S. 281 Essex
Moody L, B. basement Asiatic building
Moreland John H. 241 Essex
Riley David M. 7 Washington
Weeks Francis S, 188 Essex
Whipple Henry & Son, 190 Essex

Brass Founder & Finisher.

Gifford Geo. G. head Phillips whf.

Brewers.

Crosby G. W. 10 Derby sq. (*cellar*)
Winn B. L. Front, cor. Washington (*cellar*)

Brick Maker.

Putnam Joseph, 10 Franklin

Brokers.

[*Real Estate and Stock.*]

Archer William jr. 34 Front and 18 Washington
Nichols George, 42 Washington
Peirce N. 163 Essex

Cabinet Makers.

Appleton N. 80 Derby (*desks*)
Fellows Israel, 199 Essex
Grant Joshua B. 51 Boston.
Grant J. C. 15 Lafayette

Haskell & Lougee, 296 Essex
Henderson & Kimball, 38 Wash.
Hubon H. & H. G 48 Washington
Kimball J. 111 Essex (*chairs*)
Sanderson John, 122 Federal
Very Nathaniel jr 274 Essex
Wallis Joseph, 205½ Essex

Carpenters and Builders.
Ames Jeremiah, 32 St. Peter
Barker Jacob, 39 North
Blake A S. 29 Liberty
Bousley & Locke, 16 Mill
Brown George, 49 St. Peter
Brown George A. & T. 158 Derby
Brown Jas. M., Bridge, opp. St. Peter
Coffin C., South railway (*ship*)
Copeland R. M. 8 North
Danforth J. A. 46 Union
Danforth S. G. 33 Endicott
Day Albert, 228 Derby
Dennis D. 8 Lafayette
Dodge & Brooks, Derby whf. (*ship*)
Edwards John S. 8 North
Elwell & Potter, 38 Peabody
Fairfield James jr. 29 Essex
Fuller E. P., North Pine, c. Fowler
Gardner William F. 6 Pine
Gifford T. J. & Co. rear Carpenter
Gifford R. B., Dean
Goldthwait & Day, 20 Peabody
Haley S. 5 Prince
Hamond Wm. C. 127 Derby (*ship*)
Harris & Hutchings, 36 North
Hawes William. 127 Boston
Hill Thomas, 7 Walnut
Honeycomb Thomas P. 31 North
Honeycomb William H. 14 Cross
Honeycomb S. R. 16 Endicott
Hood David B., Turner, near Essex
Jones William, 171 Derby
Leavitt Walter, 33 North
Lovejoy John, 108 Essex
Marden Lemuel, 9 Beckford
Melcher Edward, 8 North
Morse Ebenezer, rear 123 Lafayette
Moulton N. P. 5 Mechanic
Ober Andrew, 42 Charter
Perkins E. B. 11 Cherry
Perkins Wm. E. 153 Derby
Putnam A. P. 3 Beach
Smith Aaron jr. 3 Howard
Smith James A. 10 Walnut
Stiles Dean, 23 Harbor
Symonds Charles F. 31½ Buffum
Towle Abraham, Ward
Upton Moses T. 7 Walnut
Walker P. D. 7 Boston
Whitaker William, 222 Derby
Wilkins Jason, 112 Essex

Williams John H. head Phillips wf.
Winchester Isaac. 42 Charter
Woodbury Ezra, 126 Bridge

Carpetings.
Archer, Downing & Co. 173 Essex
Goldthwait Willard, 155 Essex
Ide Edwin R. 223 Essex
Pulsifer N. 11 Spring (*painted*)

Carpet Makers.
Lovering Lydia, 14 Federal
Daland Joanna, 12 Beckford

Carriage Builders.
Andrews Gilman, 27 Beach
Brooking Thomas, 21 Mason
Dodge J. W. 30 Peabody
Loring Edward D., West place
McIntire H. 12 Sewall
Southward S. S. rear Essex House
Stimpson E. Spring, c. Webb (*dealer*)
Whitney & Tuttle, West place

Carver.
True Joseph, 42 Mill

Caterer.
Sanger Edward H. 416 Essex

Chair Manufactory.
Kimball James, 111 Essex

Cigar Makers.
Battis & Brown, 110 Derby
Francis Joseph, 140 Essex
Laskey John, 47 Mill
Skinner R. & Son, 64 Federal
Skinner S. S. 104 Derby
Smith & Bartlett, 132 Derby
Weissberger L. 2 Phœnix building
Zimmerman J. A. 35 Washington

Cigar Box Manufacturer.
Walton Joseph, 147 Boston

Clergymen.
Allen E. W. 1 Northey[1]
Beaman Charles C. 80 Bridge
Berick F. H. 6 Cross
Briggs G. W. 9 Summer
Brown Geo. W. 24 Brown
Carlton Michael, 30 Charter
Clapp Dexter, 105 Bridge
Cook William, 44 Charter
Dwinell Israel E. 65 North
Emerson B. 377 Essex
Gunner F. 346 Essex

SALEM DIRECTORY. 199

Herrick A. F. 80 Summer
Hoppin J. M. 364 Essex
Johnson S. jr. 2 Chestnut
Leeds George, 33 Summer
Lowe Charles, Lafayette
Mills R. C. 119 Federal
Russell John L. 22 Lafayette
Shahan Thomas H. 14 Mall
Thompson J. W. 40 Chestnut
Very Jones, 154 Federal
Winn Daniel D. 179 Federal
Worcester S. M. 6 Carpenter

Cloaks and Mantillas.
Hammond & Tuttle, 167 Essex
Palmer W. W. & Co. 175 Essex
Shepard J. B. & S. D. 152 Essex

Clocks.
Farless James A. 186 Essex

Clothes Cleaning.
Ryan John, 13 St. Peter

Clothing & Furnishing Goods.
Ashton William B. 211 Essex
Bennett A. 33 Lafayette
Burbeck W. H. & Co. 249 Essex
Carpenter D. P. 205 Essex
Chamberlain & McKenzie, 29 Wash.
Cross J. S. 198 Essex
Dodge George, 122 Derby
Griffen E., Liberty, cor. of Charter
Griffen T. J. 32 Derby
Henfield J. H. 10 Front
Jones S. G. 177 Essex
McCord Thomas, 146 Derby
McKey J. 189 Essex
Peck F. S. 240 Essex
Perkins & Brown. 137 Derby
Perkins Daniel, 181 Essex
Sibley M. H. 10 Front
Wilson Edward, 247 Essex

Coach Office.
13 Central street

Coal and Wood.
[See *Wood and Bark*.]
Brooks A. T. 117 Derby
Cabeen William, 211 Derby
Dike John & Co. 183 Derby
Dodge J. L. 17 Lafayette (*bark*)
Fuller B. B. & Co. 13 Front
Grover J., Brookhouse & Hunt's wf.
Hatch L. B. 113 Derby (*bark*)
Heeney & Clark, 169 Derby
Sanborn G. & F. T. 115 Derby
Wiggin & Clark, 29 Peabody

Coffin Warehouses.
Appleton N. 80 Derby
Hubon H. & H. G. 48 Washington
Very Nathl. jr. 274 Essex
Wallis Joseph, 205½ Essex
Woodberry L. 3 Sewall

Confectioners.
Carter Oliver Mrs. 15 Central
Estes G. W. 10 Newbury
Needham & Hawkes, 144 & 272 Essex
Pepper J. W. Mrs. 44 Buffum (*manuf.*)
Roberts E. F. & J. W. 203 Essex
Rogers S. F. 170 Essex
Simon J. 160 Essex
Wise G. H. 271 Essex

Consul. [*British*.]
Miller E. F. 112 Derby

Coopers.
Battis John, 147 Derby
Dalrymple Simon O. 4 Derby wharf
Farley J. L. 22 Cedar
Getchell Benj. W. h. Phillips wharf
Kehew Samuel, 47 Union
Nichols Wm. H. & Brother, Brookhouse wharf
Roundy Thomas, 10 Lafayette
Rowell Edward, Webb's wharf
Story Daniel, 4 Cambridge

Copper and Brass Founder.
Waters Andrew S. 6 Franklin

Cordage.
Chisholm Joseph, 68 Mill (*manilla*)

Counsellors.
Abbott A. A. 224 Essex
Almon A. B. 214 Essex
Andrews George, 150 Essex
Bancroft S. C. 27 Washington
Barstow Benjamin, 159½ Essex!
Chever George F. 150 Essex
Devereux Geo. H. 24 Washington
Gillis James A. 22 Asiatic Building
Huntington A., Court House
Ingersoll H. 150 Essex
Ives & Peabody, 226½ Essex
Kimball D. B. 27 Washington
Kimball E. W. 214 Essex
Lord Nathaniel J. 194 Essex
Lord Otis P. 27 Washington
Northend & Choate, 20 Asiatic Bdg.
Osgood J. B. F. 235 Essex
Perkins J. C. 243½ Essex
Perry & Endicott, 182 Essex
Phillips Stephen H. 22 Asiatic Bldg.

Phillips & Gillis, 22 Asiatic Build'g
Pingree T. P. jr. 243½ Essex
Prescott Wm. C. 27 Washington
Rantoul R. S. 22 Asiatic Building
Roberts D. 118 Essex *(master in chancery and commissioner for Maine, R. I, and Louisiana.)*
Safford D. E. 24 Asiatic Building
Stimpson T. M. 194 Essex
Story Augustus, 27 Washington
Waters Joseph G. 150 Essex
Webb Stephen P. 159½ Essex
Weed Dan, 224 Essex
Wheatland George, 1 Market ct.
Wheatland S. G. 194 Essex

Crockery, Glass, and Earthen Ware.

Bancroft T. S. 108 Boston
Bowditch William A. 221 Essex
Brooks Asa, 143 Essex
Peele Robert, 282 Essex
Ropes Timothy, 214 Essex
Simonds S. C. & E. A. 32 Front

Curriers.

[*See Leather Dressers, &c.*]

Austin William, rear 46 Boston
Bott James, rear 27 Boston
Bott John C. 9 Pope's court
Braden James, 47 Boston
Brewster Ira & Son, 11 Franklin
Buxton Joseph, jr. 1 Beach
Carleton Frazier, 14 Franklin
Conrey James H., Buffum
Conway Hugh, 79 Mason
Culliton John, Milldam
Dalton Joseph A. 61 Mason
Evans A. A. rear 9 Mason
Fanning James, rear 46 Boston
Fitzgerald John, Goodhue
Frye Daniel, rear Frye's Mills
Gibney John, 11 Beach
Harrington Charles, 428 Essex
Harrington L. B. 428 Essex
Haskell Daniel C. 71 Mason
Horton Nathaniel, Buffum
Hull A. B. & Co. rear 11 Mason
Huse John, 59 Boston
Ingalls Ira F. 13 Beach
Kenney William, May street court
Kinsman & Clough, Franklin
Looby Thomas, Grove, n. Milldam
Mshoney Jeremiah, 55 Boston
Martin Wm. P. foot of Beach
McCalley Andrew, rear 180 Feder'l
McCurdy T. G. 67 Mason
Meloney H. E. rear 97 Mason
Murphy Wm. C. foot of Buffum
Nichols Thomas, Goodhue

Nichols & Shepard, Nichols, n. Prospect
Noah Samuel jr. 34 Boston
Phipps Joseph, Franklin, n. North
Pitman J. C. 5 Pope's court
Pitman N. 24 Boston
Pitman Samuel jr., Goodhue
Putnam Jacob & Co. 63 Boston
Redmond John, Goodhue
Riley James, 91 Mason
Rupp Andrew, rear 31 Boston
Sanborn James, rear 11 Mason
Snow N. foot of Beach
Stimpson James B. rear 41 Boston
Stimpson J. C. 39 Boston
Thorndike William D., Hanson
Treadwell Nathaniel R. rear Mason
Tuttle Nathaniel, 21 Boston
Varney W., D., & S. 82 Boston
Walden Joseph F. 48 Boston
Weston Charles & Sons, May
Williams U. R., Prospect

Curled Hair Factory.

English Philip, Bridge, near March

Daguerreotype Artists.

Fullerton J. W. 224 Essex
Moulton J. W. 214 E sex
Perkins E. R. 241 Essex
Snell William, 208 Essex

Dentists.

Batchelder J. H. 20 Washington
Bowdoin W. L. 208 Essex
Farnum Joseph jr. 251 Essex
Fisk Joseph E. 11 Washington
Hurd W. W. 251 Essex

Distillers.

Chamberlin T., Charter, c. Derby
Hodges Samuel R. 17 Elm

Door Plates.

Newhall F. A. 24 Washington

Dressmakers.

Baker Harriet, 3 North
Breed Rebecca, 57 Summer
Bush Mary A. 255 Essex
Chipman Caroline, 8 Hardy
Colman F. O. 242½ Essex
Dakin R. Mrs. 77 Summer
Dewing Dolly, 2 Lynde
Dimond Abigail, Botts court
Dockham M. A. 385 Essex
Dukes H. 148 Boston
Gardner Martha, 59 Mill
Goodhue Priscilla, 55 Washington

Greenough Caroline, 12 Daniels
Harding M. T. 29 Union
Henderson Mary E. 17 Brown
Jones Abby B. 169 Essex
Laskey Mary E. 45 Mill
Mansfield N. & F 13 Cromble
McIntyre Mary E. D. 12 Carpenter
Osborn Jane F. 5 Winter
Phillips Eliza A. 10 Lafayette
Pulsifer E. F. & S. 63 Essex
Rich N. A. 238½ Essex
Roberts Hannah J. 52 Harbor
Ropes L. J. 6 Winthrop
Saddler Harriet M. 13 Church
Saunders Lydia, 6 Norman
Savory Mary, 21 Beckford
Sotchburn G. A. Mrs. 3 Central
Stone Sarah E. 7 Pleasant
Thayer Nancy, 34 Broad
Twombly E. Mrs 252½ Essex
Ward Louisa H 18 Andrew
Woodbury S. rear 95 Boston

Dry Goods.

Silks, Shawls, Hosiery, Gloves, &c.

Almy James F. 156 Essex
Archer, Downing & Co. 173 Essex
Batchelder A. & M. 202 Essex
Bray Ann R. 76 Federal
Brooks Susan, 8 Elm
Chamberlain R. H 236 Essex
Choate F & Co. 222 Essex
Cutler William, 138 Boston
Dix Asa C. 245 Essex
Gavett William R. 192 Essex
Goldthwait Willard, 155 Essex
Hammond & Tuttle, 167 Essex
Hill W. & R. 277 Essex
Ide Edwin R 223 Essex
Lynch D. 94 Derby
Mayer Joseph, 171 Essex
Nickerson A. W. 174 Essex
Paine J. A. 153 Essex
Palmer Wm. W. & Co. 175 Essex
Pillsbury Lucy A 284 Essex
Pond J. S. 29 Lafayette
Presby & Fearing, 228 Essex
Price Z. E. 220 Essex
Rose Martha A. 12 Harbor
Shepard J. B. & S. D. 171 Essex
Shillaber S. 253 Essex

Dyer.

Roles Samuel jr. 7 Franklin

Engravings.

Weeks Francis S. 188 Essex (*publisher*)

Fancy Goods.

Combs, Toys, &c., &c.

Davis Hannah L. 142½ Essex
Ives J. S. 281 Essex
Remond & Babcock, 188½ Essex
Skerry Francis jr. & Son, 180 Essex
Smith & Chamberlain, 201 Essex
Sweetser Abby E. 165½ Essex
Weeks Francis S. 188 Essex

Feather Bed Renovators.

Goodhue J. 274 Essex
Goss E. 279 Essex

Fish.

Abbott & Dummer, Phillips wharf
Cook George T. near North Bridge
Martin John N. 14 Front
Parsons & Shackelford, 64 Union
West B A. 228 Derby (*dry*)
Wright David, 20 Lafayette

Flour and Grain.

Ball William, 22 Central
Beckford & Hanson, 2 Lafayette, and Grove
Brooks A. T 117 Derby
Bowker Brothers, 227 & 229 Derby
Dodge & Jones, Pierce's wharf
Ropes R. W. & Co. 165 Derby
Steele, Blodgett & Co. 26 Front

Fruit.

Carter Oliver Mrs. 15 Central
Crocker S. P. 12 Washington
Metcalf D. D. 20 Lafayette
Needham & Hawkes, 144 and 272 Essex
Nourse Ebenezer, 41 Washington
Read J. F. 7 & 9 City Market
Roberts E. F & J. W. 203 Essex
Rogers S. F. 170 Essex
Wheeler R. P. 5 & 6 Market House

Furnaces and Ranges.

Frothingham N. & T. H. 31 Front
Ropes J. T. & Co. 17 & 19 Front
Wentworth & Fifield, 15 St. Peter

Furniture and Feathers.

Currier & Millett, 261 Essex
Fellows Israel, 199 Essex
Goss E. 279 Essex
Henderson & Kimball, 38 and 40 Washington
Hynes P. J. 25 Front
Kimball J. 111 Essex (*chairs*)
May Calvin W. 274 Essex
Wallis Joseph, 20½ Essex

Gas and Steam Pipes and Fixtures.

Small Wm. F. 273 Essex
Staten Edward H. 151 Essex

Glue Manufacturer.

Anderson J. M., Salem Turnpike

Grain Mills.

Beckford & Hanson, 1 Front, and Frye's Mills
Norfolk E. L. 13 Front (*manuf. portable*).

Granite.

Clark Nathan T. 25 Peabody
Whittier Charles C. 18 Lafayette

Grocers.

Bartlett Alexander, 82 Derby
Beckford T. F., Pleasant, c. Bridge
Boardman D. 39 Derby
Brooks Luke jr. 178 Derby
Brooks & Noyes, 121 Essex
Brooks N. H. 178 Derby
Brown Daniel, 16 Mill
Calef John, 26 Washington
Chamberlain, Harris & Co. 24 Front
Chandler & Haskell, 391 Essex
Chandler J. D. 106 Federal
Dodge George, 122 Derby
Dolan John, 171 Derby
Emerson H. G. & N. 134 Boston
Foster I. P. 109 Derby
Gardner John, 3 High
Goodhue W. P. 44 Derby (*wholesale and retail*.)
Goodwin Enoch, Derby, c. Carlton
Grant John, 18 Boston
Gray William B. 15 English
Gwinn T. W. & J. S. 410 Essex
Hale Pemberton, 27 Summer
Hardy Temple, 72 Federal
Knight Foster, 46 North
Knight Willard, 55 Harbor
Larrabee Samuel H. 13 Church
Lefavour T. H. 135 Derby
Lindsey Richard, ag't. 25 Lafayette
Mann James B. 40 Boston
Mechanics P. U. 25 Union
Millett Daniel, 67 Derby
N. E P. Union, 12 Front
Nichols Wm. F. 107 Boston
Noyes Enoch K. & Co. 6 & 8 Front
Parks & Harris, 4 St. Peter
Phippen Rebecca, 85 Bridge
Pingree Wm. G. 8 Brown
Prime James M. 15 North
Reeves William, 20 Essex
Reynolds M. C. & Co. 20 Front

Salem Independent Protective Association, 37 Endicott
Simonds Samuel, 76 Derby
Stevens William, 13 Derby square
Symonds Benjamin R. 109 North
Symonds B. R. jr., North, c. Bridge
Symonds Samuel jr. 49 North
Symonds Thomas, 74 North
Tufts Samuel C. 47 Derby
Walton Ebenezer, 89 Mason
Webster J. C. 4 Newbury and 116 Essex
Wells James, Spring, c. Webb
Whitcomb Jared P. 22 Boston
White Franklin & Co. 56 Harbor

Gum Copal Works.

Whipple S. & Brothers, 35 Turner

Gunsmith.

Perry H. B., Blaney

Hair Dressers.

Babcock Charles, 214 Essex
Cassell John M. 7½ Washington
Charnce James, 23½ Union
Colman George B. 175½ Essex
Gardner Benjamin, 4 Central
Gomes Joseph C. 22 Washington
Hovey George H. 157 Essex
Lander E. W. 9 St. Peter
Osborn J. B. 60 Derby
Pingree R. D. 16 Derby square
Ross Nathaniel, 10 Boston
Rowe J. S. 35 Wash. cor. Essex
Stewart L. 8 Washington
Williams A. 5 Arrington's Block

Hair Work, Wigs, &c.

Putnam C. E. 175½ Essex
Remond & Babcock, 188½ Essex
Skerry F. jr. & Son, 180 Essex

Hardware and Cutlery.

Adams, Richardson & Co. 207 Essex
Brooks Asa, 143 Essex
Chase William, 206 Essex
Farless James A. 186 Essex
Hale Henry, 215 Essex
Peele Robert, 282 Essex
Ropes Timothy, 214 Essex
Simonds S. C. & E. A. 32 Front

Harness Makers.

Bennett G. W. 321 Essex
Buffum Edward, 23 Buffum
Coombs F. 81 North
Cunningham J. 17 Daniels
Dayton Isaac, 4 Sewall

SALEM DIRECTORY.

Hagerty Daniel, 125½ Boston
Osgood Benjamin H. 9 Church
Price Eben N. 237 Essex (*trunks*)
Tufts Richard Palmer, 121 Boston
Watson Fenton, 414 Essex
Whitney & Tuttle, West place

Hats, Caps, Furs, &c.

Cook Humphrey, 233 Essex and 33 Washington
Kimball William, 209 Essex
Maynes William, 35 Washington
Nourse Aaron, 37 Washington
Osborne Stephen, 183 Essex
Webster Edward C. 225 Essex

Hay. (*Bundle.*)

Brown George F. & S. 33 North
Dike John & Co. 183 Derby
Hatch L. B. 113 Derby

Horse Shoers.

Brooking Thomas, 21 Mason
Clark James, West place
Drown Peter, Lummus court
Harding David, rear 25 Front
Wilkins Charles, 28 Liberty

Hosiery Manufacturer.

Wilson Jabez, 7 North

Ice.

Barton W. C. 8 Brown
Haskell Jacob, 2 Lafayette

Insurance Agents.

Archer William jr. 34 Front and 18 Washington
Clarke N. A. 27 Washington
Mackintire Samuel, 18 Asiatic Blg.
Mackintire S. A. 27 Washington
Nichols George, 42 Washington
Perkins N. B., Asiatic Building

Iron Fence Builders.

Cutts Benjamin, 8 Sewall
Cutts Richard, Endicott, c. Mill
Pierson George H., West place

Iron Foundry.

Smith J. R. & S., South Prospect, c. E. Gardner

Jewellers.

[*Manufacturing.*]

Luscomb & Pratt, 162 Essex
Mackintire J. 10 Central
Smith & Chamberlain, 201 Essex

Junk.

Crafts George, 43 Derby

Laces and Trimmings.

Filene Wm & Co. 146 Essex
Mayer J. 171 Essex
Paine J. A. 153 Essex
Palmer W. W. & Co. 175 Essex
Peabody John 238 Essex
Price A. E. 220 Essex

Lamps and Camphene.

Farless James A. & Co. 186 Essex (*lamps*)
Hale Henry, 215 Essex
Ropes T. 214 Essex (*lamps*)
Simonds S. C. & E. A. 32 Front (*lamps*)

Laundress.

Phippen Mary J. 10 Ash

Lead Pipes.

Waters Andrew S. 6 Franklin

Leather and Morocco Dresser and Colorer.

Arnold Edward B. 3 Pope's court

Line and Twine.

Chisholm Joseph, 68 Mill
Gwinn James F. 38 Bridge

Livery Stables.

[*See Stables.*]

Locksmith and Bell Hanger.

Goodell A. C. & Son, 16 Lafayette (*locks*)
Phelps Charles, 84 Federal

Lumber.

Austin Eleazer, 16 Lafayette
Austin George F. 16 Lafayette
Brown G. F. & S. 33, 35, & 37 North
Buffum David, 9 Front
Farnham J. M. 221 Derby (*lime*)
Fuller B. B. & Co. 13 Front
Putnam Nathan, 157 Derby
Rowell Thomas P. 2 Naumkeag wf.
Thayer Oliver, 190 and 199 Derby

Machine Sewing.

Mansfield M. B. 230½ Derby
Poole Nathan, 1 Holly
Pray Isaac C 16 Lafayette
Sanderson John W. 25 Daniels

Machinists.

Goodell A. C. & Son, 16 Lafayette
Newcomb Geo. L. 18 Peabody
Ropes John C. 19 Front
Smith J. R. & S. South Prospect, c. East Gardner
Smith O. C., Naumkeag Co.'s whf.
Trask Benjamin, 15 Harbor
Weston John W. rear May

Maps, Charts, &c. for Mariners.

Whipple Henry & Son, 190 Essex

Mahogany.

Prime, Kenny & Co., City Mills

Manufacturing Companies.

[*See Miscellaneous.*]

Marble Manufacturers.

Lord A. & D. Market wharf
Morgan Thomas, 14 Central
Power William A. 11 St. Peter

Masons and Colorers.

Bowditch George, jr. 9 Bentley
Farmer & Harris, 72 Washington
Flint Simeon, 223 Derby
Fowler George P. 2 St. Peter ct.
Gardner David, 5 Cambridge
Hayward Aaron, 82 Summer
Hayward Josiah, 120 Federal
Hurd Thomas, 24 Hathorne (*stone*)
Kehew Wm. B. 24 North
Mansfield Ira, 3 Lagrange
Moulton Frederick, 105 Federal
Neal Jonathan, 12 Broad
Reynolds John P. 13 Northey
Ricker Morrill, 56 Endicott
Roberts William S. 12 St. Peter
Slocum E. 4 Hardy
Stone Benjamin, 21 Williams
Stone James, Flint, cor. Warren
White Benjamin R., St. Peter ct.
Young Stephen, 95 Lafayette

Mast Maker.

Vincent A. L., rear 41 Derby

Mastic Roofing.

Saxby W. L. 153 Derby

Merchants.

Bertram John, Central wharf
Brookhouse R. 16 Asiatic Building
Brookhouse R. jr. 16 Asiatic Bldg.
Curwen James B., Central wharf
Cushing Isaac, 183 Derby
Dodge & Jones, 10 Pierce's wharf
Fabens Benjamin, 211 Derby
Fabens Charles H. 211 Derby
Fitz Daniel P. 5 Derby wharf
Frye Nathan A. 16 Asiatic Build'g
Gardner Henry, 1 Market court
Goodhue Wm. P. 44 Derby (*comm.*)
Hoffman Charles, 12 Derby wharf
Hunt William, 16 Asiatic Building
Hanson J. H. 16 Asiatic Building
Jenks H. E. & Co. 226½ Essex
McMullan Wm., Central wharf
Merritt & Co. 14 Wash. (*forward'g*)
Moore David, 21 Derby wharf
Osgood John C 63 Union
Phillips W. P., Phillips wharf
Phippen & Endicott, 61 Union
Pickman Wm. D. 14 Asiatic Build.
Pingree David, 172 Essex
Pingree T. P. 61 Union
Shatswell Joseph, 23 Front
Shepard H. F., Central wharf
Silsbee B. H. 14 Asiatic Building
Silsbee John B., Central wharf
Silsbee John H. 14 Asiatic Build'g
Stone B. W. 14 Asiatic Building
Trumbull E. H., Central wharf
Upton James, 63 Union
Upton Robert, 63 Union
Waters R. P. 182 Essex
Webb B., Webb's wharf
Webb J. B., Webb's wharf
West Benjamin A. 218 Derby

Milliners.

Baker Mary T. 3 North
Brown Catharine H. 15 Crombie
Buffum Caroline, 255 Essex
Buxton Thomas, 256 Essex
Campion Misses, 74 Federal
Copeland George A. 165 Essex
Draper A. 260 Essex
Duncklee E. 295 Essex
Field M. E. 264 Essex
Fletcher R. C. Mrs. 168 Essex
Foster M. L. 263 Essex
Gwinn Mary A. 294 Essex
Haskins S. L. 147 Essex
Jones Abby B. 169 Essex
Kelley Mary, 15 Lafayette
Morrill & Walker, 217 Essex
Paine J. A. 153 Essex
Putnam H. P. 293 Essex
Price A. E. 220 Essex
Stanwood L. M. 148 Essex
Ward Sarah A. 278 Essex
Woodman M. E. 31 Lafayette
Woodward E. S. 252½ Essex

Music Stores.

Brooks D. B. & Brother, 193 Essex
Weeks Francis S. 188 Essex
Whipple Henry & Son, 190 Essex

Nail Maker. (*Horse.*)

Burkinshaw George, rear 63 Boston

Nautical Instrument Maker.

Emery Samuel, 162 Derby

Nurseries.

Hathorne E., Hollingsworth Hill
Manning Robert, 33 Dearborn
Putnam C. F., Orne
Woods Ephraim, 122 North

Nurses.

Archer Sarah, rear 28 Church
Badger Abigail, Woodbury's court
Barron Phœbe H. 48 Charter
Beckford Melinda R. 24 Union
Berg Nancy, 5 Woodbury's court
Bright Mary, 12 Becket
Brown Lucy, 16 High
Bruce Sarah H. 24 Derby
Bryant Lydia, 14 Norman
Burbank Hannah, 31 Norman
Burrill Mary Mrs. 7 Becket
Burnham E. G. 20 Northey
Cate Mary E. 19 Warren
Cheever Mary P. 371 Essex
Clement Mary, 181 Bridge
Colburn Rebecca, 14 Howard
Cox Mary G. 16 High
Crosby Sarah, 14 Norman
Derby Susan A. 2 Dow
Dockham Elizabeth, 34 Essex
Dodge Emeline, 48 Charter
Field Louisa, 112 Bridge
Francis Maria, 39 Summer
Goss Polly, 62 North
Grover Susan, 23 Winthrop
Hammond Hannah, 12 Winthrop
Homan Abigail, 368 Essex
Isaackson Sarah A. 29 Norman
Knight Elizabeth P. 346 Essex
Littlefield Hannah, 14 Odell square
Matthews Sarah N. 7 Federal
McNeal Margaret, 19 Winter
Newport Sarah A., Cedar court
Nowell Phœbe A. 8 Norman
Odlin Mary, 25 Hardy
Peabody Sally, 6 Howard
Pepper Eliza, 1 English
Peterson Priscilla, 5½ Gedney ct.
Pitman Harriet, 14 Norman
Pope Rebecca S. 14 Peabody
Reed Sarah W. 43 Bridge
Richardson L. 108 Bridge
Russell Susan, 26 Endicott

Saunders Margaret, 343 Essex
Smith Catharine, 18 Derby
Snelling John Mrs., Porter court
Southwick Eliza, 52 Endicott
Stanton Mary, 16 Norman
Teste Mary P. 16 High
Towns Ann, 9 Federal
Tufts Sarah, 15 High street court
Vincent H. F. 59 Derby
Ware Mary, at Horace Ware's, Salem Turnpike

Oil and Candles.

Salem and S. Danvers Oil Co., Mason (*resin oil*)
Seccomb Ebenr., foot of Harbor

Oysters and Refreshments.

Abbott I. C. 12 Market square
Batchelder Geo. W. 10 Derby sq.
Chandler L. & Co. 4 Washington
Collins P. 1 Phœnix building
Cook A., Eastern Railroad Depot
Empire Oyster Saloon, 299 Essex
Estes G. W. 10 Newbury
Esty J. A. 17 Derby square
Holbrook J. 5 Derby square
Lee George, 14½ Derby square
Martin W. basement 6 Wash.
Morris Jos. B. 18 & 20 Derby sq.
Newcomb David, 24 Derby square
Perry B. 60 Boston.
Rock John, West place
Rogers S. F. 170 Essex

Painters.

House and Sign.

Abbot Philip jr. rear 9 Church
Ames Edward B. 3 Crombie
Brown C. E. 42 Charter
Brown R. L. 159½ Essex
Calley Samuel, 74 Washington
Carey Joseph W. 7 Boston
Clark S. C. 112 Essex
Davis C. H. 25 North
Felt John G. 27 Front
Ferguson J. B. 341 Essex
Ferguson John F. 9 Beckford
Foley Edward, 32 Endicott
Gage Andrew jr. 71 Derby
Hill Thomas, 7 Walnut
Henderson Daniel, 6 Newbury
Kimball & Skerry, 139 Derby
Lowd Mark, 8 North
Mansfield B. S. 8 Endicott
Mansfield Joseph, 9 Lafayette
Messervy John, 34 Lafayette
Nichols S. F. 113 Derby
Pulsifer C. H. 51 Boston
Pulsifer D. & Co. 25 Front
Pulsifer Joseph, 230 Derby

Pulsifer N. 11 Spring (carpet)
Rhodes & Pousland, 20 Peabody
Simonds Wm. H. 76 Derby
Symonds J. Shove, 41 North

Carriage.

Burbank E. G., West place
Burbank S. 3 Cambridge
Davidson Moses, 124 Boston
Hovey Charles F., Spring, corner Webb
Rhodes & Pousland, 20 Peabody
Tufts Chas. H. & Co., Endicott, cor. Margin

Portrait.

Osgood Charles, 7 Central
Southward George, 7 Central

Sign and Ornamental.

Adams & Foster, 24 Wash. (pearl glass)
Felt John G. 27 Front
Luscomb William H. 341 Essex
Mansfield J. 9 Lafayette

Paints, Oil, and Glass.

Adams, Richardson & Co. 207 Essex
Farless James A. 186 Essex
Felt John G. 27 Front
Kimball & Skerry, 139 Derby
Pulsifer D. & Co. 25 Front
Simonds S. C. & E. A. 32 Front

Paper Hangers.

Abbott Philip jr. rear 9 Church
Edwards C. W. 8 Creek
Felt J. G. 27 Front
Lowd Mark, 8 North
Mansfield J. 9 Lafayette

Paper Hangings.

Brook Asa, 143 Essex
Creamer George, 243 Essex
Ives H. P. & Smith A. A. 232 Essex
Simonds S. C. & E. A. 32 Front

Paper and Paper Stock.

Brooks D. B. & Brother, 193 Essex (wrapping)
Brown George T. 33 Lafayette
Weston P. R. 164 Derby

Patent Balance Curtain Spring Manufacturer.

Bray B. 2 Franklin Building

Patent Leather Manufactory.

Stevens H. H., Mason Hill

Perfumery, &c.

Weeks Francis S. 188 Essex

Physicians.

Choate David, 18 Church
Choate George, 251 Essex
Cox Benjamin jr. 23 Norman
Fitz Gerald Edward, 25 Lafayette
Floto J. H. 10 Liberty
Gersdorff B. 49 Washington
Gove Hiram, 26 Lynde
Hannan D. B. 122 Boston
Harris Jerome, 22 Washington
Johnson Samuel, 2 Chestnut
Lamont Daniel G. 243½ Essex
Mack William, 21 Chestnut
Peirson E. B. 13 Baton square?
Perkins George A. 5 Newbury
Quimby Elisha, 48 Federal
Quimby E. Hervey, 48 Federal
Stone H. Osgood, 314½ Essex
Stone James jr. 40 Broad
Stone L. R. over 174 Essex
Tuttle H. C 165 Federal
Wallace Thos. 9 Washington
Wheatland H. 21 Chestnut
Wheatland R. H. 374 Essex
Wiedeman A. 1 Central (homœ.)
Williams William, 110 Federal
Winsor Frederic, 14 Brown
Wood J. G. 265 Essex

Clairvoyant, &c.

Bassett J. A. 14 Webb
Charnce James, 23½ Union (Indian)
Patten J. R. 25 Harbor (eclectic)

Piano Dealer and Tuner.

Lang Benjamin, 157 Essex

Picture Frame Makers and Gilders.

Shaw X. H. 291 Essex
Weeks Francis S. 188 Essex

Pilots.

Boat Ariomedes.

Lloyd William H. 49 St. Peter
Perkins Joseph, 17 Derby

Boat Clarence Barclay.

Perry Ittai, 12 English
Powers Stephen, 9 Webb
Wallis Francis F. 15 Essex

Plaster.

Dodge & Jones, Pierce's wharf

Plumber.
Goss F. P. 7 St. Peter

Printers.
Chapman & Palfray, 185 Essex (*Salem Register*)
Foote & Horton, 191 Essex (*Salem Gazette*)
Hutchinson T. J. 175½ Essex
Ives William & Co. 226½ Essex (*Salem Observer*)
Lander B. W. over 215 & 217 Essex (*Salem Advocate*)
Moreland John H. 235 Essex

Printing Press Manufacturer.
Danforth Wm. H. 46 Union

Produce.
Chamberlain S. G. 22 Derby sq.
Read John, 7, 8, and 9 Market Ho.
Read W. A. 10 & 11 Market House (butter and cheese)
Steele, Blodgett & Co. 26 Front

Provisions.
Collins Daniel, 5 Charter
Craig Samuel, 3 Lafayette
Daniels Stephen, 70 Federal
Elliot Isaac B. 3 & 4 Market House
Forbush Jonathan C. 7½ Winter
Hayford Asa, 91 Essex
Knight F. 46 North
Mansfield D. A. 33 Endicott
Millet D. 67 Derby (salt provisions)
Newcomb C. H. 14 Newbury
Ober Samuel, 2 Norman
Perry Wm. F. 319 Essex
Pickering J. H., South Market, 37 Lafayette
Pierce Leonard, Bridge, c. Pleasant
Plander John G. 116 Derby
Porter Frederick, 17 St. Peter
Roberts J. 13 & 14 Market House
Sawyer Asa, 17 & 18 Market House
Snow Elbridge, 44 North
Tuttle Henry G. 36 Boston
Tufts Samuel C. 47 Derby
Upton Ezra, 2 Mill [House
Ward Alfred A. 15 & 16 Market
Wheeler B. S. 1 & 2 Market House
Winberry Thomas, 7½ Boston
Wright P. E. 50½ Derby
Wiggin Levi, 12 Newbury

Public Houses.
Essex House, 176 Essex, J. S. Leavitt [Skinner
Mansion House, 188 Essex, S. S.

Pump and Block Makers.
Donaldson A. 141 Derby
Felt Benjamin, 118 Derby
Russell J. 48 Union

Restorators.
Haskell S. C., Front, c. Derby sq.
Pray & Boynton, 25 Front

Rigger.
Berry Charles H. 20 Derby wharf

Rubber Goods.
Chapman Wm. H. 210 Essex
Flint Harrison O. 210 Essex

Sail Makers.
Crandell John, rear 41 Derby
Kemp S. Peabody's wharf
Lane E. B. 57 Union
Oakes Thomas, 7 Derby wharf
Whipple J. H., Phillips wharf

Salt.
Bowker Bros 227 Derby

Sash, Blind, and Door Makers.
Hardy Augustus. 26 Front
Newell Joseph, 7 Front
Phelps Wm. jr. & Co 84 Federal
Pulsifer D. & Co. 25 Front

Sewing Machines.
Griswold B. L. 17 Charter
Macintire S. 18 Asiatic building
Trefren James, 15½ St. Peter

Ship Builder.
Miller Edward F., E. Gardner

Ship Chandlers.
Goodhue Wm. P. 44 Derby
Lefavour T. H. 135 Derby

Shipping Offices.
Griffen E., Liberty, cor. Charter
Griffen T. J. 32 Derby

Shipwrights and Calkers.
Bowditch D. C. head Phillips whf.
Coffin Calvin, E. Gardner

Shoe Binders.
Chute E. 17 Barr
Pray Isaac C. 16 Lafayette
Sibley John S. 42 Lafayette
Trefren James, 15½ St. Peter

Shoe Stiffenings.
Trofatter C. H. 5 Beaver
Trofatter Samuel J. r. 10 Beaver

Soap Manufacturer.
Robertson S. W. rear 44 Boston

Stables.
Gardner S., Endicott, corner Margin (sale)
Kelman Wm. W., Church, c. Wash.
Leavitt J. S. rear Essex House
McIntire S. J., Mechanic
Price John, 8 Norman
Smith & Manning, 212 Essex, 9 Hamilton, and 47 Washington
Tuttle John, 191 Federal

Stair Builders.
Brown George, 49 St. Peter
Brown George jr., North, n. Bridge
Kendall Alvah, 11 Hathorne
Winchester Isaac, 42 Charter

Steam Sawing and Planing.
Buffum David, Front, n. Lafayette
Prime, Kenney & Co., City Mills

Slater.
Pinnock Thomas, 6 Peabody

Stevedores.
Creamer Michael, 7 Allen
Smalley R. 8 Daniels

Tailors and Drapers.
Burbank Geo. W. 235 Essex
Burbeck W. H. 249 Essex
Chamberlain & McKenzie, 29 Wash.
Cornelius A. G. 178 Essex
Dease Lawrence, 244 Essex
Edwards Benjamin, 224 Essex
Hannam Thomas, 64 Boston
Jones S. G. 177 Essex
Norris C. H. 188½ Essex
Patch Ephraim, 247 Essex
Perkins Daniel, 181 Essex
Purbeck William A. 267 Essex
Quinn & Kelley, 184 Essex
Sibley Moses H. 10 Front
Stanley J. W. 39 Washington
Webb John K. 197 Essex

Tailoresses.
Brown Frances S. 61 Essex
Churchill Abigail H. 2 Conant
Cloutman Sally and Priscilla, 15 Carlton
Daland Mary, 12 Beckford

Knight Anna, 7 Cross
Lafavour M. A. 80 North
Lander Sarah W. 242½ Essex (boys')
Laskey Esther 57 Charter
McIntyre Misses, 36 Norman
Pope Maria, 1 Hardy
Porter Ann B. 6 Ash
Smith M. 17 Lynde
Smothers Olive, 14 Norman
Vincent Letitia, 12 Essex
Walker Mary, 15 High st. court
Williams Elizabeth C. 4. St. Peter court

Tanners.
Allen Benjamin B., Goodhue
Bond Lewis, Goodhue
Bott James, rear 27 Boston
Brewster Ira A. & Son, 11 Franklin
Buxton Joseph jr. 1 Beach
Carleton Edward F 14 Franklin
Carleton Frazier, 14 Franklin
Conway Hugh, 69 Mason
Culliton John, Milldam
Dalton J. A. 69 Mason
Frye F. A. foot Beach
Frye James, Goodhue
Frye Joseph S., Goodhue
Frye Stephen N. rear Frye's Mills
Gibney John, 11 Beach
Hadley Geo. S., Goodhue
Hanson E. A. 13 Grove
Harrington R. rear 9 Mason
Hazelton John, May
Hull A. B. & Co. rear 11 Mason
Kenney Wm., Turnpike
Looby Thomas, Grove, n. Milldam
Lord James, rear 180 Federal
Lord James A., Pope's court
Maloon & Harrington, Goodhue
McCalley Andrew, r. 180 Federal
Meloney H. E. rear 97 Mason
Morse L. B. 71 Mason
Muhlig Robert, foot of Buffum
Murphy Wm. C. foot of Buffum
Nichols David, Pope's court
Nichols Daniel F. rear 44 Boston
Nichols James, Prospect
Nichols & Shepard, Prospect
Osgood N. W., Goodhue
Osgood N. W. jr., Goodhue
Pope Eleazer rear 37 Boston
Putnam Jacob & Co 17 Goodhue
Rupp Andrew, rear 31 Boston
Sanborn James, rear 11 Mason
Stimpson J. C. 39 Boston
Turner Calvin, 4 Goodhue
Varney W. D. & S. 82 Boston
Weston Charles & Sons, May
Wilkins Albert, 50 Boston
Wilkins J. H. 48 Boston

SALEM DIRECTORY.   209

Teachers.
Bowland H., Walnut, cor. Essex
Bradford G. P. 1 Cambridge
Brooks E. M. R. 112 Lafayette (music and French)
Brown Martha A. 44 Forrester
Davis R. J., Phelps ct. (dancing)
Fenollosa Manuel, 7 Central (music)
Hawkes Louisa M. 20 Andrew
Hause Carl, 9 Wash. (music)
Henderson F. A. 14 St. Peter (music)
Honeycomb Sarah E. 7 Lemon (music)
Jerome N. H. 243½ Essex (French)
Jocelyn Mary E. 224 Essex
Leavitt W. 71 Forrester (navigation)
Mann Elizabeth N. 190 Federal
Quimby A M. 48 Federal (music)
Read George F. 42 Buffum
Stevens Ann P., Hamilton Hall
Stickney Harriet, 32 Mill (music)
Upton Francis, 31 Pleasant (music)
Waters H. F. G., Franklin building
Williams Mary E. 243½ Essex (drawing)
Wood Marion, 107 North

Teamsters.
Brooks A. R. 107 Derby
Byrne Clifford C. 117 Derby
Hanson Joseph, 64 Union
Haslam Joseph, 56 Harbor
McIntire S. J., Mechanic
Moulton J. G. 1 Front
Pickering James, 194 Derby
Pitts Darling, 2 Lafayette, c. Front
Pitts Nathaniel, 5 Front
Sumner & Johnson, 132 Derby

Thread Stores.
Nickerson A. W. 174 Essex
Shillaber S. 253 Essex
Sweetser Abby E. 165½ Essex

Tin Plate and Sheet Iron Workers, Stoves, &c.
Chase William, 206 Essex
Chase & Co. 8 Lafayette
Chipman R. M. 347 Essex
Eaton John D. 40 North
Frothingham N. and T. H. 29 and 31 Front
Fuller William P. 43 Washington
Pease Samuel W. 128 Derby
Preston Jonathan, 12 Central
Ropes John T. & Co. 17 & 19 Front
Webster Gardner, 135 Boston
Wentworth & Fifield, 15 St. Peters

Tomato Catchup Manufacturer.
Estes G. W. 10 Newbury

Turning and Sawing.
Clapp Luther, 5 Front

Umbrella Makers.
Brown John B. 159 Essex
Lynch P. 92 Derby
Ottignon Firmin, 53 Washington

Undertakers.
Neal John H. 66 Federal
Woodbury L. 3 Sewall

Upholsterers.
Goss Ezekiel, 279 Essex
Mansfield George S. 50 Wash.
Mackie John, 131 Essex
Shepard S. 298 Essex

Upholsteresses.
Dodge Sarah, 8 Williams
Holt S. C. 9 Rust
Marshall Hannah, 101 Federal

Variety Stores.
Allen G. F. Mrs. 368 Essex
Bermingham C. 30 Norman
Byrne Anna E. 352 Essex
Caraway C. S. 58 Derby
Clark Sarah F. 18 Mill
Colby J. W. 46 Peabody
Fowler S. J. & E. B. 14 Boston
Geary D. J. 3 Newbury
Glover Isabella, 43 Essex
Haskell Wm. 5 Lynn
Knight M. B. & M. 5 Pleasant
Mitchell John, 44 Peabody
Phillips George Mrs. 38 St Peter
Plum Eliza P. 117 Essex
Plummer R. 148 Essex
Stephenson Elizabeth, 34 Peabody
Symonds E. G. North, cor. School
Wühr L. W. 52 Endicott
Wyman M. F. 23 St. Peter

Veterinary Surgeons.
Greenman Wm. B. 10 Boston
Saunders Robert J. 16 Buffum
Saunders Wm. 5 Buffum

Waiters and Tenders.
Drew Thomas, rear 1 Ropes
Dailey R. 8 Porter

Watchmakers and Jewellers.

Appleton G. B. 179 Essex
Kehew Wm. H. 230 Essex
Lamson Charles, 234 Essex
Luscomb & Pratt, 162 Essex
Newhall F. A. 24 Washington
Rider Joseph J. 242 Essex
Skerry F. jr. & Co. 180 Essex
Smith Jesse, 262 Essex
Smith & Chamberlain, 201 Essex
Warner Caleb, 3 Central (spectacles)

Water for Shipping.

Parsons & Shackelford, 64 Union

West India Goods.

[*See Grocers.*]

Wharfingers.

Knight E. H., Phillips wharf
King James, Derby wharf

Wheelwrights.

Andrews Gilman, 27 Beach
Barker Joseph W. 29 Liberty
Batchelder Joseph, 16 Creek
Dodge John W. 20 Peabody

Nichols John, 29 North
Noah S. 101 Boston
Patch I. H. 7 Sewall
Spiller John P., West place
Stocker John W. 23 Endicott

Wines, &c.

Batchelder G. W. 10 Derby square
Felt John, 25 Wash. (city agent)
Gowen W. 16 Derby square
Linehan D. 6 Derby square
Remond John, 5 Higginson square
Odell J. A. 23 Front

Wood and Bark.

[*See Coal, &c.*]

Brown G. F. & S. 33, 35, and 37 North
Dike John & Co. 183 Derby
Fuller B. B. & Co. 13 Front
Hatch L. B. 113 Derby
Heeney & Clark, 169 Derby
Prime Kenny & Co., City Mills (hard wood)
Putnam Nathan, 157 Derby
Sanborn G. & F. T. 115 Derby

Wood Moulding.

Straw Benjamin, 5 Front

NEW YORK STATE
BUSINESS DIRECTORY,

NOW IN PREPARATION,

ON A PLAN SIMILAR TO THE

NEW ENGLAND
BUSINESS DIRECTORY.

PRICE $3.

SALEM DIRECTORY.

CITY GOVERNMENT, 1858.

City Election, first Monday in January; Organization of the City Government, fourth Monday in January.

NATHANIEL SILSBEE, Mayor. — Salary, $800.

S. W. Robertson,
Ira A. Brewster, } ALDERMEN. { David Moore,
Daniel P. Fitz,   Brackley R. Peabody,
                                         Edward B. Lane.

COMMON COUNCIL.
President, STEPHEN B. IVES.

WARD 1.—Charles A. Putnam, Jarius W. Perry, Daniel H. Jewett, George Upton.

WARD 2.—Benjamin R. White, George Creamer, Stephen B. Ives, Charles Lamson.

WARD 3.—Dana Z. Smith, Charles Harrington, John Preston, John S. Driver.

WARD 4.—James M. Caller, George F. Putnam, Henry L. Williams, John Huse.

WARD 5.—Simeon Flint, Lewis E. Wentworth, Amos P. Day, Samuel A. Merrill.

WARD 6.—James Ropes, James H. Conrey, Stephen Curran, Charles A. Ropes.

The City Council meets regularly on the second and fourth Monday of each month, in the evening, at the City Hall.

The Committee on Accounts meets on Thursday after the first Monday in each month, at 7½ o'clock, P. M., at the City Hall.

The meetings of all the Boards and Committees are held at the City Hall.

CITY OFFICERS.

City Clerk — Joseph Cloutman,..........................$800
Clerk of the Common Council — Joseph M. Newhall,.... 125
Treasurer and Collector — Henry B. Smith,............. 800
City Solicitor — W. C. Endicott,........................
City Marshal — Thomas B. Perkins,................... 700
Assistant Marshals — James Dalrymple and Edward Collins
 (Police Office, Town Hall), each 600
Commissioner of Streets — Perley Putnam,............. 600
City Messenger — William Mansfield,.................. 550

WARD OFFICERS.

WARD 1. — Eben N. Walton, *Warden.* J. Lovett Whipple, *Clerk.* John H. Williams and Geo. W. Moreland, *Assistants.*

WARD 2. — Aaron A. Smith, *Warden.* Lyman B. Brooks, *Clerk.* Samuel Calley and Israel P. Harris, *Assistants.*

WARD 3. — Albert Day, *Warden.* David R. Peabody, *Clerk.* Hezekiah Sleeper and Thomas B. Flowers, *Assistants.*

WARD 4. — Thomas F. Odell, *Warden.* James F. Potter, *Clerk.* Chas. H. Daniels and Joseph Very, *Assistants.*

WARD 5. — Wm. A. Purbeck, *Warden.* Joseph Chisholm, *Clerk.* Chas. H. Norris and George D. Glover, *Assistants.*

WARD 6. — James Ropes, *Warden.* Joseph D. Gardner, *Clerk.* Thomas Symonds, Jr., and Thomas Ashby, *Assistants.*

Overseers of the Poor. — The Mayor and Aldermen, and Messrs. J. W. Perry, Charles Lamson, John Preston, John Huse, S. A. Merrill, and James Ropes.

The Overseers of the Poor meet on the first Tuesday in each month, at the Alms House, and on Wednesday evening of each week, at the City Hall.

Physician to Alms House, Dr. Frederic Winsor.
Chaplain to Alms House, John Carlton.
Superintendent of Alms House, Mark B. Avery.
Assessors. Jonathan Tucker, Charles E. Symonds, Thomas E. Jewett.

Assistant Assessors.—Simon O. Dalrymple, William B. Smith, Moses T. Upton, Chas. Endicott, James Stone, Alvah Kendall, Thomas F. Odell, Aaron Perkins, Mark Kimball, Thomas Simonds, Geo. F. Brown, Eleazer Pope.

The Assessors meet from 9 to 12 A. M., and 2 till 5 o'clock, P. M., at the City Hall, every business day.

SALEM DIRECTORY. 213

Board of Health. — The Mayor and Alderman, *ex-officio.*
Visiting Physician. — Dr. Frederic Winsor.
School Committee. — Nathaniel Silsbee, Stephen B. Ives, *ex-officio,* Andrew B. Almon, George Andrews, James F. Almy, George W. Briggs, William B. Brown, George F. Chever, David Choate, Henry J. Cross, Joseph Chisholm, Israel E. Dwinell, Joseph A. Dalton, Asahel Huntington, Walter S. Harris, Henry P. Ives, George Leeds, Jacob Perley, Geo. F. Reed, John B. Shepard, Gilbert L. Streeter, J. S. Symonds, Nathaniel Tuttle, Frederick Winsor.
City Watchmen. — George E. Berry, *Captain.* George S. Arrington, Payne Morse, Joseph S. Buxton, John W. Cole, John S. Wardwell, John Wheeler, John Saul, William Odell, Eben. N. Vent, Moses A. Averell, Isaac N. Colby.
Constables. — Thomas B. Perkins, Edward Collins, James Dalrymple, Ezra Osborn, William Mansfield, Thomas Saul, Rufus L. Gordon, Horace Rust, T. M. Dix, A. J. Cate, Gorham Smith, Albert Knight, Jewett J. Smith, Roland Smalley, John F. Edgerly, John Chandler, Chas. Creasy, Samuel A. Merrill, Edward C. Larrabee, Samuel Day, Alfred R. Brooks, Henry J. Lane, Alanson Kenney, Aaron Welch, Charles A. Dearborn, Otis Pitts, Walter Norris, Jacob Berry, Thomas Treadwell, J.C. Thorner, N. W. Prince, P. Littlefield, Isaac Winchester, E. G. Guilford, Nelson M. Prince, William Lewis, George W. Luscomb, Joseph Peterson, John H. Newton, Joshua L. Foster, George F. Wiggin, Amos G. Teague, William F. Chapple, Frederick H. Hunt, George E. Berry, George Pettingill, Mark B. Avery.
City Crier. — William Newhall.
Sealer of Weights and Measures. — John T. Ropes.
Superintendent of Burials. — Jeremiah S. Perkins. Charles Staniford and Charles Creasy, *Assistants.*
Surveyor-General of Lumber. — Albert Day. *Deputies,* Nathan Putnam, Amos P. Day, George A. Brown.
Superintendent of Union Street Bridge. — Richard Stickney.
Superintendent of South Bridge. — David Wright.
Fire Department. — William Chase, *Chief Engineer.* Albert Day, George Sanborn, Samuel Lewis, Andrew S. Waters, James A. Lord, William H. Honeycomb, *Assistant Engineers.*

FIRE CLUBS.

ACTIVE. A. G. Browne, *Moderator.* Jonathan Perley, *Clerk.* Annual Meeting, third Wednesday in February.
ADROIT. C. M. Richardson, *Moderator.* Humphrey Cook, *Clerk.* Annual Meeting, second Thursday in January.
ALBERT. Joseph C. Foster, *Moderator.* John S. Jones, *Clerk.* Annual Meeting, second Tuesday in January.

BOSTON STREET. William Sutton, *Moderator.* Joseph Very, *Clerk.* Annual Meeting, second Monday in January.

ENTERPRISE. J. W. Perry, *Moderator.* William B. Brown, *Clerk.* Annual Meeting, second Wednesday in January.

NAUMKEAG. Charles Upton, *Moderator.* Joseph Chisholm, *Clerk.* Annual Meeting, first Wednesday in February.

RELIEF. John Hill, *Clerk.* Annual Meeting, third Wednesday in February.

ENGINE COMPANIES.

Names.	Directors.	Clerks.	Location.
1 RELIANCE,	A. J. Tibbetts,	Wm. M. Hill,	Derby, c. Hardy.
2 YOUNG AMER.	Chas. Osborn,	S. W. Mansfield,	Forrester.
3 RELIEF,	L. E. Wentworth,	Geo. F. Austin,	South Salem.
4 LAFAYETTE,	David Hart,	J. L. Whipple,	Derby, c. Daniels
5 NAUMKEAG,	Hen. A. Farnum,	E. H. Wilson,	Federal.
6 EXCHANGE.	John Felt,	William Wallis,	Beckford.
7 SUTTON,	Henry C. Noah,	Solomon Stevens,	Boston.
8 ACTIVE,	W. T. Sanborn,	Thos. Ashby,	North Salem.
9 CONSTITUTION,	A. A. Wiggin,	John H. Wilkins,	Pleasant.
10 ADAMS,	Jas. B. Nichols,	Geo. O. Stevens,	Boston.
1 SAIL CARRIAGE	Henry Meeke,	A. R. Brooks,	Derby, c. Daniels.
3 " "	L. B. Morse,	H. G. Tuttle,	Boston.
1 HOOK & LAD'R	Samuel Calley,	H. W. Thurston,	Federal.

PUBLIC SCHOOLS.

At the organization of the Board of School Committee, each elective member is appointed to one of the three visiting Committees that have the management of the respective divisions of schools, as regards the discipline, classification, and studies.

FIRST DIVISION.

CLASSICAL AND HIGH SCHOOL.—Broad Street. Jacob Batchelder, *Principal;* salary, $1,600. Gordon Bartlett, *Usher;* salary, $1,000. Caroline Lord, Mary Ann Batchelder, Lydia Dodge, and Sarah A. Shaw, *Assistants;* salaries, $400, $350, $300, $250. Males, 93; females, 84: total, 177.

SECOND DIVISION.

GRAMMAR SCHOOLS.

BENTLEY, located between Essex and Forrester sts.; boundaries, that portion of the city between North and South rivers east of the centre of St Peter and Central streets. M. J. Fitz, *Principal.* Salary, $450. Anna Whittemore, *Sub-Principal;* Mary A. Colman, Margaret A. Dunn, *Assistants.* Females, 149.

PHILLIPS, located between Essex and Forrester Sts.; boundaries, that portion of the city between the North and South rivers east of the centre of North and Summer streets. Silas Peabody, *Principal.* Salary, $1,000. Caroline Roberts and Ellen Rideout, *Sub-Principals.* Harriet C. Gray, Ruth H. Gray, Ellen Sawyer and Aroline B. Meek, *Assistants.* Males 313.

BROWNE, located on Ropes street; boundaries, South Salem. Jacob F. Brown, *Principal.* Salary, $1000. Anne F. Chisholm, Laura A. Barron, *Assistants.* Males, 59; females, 65: total, 124.

PICKERING, located on North, corner Dearborn Street; boundaries, North Salem. William P. Hayward, *Principal.* Salary, $1,000. Sarah E. Cross and Mary Ann Cross, *Assistants.* Males, 51; females, 57: total, 108.

HIGGINSON, location, Broad Street; boundaries, that portion of the city between North and South Rivers westward of a line through the centre of St. Peter and Central Streets, and below the Town Bridge, Boston Street. M. L. Shepard, *Principal.* Salary, $450. Elizabeth A. Jelly, *Sub-Principal.* Lucy A. Shaw, P. Elizabeth Church, *Assistants.* Females, 178.

HACKER, location, Dean Street; boundaries, that portion of the city between North and South Rivers west of the centre of North and Summer Streets, and below the Town Bridge, Boston street. Thomas H. Barnes, *Principal.* Salary, $1,000. Sarah C. Pitman and Rebecca C. Southard, *Assistants.* Males, 149.

EPES, location, Aborn Street; boundaries, that portion of the city north and west of the Town Bridge, Boston Street. L. F. Warren, *Principal.* Salary, $800. Charlotte L. Forten, *Assistant.* Males, 46; females, 42: total, 88.

Salaries of sub-principals $250, and of assistant teachers $200, per annum.

THIRD DIVISION.
INTERMEDIATE AND PRIMARY SCHOOLS.

Salary of teachers of Intermediate Schools, $275; 1st Assistants, $200. Of teachers of Primary Schools, $225; Assistants, $150.

Bridge Street. Sarah H. Tibbets, *Principal.* No. scholars, 43.

Williams Street. H. N. Lord, *Principal.* M. E. Clark, *Assistant.* No. scholars, 106.

Bentley. Sarah A. Brown, *Principal.* Eliza G. Cogswell and S. E. Honeycomb, *Assistants.* No. Scholars, 130.

Phillips. Mary R. Kimball, *Principal.* Harriet N. Felton, Emeline R. Kimball, and Caroline A. Dalton, *Assistants.* No. scholars, 203.

Browne. Caroline Weeks, *Principal.* Nancy Osborne, E. A. Arrington, and Harriet N. Tyler, *Assistants.* No. scholars. 278.

Broad Street. Caroline Stevens, *Principal.* Rebecca Stacy, M. E. Stevens, and S. E. Francis, *Assistants.* No. scholars, 220.

North Street. Maria Cushing, *Principal.* Georgiana Smith, E. R. Russell, and Marian M. Wood, *Assistants.* No. scholars 223.

Fowler Street, Primary and Intermediate. Frances E. Very, *Principal.* M. E. Webb, *Assistant.* No. scholars, 92.

Mason Street.—L. L. A. Very. No. scholars, 65.

Epes.—N. R Eustis, *Principal.* Eliza A. Dix, *Assistant.* No. scholars, 105.

Expenses for the year ending March, 1858.

SALARIES of Teachers and Assistants,........................$18,809.75
ORDINARY EXPENDITURES—repairs, fuel, rent, care of houses, &c. 5,747.80

Total expenditure,........$24,557.55

The regular meetings of the Board are held at the City Hall, on the third Monday evening of each month.

PRIVATE SCHOOLS.

From the returns made in March, 1858. Number of Private Schools, then in the city, 30. Average attendance of pupils, about 900. Estimated amount of tuition paid, $11,000.

Teachers and Locations, in part, October, 1858.

Geo. P. Bradford, 1 Cambridge
Miss M. A. Brown, 44 Forrester
Miss Hannah Bowland, 1 Walnut
Miss Dalrymple, 10 Essex
Miss Deborah Foye, 4 Lynde
Miss Abigail Floyd, 28 Norman
Miss L. M. Hawkes, 20 Andrew
Charles Hobart, 95 Federal
Miss M. Roberts, Lyceum building
Miss Emeline Lord, 94 Bridge
Miss H. A. Luscomb, 41 Lafayette
William Leavitt, 71 Forrester
Miss Mary E. Jocelyn, 224 Essex
Miss E. N. Mann, 180 Federal
Miss Lucy P. Morgan, 360 Essex
Misses Peirce, 139 Essex
Miss Sarah Smith, 16 Summer
Miss E. E. Safford, 33 Essex
Miss M. P. Snow, Hamilton Hall
Miss Rebecca Thayer, 34 Broad
Miss A. M. Upton, Essex, c. Daniels
Miss Harriet Very, 1 Hardy
Mrs. Martha N. Very, 78 Federal
Miss E. W. Ward, 34 Chestnut
Miss Lucy F. Watson, 412 Essex
H. G. F. Waters, Franklin building
Miss Mary E. Williams, 243½ Essex
Edward Woodford, r. 161 Essex

Sisters of Notre Dame. School, 15 Walnut St. No. of scholars about 400. Tuition free.

STATE NORMAL SCHOOL AT SALEM.

Resolves to establish a State Normal School in the County of Essex were finally passed by the Legislature, April 16, 1853. The Board of Education, at their meeting held on Thursday, June 2, 1853, decided to locate the same in Salem. The city of Salem furnished the site formerly occupied for the Registry of Deeds, on the corner of Summer and Broad streets, erected and furnished the building to the acceptance of the Board, and received the six thousand dollars appropriated for that purpose by the Legislature. On Saturday, Sept. 3, 1853, workmen commenced to remove the old building. The new edifice, two stories high, sixty-seven feet square, built of brick, was dedicated on Thursday, Sept. 14, 1854, Gov. Washburn presiding, and the address by Ex-Gov. Boutwell.

TEACHERS.—Alpheus Crosby, *Principal*. Martha Kingman, Elizabeth Weston, Sarah R. Smith, Olive P. Bray, Ellen M. Dodge, Mary E. Webb, Gertrude Sheldon, *Assistants*. E. Ripley Blanchard, *Teacher of Music*.

Number of scholars, 117. Scholars are admitted twice a year, on the second Wednesdays of March and September. Tuition free. Scholars are required to declare their intention to teach in the schools of the Commonwealth. This school is intended for females.

CHURCHES.

FIRST CHURCH. — Unitarian Congregational.

Organized 1629. A brick edifice on Essex Street, corner of Washington.

Rev. George W. Briggs, D. D., *Pastor;* William G. Choate, *Clerk;* E. Emmerton, *Treasurer;* J. F. Allen, Nathan Frye, David Roberts, Augustus J. Archer, William A. Bowditch, *Committee;* Horace Rust, *Sexton*.

FRIENDS.

Organized 1658. A brick edifice on Pine, corner of Warren St.

William Chase, *Clerk;* Stephen A. Chase, *Treasurer;* Wm. Chase, Squires Gove, *Committee;* Stephen A. Chase, Enoch Page, Wm. Chase, *Overseers of the Poor of the Society*.

EAST CHURCH. — Unitarian Congregational.

Gathered in 1718. A freestone edifice in Washington Square.

Rev. Dexter Clapp, *Pastor;* William B. Parker, *Clerk and Treasurer;* Benjamin H. Silsbee, William B. Parker, Charles Millett, Thomas Downing, T. H. Lefavour, *Committee;* N. Berry, *Sexton*.

ST. PETER'S CHURCH. — Episcopalian.

Gathered in 1733. A stone edifice on St. Peter, corner of Brown Street.

Rev. George Leeds, *Rector;* Francis W. Pickman, Wm. R. Gavett, *Wardens;* Jona. Tucker, *Treasurer and Clerk;* Jona. Tucker, S. C. Clark, J. W. Getchell, Joshua Phippen, R. H. Chamberlain, Stephen B. Ives, Benj. Shreve, Daniel Brown, jr., *Vestrymen;* John S. Pepper, *Sexton.*

TABERNACLE. — Orthodox Congregational.

1735. Place of worship, Washington, corner of Federal. A new edifice erected, 1854.

Rev. Samuel M. Worcester, D. D., *Pastor;* Geo. D. Phippen, *Clerk;* Joseph H. Phippen, *Treasurer;* Henry Whipple, B. G. Metcalf, Israel Fellows, Pemberton Hale, William A. Purbeck, *Committee;* John H. Neal, *Sexton.*

NORTH CHURCH. — Unitarian Congregational.

Organized 1772. A stone edifice on Essex, near North street.

Rev. —— ——, *Pastor;* Stephen G. Wheatland, *Clerk and Treasurer;* George Wheatland, Jeremiah Page, A. B. Almon, Daniel Lord, Henry L. Williams, *Committee;* Abraham Very, *Sexton.*

SOUTH CHURCH. — Orthodox Congregational.

Formed 1775. Place of Worship, Chestnut, corner of Cambridge Street.

Rev. Brown Emerson, D. D., *Pastor;* Rev. Israel E. Dwinell, *Colleague;* John Chapman, *Clerk;* Charles H. Towne, *Treasurer;* Wm. P. Goodhue, John H. Stone, Geo. R. Chapman, Daniel H. Jewett, Joseph H. Towne, *Committee;* Aaron J. Cate, *Sexton.*

HOWARD STREET CHURCH. — Orthodox Congregational.

Formed as Congregational, Dec. 29, 1803; became Presbyterian, 1815; returned to Congregational in 1828. Place of worship, Howard street.

Rev. Charles C. Beaman, *Pastor;* William H. Chapman, *Treasurer;* Ezekiel Goss, *Clerk;* E. Cleaveland, B. A. Gray, Henry Hale, H. C. Tuttle, *Committee;* Joseph Kinsman, *Sexton.*

FIRST BAPTIST CHURCH.

Organized 1804. Brick edifice, 56 Federal Street.

Rev. Robert C. Mills, *Pastor;* N. Very, jr., *Clerk;* Joseph

Farnum, jr. *Treasurer;* James Upton, Charles H. Price, Alfred Peabody, George F. Brown, Frazer Carleton, *Committee;* Thos. Treadwell, *Sexton.*

FIRST UNIVERSALIST SOCIETY.
Formed 1805. A brick edifice on Rust Street.

Rev. ———— ————, *Pastor;* Charles W. Swasey, *Clerk and Treasurer;* Wm. B. Brown, Albert Wilkins, Daniel C. Haskell, Stephen Whipple, C. A. Ropes, Joseph F. Walden, William P. Martin, *Committee;* Hezekiah Sleeper, *Sexton.*

CHURCH OF THE IMMACULATE CONCEPTION.—
Roman Catholic.

Organized 1810. Place of worship, Walnut Street.

Rev. T. H. Shahan, *Pastor;* Rev. Michael Hartney, *Assistant.*

INDEPENDENT CHURCH.— Unitarian Congregational.

Organized 1824. A brick edifice, Barton Square.

Rev. James W. Thompson, D. D., *Pastor;* Samuel C. Simonds, *Clerk;* Abbott Walker, *Treasurer;* S. H. Phillips, John Jewett, Thomas Nichols, jr., Daniel Perkins, James Chamberlin, Augustus Story, Nath'l Horton, *Committee;* Jeremiah S. Perkins, *Collector;* Jacob S. Haskell, *Sexton.*

BETHEL.

Opened August, 1823. Present place of worship, Herbert St. Rev. Michael Carlton, *Pastor.*

CENTRAL BAPTIST.

Organized 1826. Brick edifice, St. Peter Street.

Rev. Daniel D. Winn, *Pastor;* Nathan Putnam, *Clerk;* Daniel Potter, *Treasurer;* W. C. Hamond, Henry F. Skerry, Levi Wiggin, D. C. Manning, William F. Gardner, Gilman Andrews, B. R. Peabody, *Committee;* E. G. Guilford, *Sexton.*

CROMBIE STREET CHURCH.—Orthodox Congregational.
Formed 1832. Brick edifice on Crombie Street.

Rev. James M. Hoppin, *Pastor;* Humphrey Cook, *Clerk;* A. A. Smith, *Treasurer;* Oliver Thayer, J. G. Waters, Charles H. Fabens, *Committee;* Charles Staniford, *Sexton.*

LAFAYETTE STREET METHODIST EPISCOPAL CHURCH.

Organized March, 1841. Place of worship, corner Lafayette and Harbor Streets.

Rev. A. F. Herrick, *Pastor;* Abraham Bennett, *Secretary and Treasurer;* Ira Mansfield, Abraham Bennett, Henry Brown, Isaac Perkins, John Roberts, Matthew Robeson, *Trustees;* Alanson Kenney, *Sexton.*

SECOND ADVENT SOCIETY.

Organized July 23, 1848. Place of worship, Endicott Street.

Rev. Frederick Gunner, *Pastor;* Charles Willey, of Danvers, *Clerk;* Elisha W. Turner, *Treasurer;* Charles H. Berry, Elisha W. Turner, J. Sweet, *Committee.*

ST. JAMES CHURCH. — Roman Catholic.

Organized 1850. Place of worship, No. 160 Federal Street.

Rev. Thomas Shahan, *Pastor.*

SECOND ADVENT SOCIETY.

Organized 1852. Place of worship, Union Street.

Rev. Francis H. Berick, *Pastor;* R. B. Reed, *Clerk;* S. F. Rogers, *Treasurer;* Temple Hardy, S. F. Rogers, *Deacons and Committee;* William Lewis, *Sexton.*

GRACE CHURCH.

Organized 1858. Gothic church, located on Essex Street, nearly opposite Monroe.

Rev. ———— ————, *Rector;* Benjamin Shreve, John Calef, *Wardens;* Charles S. Nichols, *Clerk and Treasurer;* John R. Lee, J. S. Jones, Henry F. Shepard, Samuel Pitman, jr., D. P. Ives, George D. Glover, *Vestrymen.*

CUSTOM HOUSE.

FOR THE DISTRICT OF SALEM AND BEVERLY.

No. 112 Derby Street, corner of Orange, Salem.

William B. Pike, *Collector.*
Chipman Ward, *Deputy Collector.*
Henry L. Lambert, *Clerk.*

SALEM DIRECTORY. 221

John Ryan, *Naval Officer*.
Ebenezer Dodge, *Surveyor at Salem;* Samuel Porter, *Surveyor at Beverly*..
Jonathan H. Orne, Charles H. Manning, Henry W. Perkins, *Weighers and Gaugers*.
Robert W. Gould, *Measurer*.
Connor B. Sawsey, *Public Storekeeper*.
George W. Mullet, Daniel B. Lord, William A. Phillips, Samuel Fuller, Thomas P. Kingsley, Henry Derby, Edward C. Peabody, Moses D. Randall, Salem, Stephen Lovett, Maurice C. Oby, Beverly, *Inspectors*.
Henry Meek, Henry Upton, *Boatmen*.

READING ROOM.

MERCHANTS' NEWS ROOM, Asiatic Building, 32 Washington. James Manning, *Proprietor*.

BRITISH CONSULAR AGENT.

Ephraim F. Miller, 112 Derby Street.

POST OFFICE.

Asiatic Building, 32 Washington Street.

JOSEPH S. PERKINS, POSTMASTER.
JOHN J. DALRYMPLE, CLERK.
JOHN A. CURRIN, WILLIAM H. DALRYMPLE, ASSISTANT CLERKS.

California Mails close on the 4th and 19th of each month, at 12 M.

English Mails close every Tuesday and Friday.

⁂ Office hours from 7 A. M. to $7\frac{1}{2}$ P. M.

RATES OF POSTAGE IN THE UNITED STATES, OR TO B. N. AMERICAN PROVINCES.

Letters in the U. S., per $\frac{1}{2}$ oz. (fractions same), not over 3000 miles, 3 c. prepaid; over 3000 miles, 10 c. prepaid. Letters dropped for delivery only, 1 c. prepaid or not. Advertised letters, 1 c. extra. To or from the Provinces, not over 3000 miles from the line, 10 c. per $\frac{1}{2}$ oz., over 3000, 15 c., prepaid or not.

Transient newspapers, periodicals, unsealed circulars, or other articles of printed matter, not exceeding three ounces in weight, to any part of the United States, prepaid 1 c., not prepaid 2 c.;

each additional ounce, or fraction of an ounce, prepaid 1 c., not prepaid 2 c.

Regular newspapers or periodicals, paid yearly or quarterly in advance, when circulated in the State where published, not weighing over 1½ oz., ¼ c.; over 1½ oz and not over 3 oz., ½ c.; every additional oz. or fraction, ½ c. When circulated *out of the State*, all weighing 3 oz. or *less*, ½ c. and each additional oz or fraction, ½ c. *Weekly newspapers*, within the county where printed and published, single copy free to each subscriber. Small newspapers and periodicals, monthly or oftener, and pamphlets not containing more than sixteen octavo pages, in single packages of not less than eight oz., to one address, prepaid, ½ c. for each oz.: fraction same.

Books, bound or unbound, not weighing over four pounds, under three thousand miles, 1 c. per oz. prepaid, 1½ c. not prepaid; over three thousand miles, 2 c. prepaid, 3 c. not prepaid.

Publishers of newspapers and periodicals are allowed a free exchange of one copy, and may also send to each actual subscriber, enclosed in their publications, bills, and receipts for the same, free.

All printed matter must be sent without cover, or in a cover open at the ends and sides. There must be no word or communication printed on the same after its publication, or upon the cover, except the name and address of the person to whom it is to be sent. There must be no paper or other thing enclosed in or with such printed paper.

TO OR FROM GREAT BRITAIN OR IRELAND.

Letters.—Each ½ oz., 24. c.; 5 c. extra for California or Oregon. Prepayment optional.

Newspapers.—2 c. each, payable in U. S.

Periodicals and Pamphlets.— Not over 2 oz., 2 c. each, and 4 c. each extra oz., payable in the United States; and same postage is payable in the United Kingdom, excepting that for the third oz. it rises to sixpence, and each extra oz. is twopence.

BANKS IN SALEM.

Annual meeting of the Banks in Salem, in October.
Dividends declared, first Monday in April and October.

ASIATIC BANK—Asiatic Building, No. 32 Washington St.

Capital, $315,000. Par value of share, $30.

Directors—Joseph S. Cabot, *President.* George Wheatland, G. G. Newhall, N. A. Frye, Leonard B. Harrington, James B.

SALEM DIRECTORY. 223

Curwen, G. F. Brown. W. H. Foster, *Cashier.* Charles H. Towne, *Bookkeeper.* Wm. J. Foster, *Teller.* D. E. Saunders, *Clerk.*

Discount, Mondays, Wednesdays, and Fridays. Bank hours, 9 to quarter past 1.

COMMERCIAL BANK—No. 7 Central Street.

Capital, $200,000. Par value of share, $66.66⅔.

Directors—William Sutton, *President.* Wm. P. Goodhue, M. W. Shepard, John Jewett, W. D. Waters, J. C. Stimpson, George W. Keene. E. H. Payson, *Cashier.* S. B. Buttrick, *Bookkeeper.* G. L. Streeter, *Teller.*

Discount, Mondays, Wednesdays, and Fridays. Bank hours, 9 to half past 1.

EXCHANGE BANK—No. 172 Essex Street.

Capital, $200,000. Par value of share, $66.66⅔.

Directors — John Webster, *President.* J. C. Lee, W. D. Pickman, S. G. Wheatland, Nathan Nichols, Henry L. Williams, Joseph F. Walden. John Chadwick, *Cashier.* Joseph H. Webb, *Bookkeeper.* S. G. Symonds, *Clerk.*

Discount, Mondays and Thursdays. Bank hours, 9 to quarter past 1.

MERCANTILE BANK—No. 7 Central Street.

Capital, $200,000. Par value of share, $100.

Directors—John Dwyer, *President.* William F. Nichols, John Huse, Aaron Perkins, Oliver Thayer, Wm. S. Messervy, Josiah Spalding. J. Hardy Phippen, *Cashier.* J. I. Hutchinson, *Bookkeeper.*

Discount, Tuesday and Fridays. Bank hours 8¾ to half past 1.

MERCHANTS BANK—Asiatic Building, 32 Washington St.

Capital, $200,000. Par value of share, $50.

Directors—Benjamin H. Silsbee, *President.* J. W. Peele, James Upton, Benjamin Webb, William Varney. Nathaniel B. Perkins, *Cashier.* William H. Whipple, *Bookkeeper.* B. W. Gardner, *Clerk.*

Discount, Tuesdays and Fridays. Bank hours, 8¾ to 1¼.

NAUMKEAG BANK—No. 163 Essex Street.

Capital, $500,000. Par value of share, $100.

Directors—David Pingree, *President.* W. B. Parker, E. D.

Kimball, Nathaniel Weston, Jeremiah Page, R. P. Waters, B. A. West. J. Hardy Towne, *Cashier.* Geo. R. Felt, *Bookkeeper.* John C. Towne, *Discount Clerk.* John P. Downing, *Clerk.*

Discount, Tuesdays and Fridays, 9½. Bank hours, 8½ A. M. to 1½ P. M.

SALEM BANK—No. 163 Essex Street.

Capital, $250,000. Par value of share, $100.

Directors—Wm. C. Endicott, *President.* Abbott Walker, Nathaniel B. Mansfield, J. H. Nichols, James Chamberlain, Joshua Phippen, E. S. Poor. George D. Phippen, *Cashier.* Benjamin W. Russell, *Bookkeeper.* Geo. B. Phippen, *Clerk.*

Discount, Mondays and Thursdays. Bank hours, 9 to 1.

SALEM SAVINGS BANK—Asiatic Building.

No. 32 Washington.

Incorporated, 1818. Object, to enable industrious persons of all descriptions to invest sums in a manner which will afford them profit and security. Two and a quarter per cent in interest, half yearly, is payable on the third Wednesday in April and October, which, if not withdrawn, is added to the principal as the end of three months, and at the end of every five years all extra income is divided; the interest on long deposits has generally amounted to nearly 7 per cent.

September, 1858, the amount deposited by 8,889 depositors was $1,947,201.92.

Financial Committee.—J. S. Cabot, Wm. H. Foster, J. W. Peele, Benjamin H. Silsbee, Wm. D. Pickman.

Annual Meeting, on the second Wednesday in January.

The Bank is open every day, from 8¾ A. M. till 1¼ P. M.

Officers chosen, January, 1858.—Daniel A. White, *President.* Humphrey Devereux, George Peabody, Zachariah F. Silsbee, John Bertram, Joseph F. Cabot, William Sutton, *Vice Presidents.* Benjamin P. Chamberlain, John C. Lee, Jonathan W. Peele, B. H. Silsbee, William B. Parker, William Pickman, John Dwyer, Thomas Downing, Benjamin Cox, David Putnam, Alfred Peabody, Wm. H. Foster, Leonard B. Harrington, Jas. B. Curwen, Stephen A. Chase, *Trustees.* Henry Ropes, *Treasurer.* William Wallis, *Secretary.*

SALEM FIVE CENTS SAVINGS BANK.

No. 171 Essex Street.

Commenced operations, July, 1855.

SALEM DIRECTORY. 225

Open for deposits from 9 to 1 o'clock, daily.
Edward D. Kimball, *President*. John Chapman, Asahel Huntington, Thomas Nichols, Jr., Thomas P. Pingree, Edmund Smith, Wm. S. Messervy, *Vice Presidents*. J. Vincent Browne, *Treasurer*. Nathaniel Cleaves, *Secretary*. Ephraim Brown, Francis Brown, George F. Brown, J. Vincent Browne, William Calley, Nathaniel Cleaves, William P. Goodhue, William Hunt, Samuel Endicott, of Beverly, John Jewett, William F. Nichols, Gilbert G. Newhall, David Moore, Jeremiah Page, J. W. Perry, Charles A Ropes, James C. Stimpson, Oliver Thayer, William Varney, Benjamin Webb, Benjamin A. West, Henry L. Williams, Thomas Evans, of Marblehead, *Trustees*. Edward D. Kimball, William Hunt, Edmund Smith, Henry L. Williams, J. Vincent Browne, *Committee of Investment*.

SALEM AND DANVERS LOAN AND FUND ASSOCIATION.

Organized, January, 1855. Commenced operations, May, 1855, Office, No. 16 Washington, up stairs.

Regular meetings, third Monday in each month.
Officers.—James Kimball, *President*. Stephen B. Ives, *Vice President*. Wm. Archer, *Secretary*. Steven B. Ives, Jr., *Attorney*. Thomas S. Jewett, *Surveyor*. E. B. Peirson, C. H. Manning, William Calley, E. H. Payson, T. M. Saunders, Samuel Day, T. H. Frothingham, R. Lindsey, Jacob F. Brown, Aaron Perkins, H. G. Hubon, Moses T. Upton, Chas. Greene, L. B. Hatch, Salem; Thomas A. Sweetser, S. Danvers, *Directors*.

WORKING MEN'S LOAN AND FUND CORPORATION.

Organized, December, 1854. Commenced operations, Oct. 1855. Room No. 18 Asiatic Buildidg.

Officers.—Stephen H. Phillips, *President*. John Webster, *Vice President*. Samuel Mackintire, *Secretary*. Nathaniel B. Perkins, George F. Brown, Israel Fellows, Joseph C. Foster, George W. Pease, James A. Gillis, Daniel C. Manning, Salem; Daniel E. Safford, Hamilton; John Conway, Jr., Marblehead; Stephens Baker, Beverly; Edward Staten, Gloucester; Jefferson Taylor, South Danvers; Calvin Putnam, Danvers Port; Horace Clarke, Lynn, *Directors*.

INSURANCE COMPANIES.
ESSEX MUTUAL FIRE INSURANCE CO.
No. 42 Washington Street.

Annual Meeting, Third Saturday in September.
Directors—George Nichols, *President*. David Putnam, Geo.

H. Smith, Pierce L. Wiggin, Perley Putnam, Nathaniel Appleton, Robert Peele. John Pratt, Leonard B. Harrington, John Jewett, Timothy Ropes. John H. Nichols, *Secretary*.

HAMILTON INSURANCE CO.

No. 27 Washington Street.

Cash capital, $60,000. Guarantee Capital, $360.000.

Directors—William C. Prescott, *President and Treasurer*. Elijah J. Hanson, N. D. Symonds, John Hilton, Joshua Silvester, John T. Burnham, James Kimball, A. Richardson, Wm. Brown, Caleb Smith. N. A. Clarke, *Superintendent*. John T. Burnham, *Secretary*.

SALEM MUTUAL FIRE INSURANCE CO.

No. 42 Washington Street.

Annual Meeting, 4th Monday in April.

Directors—John H. Nichols, *President*. Isaac P. Foster, Wm. Calley, Samuel Chamberlain, James Chamberlain, Charles M. Richardson, Geo. F. Brown, Eben N. Price, Francis Choate. Charles S. Nichols, *Secretary*.

SALEM MARINE INSURANCE COMPANY.

Asiatic Building.

Capital, $100,000.

Directors—Jeremiah Page, *President*. Wm. B. Parker, B. H. Silsbee, William Hunt, James B. Curwen, Benjamin A. West, Thomas Perkins, Jr. William Northey, *Secretary*.

HOLYOKE MUTUAL FIRE INSURANCE CO.

No. 27 Washington Street.

Cash Capital, $100,000.

Annual Meeting, Second Wednesday in October.

Directors — Augustus Story, *President and Treasurer*. Stephen Osborne, William Story, John T. Burnham, James Chamberlain, Salem; Fred. Mitchell, Ipswich; Joshua Silvester, Danvers; John Hilton, Lynn; Edward Todd, Rowley. John T. Burnham, *Secretary*. N. A. Clarke, *General Agent*.

SOCIETIES AND COMPANIES.

SALEM ATHENÆUM,

Incorporated in 1810, was formed by the union of the Social and Philosophical Libraries. The former was organized in 1760, the latter in 1781. Number of volumes, 12,500, which are deposited in Plummer Hall, 134 Essex street.

Annual meeting for the choice of officers, last Wednesday but one in May.

Library open every day between the hours of 9 A. M. and 1 P. M., and from 2 to 5 P. M.

Officers chosen in May, 1858.—George Choate, *President;* Henry Wheatland, *Clerk of the Corporation;* James Chamberlain, *Treasurer;* George Choate, Benjamin Barstow, William Mack, James M. Hoppin, Henry Wheatland, A. Huntington, John C. Lee, James Chamberlain, Wm. S. Messervy, *Trustees;* Henry J. Cross, *Librarian.*

ESSEX SOUTHERN DISTRICT MEDICAL SOCIETY

Consists of all those members of the Massachusetts Medical Society who reside in Lynn, Swampscott, Nahant, Saugus, Marblehead, Salem, Danvers, Middleton, Beverly, Wenham, Topsfield, Ipswich, Hamilton, Essex, Rockport, Gloucester, and Manchester.

The Society was formed in 1805, in pursuance of a vote of the Massachusetts Medical Society, authorizing the establishment of district or subordinate associations. The Library is annually increased, and contains about 1000 volumes; it is deposited in Plummer Hall, where the regular quarterly meetings of the Society are held.

Annual Meeting on Tuesday of the week preceding the meeting of the Massachusetts Medical Society.

Officers elected, 1858.—Eben Hunt, of Danvers, *President;* Augustus Torrey, of Beverly, *Vice President;* Richard H. Wheatland, of Salem, *Treasurer;* F. Winsor, of Salem, *Secretary;* L. R. Stone, of Salem, *Librarian.*

ESSEX INSTITUTE,

Incorporated in 1848, was formed by the union of the Essex Historical Society and the Essex County Natural History Society.

The Library contains about 13,000 volumes; the cabinets are well filled with specimens of Natural History. The Institute have also portraits of several of the former Presidents of the Historical Society, and some of the early settlers of New England.

Exhibitions of Fruits and Flowers are held occasionally at their rooms, in Plummer Hall.

Annual Meeting on the second Wednesday in May.

Officers chosen in May, 1858.—D. A. White, *President;* John Lewis Russell, John C. Lee, Henry M. Brooks, *Vice Presidents;* Henry Wheatland, *Secretary and Treasurer;* J. H. Stone, *Librarian;* Caleb Cooke, *Cabinet Keeper.*

Library open every day between the hours of 9 A. M. and 1 P. M., and 2 and 5 P. M.

SALEM LYCEUM

Was formed the 18th of January, 1830, and organized as an Incorporated Association on the 2d of April, 1830. The introductory lecture was delivered in the Sewall Street Meeting House, by Hon. D. A. White.

The purchase of an annual ticket makes a person a member of the corporation, and the price of a ticket has never been more than ONE DOLLAR. Nearly six hundred lectures have been delivered in the annual courses.

The Legislature, on the 20th of April, 1852, passed an act, making Daniel A. White, Stephen C. Phillips, George Peabody, their associate petitioners and successors, and the male citizens of the city of Salem, of twenty-one years of age, purchasers of tickets to the twenty-third course of lectures, a corporation by the name of the Salem Lyceum. At a meeting of the corporation, held May, 1858, the following officers were elected:—

George W. Briggs, *President;* George Andrews, *Vice President;* Joseph M. Newhall, *Recording Secretary;* H. J. Cross, *Corresponding Secretary;* G. L. Streeter, *Treasurer;* James Kimball, S. P. Andrews, S. Johnson, Jr., Wm. Silver, A. G. Brown, Jacob Batchelder, Wm. A. Bowdoin, I. E. Dwinell, *Managers;* Daniel A. White, Stephen H. Phillips, George Peabody, *Trustees.*

YOUNG MEN'S UNION.

Organized, 1855.

For the benefit of the Young Men of all avocations *in this community.*

This association occupies convenient rooms (No. 172 Essex St., over the Exchange Bank), and is in receipt of the leading daily and weekly journals, of all parts of the country; also the "London Times," and "Illustrated News," and the standard Reviews and principal perodicals of the day. It has a library of reference, comprising the latest and most accurate maps.

SALEM DIRECTORY.

No admission fee is required; and the assessments, payable in advance, is fixed at the low price of $2 per annum.

All gentlemen wishing to sustain such an institution in our city, or avail themselves of its privileges, are cordially invited to join.

Officers for the year ending April, 1859.—Richard C. Manning *President;* Justin Rideout, *Vice President;* Charles Bowker, *Treasurer;* Geo. W. Williams, *Recording Secretary;* Francis H. Lee, *Corr. Sec.;* R. H. Wheatland, James Donaldson, Ezra F. Newhall, Charles F. Robbins, *Directors.*

BIBLE SOCIETY OF SALEM AND VICINITY.

Instituted, August 22, 1810. Annual Meeting, second Wednesday in June. Depository, No. 230 Essex street.

Officers elected, June, 1856.—Rev. S. M. Worcester, *President;* Rev. J. M. Hoppin, *Secretary;* Stephen B. Ives, *Treasurer;* John Dike, R. P. Waters, John G. Waters, Alfred Peabody, *Trustees.*

HARMONY GROVE CEMETERY CORPORATION.

Organized in 1839. Incorporated in 1840. Consecrated, June 14, 1840. Contains about 65 acres.

The cemetery was formerly situated within the town of Danvers. The Legislature of 1840 passed an act so altering the boundaries between Salem and Danvers, that the whole of the cemetery now lies within the limits of the city of Salem. The sale of lots is under the charge of W. H. Foster, to whom application can be made.

Annual Meeting for the choice of Trustees, first Wednesday in January.

Officers elected, January, 1858.—Joseph S. Cabot, *President;* John C. Lee, J. W. Peele, Elijah A. Hanson, Francis Peabody, George Wheatland, Nathaniel Silsbee, William H. Foster, *Trustees;* William H. Foster, *Secretary and Treasurer;* Chas. Creasy, *Keeper.*

SALEM SOCIETY FOR THE MORAL AND RELIGIOUS INSTRUCTION OF THE POOR.

Formed, March 24, 1819. Incorporated, February, 1826.

Annual Meeting in April.

Officers elected, May, 1858.— ———————, *President;* Geo. D. Phippen, *Vice President;* John Carlton, *Treasurer;* Step'n P. Driver, *Secretary;* C. H. Price, John Carlton, E. Buswell. John B. Shepard, Benj. Shreve, Moses B. Upton, D. B. Brooks *Managers;* Rev. Michael Carlton, *Agent;* John Carlton, *Collector.*

PLUMMER FARM SCHOOL OF REFORM FOR BOYS.

This school was founded by the munificent bequest of Miss Caroline Plummer. It is a school for the instruction, employment, and reformation of juvenile offenders in the city of Salem, and is to be conducted on a plan similar to that of the State Reform School. The amount of the bequest is 25,000; present fund $28,000; and the school will go into operation as soon as adequate means are obtained to carry it on successfully, in accordance with the will of the donor.

A Board of ten Trustees was chosen by the Mayor and Aldermen of the city of Salem, in May, 1855, and incorporated by an Act of the Legislature on the 21st of May, 1855. The first meeting of the Board of Trustees was held Nov. 26, 1855, at which time a code of By-Laws was adopted, and officers were elected. The Board of Trustees for 1858 is as follows:—

Daniel A. White, *President*; George Andrews, *Secretary*; William L. Bowditch, Joseph Andrews, Eleazer Austin, *Executive Committee*; George Andrews, *Treasurer*, Danl. A. White, Wm. L. Bowditch, Joseph Andrews, James Kimball, Eleazer Austin, William Chase, George Andrews, Wm. D. Waters, David Nichols, Wm. S. Messervy, *Trustees*.

DORCAS SOCIETY.

Mrs. A. L. Peirson, *Directress*; Mrs. Rebecca C. Kinsman, Miss Lydia H. Chase, Miss Elizabeth I. Devereux, *Distributors*; Miss Mary C. Anderson, *Treasurer*; Miss Esther C. Mack, *Secretary*.

CHARITY INFANT SCHOOL.—Federal Court.

Miss Lydia H. Chase, Miss Lydia R. Nichols, *Managers*; Miss Elizabeth P. Nichols, *Treasurer and Secretary*; Miss Rebecca Thayer, *Teacher*.

SALEM SEAMEN'S ORPHAN AND CHILDREN'S FRIEND SOCIETY.

The Salem Children's Friend Society was organized February 25, 1839, for the purpose of rescuing from evil, and improving the condition of such children as are in indigent and suffering circumstances, and not otherwise provided for. Incorporated, March, 1841. In 1844, the house they now occupy, No. 7 Carpenter street, was purchased at an expense of $1,500, and presented to them by R. Brookhouse, Esq., of this city, when they took their present name.

Annual Meeting, 8th of May. Visitors admitted on Thursday.

SALEM DIRECTORY. 231

Officers – Mrs. Thorndike Proctor, *President;* Mrs. N. W. Osgood, *Vice President;* Miss Harriet L. Peirson, *Secretary;* Miss H. King, *Treasurer;* Mrs. John Bertram, Mrs. B. E. Valentine, Mrs. A. L. Peirson, Miss Margaret P. Dabney, Miss C. Fabens, Mrs. Michael Carlton, Mrs. B. Peabody, Mrs. Edward Putnam, Mrs. Joseph Winn, Mrs. Rea, Miss E. Fettyplace, Mrs. J. Rose, Jr., *Managers;* Michael Carlton, A. Huntington, John Chapman, *Board of Advisers.* Miss Lydia Babbidge, *Teacher.* Mrs. E. B. Harris, *Matron.*

SEAMEN'S WIDOW AND ORPHAN ASSOCIATION.

Formed, May 1, 1833, for the purpose of devising and adopting such measures as may seem best to ameliorate the condition of the fatherless and the widow.

Annual Meeting on the first Thursday in May.

Officers May, 1858.—Mrs. A. True, *President;* Mrs. Catharine Little, *Vice President;* Mrs. George D. Phippen, *Treasurer;* Miss Sarah E. Lakeman, *Secretary;* Mrs. Joseph Webb, Mrs. E. K. Lakeman, Mrs. Joseph Hodges, Mrs. T. B. Russell, Mrs. G. Kimball, Mrs. Ephraim Burr, Mrs. Samuel Ropes, Jr., Miss Eliza Low, Mrs. J. Emerson, Mrs. J. Kimball, Mrs. William H. Jelly, Miss Louisa Webb, *Managers.*

LADIES' SEAMEN'S FRIEND SOCIETY.

Organized, January 22, 1844.

Present Officers.—Mrs. George H. Smith, *President;* Mrs. Samuel Benson, 1st *Vice President;* ———— ————, 2d *Vice President;* Miss Sarah Hobart, *Corresponding and Recording Secretary;* ———— ————, *Treasurer;* Mrs. Robert Mills, Mrs. Andrew Ward, Mrs. Parker Brown, Mrs. N. P. Rust, Mrs. Michael Carlton, Mrs. Robert Skerry, Mrs. Ephraim Allen, Mrs. James M. Hoppin, *Managers.*

FEMALE SAMARITAN SOCIETY.

Annual Meeting for the choice of officers, on the second Monday in December.

Board of Managers.—Miss Lydia Frothingham, *President;* Mrs. Elizabeth Cheever, 1st *Vice President;* Mrs. Mary Woods, 2d *Vice President;* Miss Jane Varney, *Secretary;* Miss Mary E. Whipple, *Treasurer;* Mrs. Mary Whipple, Mrs. Mary Walden, Miss Sarah P. Davis, Miss Mary Stocker, Miss Lydia Ann Jenks, Miss Clarissa Gavett, Mrs. Matilda Nourse, Mrs. Elizabeth Brown, Miss E. Devereux, *Trustees.*

SALEM DISPENSARY.

Organized, February, 1820. Incorporated, February, 1831.

Its object is the relief of the poor by affording Medicines and Medical Advice gratuitously. The expenses to be paid by an annual subscription. All the subscribers can give certificates to the Apothecaries for such Medicine as may be prescribed by the Physicians in their behalf. To this class, much time timely and effectual aid has been rendered.

The city is divided into two districts, the Eastern and the Western, to each of which is assigned a Physician and an Apothecary.

The Eastern district includes all persons who may apply for relief, living eastward of St. Peter and Central Streets, and South Salem.

The Western district includes those living westward of the above streets, and North Salem.

Annual Meeting, first Thursday in January.

Board of Managers, elected January 7, 1858.—D. A. White, *President;* Henry Whipple, *Secretary and Treasurer;* George Peabody, Robert Brookhouse, Richard S. Rogers, Asahel Huntington, E. H. Payson, Andrew Ward, Aaron Perkins, E. B. Peirson, John Bertram, Wm. S. Messervey, Wm. D. Pickman.

Physicians.—Dr. David Choate, 18 Church street, Eastern District; Dr. L. R. Stone, Western District.

Apothecaries.—G. Barton, Eastern District; C. H. Pinkham, Western District.

SALEM FEMALE CHARITABLE SOCIETY.

This Society was one of the first of our charitable institutions, having been formed as early as 1801, and incorporated in 1804; its objects were the support of female children, and to assist that unfortunate class, the aged and infirm widows.

Its first Board were Mrs. Sarah Fiske, *First Directress;* Mrs. Lucretia Osgood, *Second Directress;* Mrs. Lydia Nichols, *Treasurer;* Mrs. Abigail M. Dabney, *Secretary;* Mrs. Elizabeth White, Mrs. Deborah Hovey, Mrs. Hannah Robinson, Mrs. Hannah Ropes, Mrs. Eunice Richardson, Mrs. Sarah Crowninshield, Mrs. Hannah Hodges, Mrs. Sarah Dunlap, *Managers.* These ladies were succeeded by others, some long since deceased; the most recent, the late Mrs. Rebecca Dodge, and Mrs. Richard S. Rogers.

The Society continued its operations, as above stated, until 1831 or 1832, when by a vote of the Board, and by the authority granted them by the Legislature, it was decided to appropriate its income for the relief of indigent females. The Society meetings are held monthly, at the houses of the officers.

The present Board consists of Mrs. R. Brookhouse, *First Directress;* Mrs. P. P. Pinel, *Second Directress;* Miss S. Frye, *Treasurer;* Miss H. O. Mack, *Secretary;* Mrs. Susan Ward, Mrs. S. P. Webb, Mrs. Emery Johnson, Mrs. S. A. Safford, Mrs. G. B. Loring, Mrs. O. P. Lord, Miss Mary C. Anderson, Miss Lydia H. Chase, Mrs. Rebecca Kinsman, Mrs. Eben Putnam, *Managers.*

SALEM EAST INDIA MARINE SOCIETY.

No. 163 Essex Street.

Founded in 1799. Incorporated in 1801.

The museum contains a fine collection of specimens in the various departments of Natural History, to which strangers have free access by first obtaining a pass from any of the members of the Society.

Annual Meeting, first Wednesday in November.

The Hall is open from June 1 to October 1, from 10, A. M., to 1, P. M., and from 3 to 5, P. M. Closed the remainder of the year.

Officers elected November, 1857.—Allen Putnam, *President;* Charles Millett, Charles Mansfield, William B. Parker, *Committee of Observation;* Nathaniel Griffin, *Treasurer;* Gilbert G. Newhall, *Corresponding Secretary;* Thomas Saul, *Recording Secretary and Superintendent;* William Story, *Distributor of Journals;* James King, *Inspector of Journals.*

SALEM MARINE SOCIETY.

Instituted, 1766. Incorporated, 1771.

Annual Meeting, last Thursday in October. Meetings are likewise held on the evening of the last Thursday of every month throughout the year. Rooms in Franklin Building.

Officers elected October, 1857.—John Dwyer, *Master;* Jeremiah Page, *Deputy Master;* Jonathan P. Felt, *Treasurer;* Edward Barnard, *Clerk;* Josiah Spaulding, Charles Mansfield, Jeremiah Page, James Buffington, *Distributing Committee;* Nath. Weston, William B. Smith, *Committee on Franklin Building;* Jonathan P. Felt, *Agent of Franklin Building.*

THE SALEM PROVIDENT ASSOCIATION.

Organized on Wednesday evening, October 27, 1852.

Object, to afford a more systematic plan of relief for the poor.

William D. Pickman, *President;* Richard S. Rogers, *Vice*

President; B. H. Silsbee, *Secretary;* John Ball, *General Agent and Treasurer;* Edward B. Pierson, John B. Silsbee, John Bertram, S. Endicott Peabody, *Committee.*

SALEM CHARITABLE MECHANIC ASSOCIATION.

Organized, Oct. 1, 1817. Incorporated, June 4, 1822.

Consists of regular apprenticed Mechanics, and of Manufacturers, citizens of the city of Salem and vicinity. Number of members about 300. Annual Meeting for the choice of officers, first Wednesday in January.

In connection with this Association is a Library containing 4000 volumes, for the use of members and their apprentices. The Library is open on Saturday evening of each week. The average weekly delivery is 150 volumes.

Officers elected Janury, 1858.—James Kimball, *President;* Aaron Perkins, *Vice President;* John Chapman, *Treasurer;* Thomas M. Dix, *Secretary;* Charles Harrington, Mark Lowd, Wm. P. Martin, James F. Potter, John P. Henderson, Josiah Crocker, Henry A. Ruee, Daniel Henderson, James A. Brown, *Trustees.*

ESSEX AGRICULTURAL SOCIETY.

Organized at Topsfield on Monday, Feb. 16, 1818, by the election of Col. Timothy Pickering, *President;* and to this office he was annually elected for ten successive years. Incorporated, June 12, 1818. The first exhibition was held at Topsfield, October 5, 1820, and they have been continued annually in the month of September or October in several towns in the county — usually twice successively in the same place. The society is receiving from year to year large accessions to its list of members; about 1500 names are on its catalogue.

This Society was the first in the State to publish in detail its transactions — which have now extended to four large octavo volumes, containing much valuable information to the agriculturist.

A Library was commenced in the Autumn of 1849, by the purchase of the agricultural portion of the library of the late lamented Henry Colman, which, with a few additions from other sources, numbers about seven hundred volumes, deposited in the Court House, Salem.

Officers elected at the annual meeting, in Danvers, September, 1858: —

Daniel Adams, Newbury, *President;* Andrew Dodge, Wenham, Dean Robinson, West Newbury, Thomas E. Payson, Rowley, Lewis Allen, S. Danvers, *Vice Presidents;* William

Sutton, South Danvers, *Treasurer;* Allen W. Dodge, Hamilton, *Secretary.*

James H. Duncan, Haverhill; Gardner B. Perry, Groveland; John W. Proctor, Danvers; Richard S. Fay, Lynn, *Honorary Trustees.*

Paul Titcomb, Newbury; John Alley, 3d, William Osborn, Lynn; I. Osgood, N. Andover; J. D. Cross, Ipswich; Jonathan Berry, Middleton; David Choate, Essex; Jeremiah Coleman, Joshua Hall, Newburyport; Jos. How, Methuen; John Keeley, Haverhill; H. K. Oliver, Lawrence; Royal A Merriam, Topsfield; Andrew Mansfield, Lynnfield; John M. Ives, Robert Brookhouse, Jr., Geo. B. Loring, Salem; Moses Pettengill, Topsfield; William R. Putnam, Chas. P. Preston, Danvers; J. B. Jenkins, Andover; Samuel Little, Georgetown; Horace Ware, Marblehead; Richard P. Waters, Beverly; Enoch Wood, Boxford; Enoch S. Williams, Newburyport; Thos. P. Gentlee, Manchester; B. Perley Poore, West Newbury; Lambert Maynard, Bradford,—*Trustees.*

ESSEX COUNTY TEACHERS' ASSOCIATION.

Organized at Topsfield, Dec. 3, 1830.

Meetings are held semi-annually, on the Friday and Saturday following the annual Fast in April, and the third Friday and Saturday of October, at such places as may be designated at the previous meeting.

Officers elected, October, 1858. — Wm. C. Todd, Newburyport, *President;* J. A. Shores, Haverhill, *Vice President;* D. M. Easton, Gloucester, *Recording Secretary;* Alpheus Crosby, Salem, *Corresponding Secretary;* Stephen Peabody, Newburyport, *Treasurer.* Wm. J. Rolfe, Lawrence; A. J. Saunders, Groveland; L. P. Brickett, South Danvers; E. E. Boynton, Lynn; W. K. Bell, Ipswich; John R. Baker, Beverly, *Councillors.*

MISSIONARY UNION OF SALEM AND VICINITY.

Annual Meeting second Wednesday in June. Board of Managers chosen June, 1858: —

Rev. Samuel M. Worcester, D. D., *President;* Rev. Parsons Cooke, D. D., *Vice President;* Rev. J. B. Clark, *Secretary;* Richard P. Waters, *Treasurer;* Henry Whipple, *Auditor.*

SALEM INDEPENDENT PROTECTIVE UNION.

Organized, August 26, 1847.

H. Luscomb, Jr., *President;* E. A. Goldthwait, *Vice President;* Benjamin A. Gray, *Secretary;* Thomas B. Flowers,

Treasurer; Henry Luscomb, S. N. Larrabee, J. P. Punchard, *Directors;* T. B. Flowers, Lewis D. Richards, C. H. Lord, *Store Keepers.*

SALEM GASLIGHT COMPANY.

23 Northey Street.

Organized, April 4, 1850. Capital $125,000.

Annual Meeting, second Monday in March. The Company carries the branch pipes into buildings to a distance of seventeen feet from the main pipe; beyond that, the pipes and the fixtures are at the expense of the consumer. The Company also places the metre to measure the quantity of gas consumed by a self-registering process of wheel-work. The price of gas is at the rate of $3.50 per 1000 cubic feet.

The stores were lighted with gas, for the first time, on Tuesday evening, December 17, 1850; the street lamps, on Wednesday evening, December 25.

George Choate, *President;* B. Frank Fabens, Stephen G. Wheatland, William Hunt, Salem; Henry Cook, Danvers, *Directors;* Francis Brown, *Treasurer and Superintendent;* Richard Gardner, *Clerk.*

SALEM AND DANVERS ASSOCIATION FOR THE DETECTION OF THIEVES AND ROBBERS.

Formed, 1833. Annual Meeting, first Wednesday in January.

Officers elected, January, 1858. — Elijah A. Hanson, *President;* Lewis Allen, Benj. F. Browne, *Vice Presidents;* Henry Whipple, Abner Sanger, Robert Brookhouse, *Trustees;* Jonathan Perley, *Clerk;* Joseph S. Leavitt, Samuel Day, Alfred R. Brooks, Rufus Wyman, Wm. C. Barton, Joseph Cloutman, — *Directors.*

SALEM FEMALE ANTI-SLAVERY SOCIETY.

Organized, June 4th, 1834.

Officers chosen, 1858. — Mrs. William Ives, *President;* Mrs. Sarah Hayward, Mrs. Caroline Putnam, *Vice Presidents;* Adaline Roberts, *Corresponding Secretary;* Caroline Balch, *Recording Secretary;* Adaline Roberts, *Treasurer;* Lydia P. Chase, *Auditor;* Lydia H. Chase, Sarah Holman, Eliza Cox, Lucy Watson, *Counsellors;* Caroline Balch, *Collector.*

SALEM LABORATORY COMPANY.

Office, 42 Washington Street. Located on Laboratory Street, North Salem. Annual Meeting, last Wednesday in July.

Charles Richardson, Wm. H. Foster, George F. Brown, John G. Felt, Stephen Curran, *Directors;* George Nichols, *Agent and Treasurer;* John H. Nichols, *Clerk;* Stephen Curran, *Chemist.*

SALEM AND DANVERS AQUEDUCT COMPANY.

Incorporated, 1797. Annual Meeting, first Thursday in May. Dividends in May and November, paid at Salem Bank. Office, No. 2 Sewall Street.

William D. Waters, *President;* J. S. Leavitt, *Vice President;* Charles M. Endicott, *Clerk and Treasurer;* William Jelly, *Agent and Collector;* David Pingree, Henry Cook, Charles M. Endicott, Robert Peele, Ebenezer Sutton, Aaron Perkins, J. S. Leavitt, J. G. Waters, *Directors.*

ESSEX MARINE RAILWAY.

Incorporated, February, 1826. First vessel hauled up, ship "Endeavor," Sept. 21, 1826. Annual Meeting, third Monday in January.

J. W. Getchell, *Superintendent.*
Nathaniel B. Perkins, *Treasurer.*
Josiah Crocker, Benj. Webb, Nathaniel B. Perkins, *Directors.*

SALEM MARINE RAILWAY COMPANY.

Incorporated, 1823. First vessel hauled up, brig "Washington," Sept. 1823. Annual Meeting in January.

J. W. Peele, George Dodge, Nathaniel Griffin, *Directors;* J. W. Peele, *Treasurer;* Daniel C. Becket, *Superintendent.*

SALEM TURNPIKE AND CHELSEA BRIDGE CORPORATION.

Officers chosen, September, 1858. — Nathaniel Griffin, *President;* Gideon Tucker, *1st Vice President;* B. F. Newhall, *2d Vice President;* William S. Cleveland, *Clerk and Treasurer.*

Directors.—William D. Waters, Gideon Tucker, Robert Peele, Nathaniel Griffin, Samuel Symonds, Thorp Fisher, Benjamin F. Newhall, John Archer, William Endicott. Samuel Knowles, *Agent.*

Annual Meeting in September. Dividends, first Wednesday in January, April, July, and October, paid at Commercial Bank.

EAST INDIA MARINE HALL CORPORATION.

Incorporated, 1824.

Annual Meeting, second Wednesday in January.

Officers elected in January, 1858. — *Directors.* — Allen Putnam, *President;* Wm. B. Parker, Charles Mansfield, Charles Millet. Nathaniel Griffin, *Clerk and Treasurer.*

MECHANIC HALL CORPORATION.

Incorporated, 1839.

Annual meeting, first Thursday in January.

Directors.—Perley Putnam, *President;* Aaron Perkins, Thos. Nichols, jr., John G. Felt, Daniel Potter. T. M. Dix, *Clerk, Treasurer, and Agent.*

NEW MARKET MANUFACTURING CO.

Incorporated in 1823.

Mills located at Lamprey Rivers, New Market, N. H. Treasurer's office, 17 Asiatic Building, Salem. Annual Meeting, second Wednesday in July.

Directors.— Nathaniel Silsbee, *President.* Benjamin W. Stone, B. H. Silsbee, David S. Brown, W. D. Pickman, Wm. B. Howes, Richard S. Fay, Henry Saltonstall. John Webster, *Treasurer.*

FOREST RIVER LEAD CO.

Formed, 1843. Incorporated, 1846.

Officers.—Benjamin Howard, *President.* William H. Chase, B. F. Fabens, George C. Chase, Elijah D. Brigham, *Directors.* George C. Chase, *General Agent.* Henry M. Brooks, *Clerk and Treasurer.*
Mills at Forest River, on the road leading to Marblehead. Counting-room 243½ Essex Street (up stairs). The Company manufacture White Lead, Sheet Lead, and Vinegar.

GREAT PASTURE COMPANY.

Annual meeting, first Monday in April.

Officers elected, April, 1858.—John Archer, *President.* Gideon Tucker, Joseph S. Cabot, Henry L. Williams, *Directors.* Caleb Foote, *Treasurer.* H. Wheatland, *Secretary.*

NAUMKEAG STEAM COTTON COMPANY.

Annual meeting, 3d Wednesday in January.

Incorporated in 1839. Building erected in 1845, in Harbor

Street, South Salem. Length, 405 feet; breadth, 55; 4 stories high. Number of Looms, 641; spindles, 32,768. Hands employed, 600. Steam Engine, 400 horse power.

Directors. — David Pingree, *President.* William D. Waters, William Sutton, Ephraim Emmerton, Joseph S. Leavitt, Richard P. Waters, B. A. West, W. B. Parker, E. F. Cutter, of Poston. A. S. Brown, *Clerk.* Edmund Smith, *Treasurer.*

NEWSPAPERS.

SALEM GAZETTE. Established weekly, 1768; semi-weekly, 1796; tri-weekly, in 1847. Enlarged and published semi-weekly, Oct. 1, 1851, every Tuesday and Friday, at 191 Essex Street. Caleb Foote, proprietor.

SALEM MERCURY. Established in 1831. Published every Wednesday, at 191 Essex Street. Caleb Foote, proprietor.

SALEM REGISTER. Established in 1800. Published every Monday and Thursday, by Chapman & Palfrey, 185 Essex St.

SALEM OBSERVER. Established in 1823. Published every Saturday, by William Ives & Co., at 226½ Essex Street.

SALEM ADVOCATE. Published every Saturday, by B. W. Lander, over 215 & 217 Essex Street.

MASONIC AND ODD FELLOW SOCIETIES.

Meetings are held at 32 Washington Street.

ESSEX LODGE OF FREE AND ACCEPTED MASONS. Chartered by the Grand Lodge of Massachusetts, June, 6, 1791.

Reorganized, June 11, 1845.

Regular communications on the first Tuesday evening in each month; other Tuesday evenings, meetings of the Lodge of Instruction.

Officers elected annually, on the first Tuesday evening in December.

Officers elected, Dec., 1857.—G. H. Pierson, *Master.* H. E. Jocelyn, *S. W.* J. F. Brown, *J. W.* Charles Harrington, *Treasurer.* William Leavitt, *Secretary.* J. S. Perkins, *S. D.* Jona. Perley, jr., *J. D.* George W. Estes, *S. S.* Hiram A. Tuttle, *J. S.* Edward Rea, *Tyler.*

WASHINGTON ROYAL ARCH CHAPTER.

Instituted, January 18, 1811.

Reorganized September 7th, 1852.

Regular communications, 1st and 3d Thursday of each month.

Officers elected annually, 1st Thursday in December.
Wm. L. Batchelder, *H. P.* Jos. S. Perkins, *K.* John R. Smith, *S.* George W. Sargent, *V. H.* Charles Greene, *P. S.* Joseph C. Cheever, *R. A. C.* Alvah Kendall, *Treasurer.* William Leavitt, *Secretary.* N. P. C. Patterson (S. Danvers), Nath'l Pickman, John E. Giddings, *M. of V.* Hiram L. Hall, John H. Chester (of Beverly), *Ss.*

INDEPENDENT ORDER OF ODD FELLOWS.

Fraternity Lodge, No. 118. I. O. of O. F.

Instituted, November 18, 1846. Meetings every Wednesday evening, at 32 Washington Street. Officers chosen semi-annually, on the last Wednesday evenings in June and December.

Officers elected Sept., 1858.—J. J. Rider, *N. G.* G. L. Upton, *V. G.* J. F. Worcester, *Secretary.* J. Farnum, jr., *Treasurer.*

Essex Lodge, No. 26. I. O. of O. F.

Instituted, Nov. 6, 1843. Meetings every Monday evening, in Asiatic Building. Officers chosen semi-annually, on the last Monday evening in June and December.

Officers elected, June, 1858.— Henry Luscomb, jr., *N. G.* David A. Clifford, *V. G.* E. B. Phillips, *Recording and Permanent Secretary.* J. P. Langmaid, *Treasurer.*

NAUMKEAG ENCAMPMENT, NO. 13.

I. O. of O. F.

Instituted at Salem, June 26, 1845. The regular sessions are held on the second and fourth Thursday evenings in each month, in Asiatic Building. Officers chosen semi-annually, in the months of June and December.

Officers elected, June, 1858. — B. W. Standley, *C. P.* J. W. Moulton, *H. P.* R. L. Woodfin, *S. W.* J. J. Rider, *J. W.* E. B. Phillips, *Scribe.* Joseph Swasey, *Treasurer.*

SALEM TOTAL ABSTINENCE SOCIETY.

Organized, 1857. Regular Meetings held every Monday evening, at Howard Street Chapel.
———— ————, *President.* John C. Forbush, *Vice-President.* Wm. H. H. Guilford. *Sec.* Henry Hale, *Treas.*

SALEM DIRECTORY.   241

SONS OF TEMPERANCE.

Henfield Division, No. 2.
Instituted, February 23, 1844.

Officers elected quarterly. Meetings in their Hall, No. 27 Washington Street, on every Thursday evening.
Officers for the quarter commencing October, 1858 : —
Philip B. Ruee, *D. G. W. P.*   James H. Putnam, *P. W. P.*   Jeremiah Knight, *W. P,*   George H. Pitts, *W. A.*   David R. Peabody, *R. S.*   Everson Hall, *A. R. S.*   Eben N. Walton, *F. S.*   James H. Doland, *T.*   Luther C. Butman, *C.*   Eleazer Pope, *A. C.*   Charles W. Dodge, *I. S.*   Thomas H. Hall, *O. S.*   James F. Almy, *Chaplain.*

ZEPHYR UNION DAUGHTERS OF TEMPERANCE.

Instituted, April 28, 1847.

Meetings every Wednesday evening, at S. of T. Hall, 27 Washington Street.
Officers for 1858. — Louisa Fields, *P. S.*   Ann Morse, *A. S.*   Mary Dowst, *R. S.*   Mary Winn, *A. R. S.*   Rebecca Francis, *F. S.*   Louisa Henfield, *T.*   Celia Larrabee, *C.*   Margaret Bowditch, *A. C.*   Lydia Dowst, *I. G.*   Eliza Fellows, *O. G.*   Eliza M. Sanborn, *P. P. S.*   Mary L. W. Melzeard, *C.*

SALEM BRASS BAND.

Room No. 5 Washington Street.

P. S. Gilmore, *Leader.*   Eben Upton, *Clerk and Treasurer.*

MILITARY.

SECOND DIVISION MASSACHUSETTS VOLUNTEER MILITIA.

William Sutton, South Danvers, *Major General.*
Lieut. Col. Daniel Perkins, Salem, *Division Inspector.*
Maj. Wm. Saunders, Salem, *Division Quarter Master.*
Maj. Alfred A. Abbott, Danvers, *Judge Advocate.*
Maj. Samuel Brown, jr., Salem,   } *Aides-de-camp.*
Maj. Jairus W. Perry, Salem,
Maj. David Moore, Salem, *Engineer.*

FOURTH BRIGADE.

Joseph Andrews, Salem, *Brigadier General.*
Henry Merritt, Salem, *Brigade Inspector.*

Samuel C. Oliver, Lawrence, *Aid-de-camp.*
John F. Fellows, Chelsea, *Brigade Quarter Master.*
William A. Williams, Chelsea, *Engineer.*

SECTION OF BATTERY ANNEXED TO FOURTH BRIGADE, SALEM.

Armory, North Street.

Charles H. Manning, *Captain.* Daniel P. Watson, *First Lieutenant.* Edward Wilson, *Second Lieutenant.* E. Harvey Quimby, *Surgeon.*

SEVENTH REGIMENT INFANTRY.

Lyman Dyke, Stoneham, *Colonel.*
Simeon Flint, Salem, *Lieut. Colonel.*
John Wiley, 2d, South Reading, *Major.*
Barnabas N. Mann, Chelsea, *Adjutant.*
——— ———, ———, *Quarter Master.*
Hadley P. Russell, Chelsea, *Paymaster.*
William H. Heath, Stoneham, *Surgeon.*
Bela N. Stevens, Chelsea, *Surgeon's Mate.*

COMPANY A.—SALEM LIGHT INFANTRY.

Armory, Phœnix Building.

J. A. Farless, *Captain.* Henry A. Brown, *First Lieutenant.* James B. Nichols, *Second Lieutenant.* N. D. Silsbee, *Third Lieutenant.* William A. Brooks, *Fourth Lieutenant.*

COMPANY B.—SALEM MECHANIC LIGHT INFANTRY.

Armory, Phœnix Building.

George H. Peirson, *Captain.* Daniel B. Lord, *First Lieut.* G. Norris, jr., *Second Lieutenant.* Israel P. Harris, *Third Lieutenant.* Edward H. Staten, *Fourth Lieutenant.*

COMPANY H.—SALEM CITY GUARDS.

Armory, Bowker Building.

Eleazer Hathaway, *Captain.* ——— ———, *First Lieut.* Charles Remon, *Second Lieutenant.* Charles H. Pinkham, *Third Lieutenant.* ——— ———, *Fourth Lieutenant.*

SALEM DIRECTORY. 243

DIVISIONARY CORPS.—SALEM INDEPENDENT CADETS.

Armory, Perkins Hall.

Samuel B. Foster, *Captain.* John L. Marks, *Captain-Lieut.* Joseph A. Dalton, *First Lieutenant.* Richard Skinner, jr., *Second Lieutenant.* Jonathan Kenney, *Third Lieutenant.* Thomas H. Johnson, *Fourth Lieutenant.* Joseph C. Foster, *Ensign.* John Pickering, jr., *Adjutant.* R. Brookhouse, jr., *Quarter Master.* J. G. Wood, *Surgeon.*

EXPRESSES.

Savory & Co.'s Eastern, Boston, and Southern Express.

Leaves Salem, No. 7 Washington St., at 9 and 11 A. M., and $2\frac{1}{2}$ P. M. Leaves Boston, Railroad Exchange, Court Square, $11\frac{1}{2}$ A. M., and $2\frac{1}{2}$ and 5 P. M.

Expresses leaving Savory & Co.'s Office, No. 7 Washington St.

Abbott's, South Danvers, 10 A. M. and 4 P. M.
Eastern Express Co., $7\frac{3}{4}$ A. M. and $3\frac{1}{4}$ P. M.
Elliot's, Hampton and Exeter, 3 P. M.
Forbes's, Newburyport, $3\frac{1}{4}$ and $5\frac{1}{4}$ P. M.
Marshall's, Manchester and Essex, 5 P. M.
Haskins's, Rockport, 5 P. M.
Jackson & Co.'s, Portsmouth, 3 and 5 P. M.
Fitz & Choat's, Ipswich, 3 P. M.
Winchester & Co.'s, Gloucester, 5 P. M.
   B. SAVORY.   J. A. GOLDTHWAIT.

Saunders's Salem and Lawrence Express.

Office 10 Washington, corner Front Street.

Leave Lawrence in the morning and noon trains. Leave Salem in the forenoon and afternoon trains.

Simon's Salem and Boston Express.

Office No. 27 Front Street.

Leaves Salem at 11 A. M., and 8 Court Street, Boston, at $3\frac{1}{2}$ P. M.

Salem and Lynn Express.

Charles Parshley, office $15\frac{1}{2}$ Central Street.

Moulton & Davis's Salem and Boston Express.
Office 10 Washington Street.

Haraden's Boston and Salem Express.
Office basement Asiatic Building.

Boston and Salem Express.
Joseph Potter, 34 Front Street.

Merritt & Co.'s Express and Transportation line.
No. 14 Washington Street, Salem.

All business entrusted to this line will receive prompt and faithful attention.
Office in Boston, No. 5 Merchants Row.
DAVID MERRITT,   DAVID MERRITT, JR.

City Express.
R. Muchmore, Essex House Stage office.

STAGES.

A stage for Boston leaves the Essex House every Sunday, at $4\frac{1}{2}$ P. M. Leaves Boston every Sunday, at 9 A. M.

General Stage Office, 13 Central Street.

For Georgetown and Haverhill, leaves 13 Central st., Salem, daily (Sundays excepted), at $2\frac{3}{4}$ P. M. Returning, leaves Haverhill at $6\frac{1}{2}$ o'clock, A. M., and arrives in Salem at $10\frac{1}{2}$ A. M.
SPALDING & PERKINS, *Proprietors.*

For Gloucester, leaves 13 Central st., every day (Sundays excepted), at 1 P. M., and arrives in Salem, at 10 A. M.
J. C. TRASK, *Proprietor.*

For North Danvers, leaves 13 Central st. seven times daily.
SPALDING & PERKINS, *Proprietors.*

For Tapleyville, a coach leaves 13 Central st., Salem, at $9\frac{1}{2}$ A. M., and $4\frac{1}{2}$ and 7 P. M. Leaves North Danvers at 7 A. M., and 1 and 5 P. M.   JACOB PALMER, *Proprietor.*

Leave 13 Central st., three times daily for Marblehead.

Leave 13 Central st., three times daily for Beverly.

For South Danvers, leaves 13 Central st., at 8 A. M., and every half-hour through the day, till 9 P. M. Leaves S. Danvers at 7 A. M., and every half-hour through the day till 8 P. M.   SHACKLEY & MERRILL.

Railroad Coach office, rear Essex House.

TAXATION IN SALEM.

The rate of Taxation in Salem, for 1858, is 74 cts. per $100. The valuation is as follows:—

Real estate,..............$7,054,620
Personal estate,.......... 7,159,100

$14,213,720

Ratable polls, 4,336.

The whole tax of the city this year is $114,980.89, less than one-quarter of which is for State and county tax, namely,

State tax,..................$7,999.00
County tax,............... 18,079.46
City demand,............. 88,903.43

$114,980.99

Valuation, 1857,......................................$14,628,850
" 1858,...................................... 14,213,720

Decrease............... $415,130

CENSUS OF ESSEX COUNTY.

	1850.	1855.		1850.	1855.
*Amesbury,.........	3143	3585	*Nahant, set off from		
Andover,...........	6945	4810	Lynn, 1853,		270
*Beverly,...........	5376	5944	*Newbury,..........	4426	1483
Boxford,...........	982	1034	*Newburyport,......	9572	13354
Bradford,..........	1328	1372	North Andover, set off		
Danvers,...........	8110	4000	from Andover, 1855,		2276
*Essex,............	1585	1668	*Rockport,..........	3255	3498
*Georgetown,......	2052	2042	*Rowley,...........	1075	1315
*Gloucester,.......	7805	8935	*Salem,............	20263	20934
*Groveland,........	1286	1367	*Salesbury,.........	3100	3185
*Hamilton,........	889	896	Saugus,............	1552	1788
Haverhill,..........	5877	7940	South Danvers, set off		
*Ipswich,..........	3349	3421	from Danvers, 1855,		5348
Lawrence,.........	8283	16081	*Swampscot, set off		
*Lynn,............	14257	15713	from Lynn, 1852,		1335
Lynnfield,.........	1723	883	Topsfield,..........	1171	1250
*Manchester,......	1638	1878	*Wenham,..........	977	1073
*Marblehead,......	6167	6933	*West Newbury,....	1746	2094
Methuen,..........	2543	2582			
Middleton,.........	832	880		131,807	151,167

In April, 1852, a law was passed, dividing the State into eleven districts, each district to elect one representative to Congress. The above cities and towns having a * form District No. 6. The remaining towns in the county of Essex, with Charlestown, Burlington, Lexington, Malden, Medford, Melrose, Reading, Somerville, South Reading, Stoneham, Waltham, West Cambridge, Wilmington, Winchester, and Woburn, in the County of Middlesex, form District No. 7.

COURTS

SUPREME JUDICIAL COURT.

Lemuel Shaw, Boston, *Chief Justice*, Salary, $4,500
    Associate Justices.
    Charles A. Dewey, Northampton, Salary, 4,000
    Theron Metcalf, Boston, " 4,000
    George T. Bigelow, Boston, " 4,000
    Pliny Merrick, Worcester, " 4,000
    Benjamin F. Thomas, Worcester, " 4,000
    Horace Gray, jr., Boston, *Reporter*, " 500
Stephen H. Phillips, of Salem, *Attorney General.*
Asahel Huntington, of Salem, *Clerk of the Courts for the County of Essex.* (Office in the Court House, Salem.)

Law Term.—At Salem, on the 6th Tuesday after the 4th Tuesday in September. *Nisi Prius Term.*—At Salem, immediately after the law term, and on the 8th Tuesday after the 1st Tuesday in March.

COURT OF COMMON PLEAS.

Edward Mellen, Wayland, *Chief Justice*, Salary, $2,700
Jonathan C. Perkins, Salem,
George N. Briggs, Pittsfield,
Henry W. Bishop, Lenox,   *Asssociate Justices*, 2,500
Geo. P. Sanger, Boston,
Henry Morris, Springfield,
David Aiken, Greenfield,

This Court is held for civil business, at Salem, on the third Monday of June, and third Monday of December; at Newburyport, on the third Monday of September; at Lawrence, on the third Monday of March;—and for criminal business at Salem, on the fourth Monday of January; at Newburyport, on the fourth Monday of May; and at Lawrence, on the second Monday of October.

A. A. Abbott, of South Danvers, *District Attorney for Essex County.*

Commissioners of Insolvency for Essex County.—William G. Choate, Salem; D. E. Safford, Hamilton; Lonson Nash, Gloucester.

SALEM DIRECTORY.

Masters in Chancery for Essex County.—Henry B. Fernald, Lynn; William G. Choate, 25 Asiatic building, Salem; David Roberts, Salem, office 118 Essex st. Salem; Dan Weed, 224 Essex st. Salem; N. W. Harmon, Lawrence.

Notaries Public in Salem —George Andrews, Joseph Cloutman, Wm. C. Endicott Ephraim F. Miller, J. B. F. Osgood, William C. Prescott, David Roberts, Thos. M. Stimpson, Isaac Story, Joseph G. Waters, S. P. Webb, Dan Weed, Stephen G. Wheatland.

Commissioners for other States.—J. B. F. Osgood, for California, Iowa, and New York. T. P. Pingree, jr., for Maine, New Hampshire, Vermont, New York, Illinois, Maryland, Tennessee. Wm. C. Endicott, for Michigan. J. W. Perry, for Maine. S. H. Phillips, for New Hampshire, Vermont, Maryland. David Roberts, for Maine, Rhode Island, and Louisiana. R. S. Rantoul, for Illinois, Iowa, Pennsylvania, and Ohio. S. P. Webb, for California.

COURT OF INSOLVENCY FOR ESSEX COUNTY.

George F. Choate, Salem, *Judge.*
A. C. Goodell, Salem, *Register.*

The Court of Insolvency sits at the Court House in Salem on the first and second Wednesday, in Lawrence on the third Wednesday, at Newburyport on the fourth Wednesday, in each month.

PROBATE COURT FOR ESSEX COUNTY.

George F. Choate, Salem, *Judge.*
A. C. Goodell, Salem, *Register.*

The records are kept at the Court House in Salem.
The Court sits as follows:

Salem, 1st Tuesday in every month. Ipswich, 3d Tuesday in Feb., May, Aug., and Nov. Lynn, 1st Wednesday following 1st Tuesday in Jan. and July. Marblehead, 1st Wednesday following 1st Tuesday in April and Oct. Newburyport, last Tuesday in March, June, Sept., and Dec. Gloucester, 3d Tuesday in Jan. and July. Andover, 2d Tuesday in Aug. North Andover, 2d Tuesday in Feb. Haverhill, 3d Tuesday in April and Oct. Lawrence, 2d Tuesday in March, June, Sept., and Dec.

County Commissioners.—Geo. Haskell, Ipswich, *Chairman.* Ebenezer B. Currier, Lawrence. Geo. Wilson, Marblehead.

Special Commissioners.—John I. Ladd, Groveland; Chas. B. Holmes, Lynn.

SALEM DIRECTORY.

Clerk of County Commissioners.—Asahel Huntington, Salem.

Their meetings are held as follows: At Ipswich, on the 2d Tuesday of April; Salem, 2d Tuesday of July; Newburyport, 2d Tuesday of October; and on the 4th Tuesday of December, at Salem, Ipswich, or Newburyport, as may be determined at the preceding meeting.

County Treasurer.—A. W. Dodge, Hamilton. Office, Court House, Salem.

Register of Deeds.—Ephraim Brown, Salem. Office, Court House, Salem.

Sheriff of Essex County.—James Cary, Lawrence.

Deputy Sheriffs.—John Rowell, Amesbury; Jacob S. Fullington, West Amesbury; Rufus S. Morton, Andover; Richard Hood, Danvers; Ezra Perkins, jr., Essex; Otis Thompson, George W. Boynton, Georgetown; Jacob Howe, Phineas E. Davis, Haverhill; Joseph Spiller, Ipswich; Bailey Bartlett, Leonard Stoddard, Lawrence; Chas. Merritt, Lynn; John Dixey, Marblehead; John Akerman, Wooster Smith, Newburyport; Henry Dennis, Rockport; Daniel Potter, Ebenezer D. Kimball, Salem; Stephen Upton, South Danvers.

Ebenezer D. Kimball, *Jail Keeper in Salem.*
Ira Worcester, *Jail Keeper in Ipswich.*
John Akerman, *Jail Keeper in Newburyport.*
Ira Worcester, *Keeper House of Correction in Ipswich.*
James Cary, *Keeper of Jail and House of Correction, Lawrence.*

Frederick Winsor, *Physician to the Salem Jail.*

Coroners in Salem.—Eben N. Walton, Nehemiah Brown.

Commissioner for the City of Salem of the State Industrial School for Girls.—George Andrews.

Commissioners to qualify Civil Officers. John Chapman, Asahel Huntington, Charles Kimball, Joseph B. F. Osgood, Dan Weed, Geo. Wheatland, Henry Whipple, Daniel A. White.

Justices throughout the Commonwealth.—Alfred A. Abbott, Albert G. Browne, John Chapman, Caleb Foote, Asahel Huntington, Otis P. Lord, Jonathan C. Perkins, Stephen H. Phillips.

Justices of the Peace and Quorum.—Sam'l P. Andrews, Benj. F. Browne, Geo. H. Devereux, Horace Ingersoll, Stephen B. Ives, jr., Nath'l J. Lord, Ephraim F. Miller, Wm. D. Northend, Wm. C. Prescott, David Roberts, Augustus D. Rogers, Nath'l Silsbee, Isaac Story, Joseph G. Waters, Stephen P. Webb, Dan Weed, George Wheatland, Henry Whipple, Daniel A. White.

SALEM DIRECTORY. 249

Justices of the Peace.

Nathaniel K. Allen,
Geo. Andrews,
Joseph Andrews,
Nathaniel Appleton,
Wm. Archer, jr.
John Ball,
Sidney C. Bancroft,
Benj. Barstow,
John Bertram,
James B. Briggs,
Robert Brookhouse,
Ephraim Brown,
Nehemiah Brown,
J. Vincent Browne,
John F. Burnham,
Samuel B. Buttrick,
Joseph S. Cabot,
William Calley,
Michael Carlton,
John Chadwick,
Geo. F. Chever,
Geo. F. Choate,
Wm. G. Choate,
Wm. S. Cleveland,
Jos. Cloutman,
Humphrey Cook,
Francis Cox,
Geo. R. Curwen,
Joseph A. Dalton,
Humphrey Devereux,
John Dwyer,
Charles M. Endicott,
Wm. C. Endicott,
John G. Felt,
William H. Foster,
James A. Gillis,
Benj. A. Gray,

Henry B. Groves,
Leonard B. Harrington,
Mark H. Skell,
Wm. P. Hayward,
Moses Hill,
Edward Hodges,
Jacob Hood,
John Jewett,
Charles Kimball,
Eben W. Kimball,
James Kimball,
Henry L. Lambert,
Joseph S. Leavitt,
Geo. B. Loring,
Samuel Mackintire,
John Masury,
William Maynes,
Jas. McGeary,
Wm. S. Messervy,
Geo. L. Newcomb,
Gilbert G. Newhall,
David Nichols,
John H. Nichols,
Thos. F. Odell,
Joseph B. F. Osgood,
Jeremiah Page,
Wm. W. Palmer,
Geo. A. Parker,
John Brooks Parker,
Wm. B. Parker,
Ira J. Patch,
Edward H. Payson,
Francis Peabody,
Geo. Peabody,
John B. Peabody,
Robert Peele,
Aaron Perkins,

Daniel Perkins,
Jonathan Perley, jr.
Jairus W. Perry,
Willard P. Phillips,
David Pingree,
Thomas P. Pingree,
Thomas P. Pingree, jr.
Daniel Potter,
David Putnam,
Perley Putnam,
Moses D. Randall,
Robert S. Rantoul,
Stratton W. Robinson,
James Ropes,
Edmund Smith,
Geo. H. Smith,
Henry B. Smith,
Edward Stimpson,
James C. Stimpson,
Thomas M. Stimpson,
Augustus Story,
Gilbert L. Streeter,
John D. Symonds,
Nathaniel D. Symonds,
Charles W. Upham,
Abbott Walker,
Eben N. Walton,
Wm. D. Waters,
Benj. Webb,
Nath'l Weston,
Henry Wheatland,
Stephen G. Wheatland,
John Whipple,
Henry L. Williams,
Wm. Williams,
Jonathan F. Worcester,
Isaac Wyman.

POLICE COURT.—Jos. G. WATERS, *Justice.*

Associate Justices, George Andrews, William C. Prescott.

Clerk, Samuel P. Andrews.

The Police Court is held in the Court Room in Bowker Place, No. 150 Essex Street, for criminal business, every day at 9 o'clock, A. M.; and for civil business on each Monday at 10 o'clock, A. M.

Public Administrators, Michael Carlton, Benj. A. Gray, Nehemiah Brown.

EASTERN RAILROAD.

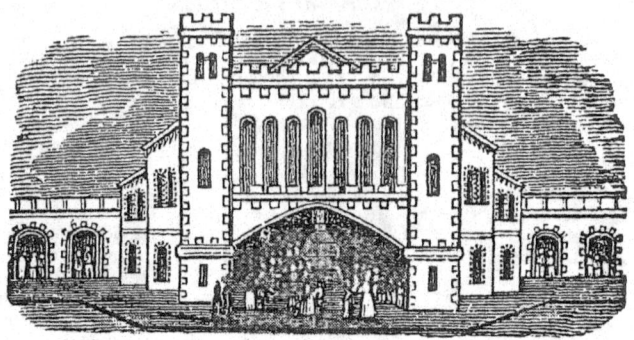

View of the Eastern Railroad Depot at Salem.

Depot in Boston, on Causeway street, foot of Friend and Canal streets.

Annual Meeting, 2d Monday in July.

Incorporated, April 14, 1836. The track from Boston to Salem was opened August 27, 1838. December 10, 1839, a Branch Railroad was opened from Salem to Marblehead; Dec. 18, 1839, the cars commenced running to Ipswich Depot; June 19, 1840, they ran to Newburyport; and to the New Hampshire line, Nov. 9, 1840,—distance 56 miles. Opened for travel to Portland, 1841.

Directors.—George M. Browne, *President;* John Howe of Brookline, G. M. Browne of Boston, Samuel Hooper of Boston, N. D. Chase of Lynn, J. C. Lee of Salem, Micajah Lunt of Newburyport, H. H. Ladd of Portsmouth. J. Prescott, *Superintendent,* Somerville.

EASTERN RAILROAD, from Boston, through Lynn, Salem, and Newburyport, to Portsmouth.

PORTLAND, SACO, & PORTSMOUTH RAILROAD, to Portland. Thence by steamboats and railroads to Bath, Gardiner, and Hallowell, on the Kennebec, and Thomaston, Camden, Belfast, Frankfort, and Bangor, on the Penobscot River.

This Railroad affords access to many splendid sea-side locations, and passes through many pleasant towns, opening magnificent views of the ocean, leading to the most retired spots for sea-bathing, and to the most delightful walks and drives to be found in the native forests in New England.

Season Tickets, Family Tickets, and Tickets to Scholars, are sold at greatly reduced prices from single fares.

SALEM DIRECTORY. 251

STATIONS, DISTANCES, AND FARES ON THE EASTERN RAILROAD FROM BOSTON.

Stations.	Miles.	Fares.	Stations.	Miles.	Fares.
From Boston to			Rowley	31	$0 95
Somerville	2	$0 5	‡Newburyport	36	1 00
South Malden	4	8	Salisbury	38	1 15
Chelsea	5	15	Salisb'y Mills	42	1 25
North Chelsea	7	20	Seabrook	42	1 25
West Lynn	10	30	Hamp'n Falls	44	1 30
Lynn	11	30	Hampton	46	1 35
Swampscott	13	35	N. Hampton	49	1 45
*Salem	16	50	Greenland	51	1 55
Marblehead	20	55	Portsmouth	56	1 65
†Beverly	18	55	Eliot	58	
West Beach	21	65	S. Berwick	66	
Manchester	25	75	N. Berwick	72	
West Parish	28	1 00	Wells	77	
Gloucester	32	1 00	Kennebunk	82	
N. Beverly	21	60	Saco	92	
Wenham	22	65	Scarboro'	100	
Ipswich	27	80	Portland	105	

* Marblehead Branch intersects.
† Gloucester Branch intersects.
‡ Salisbury Mills Branch intersects.

ESSEX RAILROAD.
From Salem to Lawrence.
This road is under the management of Eastern Railroad.

SOUTH READING BRANCH RAILROAD.
From Danvers to the Boston and Maine Railroad at South Reading.
Directors the same as the Eastern Railroad Company.

SALEM AND LOWELL RAILROAD.
Incorporated in 1848. Opened August 1, 1850. This Road is leased and operated by the Boston & Lowell Railroad Co.

DANVERS RAILROAD.
Incorporated 1852. From Danvers to South Reading. This Road is managed by the Boston & Maine Railroad Co.

TELEGRAPH OFFICES.
Eastern Railroad Depot, J. R. Bagnall, *Operator*. Asiatic Building, Boston, Salem & Lynn, Miss H. P. French, *Operator*.

PLUMMER HALL.

This building, located on the north side of Essex Street, between Newbury and St. Peter Streets, was erected in 1856 from funds left by the late Miss Caroline Plummer to the Proprietors of the Salem Athenæum. It is in the form of a parallelogram, 97 feet 3 inches long by 53 feet wide. The exterior walls are of brick, 45 feet in height above the underpinning, which is 4 feet 6 inches high, and is of brown sandstone. The steps, doorway, window-dressings, balcony, belts, &c., are of the same material. The style is Romanesque. The first story is appropriated to the collections of the Essex Institute, and has two ante-rooms, 34 by 16, — one contains the herbarium, the other the historical collections. A large hall in the rear, 58 by 48, has been finished expressly for the arrangement of the specimens in geology, mineralogy, and zoology.

The second story has a similar arrangement of rooms. The western ante-room is appropriated to the use of the librarian, and some of the principal books of reference, and the new books, belonging to the Salem Athenæum; the eastern to the bound volumes of newspapers belonging to the Essex Institute, and the Library of the Essex South District Medical Society, numbering about 700 volumes.

The large Library Room, in the rear, is 58 by 48. The cases on the sides of the alcoves are of a peculiar arrangement, commencing narrow at the back of the columns (a range of corinthian columns being on each side, about 12 feet from the walls), and widening as they extend towards the sides of the room; the shelving being on each side and on the rear of the cases, also in the spaces between the windows. The centre is used for tables. A light balcony or gallery is constructed at the height of eight feet from the floor, and is finished between the columns in a serpentine form, with a neat iron railing (a similar gallery in the hall on the first story). The alcoves on the western side contain the Library of the Salem Athenæum; those on the eastern, that of the Essex Institute.

INDEX TO THE ADVERTISING DEPARTMENT.

Agricultural Warehouses.
Henry Hale,............................37
Hovey & Co.,..........................24
Parker, White & Gannett,............3

Ale, Porter, &c.
G. W. Crosby,.........................73

Ambrotypists.
E. R. Perkins,........................35
W. Snell,.............................65

Amusements.
Boston Museum,........................29

Apothecaries.
George P. Farrington,.................42
T. A. Sweetser,.......................91

Artists' Materials.
M. J. Whipple & Co.,..................24

Auctioneer.
William Archer, jr.,..................35

Bakers.
Edward H. Sanger,.....................74
Charles Watts,........................57

Bedding.
Blake & Davenport,....................19
Ezekiel Goss,.........................58
James H. Hallett,.....................10

Bell Hangers.
S. W. Fuller,.........................68
Charles Phelps,.......................74

Bible. (*New Translation.*)
J. P. Jewett & Co.,....................9

Blacksmiths.
Jacob Aggee,..........................47
Benjamin Cutts,.......................49
George H. Peirson,....................45
A. A. Raymond,........................70

Boiler Manufacturer.
James Tetlow,.........................38

Bookbinders.
H. P. Ives & A. A. Smith,.............77
J. Perley, jr., & Co.,................75

Books and Stationery.
D. B. Brooks & Brother,....front cover.
Crosby, Nichols & Co.,................23
H. P. Ives & A. A. Smith,.............77
J. P. Jewett & Co.,....................9
H. F. Marsh,..........................21
H. Whipple & Son,.......front, colored.

Boots, Shoes, and Rubbers.
Abraham Bennett,......................82
Thomas Bott,..........................81
John J. Ashby,........................66
J. H. Carty,..........................54
Harrison O. Flint,....................81
A. Hammond,...........................94
J. George Hubbard,....................81
T. Nicholson, jr.,....................52
Theron Palmer,........................54
Perkins & Brown,......................53
G. V. Sibley (manuf.),................50
J. Stetson,...........................51

Brass Founder.
Andrew S. Waters,.....................38

Brewer.
G. W. Crosby,.........................73

Brick.
Wiggin & Clark,.......................71

Brokers.
William Archer, jr.,..................35
Nathan Peirce,........................35

Card Engraving.
N. S. Dearborn,.......................20

Carpenters.
G. A. & T. Brown,.....................42
Clark & Giddings,.....................94
S. G. Danforth,.......................54
Devereux Dennis,......................46
W. F. Gardner,........................44
Wm. C. Hamond,........................54
John H. Williams,.....................44

Carriage Builders.
Gilman Andrews,.......................51
Edward D. Loring,.....................46
Thomas Brooking,......................49
John P. Spiller,......................70
John W. Stocker,......................51

Carriage & Sign Painters.
Moses Davidson,.......................44
C. F. Hovey,..........................48

Carriage Repository.
W. W. Kelman,.........................49

Carriage Smith.
George H. Peirson,....................45

Cement.
Wm. P. Goodhue,.......................72

Charts & Nautical Works.
Henry Whipple & Son,..front, colored.

Cigars, Tobacco, &c.
Battis & Brown,.......................55
D. J. Carruth,........................22
S. S. Skinner,........................55

Clothing and Furnishing Goods.
Abraham Bennett,......................82
W. H. Burbeck,........................82
C. A. Collins,........................17
Cressey & Hale,.......................93
Geo. N. Nichols, opp. C. H. Almanac.
Perkins & Brown,......................53
J. W. Read (boys'),....................3
G. W. Simmons, Piper & Co.,...........32
J. W. Smith & Co.,....................31
L. G. Smith,..........................21
Edward Wilson,........................66

Coal and Wood.
Augustus T. Brooks,...................60
John Dike & Co.,......................63
Benj. B. Fuller & Co.,................71
John Grover,..........................71
L. B. Hatch,..........................63
N. Putnam,............................71
Wiggin & Clark,.......................71

Coffin Warerooms.
H. & H. G. Hubon,.....................69
Joseph Wallis,........................57
L. Woodberry,.........................50

Confectioners.
George H. Wise,.......................65

Coopers.
John Battis,..........................46
Samuel Kehew,.........................47

17

Copper Smith.
Andrew S. Waters, ...38
Cordage.
Joseph Chisholm, ...38
Corsletts.
Dr. Abbe, ...28
Crockery.
S. C. & E. A. Simonds, ...39
Curriers' Tables & Tools.
Joshua B. Grant, ...42
Curtains and Fixtures.
Geo. S. Mansfield, ...58
Daguerreotypist.
Samuel Masury, ...16
Dentists.
W. L. Bowdoin, ...79
Wm. W. Hurd, ...79
Desks, &c.
Stephen Smith, ...26
Drugs.
George P. Farrington, ...42
G. E. Meacom, ...91
Dry Goods.
James F. Almy, ...back, colored.
R. H. Chamberlain, ...40
J. S. Chase & Co., ...8
G. P. Daniels, ...92
J. Mayer, ...41
A. E. Price, ...41
Dye House.
Barrett's, ...14
Embroideries and Laces.
R. H. Chamberlain, ...40
J. Mayer, ...41
John P. Peabody, ...40
A. E. Price, ...41
Engravers.
Chas. D. Andrews, ...13
N. S. Dearborn, ...20
Taylor & Adams (wood), ...12
Fertilizers.
Geo. Davenport, ...20
Hovey & Co., ...24
Parker, White & Gannett, ...33
Fire Works.
J. G. Hovey & Co., ...5
Fish. (Fresh and Salt.)
Parsons & Shackelford, ...6
Flour and Grain.
Bowker Brothers, ...60
Augustus T. Brooks, ...60
Dodge & Jones, ...72
E. K. Noyes & Co., ...64
M. C. Reynolds & Co., ...67
Steele, Blodgett & Co., ...62
Fruit and Vegetables.
C. H. Newcomb, ...64
R. P. Wheeler, ...61
Furniture.
Blake & Davenport, ...19
Currier & Millett, ...59
Gahery, Gendrot & Co., ...29
Ezekiel Goss, ...58
Haskell & Lougee (patent tables), ...52
P. J. Hynes, ...58
Joseph Wallis, ...57

Fur Goods.
Humphrey Cook, ...41
W. M. Shute & Son, ...25
Edward C. Webster, ...66
Gas and Steam Fixtures.
W. F. Small, ...39
E. H. Staten, ...80
S. A. Stetson & Co., ...10
Gas Holders Manuf.
James Tetlow, ...38
Gent.'s Furnishing Goods.
J. P. Draper, ...4
F. B. Locke, ...14
Glass. (Stained.)
J. M. Cook, ...14
Gold Pens.
F. W. Snow, ...
Groceries.
Augustus T. Brooks, ...60
Brooks & Noyes, ...63
Chamberlain, Harris & Co., ...63
H. G. & N. Emerson, ...61
Wm. P. Goodhue, ...72
Pemberton Hale, ...62
E. S. Howard, ...91
Foster Knight, ...61
Willard Knight, ...62
E. K. Noyes & Co., ...64
Newman & Symonds, ...93
M. C. Reynolds & Co., ...67
J. C. Webster, ...60
Guns, Fishing Tackle, &c.
Richardson & Dexter, ...22
Hair Work.
Remond & Babcock, ...59
Hardware.
Adams, Richardson & Co., ...36
James A. Farless, ...back, colored.
Henry Hale, ...37
S. C. & E. A. Simonds, ...39
Harness Makers.
Isaac Dayton, ...51
Eben N. Price, ...48
John Tuttle, ...70
Hats, Caps, &c.
Humphrey Cook, ...41
Wm. M. Shute & Son, ...25
Edward C. Webster, ...66
Edward Wilson, ...66
Hay.
John Dike & Co., ...63
L. B. Hatch, ...63
Wiggin & Clark, ...71
Horse Shoer.
Thomas Brooking, ...49
Hosiery, Gloves, &c.
R. H. Chamberlain, ...40
J. S. Chase & Co., ...8
Wm. Clapp, ...24
J. Mayer, ...41
John P. Peabody, ...40
Ink.
F. W. Snow, ...7
Insurance.
William Archer, Jr., ...35
New England Mutual Life, ...15

Dorchester Mutual Fire Ins., ...98
John H. Nichols, ...56
Iron Railing.
Benjamin Cutts, ...49
George H. Peirson, ...45
Iron Safes.
Adams, Richardson & Co., ...36
Jewelry.
George B. Appleton, ...96
Smith & Chamberlain (manuf.), ...96
Lamps.
Henry Hale, ...37
S. A. Stetson & Co., ...10
Last Manufacturers.
Brown and Stanley, ...93
Lightning Rods.
Thomas Trask, ...95
Looking Glasses.
Blake & Davenport, ...19
Williams & Everett, ...27
Lumber Dealers.
Benj. B. Fuller & Co., ...71
Prime, Kenny & Co. (hard), ...56
N. Putnam, ...71
Wiggin & Clark, ...71
Mahogany, Veneers, &c.
Prime, Kenny & Co., ...56
Marble Worker.
W. A. Power, ...50
Masons.
Simeon Flint, ...42
Ira Mansfield, ...42
Benj. R. White, ...67
Mastic Roofing.
W. L. Saxby, ...44
Mattresses.
Blake & Davenport, ...19
Currier & Millett, ...59
James H. Hallett, ...10
Ezekiel Goss, ...58
S. Sheppard, ...57
Joseph Wallis, ...57
Medicines.
Dr. Langley, ... 4
J. A. Page, ...16
Merchant Tailors.
W. H. Burbeck, ...82
C. A. Collins, ...17
Benjamin Edwards, ...53
Maguire & O'Leary, ...69
G. W. Simmons, Piper & Co., ...32
H. M. Smith & Co., ...68
J. W. Smith & Co., ...31
L. G. Smith, ...21
Millinery.
J. S. Chase & Co., ... 8
A. E. Price, ...41
Mourning Goods.
J. S. Chase & Co. 8
Music Dealers & Publishers.
D. B. Brooks & Brother, ...front cover.
Newspapers.
Salem Advocate, ...79
Salem Gazette, ...78
Salem Observer, ...76
Salem Register, ...77

Oil and Candles.
Seccomb Ebenezer, ...39
Painters and Glaziers.
C. E. Brown, ...43
M. Davidson (carriage), ...44
B. S. Mansfield, ...47
Joseph Mansfield, ...42
S. F. Nichols, ...43
J. W. Osborne, ...94
D. Pulsifer & Co., ...43
H. L. Whidden, ...91
Paints, Oil, Glass, &c.
Adams, Richardson & Co., ...36
C. E. Brown, ...43
Henry Hale, ...37
S. F. Nichols, ...43
D. Pulsifer & Co., ...43
S. C. & E. A. Simonds, ...39
Paper and Paper Bags.
G. T. Brown, ...54
Paper Hangers.
C. E. Brown, ...43
B. S. Mansfield, ...47
Joseph Mansfield, ...42
S. F. Nichols, ...43
D. Pulsifer & Co., ...43
Paper Hangings.
H. P. Ives & A. A. Smith, ...77
S. C. & E. A. Simonds, ...39
Paper and Paper Stock.
D. B. Brooks & Brother, ...front cover.
Patent Agency.
Samuel Cooper, ...11
Patent and Enamelled Leather.
H. H. Stevens, ...46
Patent Tables.
Haskell & Lougee, ...52
Photographists.
Samuel Masury, ...16
E. R. Perkins, ...35
W. Snell, ...65
Physicians.
Alfred G. Hall, ... 8
Jerome Harris, ...65
J. A. Page, ...16
Pianos.
Timothy Gilbert & Co., ...opp. preface.
Picture Frames.
Williams & Everett, ...27
Pipe.
J. F. Banister, ...94
Plaster.
Dodge & Jones, ...72
Wm. P. Goodhue, ...72
Plumbers.
Benj. F. Dudley, ... 6
Francis P. Goss, ...45
Andrew S. Waters, ...38
Printers.
Chas. D. Andrews (plate), ...13
Chas. H. Crosby, ... 6
N. S. Dearborn (card), ...20
Chapman & Palfray, ...77
Foote & Horton, ...78
William Ives & Co., ...76

B. W. Lander,..................79
J. H. Moreland,................73
Printing Presses.
Lowe Press Co.,................30
Produce.
E. K. Noyes & Co.,..............64
Frederic Porter,................73
Steele, Blodgett & Co.,.........62
Provisions.
Samuel Craig, ...64
Asa Hayford,...................96
Foster Knight,..................61
C. H. Newcomb,.................64
John G. Plander,................72
Frederic Porter,................73
John Roberts,...................61
Public Houses.
Essex House, J. S. Leavitt,......34
Simonds Hotel,..................92
Real Estate Broker.
William Archer,................35
Restorants.
Haskell's,......................73
Pray & Boynton,.................53
Rubber Goods.
Harrison O. Flint,...............81
Edward Wilson,..................66
Salt.
Bowker Brothers, ...60
Sawing.
Prime, Kenny & Co.,.............56
Scales and Balances.
Adams, Richardson, & Co., ...36
Greenleaf & Brown (Fairbanks'), back colored.
Seed Stores.
George Davenport, ...20
Hovey & Co.,....................24
Parker, White & Gannet, ... 3
Sewing Machines.
B. L. Griswold,.................67
J. Trefren,............back colored.
Wheeler & Wilson,......back colored.
Sewing Machine Threads.
Ross & Pearce,..................12
Ship Chandler.
Wm. P. Goodhue,................72
Ship Tanks Manufacturer.
James Tetlow,...................38
Shirt Manufactory.
J. P. Draper,................... 4
F. B. Locke, ...14
H. P. Wilbur,...................68
Slater.
Thomas Pinnock,.................45
Soap and Candles.
Paul Hildreth,..................94
Spectacles.
Geo. B. Appleton,...............81
Sporting Apparatus.
James A. Farless, ...back colored.
Richardson & Dexter,............22
Stables.
W. W. Kelman,..................49
C. Simonds,....................92
Stair Builder.
Isaac Winchester,...............47

Stationery.
D. B. Brooks & Brother, ...front cover.
Crosby, Nichols & Co.,..........23
H. P. Ives & A. A. Smith,.......77
H. F. Marsh,...................21
Henry Whipple & Son,...front colored.
Stitching. (Machine.)
Isaac C. Pray,.................53
Stone Dealers and Cutters.
Nathan T. Clark,................75
C. C. Whittier,.................75
Stoves, Furnaces, &c.
Gardner Chilson,........front colored.
J. M. Read (gas),...............18
John T. Ropes & Co., ...46
E. H. Staten (gas),.............80
Gardner Webster,...............69
Wentworth & Fifield,....front colored.
Teacher of Navigation.
William Leavitt,................75
Teas.
Brooks & Noyes, ...63
Chamberlain, Harris & Co.,......63
E. K. Noyes & Co.,..............64
Telegraphic Engineer.
Moses G. Farmer,................29
Tin Plate and Sheet Iron Workers.
Richard M. Chipman,............43
John T. Ropes & Co.,............46
Gardner Webster,...............69
Trees and Shrubs.
Geo. Davenport, ...20
Hovey & Co.,...................24
Parker, White & Gannett, ... 3
Trunks.
Abraham Bennett,................82
Perkins & Brown,................53
Ebenezer N. Price,..............48
Twine, &c.
G. T. Brown,...................54
Joseph Chisholm,................38
Ross & Pearce,..................13
Upholsterers.
Ezekiel Goss, ...58
Geo. S. Mansfield,..............58
S. Sheppard,...................57
Upholstery Goods.
Blake & Davenport, ...19
James H. Hallett,...............10
George S. Mansfield,............58
Varnishes.
Stimson, Valentine & Co., ... 2
Venetian Blinds.
C. B. Locke,...................18
Veterinary Surgeon.
Wm. B. Greenman,...............70
Watches.
Geo. B. Appleton, back cover, and...96
Jesse Smith,...................52
Smith & Chamberlain,............96
Water. (For vessels.)
Parsons & Shackelford, ...60
Window Shades.
George S. Mansfield,............58
Wood Mouldings.
Benjamin Straw,................58

ADVERTISEMENTS

OF

MERCHANTS AND MANUFACTURERS

IN

BOSTON.

BAY STATE VARNISH WORKS.

STIMSON, VALENTINE & CO.,
Varnish Manufacturers,

Store, — No. 36 India Street, Boston.
Factory, — Riverside, Brighton.

COACH VARNISHES.

IMITATION ENGLISH BODY.
RAILROAD CAR.
ENGINE. (For Locomotives.)
BABCOCK'S ELASTIC BODY. (Very durable.)
IMPERIAL "
No. 1 COACH "
No. 2 " "
ENAMEL LEATHER. (For carriage tops.)

FURNITURE VARNISHES, &c.

EXTRA POLISHING. (For Pianos).
No. 1 " " "
BABCOCK'S BEST FLOWING.
No. 1 "
WHITE COPAL. (For chamber sets).
DAMMAR. (White).
PAPER VARNISH. (For walls.)
EXTRA FURNITURE.
No. 1 "
SCRAPING VARNISH.
BLACK "
SHELLAC "
TRUNK "
LOOM HARNESS VARNISH.
WALNUT STAIN.
COACH PAINTERS' JAPAN.
HOUSE " "
BAKING JAPAN.
BABCOCK'S IRON LACQUER.

THE ORIGINAL
BOYS' CLOTHING STORE.

J. WALTER READ,

(LATE HUDSON & READ,)

BOYS' CLOTHING ONLY,

No. 4 Brattle, near Court Street,
BOSTON.

PARKER, WHITE & GANNETT,

Wholesale and Retail Dealers in

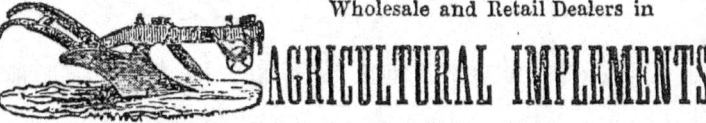

AGRICULTURAL IMPLEMENTS,

MACHINES AND SEEDS,

Comprising the following: — Horse Power and Threshing Machines, Allen's Patent Mowing Machines, Hay, Straw, and Corn Stalk Cutters, Corn Shellers, Plows of different patterns, Cultivators, Horse Hoes, Harrows, Cider Mills and Presses, Lard and Wine Presses, Seed Sowers, Fan Mills, Field and Garden Rollers, Sausage Meat Cutters and Stuffers, Store Trucks, Draft and Trace Chains, Shovels, Hoes, Spades, Hay and Manure Forks, Scythes, Snaths, Horse and Hand Rakes, Wheelbarrows, Churns, Vegetable Cutters, Axes, Axe and Pick Handles, Apple Parers, Self Sealing Cans and Jars for Fruit, Ox Yokes, Ox Bows, Grindstones, Garden Engines, &c., &c.

Also, Grass, Field, and Garden Seeds, Trees, Shrubs, Vines, &c. Pure Peruvian Guano, Coe's Super Phosphate of Lime, Ground Bone, Poudrette, &c.

47, 59, & 63 Blackstone St., Boston, Mass.

BOSTON ADVERTISEMENTS.

J. P. DRAPER,
CUSTOM SHIRT AND COLLAR STORE,

DEALER IN

GENT'S UNDER-GARMENTS,
HOSIERY, ETC.,
No. 120 Washington Street,
BOSTON.

☞ Orders executed promptly, and satisfaction guaranteed.

"BUY ME AND I'LL DO YOU GOOD."

The Best Medicine in the World and for the least Money.

DR. LANGLEY'S
ROOT AND HERB BITTERS,

The standard remedy for Jaundice, Dyspepsia, Costiveness, Indigestion, Piles, Humors of the Blood and Skin, Headache, Nervousness, Weakness, Impure Blood, Liver Complaints, General Debility, &c. They strengthen, warm, invigorate, nourish, and build up the whole system.

☞ Only 25 cents for a pint, or 37 1-2 cents for a quart, bottle.

Office, No. 11 MARSHALL STREET,
BOSTON.

☞ Sold by all Dealers in Medicine everywhere.

ADVERTISING DEPARTMENT. 5

Novel and appropriate Exhibitions furnished at the shortest notice, for Political Demonstrations, Agricultural Fairs, Public and Private Occasions, and for the

FOURTH OF JULY.

Also, constantly on hand, imported by ourselves,

A LARGE VARIETY OF

TRANSPARENT LANTERNS,

Of brilliant colors, representing our NATIONAL FLAG, U. S. SHIELDS, EAGLES, &c., &c , arranged for immediate use, and particularly appropriate for the decoration of Buildings, Garden Illuminations, and for Street Processions.

ALSO, AT WHOLESALE AND RETAIL,

Rockets, Candles, Bengal Lights, Floral Shells, Balloons, Wheels, Mines, Batteries, Pigeons, Flower Pots, Serpents, Pin Wheels, Grasshoppers, Garden Pieces, Hand Illuminations burning ten minutes, &c. &c., at reduced prices.

ADDRESS AT OUR SALESROOM,

JAMES G. HOVEY & CO.,

No. 149 WASHINGTON STREET, - - BOSTON.

(Laboratories at Cambridgeport and Brighton, Mass.)

BOSTON ADVERTISEMENTS.

BENJ. F. DUDLEY,
PLUMBER,
SAVINGS BANK BUILDING,

No. 38 School Street,

Opposite the City Hall,

BOSTON.

Orders from any part of the city or country for fitting up Bathing Rooms, Wash Basins, Shower Baths, Wash Trays for hot and cold water, Bath Boilers, Water Closets, Force Pumps, Marble Slabs, Repairing, &c., or for the purchase of any article in the Plumbing line, will be promptly and faithfully attended to.

☞ *A share of public patronage respectfully solicited.*

PRINTING OF EVERY DESCRIPTION.

BOOK, JOB, PLATE,
AND
LITHOGRAPHIC PRINTING,

Of every description, handsomely executed at the lowest remunerative prices (and warranted equal if not superior to Printing from any other establishment), by

CHARLES H. CROSBY,

No. 3 Water Street,

(In the New Block,)   BOSTON.

Particular attention is given to Factory Tickets, Tags, Plans, Views, Designs, Show Cards, Pattern Books,

And every description of *Factory Printing, Designing, and Engraving*, in which this Establishment is more largely engaged than any other concern in the country.

ADVERTISING DEPARTMENT. 7

STIMPSON'S
COMMERCIAL WRITING FLUID.

The undersigned respectfully invites attention to the following Report of the Massachusetts Charitable Mechanic Association, for 1856 :—

"No. 1649.—Nine bottles WRITING and COPYING FLUID. This Fluid is *known* to the Committee to be of excellent quality, and they recommend an award of a Diploma."

We have been three years perfecting this Fluid, and have submitted it to the use of practical men since the year 1854, and can now, without hesitation, warrant it to be the *best Black Writing* and *Copying Fluid* ever offered to the public. In durability and brilliancy of color, we are confident it is not equalled by any other preparation of the kind.

BOSTON, March 17, 1857.

Dear Sirs,—Nearly three years since, we began the trial of your Ink, and having made use of it ever since, we have no hesitation in pronouncing it superior to any ink that we have ever used. At first it flowed so easily from the pen, that we doubted whether we could obtain a copy from it, but by daily trials we find it as good as any copying ink in the market, and we therefore unhesitatingly recommend it to the public.

With great respect, yours,
S. M. PETTINGILL & CO.
Messrs. STIMPSON & Co., over 91 Washington St.

20 CONGRESS STREET,
Boston, May 16, 1857.

Messrs. STIMPSON & Co.

Gentlemen.—The specimen of Ink, "Commercial Writing Fluid," that I received from you a few days since, I find to be excellent. In an experience of many years, during which I had occasion to use a large quantity of black ink, and always strove to get the best, I never found any superior to yours, if any quite equal to it. Please send me some more of the same quality as the specimen, and oblige Yours, respectfully,
G. F. THAYER.

NEWPORT, R. I., Dec. 8, 1857.

Messrs. STIMPSON & Co.

Please send us some Ink like the last you sent. It flows free from the pen, and dries a beautiful black. Yours, truly,
WM. A. BARBER, Stationer.

Banking House of
CLAPP, FULLER & BROWNE,
1 & 3 Kilby St., Boston, March 7, 1857.

Messrs. STIMPSON & Co.

Gentlemen,—We have been troubled a great deal to get Ink that could copy well, and at the same time to flow freely, but have at last found it in your COMMERCIAL WRITING FLUID. It is vastly superior to anything we have ever seen, and we find no difficulty in taking even three distinct copies. It is invaluable to the business community, and we shall be ready at all times to recommend it. Very truly yours,
CLAPP, FULLER & BROWNE.

BOSTON, June 1, 1857.

Gentlemen,—I have been using your "Commercial Writing Fluid," for some time past, and do not hesitate to say, that I consider it superior to any other Ink that I have ever used.
Yours, very respectfully,
Messrs. STIMPSON & Co. WM. D. SWAN.

BRIDGEWATER, June 1, 1857.

Gentlemen,—Please accept the hearty thanks of an old friend, for the bottle of very nice "Writing Fluid." I have put it to immediate use, and finding it to run remarkably well shall recommend its use to the Normal School in this place. Very truly yours,
MARSHALL CONANT, Principal.

Manufactured and for sale, together with an assortment of the well-known,

IONIC GOLD PENS,
BY
F. W. SNOW,
SUCCESSOR TO STIMPSON & CO.,
91 Washington Street, ... Boston.

J. S. CHASE & CO.,
Cash Jobbers and Retailers of
MOURNING GOODS
EXCLUSIVELY.

EVERY DESCRIPTION OF

MOURNING DRESS GOODS,

Cloaks, Mantillas & Shawls.

Hosiery, Gloves, & Trimmings.

MILLINERY AND DRESS MAKING ROOMS are connected with the store, and all orders for work done promptly and faithfully.

254 Washington St., - Boston.

New Theory of Medical Practice on the Nutritive Principle.

ALFRED G. HALL, M. D.,
365 WASHINGTON ST.,
BOSTON, MASS.,

May be consulted, either in person or by letter, from any part of the Union, for the successful treatment of every form of humor, weakness, or disease.

This popular treatment is restorative in its effects, reliable in the most delicate cases, truly safe and satisfactory to invalids of every class. It is a discovery which affords immediate and progressive relief, is justly worthy the confidence of the afflicted, which THREE MONTHS' TREATMENT will practically secure. All necessary directions, prescriptions, and medicines forwarded by mail, every week during the term. Examinations made personally or by letter, when the terms, with the best references of its success, will be fully explained.

THE NEW
TRANSLATION OF THE BIBLE,
BY REV. LEICESTER AMBROSE SAWYER.

MR. SAWYER, the learned translator of this new version of the HOLY BIBLE, has devoted the past twenty years of his life to Biblical studies, with especial reference to the independent revision and translation of the Bible from the original languages, with a chronological arrangement of the SACRED BOOKS, and improved divisions of chapters and verses. Nearly all are agreed that the time has fully come for a new and thorough translation of the Bible; and the testimony of many of our most learned Theologians is conclusive in regard to Mr. SAWYER'S rare qualifications for such a work.

The principles of this translation are the following:—

1. To translate from the most improved texts of the originals. Great attention has been paid to the text of the Greek Testament, during the last two hundred and fifty years, and many inaccuracies have been detected and removed. A perfect text is not yet attained, and, from the nature of the case, cannot be; but very great improvements have been made in it, and these ought to be made available to the English reader.

2. To translate with the utmost precision and accuracy word for word and particle for particle, but without servility in respect to idiomatic forms and modes of expression.

3. To translate the same words by the same when they mean the same thing, as far as may be, and by different words only when they have different meanings which require a change.

4. To translate different words as far as may be by different words of corresponding meanings, and each word by the same word.

5. To translate general terms by those equally general, and not the more general by the less general, or the less general by the more general.

6. To avoid all needless indelicacy in the translation.

7. To translate chiefly into the recent and improved style of the language, in preference to the antique. This involves the rejection of all obsolete words and modes of expression.

8. To interpolate as little as possible; and leave what is implied in the original to be implied in the translation; and make the translation conform, as far as may be, to the style of the original.

9. To transfer the names of weights, measures, coins, &c., with expressions of their value, in brackets, and to include all interpolations in brackets.

10. To arrange the Sacred Books according to their characters and dates, and not arbitrarily or according to their lengths.

11. To divide the Sacred Books into chapters and verses according to their natural divisions, and not to allow chapters to break up closely connected discourses, or verses to separate sentences.

It is proposed to publish the entire Bible in three handsome 12mo. volumes, of from 400 to 450 pages each, at $1.00 per volume bound in cloth, or $1.25 in embossed morocco, marble edges.

The New Testament, which is now in press, will be published first, and independent of the Old, which will be issued during the year 1859.

The New Testament will be ready in October. Clergymen and others forwarding the amount, by mail, will have the New Testament sent to them *postpaid*; and in ordering will please state whether or not they wish to be considered as subscribers to the Old Testament when published.

JOHN P. JEWETT & COMPANY,
PUBLISHERS,
No. 20 Washington Street, Boston.
To whom all Orders may be addressed.

BOSTON ADVERTISEMENTS.

GAS FIXTURES AND LAMPS.

S. A. STETSON & CO.,

Nos. 350 & 352 Washington St.,

Hayward Block, Boston.

CHANDELIERS,

PENDANTS,

BRACKETS,

LAMPS,

CANDELABRAS, &C.

GAS CONDUCTING PIPE put into Buildings in the most thorough and substantial manner.
GAS STOVES, for Heating and Cooking, of the most approved patterns.

JAMES H. HALLETT,

Nos. 16 Dock Sq., and 31 Faneuil Hall Sq.,

DEALER IN

FEATHERS,

MATTRESSES, CURLED HAIR, MOSS,

PEW CUSHIONS, UPHOLSTERY GOODS,

AND

OF ALL KINDS.

Mattresses Refitted and Beds Renovated in a Superior Manner.

U. S. AND FOREIGN PATENT AGENCY,

Room, No. 11 Webster Bank Building,

13 EXCHANGE STREET, BOSTON.

SAMUEL COOPER,

LATE CHIEF EXAMINER IN THE U. S. PATENT OFFICE,

PROCURES PATENTS IN THIS AND FOREIGN COUNTRIES.

His long official connection with the Patent Office has rendered him familiar with its rules and practice, and with the history of invention in this and other countries; and this experience, with the frequent visits which he proposes making to the Patent Office, justifies him in saying that his Agency will offer to inventors all the advantages of one located in Washington; and, in addition, those which result from a residence in the midst of mechanical and manufacturing industry.

Advice given upon all matters relating to the validity, &c., of patents, the novelty and patentability of inventions. Specifications and drawings prepared, — Caveats filed, — Reconsiderations procured of applications that have been rejected upon imperfectly prepared papers, Cases of interference, and applications for extension and re-issue prosecuted, — and in general all business connected with the Patent Office transacted with care and promptness.

British and other foreign patents procured, through prompt and confidential agents in London and Paris.

Persons residing at a distance may obtain all necessary information, and have their business transacted, by writing to the subscriber, without the trouble or expense of a visit to Washington.

He begs leave to refer those unacquainted with him to the following testimonial:

From the Hon. Charles Mason, Commissioner of Patents.

U. S. PATENT OFFICE, FEB. 28, 1855.

I take great pleasure in stating that during the time I have been acting as Commissioner of Patents, Samuel Cooper, Esq., of Boston, has been engaged as Solicitor, and has been in that capacity in constant correspondence and intercourse with the Office; he has evinced a thorough acquaintance with the Patent Law, and with the rules and practice of the Office, a close attention to the interests of his clients, and a marked candor and courtesy that have rendered the transaction of business with him a pleasure. I have no hesitation in stating that I regard him as one of the very best agents for the transaction of business with this Office with whom I am acquainted.   CHARLES MASON, *Commissioner*.

THREADS,
LINEN, COTTON, & SILK,
FOR EVERY DESCRIPTION OF
SEWING MACHINES.

ALSO,

SHOE THREAD.	CABLE THREAD.
SADDLERS' do.	SEA ISLAND COTTON.
GILLING do.	ERMEN'S DIAMOND do.
MARSHALL'S do.	PHILIP'S WAXED do.

ROSS & PEARCE,
No. 7 LIBERTY SQUARE,
BOSTON, MASS.

P. S. — Personal attention given to all Orders sent by Mail, Express, or otherwise, accompanied by a Daguerreotype view, sketch, o. an accurate description of the object to be engraved.

FLAX AND COTTON TWINE,

OF EVERY DESCRIPTION.

COTTON SEINE TWINE,

4 TO 64 THREADS.

FLAX SAIL TWINE.	FLAX BROOM TWINE.
" BALING "	" BRUSH "
" HAM "	" HERRING "
" WOOL "	" GILLNET "
" SEINE "	" DRUGGIST "

Marline, Lea Bands, Venetian Filling, Loom Cord, Curtain Cord, Squaring Bands, Bale Rope, Cotton Skirt Cord, Seaming Cord.

ALSO,

UPHOLSTERERS AND CARRIAGE MAKERS' WEB AND TWINE.

SEINES AND NETS MADE TO ORDER.

ROSS & PEARCE,

No 7 LIBERTY SQUARE, BOSTON.

CHARLES D. ANDREWS,

(SUCCESSOR TO THE LATE R. ANDREWS),

ENGRAVER,

PLATE PRINTER, & LITHOGRAPHER,

116 WASHINGTON ST., BOSTON.

Marriage, Address, and Business Cards, Diplomas, Portraits, Maps, Copies, Labels, Plans, Notes, Bill and Letter Heads, done in the best manner, and on favorable terms.

Constantly on hand, a good assortment of PLATES suitable for Book Illustrations.

BOSTON ADVERTISEMENTS.

SHIRTS MADE TO FIT
AT
LOCKE'S SHIRT DEPOT,
177 Washington Street, near Milk Street, Boston.

Shirts, Collars, and Stocks, of every variety, — the largest assortment in the United States, at the lowest prices, wholesale and retail.

Fine Shirts made to order, to fit, at short notice. Gentlemen's Furnishing Goods, of every description.

STAINED AND CUT GLASS,
J. M. COOK,
MANUFACTURER,
No. 125 Congress Street, Boston, Mass.

Side Lights, Ship Windows, Shades, Entry Lanterns, Door Plates, Coach and Lantern Lights, Ground, Enamelled, Flock, and Stained Glass, wholesale and retail. Church and other ornamental Windows to order. Lead and Metal Sashes made to order, at the lowest prices. Window Glass of all kinds.

BARRETT'S DYE HOUSE,
No. 140 WASHINGTON ST., BOSTON.

Ladies' Dresses, Cloaks, Shawls, &c., of all kinds, Gentlemen's Coats, Overcoats, Pants, and Vests, Dyed or Cleansed in the very best manner.

Silks, Cloths, Thibets, Alpacas, and other piece goods, of unsaleable colors, dyed, finished, and put up in the style of new goods.

Goods sent by Express, directed as above, will receive prompt and faithful attention.

MUTUAL LIFE INSURANCE.

NEW ENGLAND

Mutual Life Insurance Co.

OFFICE, in the Company's Building,

Corner STATE and CONGRESS STS.,

BOSTON.

Since commencing, February 1st, 1844, to Dec. 1858, has made out 7500 policies.

The amounts from $200 to $15,000 each. Largest amount taken on one risk, $15,000. Insures lives only.

Fund accumulated, owing to the favorable turn of the risks thus far, over $1,350,000, invested for the proportionate benefit of those who shall become, as well as those already, members.

Surplus to be refunded to members at the end of every five years from Dec., 1843. Premiums may be paid quarterly, or semi-annually, when desired, and amounts not too small. All the premiums earned by the Company are paid to it, and no member pays in his note or money against the notes (good or bad) of other members.

Forms of application, and pamphlets of the Company and its reports, to be had of its agents, or at the office of the Company, or forwarded by mail, if written for, post-paid.

DIRECTORS:

Willard Phillips,	M. P. Wilder,	Sewell Tappan,
Charles P. Curtis,	Thomas A. Dexter,	Charles Hubbard,
W. B. Reynolds,	G. H. Folger,	A. W. Thaxter, Jr.

WILLARD PHILLIPS, Pres.   **BENJ. F. STEVENS, Sec.**

JOHN HOMANS, Consulting Physician.

Boston, Sept. 1858.

SAMUEL MASURY,

Photograph & Daguerreotype

ARTIST,

Up one flight of Stairs,

289 Washington St.,
BOSTON.

Photographs taken of every size, and finished in Oil, Water, India Ink, and Pastel Colors.

DAGUERREOTYPES

TAKEN IN THE MOST SUPERIOR MANNER.

DR. TILTON'S

Genuine, Original, and now Improved

EXTRACT OF CANNABIS INDICA

FOR CONSUMPTION.

Beware of the impositions of parties occupying my former office, 365 Washington street, Room No. 1, which was vacated by me last May, and

Removed to 120 Court Street,

The only place in Boston where the above invaluable specific can be had, and where sufferers can at all times see and converse with patients who have been cured, after all other remedies had for years failed to afford relief.

DR. J. A. PAGE,

Proprietor of the original Prescription introduced by Dr. Thomas Tilton,

120 COURT STREET, BOSTON.

Post Office address, Box 1848.

GREAT CHANCE TO SAVE MONEY

BY HAVING YOUR CLOTHES MADE BY

C. A. COLLINS,

No. 203 WASHINGTON STREET, BOSTON,

(CORNER OF BROMFIELD STREET, UP STAIRS.)

REASONS WHY:

1st.—My rent is less than any other Custom Tailor in Boston.
2d.—I buy my Goods for Cash, taking advantage of the markets.
3d.—I sell my Goods for Cash only.
4th.—I make no bad debts for customers to pay for.
5th.—I work for the interest of my customers.

Gentlemen can depend on having garments which, for style, fit, nice trimmings, and faithful work, cannot be surpassed.

I pay particular attention to making Pants, being the most difficult of all garments to fit nicely, and at the same time be perfectly easy.

My Pants are cut by a system original with myself, and used by no other person. I warrant my pants to retain their shape at the boot till worn out, and to fit handsome and be easy in every particular.

SOME OF THE PRICES.

I sell a nice Frock or Dress Coat, from German black or colored Broadcloth, made to order, for from	$15.00 to $23.00
Black German Doe Pants,	5.00 to 8.00
Side Band, and other style Pants,	5.00 to 8.00
Best quality Silk Vests,	4.50 to 5.00
Cloth, Valencia, and Plaid Vests,	2.50 to 5.00
Business Coats,	9.00 to 13.00
Spring and Fall Over Coats,	10.00 to 15.00
Winter Over Coats,	12.00 to 20.00

Where gentlemen furnish their own Cloth, I make and trim it for them into Garments, in the best style, at less prices than any other tailor in Boston.

Always on hand, *the newest and best goods* of all the manufactories of this and foreign countries.

CHESTER A. COLLINS,

203 WASHINGTON STREET,

(Corner of Bromfield Street, Up Stairs,)

BOSTON.

WELL KNOWN AS THE PLACE TO SAVE MONEY.

BOSTON ADVERTISEMENTS.

VENETIAN BLINDS

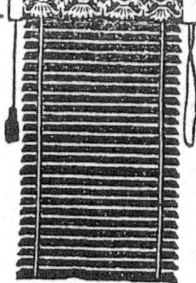

Manufactured in the best manner for

Parlors, Bay Windows, French and Oriel Windows, Halls, Conservatories, &c.

BY

CHARLES B. LOCKE,
No. 47 Cornhill, Boston.

Old Blinds Repaired and Trimmed. ..... Cash on delivery.

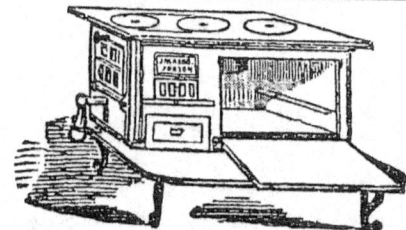
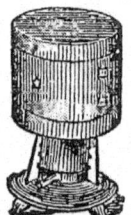

GREAT IMPROVEMENT IN
VENTILATING GAS COOKING STOVES.

Baking is done in the nicest manner by using only one six-foot burner. The arrangement for Boiling is simple, and adapted to the use of Stove Furniture. Those in want of the best Gas Stove, be sure to call and examine this before purchasing.

FOR SALE BY THE INVENTOR,

J. M. READ,
NO. 31 UNION STREET, BOSTON.

No. 11 Border Street, East Boston.

ADVERTISING DEPARTMENT. 19

BLAKE & DAVENPORT,

Manufacturers of and Dealers in every description of

FURNITURE,

IMPORTERS OF

UPHOLSTERY, PLUSHES, DAMASKS,

HAIR SEATING, ETC.,

NOS. 12 TO 24 CORNHILL,

BOSTON.

JAMES G. BLAKE. C. W. DAVENPORT.

DEPOT FOR FASHIONABLE

Card Engraving and Plate Printing,
24 SCHOOL STREET, BOSTON.

WEDDING, VISITING, BUSINESS CARDS,
Executed in the first style of the art.

Cards printed from old Plates at one hour's notice.

WEDDING STATIONERY

On hand and for sale. A large assortment of Cake Boxes, Envelopes and Note Paper.

Initials Embossed on Note Paper at short notice.

N. S. DEARBORN.

TO FARMERS, GARDENERS, AND FRUIT GROWERS.

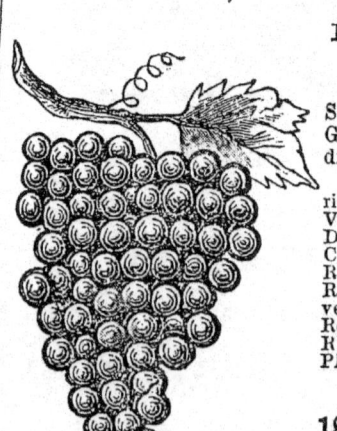

Fertilizers, Grass Seeds, Fruit Trees, Grape Vines, &c.

Best Peruvian and Mexican Guano, Super Phosphate of Lime, Ground Bone, Ground Plaster, Muriate of Lime, Poudrette, Pulverized Charcoal, &c., &c.

GRAPE VINES—Hardy Choice Native Varieties, including Rebecca, Delaware, Union Village, Brinckle, Clara, Raabe, Amelia, Diana, Hartford, Prolific Concord, Curtis, Carter, Clinton, Isabella, &c. BLACKBERRIES—Lawton and Dorchester Seedling. RASPBERRIES—Brinckle's Orange, Knevet's Giant and Franconia. CURRANTS—Red and White Dutch, and Black Naples. RHUBARD—Myatt's Linnæus and Victoria. PEAR TREES—Standard and Dwarfs.

GEORGE DAVENPORT,
18 S. Market & Chatham Sts.,
Opp. Chatham Row, BOSTON.

ADVERTISING DEPARTMENT. 21

MARSH'S STATIONERY WAREHOUSE,
No. 77 Washington Street, . . Boston,
(Opposite head of State Street.)

H. F. MARSH,
(Successor to John Marsh,)

MANUFACTURER OF

FIRST CLASS ACCOUNT BOOKS,

Check, Note, Draft, Bill, and Memorandum BOOKS; Marsh's Blank DIARIES, and Family EXPENSE BOOK. Also, a Superior Quality of BANKERS' CASES and POCKET BOOKS.

MARSH'S CREAM LAID WRITING PAPERS,

Of various sizes and qualities; some, of the finest texture and finish, fully equal to any of foreign manufacture, and less in price. These papers will be stamped with initials *free of charge*. Also, MARSH'S INITIAL STATIONERY PACKET, containing an assortment of PAPER & ENVELOPES ready stamped—a very convenient and desirable article—and a complete assortment of STATIONERY in all its branches, for sale at the lowest market prices, *wholesale or retail*. Orders solicited, which will meet prompt attention.

No. 77 WASHINGTON STREET. No. 77.

L. G. SMITH,
CLOTH
AND
CLOTHING STORE,
31 DOCK SQUARE,
BOSTON.

This is one of the largest fashionable ready-made Clothing Establishments in the city, and contains every variety of Garments, made in the best style, and at the cheapest rates. Purchasers at wholesale or retail are requested to call and examine for themselves.

CUSTOM WORK.

Garments made to order from American, German, and French Broadcloths and Doeskins, in the neatest and most fashionable style.

RICHARDSON & DEXTER,

IMPORTERS OF

GUNS, FISHING TACKLE,

AND

POCKET CUTLERY,

44 WASHINGTON STREET, - - - BOSTON.

Just received, a fine assortment of English and American FISHING TACKLE, which we will sell at wholesale and retail.

Trout, Salmon, Bass, and Bamboo RODS ; Trout Baskets, Bait Boxes and Pails ; Reels ; Silk, Linen, and Hair Lines ; Artificial Frogs, Minnows, and Bugs ; Trout, Salmon, and Bass Flies ; Hooks on Gut and Gimp, Fly Hooks, &c. ; Calcutta, Bamboo, and Cane Poles.
GUN MATERIAL—Double and Single Guns and Pistols. Sole Agents for ALLEN & WARNER'S NEW MODEL PISTOL.

SPORTING AND TARGET RIFLES
CONSTANTLY ON HAND AND MADE TO ORDER.

DANIEL J. CARRUTH,

 DEALER IN

TOBACCO, SNUFF, CIGARS, PIPES,

WINES, ALE, PORTER,

AND

CIDER.

49, 51, & 53 BLACKSTONE ST., BOSTON.

CROSBY, NICHOLS & CO.,
BOOKSELLERS, PUBLISHERS,
AND
STATIONERS,
Dealers at Wholesale and Retail in
BOOKS IN EVERY DEPARTMENT OF LITERATURE,
No. 117 Washington Street, Boston.

C, N. & Co. publish some of the most valuable and popular School Books used in the United States, among which are,

TOWER'S ELEMENTS OF ENGLISH GRAMMAR,

Universally approved, extensively used, and considered by many teachers the best treatise in print.

TOWER'S GRADUAL READERS.

STEARNS'S PRACTICAL GUIDE TO ENGLISH PRONUNCIATION.

A work just introduced into the Schools of Boston, and many other places; filling an entirely new and important place in education, and receiving the highest praise from the most competent judges.

WILSON'S TREATISE ON ENGLISH PUNCTUATION.

The best and most complete work ever published upon the subject, and approved by all who have examined it.

PAYSON, DUNTON, & SCRIBNER'S COMBINED SYSTEM OF RAPID PENMANSHIP.

In Eleven Parts. With copies at the head of each page. A Series of Copy-Books, probably better known, and more extensively used, than any other published. Its merits have secured its introduction into all the States of the Union, and it is well known to the Trade as the most popular Series in the country.

BOOK-KEEPING, ADAPTED TO PAYSON, DUNTON, AND SCRIBNER'S COMBINED SYSTEM OF PENMANSHIP.

A new and beautiful book, combining instruction in Book-Keeping by Double and Single Entry and Penmanship. This work has been examined by competent persons, who pronounce it one of the best works ever published upon the subject. It has already been widely introduced, and will commend itself wherever the system of penmanship is known.

*** Teachers and country dealers are requested to send us their orders.

24   BOSTON ADVERTISEMENTS.

ARTISTS' MATERIALS.

WINDSOR & NEWTON'S
SUPERFINE OIL COLORS,

Prepared in Tubes; Fine Linen English Canvas; Brushes, and every article required for OIL PAINTING. Also,

DRAWING MATERIALS,

In every variety, imported and for sale, Wholesale and Retail, by

M. J. WHIPPLE & CO., 35 Cornhill, . . . BOSTON.

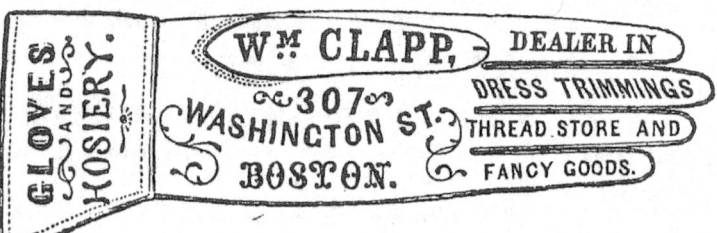

SEEDS! TREES! PLANTS!

The subscribers offer for sale an unrivalled stock of

Agricultural, Garden, and Flower Seeds,

Which are annually received from the most celebrated growers of Seeds in Europe and America, and embrace all the choicest and most esteemed varieties of

FRUIT TREES.

One of the most extensive collections to be found in this country; containing all the leading and choice varieties of Pears, Apples, Plums, Peaches, Cherries, Strawberries, Currants, Raspberries, Gooseberries; all the standard and new varieties of native and foreign Grapes, &c., &c.

ORNAMENTAL AND SHADE TREES,

Evergreen Trees; Hedge Plants; Flowering Shrubs; Roses; and Climbing Plants; also, a very large collection of

Green-House Plants, of Every Description.

Purchasers will find at this Establishment every desirable variety of Seeds, Trees, and Plants necessary for the Farm or Garden; Catalogues of which will be furnished gratis, on application, post paid.

The best Peruvian Guano, Super-Phosphate of Lime, Bone Dust, and other fertilizers, constantly for sale, at low prices.

HOVEY & CO.,
7 Merchants Row, ... Boston.

ADVERTISING DEPARTMENT.   25

W. M. SHUTE & SON'S

Hat and Fur Store,

(ESTABLISHED 1838,)

173 & 175 Washington St., Boston.

The subscribers would invite the attention of the citizens of this place and vicinity to their extensive and varied assortment of

HATS, CAPS, AND FURS,

Which, in point of

STYLE, QUALITY, AND PRICE,

Will be found to compare favorably with any in town.

☞ Every article warranted as represented.

N. B. — OLD FURS ALTERED and REPAIRED by experienced workmen.

W. M. SHUTE, ... JUDSON SHUTE.

BANK & COUNTING-ROOM FURNITURE.

SITTING DESKS. **STANDING DESKS.**

DESKS, OF ALL DESCRIPTIONS,
Constantly on hand, and made to order, and warranted,

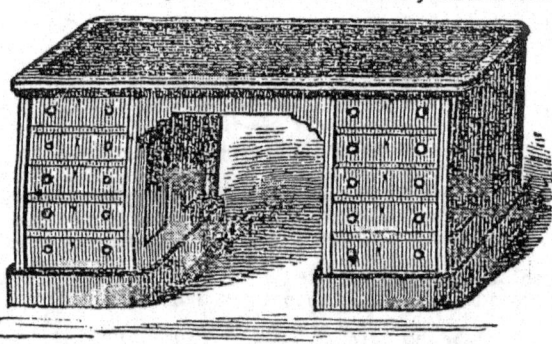

ARM CHAIRS. **BOOK CASES.**

BY
STEPHEN SMITH,
DESK MANUFACTURER,
Nos. 51 & 53 CORNHILL,
BOSTON.

WILLIAMS & EVERETT,

Manufacturers and Dealers in

LOOKING GLASSES,

PORTRAIT

AND

PICTURE FRAMES.

OIL PAINTINGS, ENGRAVINGS.

IMPORTERS AND DEALERS IN

Looking Glass Plates,

AND

PLATE GLASS FOR WINDOWS.

GILDING IN ALL ITS BRANCHES.

Looking Glass Plates Re-Silvered.

Warerooms, 234 Washington Street,

BOSTON.

DORCHESTER
MUTUAL FIRE INSURANCE COMPANY,
OF DORCHESTER, MASS.
NET AVAILABLE ASSETS, $160,000.

DIRECTORS.

Asaph Churchill, Dorchester.		Charles Hunt, Dorchester.
Marshal P. Wilder,	"	Laban Pratt, "
John H. Robinson,	"	Charles Stearns, Brookline.
Henry Humphreys,	"	Samuel Babcock, Milton.
Edward H. R. Ruggles,	"	Henry O. Hildreth, Dedham.
Otis Wright,	"	Charles Endicott, Canton.
Charles A. Wood,	"	Norton Pratt, Braintree.
William F. Temple,	"	James Torrey, Weymouth.

WM. F. TEMPLE, Secretary.   **ASAPH CHURCHILL, President.**

REFERENCES BY PERMISSION.

Henry J. Gardner, Enoch Train, Enoch Baldwin, Alpheus Hardy, Daniel Denny, Dorchester; Robert B. Forbes, Amor Hollingsworth, Dr. C. C. Holmes, Milton; F. W. Lincoln, Canton; Martin Wales, Stoughton; A. & A. Lawrence & Co., Dana, Farrar, & Hyde, Boston.

This Company insures Dwellings, Churches, Stores, Buildings, and Household Furniture, against loss or damage by **FIRE** and **LIGHTNING**, for the term of One, Three, or Five Years, and on Manufacturing and Mechanics' Risks, Stocks of Goods, and other Personal Property, for One Year, on as favorable terms as any other sound dividend-paying Company.

Office at Dorchester, Mass.
Boston Agency, No. 1 Phœnix Building, rear of No. 27 State Street.

CORSLETTS.
We call the attention of our patrons to the
IMPROVED FRENCH CORSET,

by Dr. Abbe. It is so arranged that all the natural actions of the Chest are secured, and, like the common Corset, can be and is worn with great benefit to the health; while the tendency of common Corsets is to much, and often great, injury.

THESE CORSETS CAN BE FOUND AT
No. 24 BOYLSTON STREET, BOSTON.

Dr. Abbe has, for the last twenty-five years, given his attention to

SPINAL DISEASES AND DEFORMITIES,

And has thus been compelled to give much attention to the use and effect of Corsets, and has invented this great improvement so that the multitude who are not deformed may have a Corset that will give a good figure, give every requisite support, and be worn not only without injury, but with great benefit.

Dr. Abbe still gives his attention to the treatment of all Deformities.

Premium Gold Medal,

At the Exhibition of the Massachusetts Charitable Mechanic Association of 1853, for the BEST CARVED FURNITURE, was awarded to

GAHERY, GENDROT & CO.
FROM PARIS,
MANUFACTURERS OF AND DEALERS IN

Fashionable Furniture,

324 Washington Street,

Opposite the Adams House,   **BOSTON.**

Manufactory, corner of Plymouth and Eustis Streets, Roxbury.

MOSES G. FARMER,
TELEGRAPHIC ENGINEER,
AND
CONSULTING ELECTRICIAN,
156 WASHINGTON ST., BOSTON.

THE BOSTON MUSEUM

Was erected in 1845, and cost nearly $250,000. It is the largest, most valuable, and best arranged in the United States. It comprises no less than SEVEN DIFFERENT MUSEUMS, one half of the celebrated PEALE'S PHILADELPHIA MUSEUM, swelling the collection to upwards of Half a Million of Articles, the greatest amount of objects of interest to be found together at any one place in America; and an entirely NEW HALL OF WAX STATUARY, one hundred feet in length, completely filled with Wax Figures. In addition to the attraction, and *without extra charge* visitors are admitted to the gorgeous Exhibition Hall, where they can witness the magnificent THEATRICAL ENTERTAINMENTS, given every evening, and on Wednesday and Saturday afternoons.

Admission, Twenty-Five Cents.

ECONOMY. EVERY MAN HIS OWN PRINTER.
LOWE'S PATENT PORTABLE PRINTING and LETTER-COPYING PRESS.

By which the people can do their own Printing, from Type, Stereotype, Electrotype, Dies, Wood Cuts, or Plate Engravings, giving as perfect an impression, and will do all the varieties of printing that can be worked on any press in the world.

It prints beautifully in Gold, Silver, or Copper Bronze; and various kinds of Fancy and Ornamental Printing may be done in the neatest manner, on dry or damp paper, or on any material capable of taking an impression.

It is admirably adapted for printing *Circulars, Labels, Bill-Heads, Visiting or Business Cards, Envelopes, Bills of Lading, Receipts, &c.*, and as a *Letter-Copying Press* is superior to any press now in use. *It must be seen to be appreciated.*

The largest size will be found useful to printers for taking proof-sheets, and for doing job work of all kinds. It will recommend itself by its working; and all those who are desirous of saving money and obtaining knowledge, or amusing themselves in this way, will be highly benefited by its use.

We wish to impress upon the minds of the *people* the *importance* of doing their own printing with one of *Lowe's Presses*, and thereby make a saving of over one-half. Send in your orders, and we will convince you that what we say here is true to the letter. Any person of common capacity can print *five hundred sheets of paper in one hour* (which is a fair average of the working of the press), gain information, and save money.

It is simple, strong, and durable, and easily kept in order. The smallest size, No. 1, price $5, will print a sheet 5 by 6 inches. No. 2, $10, will print a sheet 8 by 12 inches. No. 3, $15, will print a sheet 12 by 14 inches. No. 4, $25, iron cone, 13 by 17, braced. No. 5, $50, for engraved plate, 19 by 23, braced.

We desire to call the attention of the *whole world* to this WONDER OF THE AGE!

A few days' labor by a boy will save the cost of a press, and do the work as well as the most skillful workman.

Print your own Cards, and they will cost only *75 cents per thousand!* for as good an article as you would get by paying the printer two dollars and fifty cents. The cards we will furnish in any quantity, 2¼ by 3¼ inches, for 75 cents per thousand; larger or smaller in proportion. Printed *directions*, giving *all the particulars* as to the working, regulating, and using the press, and information in regard to printing generally, setting types, &c., will always accompany every press.

☞ All kinds of printing materials furnished to order.

We will furnish a good article of printing paper, for circulars, 19 by 24 inches, for ten cents per quire, or two dollars per ream of twenty quires; other qualities and sizes in proportion. The cards or paper we will cut to any size to suit customers, at the shortest notice.

Our presses may be exchanged any time within twelve months. Old presses taken in part pay for new ones. Other articles sold by us, if not satisfactory, may be returned within thirty days, if returned in as good condition as when purchased of us.

N.B.—We will furnish to our customers all kinds of printing papers and card board at cost! We have but one price for our goods, and the public can rely on their being just what we represent them to be, in the strictest sense of these terms.

PRINTING OFFICE, No. 1.—We furnish a Printing Press, 5 by 6 inches, $5; One font of Types, with all of the marks in common use, large and small letters, with spaces, containing 1742 types, $3; Ink Roller, $0.25; Ink Box, $0.25; Can of Black Ink, $0.50; Iron Chase, for fastening the type, $0.50; Blocks and bearers, $0.50. Printing Office complete, for $10.

PRINTING OFFICE, No. 2.—Printing Press, 8 by 12 inches, $10; Two fonts, containing 3,484 types, with all marks, $6; Ink Roller, $1.25; Can of best Black Ink, $1.50; Iron Chase, $0.75; Blocks and bearers $0.50. Office complete, $20.

PRINTING OFFICE, No. 3.—Printing Press, 12 by 14 inches, $16; Three fonts, containing 5,226 types, $9; Ink Roller, $1.50; Can of best Black Ink, $1.50; Iron Chase, $1; Blocks and bearers, $1. Office complete, $30.

PRINTING OFFICE, No. 4.—Our Improved Printing Press, all iron, $25; Four fonts, containing 6,968 types, and all the marks in common use, $12; Can of best London Jet Black Ink, $1.50; Ink Roller, $1.50; Iron Chase, $1; Marble Slab, for ink table, $1; Blocks and bearers, $1. Office complete, $43. Address,

LOWE PRESS COMPANY, 144 *Washington Street, Boston, Mass.*

J. W. SMITH & CO.,

MANUFACTURERS AND RETAILERS OF

FINE READY-MADE

CLOTHING,

AND

MEN'S FURNISHING GOODS,

DOCK SQUARE, cor. ELM STREET,

BOSTON.

This establishment is one of the largest, best, and most reliable in Boston, having always on hand a large stock of

CLOTHS, DOESKINS, AND VESTINGS,

Which are made to order in the best manner and at short notice. Also,

READY-MADE CLOTHING,

Got up in the latest style, of good material, and well put together.

ALWAYS ADHERING TO THE

LOW PRICE SYSTEM.

UNRIVALLED EMPORIUM

FOR

GENTLEMEN'S, YOUTHS', AND LITTLE CHILDREN'S

READY-MADE CLOTHING,

Furnishing Goods, Hats, Caps, &c.

WHOLESALE AND RETAIL.

An extensive and desirable assortment of **Rich Cloths, Doeskins, Cassimeres, Vestings, &c.**, always to be found in the **Custom Department**, with unusual facilities for prompt and faithful execution of all orders for **Genteel Clothing.**

Military and **Naval Officers' Dresses, Military and Firemen's Uniforms**, furnished at the shortest notice; and all garments warranted to give perfect satisfaction.

GEO. W. SIMMONS, PIPER & CO.,
OAK HALL, 32 and 34 North Street, Boston.

ADVERTISEMENTS

OF

MERCHANTS AND MANUFACTURERS

IN

S A L E M .

ESSEX HOUSE,

J. S. LEAVITT, Proprietor,

No. 176 ESSEX STREET, SALEM.

This House is centrally located on Essex street, and is the general head quarters for business men. It has excellent accommodations, and charges reasonable.

Coaches are in readiness to convey passengers to and from the Depot at all hours.

There is also a good Livery Stable in the rear of the Hotel, where fine Horses and easy Carriages may be found. Also, Stabling for Horses on reasonable terms.

ADVERTISING DEPARTMENT.   35

WILLIAM ARCHER, JR.,
Auctioneer & Commission Merchant,
AND
STOCK, REAL ESTATE, AND INSURANCE BROKER,
Nos. 34 Front and 18 Washington Streets.

E. R. PERKINS,

PHOTOGRAPHIC ARTIST,
241 ESSEX STREET, SALEM.

Patent Ambrotypes, Stereoscopes, Photographs, Sphereotypes, Melainotypes and Patent Leather Pictures, of various sizes, taken with all the improvements of the art.

Portraits, Miniatures, Engravings, &c., accurately copied. Views taken when desired.

NATHAN PEIRCE,
STOCK AND LOAN OFFICE,
NO. 163 ESSEX STREET,

East India Marine Society's Building,   SALEM.

SALEM DIRECTORY.

Adams, Richardson & Co.

207 ESSEX STREET,

IMPORTERS AND DEALERS IN

FOREIGN AND DOMESTIC HARDWARE,

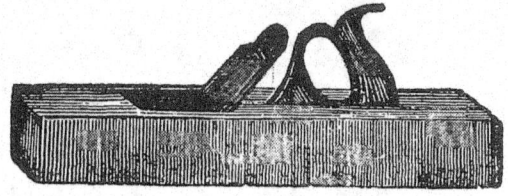

WINDOW GLASS,
CUT NAILS,
ZINC, SHEET LEAD,
WHITE LEAD,
LEAD PIPE, PUMPS, &c.

Agents for Fairbanks'

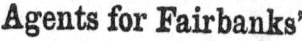

PLATFORM SCALES,
AND
DENIO & ROBERTS' IRON SAFES.

HENRY HALE,
IMPORTER AND DEALER IN
HARDWARE GOODS AND CUTLERY,
FOREIGN AND DOMESTIC.
HOUSEKEEPING ARTICLES, AND FANCY GOODS.

AGRICULTURAL TOOLS AND PLOUGHS,
Plough Castings, Friction Rollers and Cranks, Iron, and
CHAIN PUMPS AND LEAD PIPE.
KEROSENE ILLUMINATING & LUBRICATING OILS.
KEROSENE LAMPS
IN EVERY VARIETY.

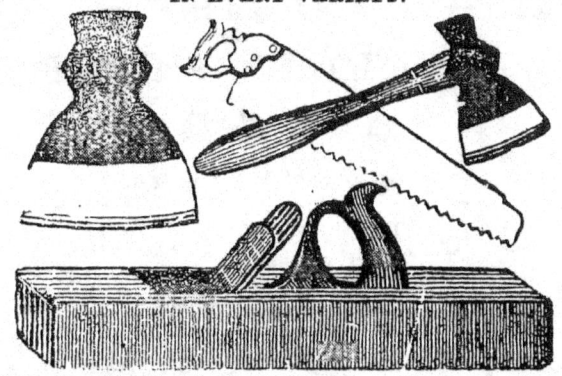

No. 215 — ESSEX STREET.

CARPENTERS' TOOLS,
House Trimmings, Shoe Makers' Tools, Nails, Thread, and Pegs, Boiler Doors, and Oven Mouths, Furnaces, Cast Iron Hollow Ware, Tubs, Pails, Mats, Cut Nails, Emery, Zinc, Lead, Japan and Sponge Blacking, &c., &c.

No. 215 Essex Street, Salem.

ANDREW S. WATERS,
BRASS FOUNDER, COPPERSMITH, AND PLUMBER.

Copper Work and Plumbing of every description promptly attended to. Casting, &c.

6 FRANKLIN STREET,
NORTH SALEM, MASS.

JAMES TETLOW,
Manufacturer of all kinds of
MARINE AND STEAM BOILERS,
HIGH AND LOW PRESSURE;
LOCOMOTIVE BOILERS;
SHIP TANKS;
GAS HOLDERS, &c.
NAUMKEAG WHARF,
SALEM.

☞ Orders from any part of the country attended to.

JOSEPH CHISHOLM
Manufactures and offers for sale

Log, Hand, Deep-sea, Fishing, Window (bleached or unbleached) and Clothes Lines; Twine; Marlines; Bedcords; Rope from Russian, American, and Manilla Hemp; Engine Packing from Hemp or Flax.

Head of Factory, 68 Mill Street.

ADVERTISING DEPARTMENT. 39

S. C. & E. A. SIMONDS,
DEALERS IN
CROCKERY & HARDWARE,
WINDOW GLASS,
Paper Hangings, Solar and Entry Lamps, White Lead, Oils, Dry and Ground Paints, &c., &c.,

No. 32 FRONT STREET.

WM. F. SMALL,
DEALER IN
GAS & STEAM PIPE,
AND
GAS FIXTURES,
273 ESSEX STREET,
SALEM.

Orders for Gas and Steam Fitting for Dwellings, Stores, &c., will be executed in the most faithful manner. Being a practical workman, he flatters himself that all work issued from his establishment will give perfect satisfaction.

E. SECCOMB,
MANUFACTURER OF
Adamantine & Imperial Sperm Candles
AND
OLEINE OIL,
Foot of Harbor Street, ... SALEM.
Office in Boston, 89 COMMERCIAL STREET.

R. H. CHAMBERLAIN,
DEALER IN
HOSIERY, GLOVES, YARN, FANCY GOODS,
AND
EMBROIDERIES,
No. 236 Essex Street, . . . SALEM.

JOHN P. PEABODY,
DEALER IN
WHITE GOODS, EMBROIDERIES,
TRIMMINGS, HOSIERY,
GLOVES,
AND
FANCY GOODS,
No. 238 Essex Street,
SALEM, MASS.

J. MAYER,

Wholesale and Retail Dealer in

EMBROIDERIES,

Trimmings, Hosiery, and Fancy Goods,

171 ESSEX STREET.

A. E. PRICE,

DEALER IN

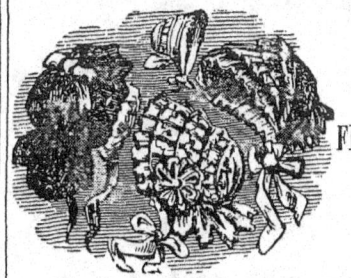

MILLINERY,

TRIMMINGS,

FRENCH FLOWERS & BONNET RIBBONS,

EMBROIDERIES,

Cloak Materials.

CLOAKS, CAPES, and TALMAS made to order.

No. 220 ESSEX STREET.

GRAVE CLOTHES CONSTANTLY ON HAND.

HUMPHREY COOK,

FASHIONABLE

HAT, CAP,

AND

FUR ESTABLISHMENT,

233 ESSEX & 33 WASHINGTON STS.

GEO. P. FARRINGTON,

310 Essex Street, corner of North,

Where may be found a large assortment of

PURE DRUGS & FAMILY MEDICINES,

Perfumery and Toilet Articles of every variety, &c.

Particular attention paid to the compounding of Physicians' prescriptions, and the dispensing of family medicines. A full assortment of Drugs and Medicines, including all the latest preparations, constantly on hand. Medicine dispensed at all hours.

G. A. & T. BROWN,
CARPENTERS,
AND
BUILDERS,
No. 158 Derby Street,
SALEM.
Orders promptly executed.

JOSHUA B. GRANT,
Manufacturer of
CURRIERS' TABLES
AND
TOOLS,
51 Boston Street,
SALEM.

IRA MANSFIELD,
MASON,

Mason Work in all its branches done in a thorough and workmanlike manner.

Shop, Congress St., Residence, 3 Lagrange St.,

SOUTH SALEM.

SIMEON FLINT,
MASON,
No. 223 Derby Street.

Mason work of every description done in a thorough and workmanlike manner. Hot-Air Furnaces, Cooking Ranges, &c., furnished at manufacturers' prices, and set to order in the best manner.

JOSEPH MANSFIELD,
Sign & House Painter,
Glazier and Paper Hanger,

Imitation of Wood and Marble,

No. 9 Lafayette St.

D. PULSIFER & CO.,
HOUSE, SHIP, AND SIGN PAINTING,
PAPERING, GLAZING, ETC.,
No. 25 Front St., opp. the Market.

For sale, at low prices, a general assortment of Paints. Oils, Coach, Furniture, and Demar Varnishes; Glazed Sashes, Blinds, Brushes, &c.

RICHARD M. CHIPMAN,
TIN PLATE AND SHEET IRON WORKER,
NO. 256 ESSEX STREET,
SALEM.

Tin Roofing, Furnace Work, and all kinds of work in his line, done in a faithful and superior manner.

S. F. NICHOLS,
HOUSE, SHIP, AND SIGN PAINTER,
No. 113 Derby Street.

Glazing & Paper Hanging.
IMITATION OF WOOD AND MARBLE.
For sale, all kinds of Glazed Sashes, Window Blinds, Paints, Oils, Glass, &c.,

C. E. BROWN,
HOUSE, SHIP, & SIGN PAINTER,
Glazier, Grainer, Paper Hanger,
AND DEALER IN
PAINTS, GLASS, & PUTTY,
No. 42 Charter Street, Salem.

JOHN H. WILLIAMS,
HOUSE CARPENTER,
AND
SHIP JOINER,
Head Phillips Wharf,
SALEM.

Jobbing and Repairing attended to promptly.

E. P. RUSSELL'S
PATENT
MASTIC ROOFING,
IN AND FOR THE COUNTY OF
ESSEX, MASS.

We invite the attention of Architects, and all interested in building, to our Roofing, as being an article superior to any Roofing now in use, both for durability and service, as it is perfectly

Fire and Water Proof.

All orders addressed to W. L. SAXBY, Salem, Mass., will receive prompt attention, and all work warranted to give satisfaction.

Testimonials and Samples may be seen by calling at

No. 153 Derby Street,
SALEM, MASS.

WM. F. GARDNER,
CARPENTER
AND
BUILDER,
NO. 6 Pine St., Salem.
Orders promptly executed.

MOSES DAVIDSON,
CARRIAGE & SIGN
PAINTER,
134 Boston St.,
SALEM.

ADVERTISING DEPARTMENT. 45

THOMAS PINNOCK,
SLATER,
HOUSE AND SLATE-YARD,
No. 3 Ward Street, South Salem.

☞ Roofs covered with Vermont, Welsh, or Eastern Slate, to order, at reasonable prices, and in the best manner. All work warranted.

FRANCIS P. GOSS,

PLUMBER,
No. 7 St. Peter Street, Salem, Mass.,

Manufacturer and Dealer in the following articles:

Sheet Lead, Lead Pipe, Bath Boilers, Wash Boilers, Water Closets, Basins, Marble Slabs, Bathing Tubs, Silver Plated Work, Shower Baths, Force and Lift Pumps, Brass Cocks.

GEORGE H. PEIRSON,
CARRIAGE SMITH,
AND MANUFACTURER OF
STEEL SPRINGS, IRON FENCE, & BALUSTRADES,
WEST PLACE.

☞ Particular attention paid to all kinds of Iron Work for Buildings.

DEVEREUX DENNIS,
CARPENTER
AND
BUILDER.
No. 8 Lafayette Street,

All kinds of jobbing executed on reasonable terms.

EDW. D. LORING,
COACH & CHAISE
MANUFACTURER,
WEST PLACE,
Rear of the Mansion House.

Repairing done in the best manner, at short notice.

H. H. STEVENS,
MANUFACTURER OF
PATENT AND ENAMELLED LEATHER,
MASON HILL,
NORTH SALEM.

Orders received for ENAMELLING, and promptly attended to.

JOHN BATTIS,
MANUFACTURER OF
KEGS & CASKS,
OF ALL KINDS,
Nos. 147 and 149 Derby Street,
Foot of Charter Street.

☞ All orders answered with dispatch.

JOHN T. ROPES & CO.,
Wholesale and Retail Dealers in
STOVES, STOVE PIPE,
TIN WARE, &c.,
Nos. 17 & 19 Front Street,
SALEM.

JOHN T. ROPES. WM. ROPES.

ADVERTISING DEPARTMENT. 47

ISAAC WINCHESTER,
STAIR BUILDER,
42 Charter Street,
SALEM.
Orders promptly attended to.

B. S. MANSFIELD,
HOUSE AND SIGN
PAINTING,
AND
Imitation of Wood & Marble,
AND PAPER HANGER,
No. 8 Endicott St., Salem, Mass.
All orders executed with promptness.

SAMUEL KEHEW,
COOPER,
And Manufacturer of
CASKS OF ALL KINDS,
NO. 47 UNION STREET, SALEM.
Repairing and Jobbing done at short notice.

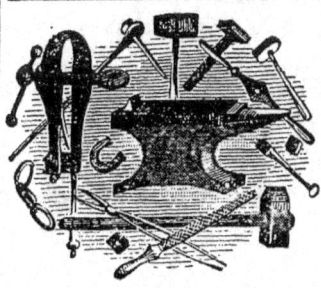

JACOB AGGEE,
BLACKSMITH,
51 Harbor Street,
SALEM.
Machine Forging and Jobbing of all kinds.

EBEN. N. PRICE,

Manufacturer and Wholesale & Retail Dealer in

HARNESSES AND TRUNKS,

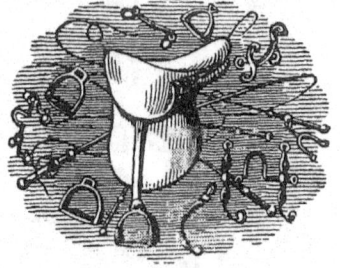 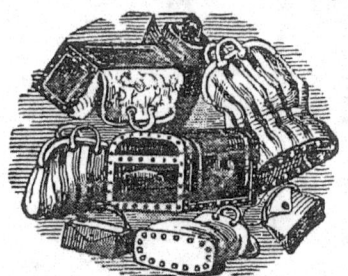

Saddles, Bridles, Valises, Carpet Bags, Whips, Robes, Blankets, Nets, and every article for the accommodation of Travellers, constantly on hand.

No. 237 Essex, near Washington Street.

CHAS. F. HOVEY,

COACH, CHAISE, AND SIGN

Corner of Spring & Webb Streets,

SALEM, MASS.

All orders promptly attended to.

ADVERTISING DEPARTMENT. 49

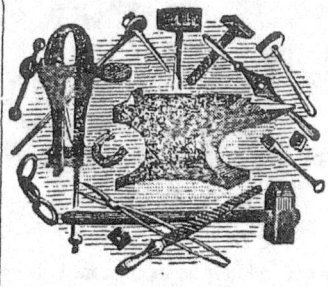

BENJAMIN CUTTS,
BLACKSMITH,
AND MANUFACTURER OF
Iron Fence, Snow Fenders,
AND BALUSTRADES,
No. 8 Sewall Street.
AGENT FOR CHASE'S WIRE RAILING, &c.

CARRIAGE  **REPOSITORY.**

Carriages and Harnesses of all kinds (including some from the most celebrated manufacturers in the State) for sale or exchange.
Horses and Carriages to Let. Boarding for Horses.
W. W. KELMAN,
WASHINGTON, COR. OF CHURCH STS., SALEM.

THOMAS BROOKING,
CARRIAGE MANUFACTURER
AND
HORSE-SHOER,
No. 21 MASON STREET, - - - SALEM.
All kinds of Carriage Work promptly attended to.

s—4

50   SALEM DIRECTORY.

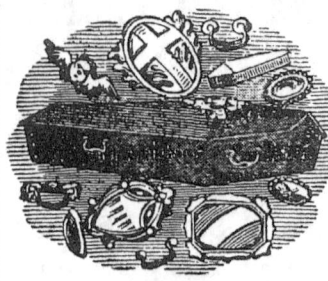

L. WOODBERRY,
Coffin & Casket
WAREROOMS,
No. 3 SEWALL STREET,
Street opp. Mechanic Hall,
SALEM, MASS.

Robes of all kinds on hand or made to order

W. A. POWER'S

MARBLE WORKS,
No. 11 ST. PETER STREET,
SALEM.

Monuments, Grave-Stones, Chimney Pieces, Table Tops, &c., &c., furnished at reasonable prices, and at short notice.

ADVERTISING DEPARTMENT. 51

G. V. SIBLEY,
Manufacturer of
LADIES' GAITER BOOTS,

Corner of Central and Charter Streets.

J. STETSON,
DEALER IN
BOOTS, SHOES, and RUBBERS,
No. 31 North St., N. Salem.
Manufacturer of
Ladies', Misses' and Children's
BOOTS & SHOES.
Repairing done at short notice.

JOHN W. STOCKER,
COACH & CHAISE
MANUFACTURER,
AND
WHEELWRIGHT,
No. 23 Endicott St.

Repairing done in the best manner at short notice. Also, Lancewood Shafts and Poles constantly on hand.

GILMAN ANDREWS,
CARRIAGE MANUFACTURER,
No. 27 Beach Street, opp. Carltonville Depot,
SALEM, MASS.

☞ *Repairing in all its branches neatly executed.*

ISAAC DAYTON,
CARRIAGE TRIMMER,
AND
HARNESS MAKER,
No. 4 SEWALL ST., (Street opposite Mechanic Hall,)
Repairing promptly attended to. SALEM.

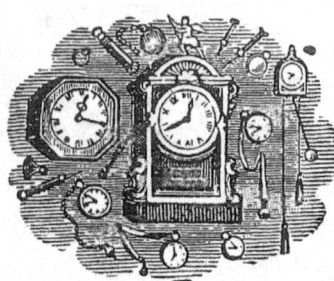

JESSE SMITH,
WATCHMAKER

And dealer in Gold and Silver Lever and Lepine

WATCHES, ETC.,
No. 262 ESSEX STREET.

Also, Marine Chronometers, Barometers, Thermometers, Nautical Almanacs, Spy Glasses, &c., &c.

Chronometers adjusted and rates ascertained by Transit Observations.

JACOB S. HASKELL & JOSEPH L. LOUGEE,
296 ESSEX STREET, SALEM.

FURNITURE

MADE AND REPAIRED IN THE BEST MANNER.

Haskell & Lougee have just obtained a PATENT for an improved

REVOLVING TABLE,

For Parlors, Offices, and Counting Rooms; including Draws for papers, &c. A specimen may be seen as above.

T. NICHOLSON, JR.,
DEALER IN
BOOTS, SHOES, & RUBBERS,
164 ESSEX ST.,
SALEM.

ADVERTISING DEPARTMENT. 53

PERKINS & BROWN,
DEALERS IN
READY-MADE CLOTHING,

Cloths, Boots, Shoes, Hats, Caps, Trunks, Furnishing Goods, and Manufacturers of and Wholesale Dealers in Oil Clothing,

137 Derby and 36 Union Streets, Salem, Mass.

BENJAMIN EDWARDS,
Merchant Tailor,
SECOND STORY,

No. 224 ESSEX STREET,

SALEM.

ISAAC C. PRAY,
NO. 16 LAFAYETTE STREET,
SECOND AND THIRD FLOORS,

ALL SORTS OF STITCHING

Usually done by hand for family use, done here with neatness and dispatch. Also, Ladies', Gentlemen's, Misses', and Children's Boots and Shoes, Gaiters, and Congress Gaiters, of every kind and description, STITCHED and BOUND in the neatest possible manner, with great dispatch.

FARMERS' EXCHANGE
EATING HOUSE,
NO. 25 FRONT STREET,

SALEM, MASS.

PRAY & BOYNTON, - - - - PROPRIETORS.

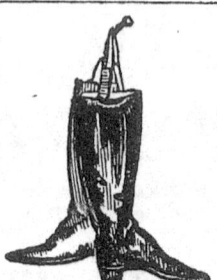

THERON PALMER,

DEALER IN

Boots, Shoes, & Rubbers.

No. 216 ESSEX STREET,

SALEM.

BOOTS & SHOES

REPAIRED HERE,

Prompt, Neat, and on Reasonable Terms.

J. H. CARTY,

Union Bridge, So. Salem.

PAPER, TWINE,

AND

MACHINE PAPER BAGS.

G. T. BROWN, AGENT,

33 LAFAYETTE STREET, ... SALEM.

DEALERS SUPPLIED AT BOSTON PRICES.

WM. C. HAMOND,	S. G. DANFORTH,
Carpenter, Builder,	**CARPENTER**
AND	AND
SHIP JOINER,	BUILDER,
127 DERBY STREET,	33 ENDICOTT STREET,
SALEM.	SALEM.
	☞ Orders promptly executed.

ADVERTISING DEPARTMENT.   55

BATTIS & BROWN,
Manufacturers and Importers of
CIGARS,
And dealers in all kinds of Leaf and Manufactured Tobacco,
WHOLESALE AND RETAIL.
NO. 110 DERBY STREET,
Sign of the Scottish Chief.

JAMES H. BATTIS.   WILLARD H. BROWN.

STEPHEN S. SKINNER,
Manufacturer and Dealer in

CIGARS, SNUFF, TOBACCO,
PIPES, ETC.,
NO. 104 DERBY STREET,
SALEM, MASS.

JOHN H. NICHOLS,

No. 42 Washington Street,

AGENT FOR

National, Fireman's, North American, & Eliot Insurance Companies

OF BOSTON;

SPRINGFIELD FIRE & MARINE, HAMPDEN & MASSASOIT INSURANCE COMPANIES IN SPRINGFIELD;

OLD COLONY INS. CO. IN PLYMOUTH;

Ætna Ins. Co. in Hartford;

CITY INSURANCE CO. IN NEW HAVEN,

AND

Home Ins. Co. in New York.

PRIME, KENNY & CO.,

Wholesale and Retail Dealers in

MAHOGANY & FANCY WOOD,

FURNITURE AND VENEERS.

SAWING EXECUTED TO ORDER.

CITY MILLS, 35 to 43 MILL STREET, SALEM.

DEALERS IN

MAHOGANY, FANCY WOOD, AND FURNITURE,

Mahogany Branch, Mottled and Plain Veneers; Rosewood, Zebra, Black Walnut, Satin, and Maple Veneers; Spanish and Southern Cedar and Mahogany; Cherry and Black Walnut Boards; Plank and Joist;

AT THEIR WAREROOMS,

No. 14 Charlestown Street, . . BOSTON.

CHARLES WATTS,

CAKE, PASTRY, AND BROWN BREAD

BAKER,

Wholesale and Retail.

No. 53 Derby Street.

Wedding Cake constantly on hand. Brown Bread for sale on Sunday Mornings. Luncheons furnished at any part of the day.

JOSEPH WALLIS,

DEALER IN

NEW AND SECOND HAND FURNITURE,

No. 205½ ESSEX STREET,

Second door East from the Market.

Coffins Ready Made, and Made to Order at Short Notice.

A large assortment of Sofas, Sofa Beds, Bedsteads, Bureaus, Secretaries; Cane Seat and Common Chairs; Mahogany, Rocking and Parlor Chairs, Flag Seat and Children's Toy Chairs; Settees and Settee Cradles; Wash Stands; Swing and Toilet Glasses; Hair, Moss, and Palm Leaf Matresses; Fancy Boxes, &c., constantly on hand and for sale at the lowest Cash Prices, wholesale and retail.

Also Palm Leaf and Excelsior for filling Under Beds, the best articles now in use. Old Furniture received in exchange for new.

S. SHEPPARD,

UPHOLSTERER,

(SUCCESSOR TO ASA LAMSON,)

No. 298 Essex St., Salem, Mass.

Mattresses, Pew and Chair Cushions, made to order, and all work in the Upholstery Business executed in the best manner.

58 SALEM DIRECTORY.

EZEKIEL GOSS,
FURNITURE, BEDDING,
AND
UPHOLSTERY ESTABLISHMENT.

Refrigerators of all kinds.

☞ Beds and Feathers renovated.

279 ESSEX ST., SALEM, MASS.

FASHIONABLE UPHOLSTERY ROOMS.

GEORGE S. MANSFIELD,

UPHOLSTERER,

And dealer in every description of

Upholstery Goods & Trimmings.

SHADES painted to order at short notice from my own patterns.
DRAPERY arranged according to the latest style.
Constantly on hand, or furnished to order, every description of Shade Fixture, that he feels justified in warranting to the public.
CARPET WORK at Boston prices, and warranted to give perfect satisfaction.
☞ Repairing of every description executed in the most workmanlike manner.

At No. 50 Washington St., Salem.

P. J. HYNES,
CABINET MANUFACTURER,
AND DEALER IN
New and Second-hand Furniture.

☞ Custom work made on reasonable terms. A large assortment of Second-hand Furniture always on hand, and will be sold cheap.
Furniture Repaired and Varnished without the trouble of moving it off. Second-hand Furniture bought.

At 25 Front Street, Salem.

REMOND & BABCOCK,

Manufacturers of all kinds of

HAIR WORK,

Dyeing and Champooing Ladies' Hair
IN THE BEST MANNER. ALSO,

CUTTING CHILDREN'S HAIR.

No. 188 Essex St. (under the Mansion House), Salem, Mass.

MISS M. J. REMOND.   MRS. C. BABCOCK.

CURRIER & MILLETT,
DEALERS IN

FURNITURE, CHAIRS,

Mattresses, Feathers, &c.,

259 & 261 ESSEX STREET,
SALEM, MASS.

BENJAMIN STRAW,
MANUFACTURER OF

WOOD MOULDINGS,
OF ALL PATTERNS,

For Carpenters, Ship Builders, Frame Makers, and all other uses.

Orders promptly attended to, and put on board cars for any part of the County.

No. 5 FRONT STREET, SALEM.

BOWKER BROTHERS,
DEALERS IN
FLOUR, GRAIN, AND MEAL,
COARSE AND FINE SALT,
Nos. 227 & 229 DERBY STREET,
(Formerly 8 and 10 Fish Street,)   SALEM.

J. C. WEBSTER,
WHOLESALE AND RETAIL DEALER IN
WEST INDIA GOODS AND GROCERIES,
PACKER OF
Ship Stores and Goods for Shipping,
NO. 4 NEWBURY STREET, AND 116 ESSEX,
(Franklin Place,)   SALEM, MASS.

AUGUSTUS T. BROOKS,
DEALER IN
FLOUR AND GRAIN,
COAL,
WEST INDIA GOODS, ETC.
No. 117 DERBY STREET,
Head of Central Wharf.

PARSONS & SHACKELFORD,
DEALERS IN
FRESH AND SALT FISH,
OF ALL KINDS,
NO. 64 UNION STREET.

Families supplied with FRESH FISH every day. Shipping supplied with WATER at short notice.

JOHN M. PARSONS.   WM. SHACKELFORD.

JOHN ROBERTS,
DEALER IN
BEEF, PORK, LARD, HAMS,
AND
POULTRY OF ALL KINDS,
Nos. 12, 13, and 14 City Market, . . . SALEM, MASS.

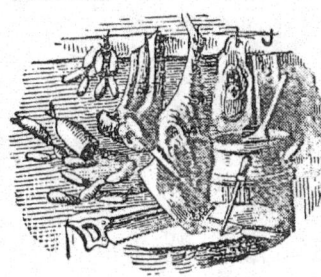

FOSTER KNIGHT,
PROVISIONS, VEGETABLES,
Fruits & Groceries,
48 NORTH ST., NORTH SALEM.

H. G. & N. EMERSON,
WEST INDIA GOODS
AND
GROCERIES,
No. 134 Boston Street,
SALEM.

R. P. WHEELER,
DEALER IN
FRUIT AND VEGETABLES,
STALLS 5 & 6 CITY MARKET,
SALEM, MASS.

PEMBERTON HALE,
DEALER IN
FAMILY GROCERIES,
NO. 27 SUMMER ST.,

A large assortment of Family Groceries of the best kinds kept constantly on hand, and delivered promptly and without extra charge in any part of the city.

STEELE, BLODGETT & CO.,

General Commission Salesmen,

AND WHOLESALE DEALERS IN

FLOUR, GRAIN, BUTTER, CHEESE, PORK, POULTRY,

And all kinds of

COUNTRY PRODUCE.

Store, No. 26 FRONT STREET,

SALEM, MASS.

E. STEELE.   P. D. BLODGETT.

WILLARD KNIGHT,
DEALER IN
FAMILY GROCERIES,
NO. 55 HARBOR STREET.

A large assortment of Family Groceries of the best kinds kept constantly on hand, and delivered promptly in any part of the city, without extra charge.

CHAMBERLAIN, HARRIS & CO.,
Dealers in
WEST INDIA GOODS,
CHOICE TEAS, ETC.,
Wholesale and Retail,
No. 24 FRONT STREET,
Corner of Derby Square.

L. B. HATCH,
Dealer in
COAL, WOOD, BARK,
HAY, ETC.,
NO. 113 DERBY STREET.
A general assortment constantly on hand, of the best quality, at the lowest market prices.

JOHN DIKE & CO.,
Dealers in
COAL, WOOD, BARK, HAY, &c.,
No. 183 DERBY STREET, SALEM.

JOHN DIKE.   RICHARD C. MANNING.

BROOKS & NOYES,
Dealers in
WEST INDIA GOODS,
SHIP STORES, TEAS, ETC.,
Wholesale and Retail,
No. 121 Essex Street.

SAMUEL CRAIG,

Dealer in

BEEF, PORK, LARD, HAMS,

And Vegetables of all kinds;

HOG'S HEAD CHEESE, SAUSAGES, AND PIGS' FEET,

OF MY OWN MANUFACTURE.

Phœnix Market, 3 Lafayette & 231 Derby Streets,   SALEM, MASS.

E. K. NOYES & CO.,

DEALERS IN

WEST INDIA GOODS

AND GROCERIES,

TEAS, FLOUR, GRAIN AND MEAL,

Eastern & Western Produce,

Nos. 6 & 8 Front Street, Salem.

E. K. NOYES.   E. F. BAKER.

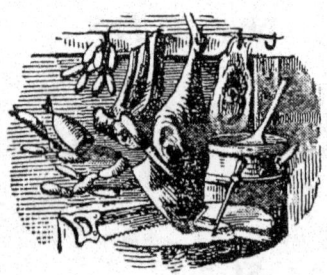

C. H. NEWCOMB,

Dealer in

BEEF, PORK, LARD, AND HAMS,

POULTRY OF ALL KINDS.

ALSO,

FRUITS & VEGETABLES.

FRANKLIN MARKET,

Cor. of Newbury & Forrester Sts.,

SALEM.

JEROME HARRIS, M. D.,

HOMŒOPATHIC PHYSICIAN,

Office and Residence, 22 Washington Street,

Office Hours from 7 to 9, A. M., 2 to 4 and 7 to 9, P. M.   **SALEM.**

W SNELL'S
PHOTOGRAPHIC GALLERY,

No. 208 Essex Street,

OPPOSITE THE MARKET,

SALEM, MASS.

The largest and longest established, containing three times the number and variety of specimens of any Rooms in the County.

The HALLOTYPES,—beautiful Colored Portraits, rivalling the best Oil or Ivory Painting, and is made at no other place in the County.

The MELAINOTYPE,— also a new Picture, and can be sent in a letter without extra postage.

PHOTOGRAPHS taken by a new Apparatus, more than twice the size of any in this city, and by a superior process.

P. S.—The only place in the city where an Artist is employed to work up and color Photographs. Photographs made from Daguerreotypes, in any size or style.

GEORGE H. WISE,
Wholesale and Retail Dealer in
CONFECTIONERY, WEDDING CAKE,
CAKE, PASTRY, ICE CREAM,
SODA SYRUPS, ETC.,

No. 271 ESSEX STREET, SALEM, MASS.

Parties, Pic-Nics, Families, &c., supplied at short notice. Wedding Cake of a superior quality, frosted and ornamented in the latest styles.

EDWARD WILSON,

DEALER IN

CLOTHING

And Furnishing Goods,

RUBBER CLOTHING, HATS, CAPS, &c.

No. 247 Essex Street, ... SALEM, MASS.

EDWARD C. WEBSTER'S
ONE PRICE

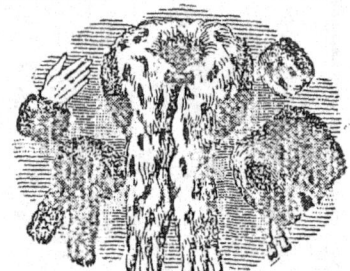

Hat, Cap, and Fur Store,

225 Essex and 34 Washington Streets,
SALEM, MASS.

JOHN J. ASHBY,

Manufacturer and Dealer in

BOOTS, SHOES, & RUBBERS

276 ESSEX STREET,
SALEM.

Ladies' and Misses' Boots and Shoes made to order. Repairing neatly done.

ADVERTISING DEPARTMENT. 67

M. C. REYNOLDS & CO.,
DEALERS IN
WEST INDIA GOODS, GROCERIES, TEAS,
FLOUR, GRAIN, & MEAL, CAMPHENE & FLUID,
No. 20 Front Street, cor. of Derby Square,

M. C. REYNOLDS,
D. B. GARDNER, JR.

SALEM, MASS.

B. L. GRISWOLD,
DEALER IN
NEW AND SECOND-HAND
SEWING MACHINES,
Of all approved kinds.
Agent for the sale of all First-Class Machines.

NEW AND SECOND-HAND MACHINES

BOUGHT, EXCHANGED, OR SOLD
ON COMMISSION.

REPAIRING
In all its branches attended to promptly.

No. 17 CENTRAL STREET, SALEM,
Two doors below the Omnibus and Stage Office.

BENJ. R. WHITE,
MASON AND BUILDER,
ST. PETER COURT,

Keeps constantly on hand, Lime, Cement, Brick, and Stone of the best qualities. Also, Hot-Air Furnaces of the various sizes, together with the necessary fixtures, furnished at Manufacturers' prices. Particular attention paid to setting Furnaces.

Residence, No. 62 Washington Street.

HORACE PRESTON WILBUR,
MANUFACTURER OF
Shirts, Bosoms, Collars, &c.

WHOLESALE AND RETAIL,
115 1-2 Washington Street, Boston.

Shirt Patterns cut in the most approved Styles, and warranted to fit.
SHIRTS MADE TO MEASURE.
Stitching of all kinds done at short notice, and satisfaction guaranteed.

H. M. SMITH & CO.,
MERCHANT TAILORS,

115 1-2 Washington Street, Boston.

The inhabitants of Salem are invited to call, when in the city, and examine our large stock of Cloths. All our garments are made by Journeymen Tailors, and warranted to give *perfect satisfaction in every particular*

H. M. SMITH.   EDWARD GAY.

SETH W. FULLER,
BELL HANGER,

25 DEVONSHIRE STREET,
BOSTON.

HOUSE BELLS,

Put up in the most approved manner. Also,

SPEAKING TUBES,

Put up to order.

Hotels and Private Houses fitted up with JACKSON'S PATENT ANUNCIATOR AND SPEAKING TUBES.
Orders from any part of the Union promptly attended to.

MAGUIRE & O'LEARY,
FASHIONABLE TAILORS,
No. 41 Charter Street,
(CORNER OF LIBERTY ST.)

SALEM,   MASS.

H. & H. G. HUBON,
COFFIN WAREHOUSE,

No. 48 WASHINGTON ST.,

SALEM.

METALLIC

And other

COFFINS,

Constantly on hand.

GRAVE CLOTHES FURNISHED AT SHORT NOTICE.

FURNITURE REPAIRED.

Residence, ... JEFFREY COURT, REAR OF WAREROOMS.

GARDNER WEBSTER,
TIN PLATE AND SHEET IRON WORKER,

AND DEALER IN

Stoves, Sheet Iron, Tin, Glass, and Wooden Ware,

No. 135 BOSTON ST., SALEM.

Particular attention paid to Tin Roofing, Furnace, Stove Work, Jobbing, &c.

JOHN TUTTLE,
HARNESS MAKER,
No. 191 Federal Street,

SALEM.

HORSES & CARRIAGES TO LET.

WM. B. GREENMAN,
Veterinary Physician
AND
SURGEON,
No. 10 BOSTON ST., SALEM.

Good Stabling furnished for horses.

JOHN P. SPILLER,
CARRIAGE MAKER
AND
WHEELWRIGHT,
WEST PLACE,

Rear of the Mansion House,

SALEM.

All kinds of Repairing promptly attended to

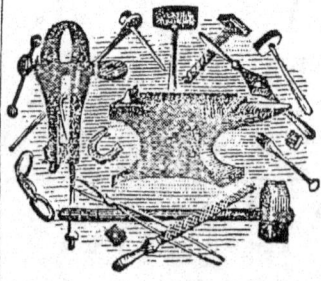

A. A. RAYMOND,
BLACKSMITH
AND
GENERAL JOBBER,
35 North Street,

NORTH SALEM.

Every description of work done to order at short notice.

BENJ. B. FULLER & CO.,
DEALERS IN
LUMBER, LIME, WOOD,
COAL, BARK, &c.,
NO. 13 FRONT ST., SALEM.

B. B. FULLER.   N. FULLER.

JOHN GROVER,
DEALER IN
WOOD, COAL & BARK,
BROOKHOUSE & HUNT'S WHARF,
(REAR 53 DERBY STREET,)
SALEM.

WIGGIN & CLARK,
DEALERS IN
COAL, WOOD, BARK, LUMBER, LIME, BRICKS,
AND PRESSED HAY,
By the Cargo and Retail,
NO. 29 PEABODY STREET, SOUTH SALEM.

NATHANIEL WIGGIN.   CHARLES S. CLARK.

N. PUTNAM,
DEALER IN
WOOD, LUMBER, ETC.,
157 DERBY STREET,
SALEM, MASS.

☞ Grateful for past favors, he most respectfully solicits a continuance of the same.

SALEM DIRECTORY.

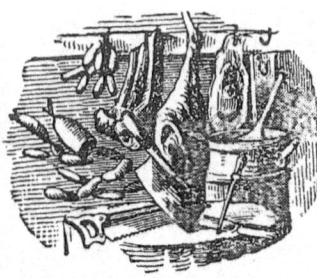

CENTRAL MARKET,
No. 116 Derby Street.

JOHN G. PLANDER,
DEALER IN
PROVISIONS,
HAMS & SAUSAGES,

Keeps constantly on hand a large assortment of Meats, Vegetables, Eggs, and Fruits.

Goods sent to any part of the city.

WM. P. GOODHUE,
Wholesale and Retail Dealer in

SHIP CHANDLERY,
SHIP AND FAMILY STORES,
Lime, Cement, and Plaster,
NO. 44 DERBY STREET,
SALEM, MASS.

Freight obtained for Vessels, and produce received on Commission.

DODGE & JONES,
COMMISSION MERCHANTS,
DEALERS IN
FLOUR, GRAIN, & PLASTER,
PIERCE'S WHARF,
SALEM, MASS.

J. A. DODGE.   J. S. JONES.

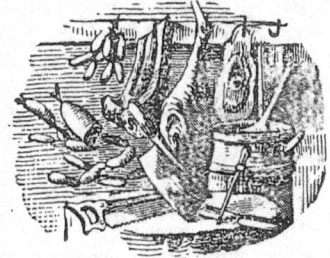

FREDERIC PORTER,

DEALER IN

PROVISIONS & PRODUCE,

At the St. Peter Street Market,

No. 17 St. Peter St.,

SALEM, ... MASS.

HASKELL'S
EATING ROOM,

Corner of Derby Sq. and Front Street,

SALEM, MASS.

☞ Meals served at all hours of the day and evening.

J. H. MORELAND,
BOOK & JOB PRINTER,
235 ESSEX STREET,

Corner of Washington St.   SALEM.

JOB PRINTING of every kind done to order, from new type, at as low prices as at any other office. Printing in COLORED INKS and BRONZE.

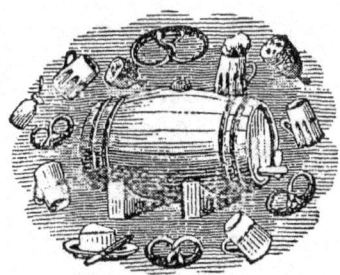

G. W. CROSBY,

Root Beer Brewer,

AND DEALER IN

BOTTLED PORTER, ALE, CIDER, ETC.,

Cellar under No. 10 Derby Sq.

SALEM, MASS.

☞ Goods delivered in the city free of expense.

EDWARD H. SANGER,

BAKER AND CATERER,

No. 416 ESSEX STREET,

Is prepared to furnish DINNERS and GAME SUPPERS for private and public parties, balls, &c., at short notice, at Nonantum Hall, No. 47 WARREN STREET.

Also, TENTS furnished (with Dinners) for Pic-nics and Excursions, capable of seating 1200 persons, which he will send to any part of the State.

Mr. S. has a large variety of

Crockery, Knives, Forks, Spoons, Tables, Table Cloths, &c.,

Which he will loan in large or small quantities.

CHARLES PHELPS,

BELL HANGER,

NO. 84 FEDERAL STREET,

SALEM, MASS.

SPEAKING TUBES
FURNISHED AND PUT UP.

Signal Bells, Table (Foot) Bells and Common House Bells, Bell Pulls, Cranks,

And all materials used in the business.

MOUTH PIECES

Of various kinds furnished to order.

ALL WORK DONE IN A NEAT AND DURABLE MANNER.

J. PERLEY, JR., & CO.,
BOOKBINDERS
AND
BLANK BOOK MANUFACTURERS,
NO. 191 ESSEX STREET,
Directly opposite the Mansion House.

J. PERLEY, JR.   Magazines neatly bound.   J. CARTER.

WILLIAM LEAVITT,
TEACHER OF NAVIGATION,
IN ALL ITS BRANCHES.
NO. 71 FORRESTER STREET,
SALEM.

C. C. WHITTIER,
STONE CUTTER.
DEALER IN
Rockport Edge Stones, Underpinnings, Monuments, Cemetery Posts, Cellar Stones, &c. Rockport and Quincy Granite.

Buffum's Wharf, near South Bridge,
SALEM, MASS.
☞ All orders executed with promptness and fidelity.

NATHAN T. CLARK,
DEALER IN
ROCKPORT AND QUINCY GRANITE,
Posts, Caps, and Sills; Door Steps, Underpinning of all kinds. Gate Posts, Bases Monuments, plain and ornamental, &c., &c. Also, Cellar Stone, of all kinds.

No. 25 PEABODY ST., - - - - SALEM.

SALEM OBSERVER
Printing Establishment,

No. 226½ Essex Street, Stearns Building,

Opposite the Eastern Railroad Depot.

This Office being furnished with all the desirable modern improved **FAST PRESSES**, adapted to every description of work, from a Poster down to the genteel Visiting Card, together with an ample supply of well chosen varieties of handsome **PLAIN AND FANCY JOB TYPE AND BORDERS**, the Proprietors believe that their facilities for executing every description of

Are such as to enable them to answer all orders to the entire satisfaction of those who may favor them with their patronage. They are prepared to execute promptly, and at as

LOW PRICES AS ANY OFFICE IN THE CITY,

Posters, Shop Bills, Programmes, Catalogues, Bill Heads, Blanks, Books, and Pamphlets; Business, Visiting, Ticket, and Check Cards; Plain or Fancy Labels, &c.

WILLIAM IVES.   GEORGE W. PEASE.

THE SALEM OBSERVER

Is published at the above office every Saturday morning. It is the design of the Publishers to give a condensed summary of the latest foreign and domestic intelligence, and such local matters of importance as will be found interesting to the public. Its large and increasing circulation both in this city and county renders it a most desirable medium for Advertising.

Terms, $2 per annum in advance.

H. P. IVES & A. A. SMITH,

(SUCCESSORS TO W. & S. B. IVES,)

Stearns's Building, opposite Railroad Station,

232 ESSEX & 36 WASHINGTON STS.,

BOOKSELLERS, STATIONERS,

AND DEALERS IN

PAPER HANGINGS,

WHOLESALE AND RETAIL.

WRITING PAPERS OF EVERY DESCRIPTION.

BLANK ACCOUNT BOOKS

RULED AND BOUND IN THE BEST MANNER.

BOOKBINDING,

In all its variety, done with neatness and dispatch.

THE SALEM REGISTER

Was established in the year 1800, and is published on Mondays and Thursdays

At No. 185 Essex, cor. of Central Street,

BY

JOHN CHAPMAN and CHARLES W. PALFRAY,

Terms, $4 per year, $3.50 if paid in advance.

TERMS OF ADVERTISING.

Advertisements of more than half a square, $1.50 for three insertions, once a week, or in three papers in succession, at the option of the advertiser. 16¾ cents for every additional insertion.

Advertisements not exceeding half a square, $1 for three insertions as above. 12½ cents for every additional insertion.

For notices of meetings, cards of acknowledgements, &c., for one insertion 6¼ cents. The privilege of annual advertisers is limited to their own immediate business. For Advertisements ordered to be published in the inside, 10 per cent extra will be charged for each insertion.

JOB PRINTING,

OF EVERY DESCRIPTION,

Neatly and expeditiously done at this office.

BOOK, JOB, AND FANCY PRINTING

EXECUTED AT THE OFFICE OF THE

SALEM GAZETTE

AND

ESSEX COUNTY MERCURY,

In the best style and on favorable terms.

THE SALEM GAZETTE,

Established Weekly, 1768; Semi-Weekly, 1796,

Is printed on TUESDAY and FRIDAY mornings, at $3.50 per year when paid in advance,—$4 when not in advance. The length of time which it has been before the public, and the extensive circulation it has obtained for the larger part of a century, render it unnecessary here to enter into a formal exposition of its character. The intention is that it shall always contain the most important foreign and domestic intelligence, political, moral, and literary; original communications upon all subjects connected with the public welfare; a full and correct shipping list; business advertisements; and, in short, everything that is usually found and expected in a Family Newspaper.

The large country circulation of the Gazette (including the Mercury, in which all new advertisements of the Gazette are published) renders it particulary valuable as a medium for the publication of Probate advertisements, sales of Real Estate, and other notices of interest to the farming population.

THE ESSEX COUNTY MERCURY,
OR WEEKLY SALEM GAZETTE,
ESTABLISHED A. D. 1832,

Is made up from the reading matter of the Salem Gazette, and is one of the largest and cheapest papers in New England. The subscription price is $1.50 per year, when paid in advance. The quantity of reading afforded is much greater than is usually found in a Newspaper; and as it circulates extensively in all parts of the County of Essex, particular pains are taken to present all the local matters of the county. The Mercury is published every Wednesday morning; the price, when not paid in advance, is $2 per year, payable semi-annually.

No. 191 ESSEX STREET,
Opposite the "Mansion House Hotel."

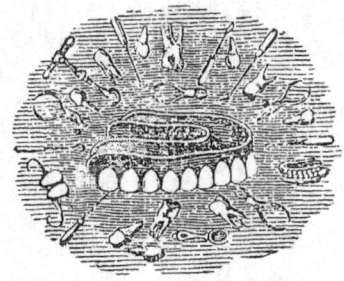

W. L. BOWDOIN,
Surgeon Dentist,
Rooms, 208 Essex Street,
Residence, 57 Washington Street,
SALEM.

WM. W. HURD,
SURGEON DENTIST,
NO. 251 ESSEX STREET,
SALEM, MASS.

SALEM ADVOCATE.

BOOK, CARD, AND ORNAMENTAL

Job Printing Establishment,

Over Nos. 215 & 217 Essex Street,

ENTRANCE FROM MARKET COURT.

By paying attention to his business, the Proprietor hopes to merit and obtain a share of public patronage.

PRICES REASONABLE,
And all work delivered promptly.

GAS & STEAM PIPES & GAS FIXTURES.

E. H. STATEN,
Gas, Steam, and Water Fitter,

151 ESSEX STREET, LYNDE BLOCK,

SALEM, MASS.

DEALER IN

GAS FIXTURES,

Of every description, for lighting Stores, Dwellings, Churches, Public Buildings, &c. Old Gas Fixtures and Lamps reburnished to look as well as new. Galvanized Wrought Iron Pipes for water. Rubber Hose Man-head Gasketts; Sheet and Ring Packings for steam-work, constantly on hand.

Agent for GEO. B. FOSTER'S CARCEL GAS BURNER (Wood's Patent), the best and most economical gas burner in existence.

SOLE AGENT FOR
W. F. SHAW'S PATENT GAS STOVES,

For heating rooms of every description and size; parlors, bath-rooms, sleeping-rooms, extension-rooms, where there are no chimneys, &c., &c. Halls, bed-rooms, bath-rooms, and all small rooms heated by the gas drawn from the common bracket, at a less expense than by the ordinary methods. The only true principle whereby all unpleasant and injurious odors are avoided. Warranted by far superior to any other invention for cooking or heating by gas ever offered to the public. Patented by the inventor, Wm. F. Shaw, in America, England, and France.

E. H. Staten, 151 Essex St., Lynde Block, Salem, Mass.

HARRISON O. FLINT,

DEALER IN

BOOTS, SHOES, RUBBERS,

AND

RUBBER GOODS,

No. 210 Essex Street, Salem.

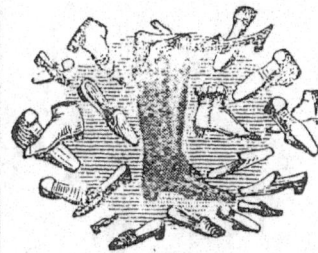

J. GEORGE HUBBARD,

Manufacturer and Wholesale and Retail Dealer in
LADIES' AND GENTLEMEN'S

BOOTS & SHOES,

Of all kinds, Custom Made.

No. 246 ESSEX STREET, SALEM, MASS.

☞ Measures taken, and all work warranted. ☜

THOMAS BOTT,

DEALER IN

BOOTS, SHOES,

AND RUBBERS,

NO. 46 DERBY ST.,

SALEM.

ABRAHAM BENNETT,

DEALER IN

CLOTHING, FURNISHING GOODS,

TRUNKS, BOOTS, SHOES,

HATS, CAPS, &c.

No. 33 Lafayette Street, . . . South Salem.

W. H. BURBECK,

MERCHANT TAILOR,

AND DEALER IN

CLOTHS, CASSIMERES, VESTINGS,

AND GENT.'S FURNISHING GOODS,

NO. 249 ESSEX STREET, SALEM.

Mr. Ephraim Lord may be found at this establishment.

SOUTH DANVERS DIRECTORY.

Since the introduction of the business of Danvers into the Salem Directory, eight years ago, the southerly part of the town has been separated and incorporated as South Danvers, which includes the tanning and currying, which was the principal part of the business of the former town, and still continues to employ a large amount of capital and labor.

The town being so closely connected with Salem, it was thought that the continuation of the business in the work, this year, might be of mutual benefit to both places; the publishers therefore, in order to make it as useful as possible, have been at considerable expense in making the addition, and hope it will prove satisfactory to all interested.

SOUTH DANVERS TOWN OFFICERS, 1858.

Selectmen and Assessors.—William Wolcott, Daniel Taylor, Nathan H. Poor.
Treasurer.—Francis Baker.
Collector.—William Wolcott.
Town Clerk.—N. H. Poor.
Overseers of the Poor.—Wingate Merrill, James P. King, William Sutton.
Constables.—Moses A. Shackley, Adino Page, William Wolcott, Bowman Viles, John G. Walcott, Stephen F. Reed, Samuel B. Farnsworth, Amasa P. Blake, Sampson W. Bowers, Horace Tibbetts, William S. Osborne, James B. Newhall.
Fence Viewers.—Asa Bushby, Augustus H. Sanger, Daniel Taylor.

Field Drivers.—Edmund Hayward, William I. Hayward, Bowman Viles, N. P. C. Patterson, George C. Buxton, Jacob S. Berry, Joseph F. Peabody, Isaac B. Cowdrey.

Surveyors of Highways.—Ward 1, Ebenezer Goldthwait; Ward 2, Philip L. Osborn; Ward 3, James Boynton; Ward 4, James B. Newhall; Ward 5, Caleb W. Marsh; Ward 6, John G. Walcott; Ward 7, Benjamin Needham; Ward 8, Hiram B. Allen; Ward 9, David W. Putnam.

Surveyors of Lumber.—Daniel Taylor, Mayhew S. Clark.

Pound Keepers.—Joseph F. Peabody, Benjamin Taylor, Geo. C. Buxton.

Board of Health.—N. P. C. Patterson, Isaac Munroe, Benj. Huntington.

School Committee.—Charles H. Wheeler, Fitch Poole, for 3 years; James O. Murray, Sydney C. Bancroft, for 2 years; Orville Brayton, Daniel W. King, for 1 year.

Engineers of Fire Department.—Jona. E. Osborne, Stephen Osborne, Horace Tibbetts, D. S. Littlefield, Benjamin Huntington.

Weigher of Hay and Coal.—Franklin Walker.

Measurers of Wood and Bark.—David Marstin, Samuel Welsh, Daniel Taylor.

Sealer of Weights and Measures.—Thomas Trask.

Liquor Agent.—Samuel Newman.

DANVERS BANK.—Main Street.

Capital, $150,000. Par value Shares, $100.

Directors.—Ebenezer Sutton, *President.* Robert S. Daniels, David Daniels, Joseph Osgood, Jonathan King, W. M. Jacobs, E. T. Osborne. G. A. Osborn, *Cashier.*

Discount days, Tuesdays and Fridays. Bank hours, from 9, A. M., to 12, M., and from 2 to 3, P. M.

WARREN BANK.—No. 11 Main Street.

Capital, $220,000. Par value of Shares, $100.

Directors.—Lewis Allen, *President.* Sylvester Osborn, Gilbert Tapley, Benj. Wheeler, Levi Preston, Franklin Osborne, George Osborne, Francis Dane, Elijah W. Upton, Miles Osborne. Francis Baker, *Cashier.*

Discount days, Mondays and Thursdays. Bank hours, 9 to 12, A. M., 2 to 3, P. M.

WARREN FIVE CENTS SAVINGS BANK.

Warren Bank Rooms.

Incorporated, April 27, 1854.

Deposits received from 5 cents to $1000.

George Osborne, *President.* Francis Baker, *Treasurer.*

DANVERS MUTUAL FIRE INSURANCE CO.

Office at Danvers Bank. Annual Meeting 1st Monday in Oct.

Directors.—Henry Cook, *President.* R. S. Daniels, Benjamin Wheeler, George Osborne, Joseph Osgood, Henry Poor, John Whitney, John Safford, N. P. C. Patterson. G. A. Osborne, *Secretary.*

CHURCHES.

UNITARIAN.

Rev. Charles H. Wheeler, *Pastor.*

FIRST CONGREGATIONAL.

Rev. James O. Murray, *Pastor.* George A. Osborne, *Clerk.*

BAPTIST.

Rev. Thomas E. Keely, *Pastor.* H. C. Marshall, *Clerk.*

METHODIST.

Rev. H. C. Dunham, *Pastor.*

UNIVERSALIST.

Rev. Orville Brayton, *Pastor.* Amos Merrill, *Clerk.*

POST OFFICE.

Albert R. Fiske, *Post Master.* Charles Dodge, *Clerk.*

PEABODY INSTITUTE.

The foundation of this Institution is due to the munificence of GEORGE PEABODY, Esq., now of London, but a native of this town.

Its origin dates from June 16, 1852, at which time Mr. Peabody proffered his first gift of $20,000. By several successive bestowments he has since increased its endowment equivalent to the aggregate sum of $80,000. The building, which was dedicated to its appropriate uses Sept. 29, 1854, — Hon. Rufus Choate delivering the address, — cost with the site about $20,000. The annual increase from all sources is about $2,500, which is applied to the increase and care of the Library, and sustaining an annual course of lectures.

The government of the Institute consists of a Board of Trustees, chosen by the inhabitants of the town, two each year, for a term of six years, thus giving a character of permanance to this body. The Trustees have the care and responsibiltity of the management of the funds and the general oversight of the Institution.

There is also a "Library and Lyceum" Committee. whose members are annually appointed by the Trustees. To this Committee is entrusted the entire management of the Institution in its two great departments of Library and Lectures.

There is a "Branch Library" connected with the Institute, which is located in Danvers, and containing over 2500 volumes. The principal Library contains over 6300. There have been four courses of Lectures delivered, and a fifth is now in progress.

The following are the present officers of the Institute : —

Trustees, 1858-9.—Henry Poor, *President*. Francis Dane, Isaac Hardy, Henry A. King, Joel Putnam, Ebenezer p Johnton, Israel M. Andrews, Alfred A. Abbott, Eben S. Poor, U -S. B. Peabody, Franklin Osborn, Philemon Putnam. John B. Peabody, *Clerk*. Franklin Osborn, *Treasurer*.

Library and Lyceum Committee.—Robert S. Daniels, *Chairman*. George A. Osborne, Benj. C. Perkins, Francis Baker, Eugene B. Hinkley, Fitch Poole, George F. Osborne, Thomas B. Stimson, Amos Merrill, Joshua Silvester, Samuel Preston, Wm. L. Weston, James D. Black, Moses Black, Jr., Eben Flint. Thos. B. Stimson, *Secretary*. George A. Osborne, *Treasurer*. Fitch Poole, *Librarian*. Nathaniel Hills, *Librarian of Branch Library*.

BUSINESS DIRECTORY OF SOUTH DANVERS.

Apothecaries.
Meacom George E. 126 Main
Sweetser Thomas A. 37 Main, near Park

Auctioneers.
Shove Squire, Sewall
Trask Thomas, 50 Main

Bakers.
Hathaway John, rear 23 Main
Pratt Leonard, 162 Main
Stimpson & Floyd, rear 50 Lowell

Blacksmiths.
Annable Nathaniel, 164 Main
Dodge W. A. & C. H. 48 Central
Dole William T. rear 11 Wash.
Jones A. W., Wallace, opp. Walnut (*edge tools*)
Jones Thomas J. 32 Elm (*edge tools and tanners' shovels*)
Smith William, Spring

Bleachery.
South Danvers Bleaching Co. rear Foster

Booksellers.
Brooks D B. & Brother, S Danvers square

Boots and Shoes.
Dealers.
Bott S. R. 13 Main
Cressey & Hale, 52 Main
Goldthwait E. P. & Co. 94 Main
Newman & Symonds, Lowell, opp. Cong. Church

Makers.
Hammond Augustus, rear 16 Main
Meacom Ebenezer, 96 Main
Walker Franklin, 38 Central

Manufacturers.
Cressey & Hale, 52 Main
Dane Francis & Co., S. Danvers sq.
Daniels David & Co. 1 Wash. cor. Main
Fuller Edward, rear 76 Main
Hardy & Osborn, Lowell, opposite Chestnut
Hill Benj. B. rear 76 Main
Morrison Joseph, Lowell
Phillips A. P. & Co 6 Main
White & Fiske, Lowell, c. Chestnut

Stiffenings.
Cottle Daniel P., Mill, near Main (*heels*)
Hunt Sylvester, Foster

Stock.
Goldthwait E. P. & Co , Grove, n. Main

Butchers.
Butman Josiah, Lowell
Cook E. G., Mason (*wholesale*)
Cook James, Washington
Elliot Isaac B., Main
Emerson Robert, Lowell (*wholesale*)
Perry Wm. F., Stevens
Prescott George, Mason
Sawyer Asa, Lowell
Tilton C. D. rear Lowell
Tilton George, Lowell
Ward A., Elm
Ward A. A., Central
Wheeler Benj S., Mason
Wilkins James, Lowell (*wholesale*)

Cabinet Maker.
Eustis Ebenezer, Grove, near R. R.

Carpenters.
Beckett Benjamin, near R R depot
Clark & Giddings, Wallace, n. Essex depot

Folsom Charles, Central
Hills Benj. M. rear R. R. depot
Parsons Samuel S., Grove, n. Main
Preston Abel, Main
Safford Joseph, Wallace, n. Hardy
Spalding Levi, Sewall

Carriage Builders.
Brine Charles W., Central, n. R. R.
Poland Oliver, 11 Washington

Clergymen.
Brayton Orville, Main
Dunham H. C., West
Keely Thomas E., Franklin
Murray James O., Main
Wheeler Charles H., Chestnut

Clothing & Furnishing Goods
Bott S. R. 13 Main
Cressey & Hale, 52 Main
Daniels George P. 83 Main
Newman & Symonds, Lowell, opp. Cong. Church

Coal and Wood.
Black M. jr., Lowell, opp. Cong. Ch.

Coffin Warerooms.
Eustis Ebenezer, Grove, near R. R

Confectioners.
Roberts E. F. & J. W., South Danvers Square
Wise William, 21 Main

Counsellors.
Abbott Alfred A., 130 Main
Perkins Benj. C. 10 Allen's building
Proctor John W. 9 Washington
Wiley H. O. 10 Allen's building

Crockery, Glass, & China Ware.
Merrill Amos, S. Danvers Square

Curriers.
[See Tanners and Curriers]

Dentists.
Crawford Aaron S. 4 Main

Dress Makers.
Hyde M. J. Mrs. 36 Main
Marshall P. 23 Main

Dry Goods.
Daniels George P. 83 Main
Merrill Amos, South Danvers Sq.
Spiller R. O. 134 Main

Expresses.
Abbot Samuel C. 81 Main
Townsend D. H. 45 Main

Fancy Goods.
Lord Mary, 33 Main

Flour and Grain.
Newman & Symonds, Lowell, opp. Cong. Church

Fruit and Vegetables.
Flint Eben S. 2 Main

Furniture.
Trask Thomas, 50 Main

Glue Manufacturers.
Brown Thos. H. r. Old Boston Road
Essex Glue Co. (Upton & Walker) rear Foster
Sanger A. H., Lowell

Grocers.
Baldwin Wm. H. Old Boston Road, above Lynnfield Road
Flint E. S. 2 Main
Goldthwait J. E. 90 Washington
Howard Ebenr. S 81 Main, c. Wash
Mutual Union Store, B. Poland, agent, 76 Main
Newman & Symonds, Lowell, opp. Cong. Church
O'Connell John. 98 Main
Osborn H. M. 121 Central
Putnam Joseph W., O. B. Road, c. Lynnfield Road
Southwick Edward, Lowell
Spiller R. O 138 Main
Welch & Fairfield, Lowell
Woodbury & Lane, 48 Main

Hair Dressers.
Davis Samuel, 7 Main
Heylingberg J. J. 26 Main

Hardware.
Merrill Amos, South Danvers Sq.

Harness Makers.
Cheever Samuel, 71 Central

Hats, Caps, and Furs.
Bott S. R. 13 Main
Cressey & Hale, 52 Main

Last Manufacturers.
Brown & Stanley, Spring

Lightning Conductors.
Copper.
Trask Thomas, 50 Main

Lumber.
Clark A. F. r. Main, n. Grove

Masons.
Bancroft Alpheus, Wash.
Manning John, Lowell
Trask Samuel, Lowell
Goodridge Zachariah, Mason
Gray Andrew W., Mason

Milliners.
Buxton Abby, 95 Main
Hyde M. J. Mrs. 36 Main
Symonds Paulina, 46 Main

Millwrights.
Bomer Caleb P. 7 Summer
Whitney John, 13 Chestnut
Perkins James, Wash.

Morocco Manufacturers.
Clark & Co. 148 Main (*bindings*)
Draper William, Wash. (*tanner*)
Gardner Chas. A., Wallace, near Hardy [*linings*
Jacobs W. M. & Son, 148 Main
Merrill G. H., Wallace, n. Tremont
Pemberton F. K. 40 Central
Pender Josiah A., Hardy, n. Wallace
Pender S. D., Walnut
Poole Joshua H., Pierpont
Putnam Jeremiah, Foster
Roberts & Moore, Walnut
Roberts Samuel, Walnut
Woodbury Daniel, Walnut

News Room.
Exchange News Room, 11 Main

Painters.
Blaney Philip, 118 Main
Jewett Moses, High, near Fulton
Osborne Jona. W. 88 Main
Price Edward, Foster
Searl George, Main, corner Grove
Whidden Henry L., Central, opp. Cong. Church

Paper Hangings.
Brooks D. B. & Brother, So. Danvers Square
Merrill Amos, So. Danvers Square

Patent & Enamelled Leather.
Bascom E. F., Foster

Physicians.
Lord Samuel A. 89 Main
Osborne George, 19 Main
Osgood Joseph, Main, cor. Park
Perkins D. C., So. Danvers Square

Potteries.
Osborn Richard, 92 Central
Reed J. W. 124 Central

Produce.
Blake & Holman, 90 Main
Flint E. S. 2 Main
Perkins P. D., Lowell (*butter & eggs*)
Southwick Edward, Lowell
Spiller R. O. 138 Main

Provisions.
Patterson N. P. C. 109 Main
Teel & Fairfield, 5 Main

Public Houses.
Naumkeag House, P. R. Bradford, Washington
Simonds Hotel, Wash'ton Simonds, S. Danvers Square

Pump Maker.
Peabody Stephen, Central, near School House

Soap & Candle Manufacturer.
Burbeck John C., Grove, n. Main
Hildreth Paul, 142 Main

Stables.

Goldthwait Wm. 71 Wash. (*sale*)
Ham Samuel, 75 Main
Simonds Charles, S. Danvers Sq.
Teel Geo. M. 42 Central

Steam Sawing & Planing.

Clark A. F. r. Main, near Grove
Taylor Jefferson, Wallace, c. Walnut

Stone Cutters.

Brown Saml. jr., O. B. Road, near Lynnfield Road
Galencia Danl. S., O. B. Road, near Lynnfield Road
Larrabee Hersey, O. B. Road, near Lynnfield Road
Newhall Henry H., O.B Road, near Lynnfield Road
Putnam David, O.B. Road, n. Lynnfield Road
Shaw Wm., O.B. Road, n. Lynnfield Road

Stoves & Tin Ware.

Haven & Whitten, Lowell

Tailors & Drapers.

Farrell John, 136 Main
Thompson G. B. 8 Main

Tanners and Curriers.

Brooks & Messer, Wallace, n. Walnut (*curriers*)
Currier Caleb, Walnut, n. English
Elliot L. W., Foster
Emerson Oliver, Hardy, n. Wallace (*currier*)
Fernald Luther, Foster (*currier*)
Fernald Stephen, Spring (*currier*)
Giddings Joshua, Spring
Hardy Isaac, Hardy, near Wallace
Harris Nathaniel, Wallace, corner Walnut
Harris Samuel, rear Main
Hodgkins Joseph S., Chestnut
Houghton E. H., Walnut (*currier*)
Jacobs Joseph & Son, Foster
Kimball Obadiah, Mason
Little William H., Foster
Lord J. A., Hardy, near Wallace
Lord William N. 40 Foster
Mahoney & Relihan, Wallace, cor. Walnut (*curriers*)
Monroe Isaac, Lowell
Nelson & Merrill, Foster
Osborn C. W., Lowell
Osborn D. W., Walnut, near Grove
Osborn Franklin, Foster
Osborn Miles & Co., Lowell
O'Shea Timothy, r. Main, n. Grove
Pierce William, Foster
Pindar & Brown, Grove, n. Main
Plummer Hiram, Lowell (*currier*)
Poole Lemuel, Grove, near R. R.
Poor Henry & Son, 36 Central
Poor Joseph, Hardy
Porter Andrew, Hardy (*currier*)
Rust Elbridge, Wallace, c. Walnut
Searles Joseph, rear Main
Southwick James M. rear 76 Main
Southwick S. A., Grove, near R. R
Stevens John V., Central, n. Hardy
Stevens John W., Central, near Hardy (*currier*)
Symonds R. S., Spring (*currier*)
Tibbetts Horace, rear 90 Wash.
Torr Andrew, Foster
Torr J. S. & H. L., Foster
Turrell & Cook, Foster (*curriers*)
Upton & Nichols, Foster
Wheeler & Adams, Foster (*curriers*)
Wilson Warren, Foster
Woodbury Dana, Wallace, n. Walnut (*currier*)

Variety Store.

Very S., Central, near R. R.

Watchmaker and Jeweler.

Stevens Benj. F. 16 Main

Wheelwright.

Berry William, 46 Central

Wool Dealers.

Blaney Stephen, Foster
Goodridge Benj. rear Foster
Sutton William jr. 141 Main
Tufts Joseph W., Foster

T. A. SWEETSER,
DRUGGIST AND APOTHECARY,
No. 37 Main, near Park Street, South Danvers,

Has on hand a complete and well-selected stock of Family Medicines. Also, Drugs, Chemicals, Foreign Leeches, Shakers' Herbs, Gums, Acids, Dye Stuffs, Sponges, and Genuine Patent Medicines. Perfumery, Toilet Articles, and Stationery. Physicians' Prescriptions accurately prepared by experienced persons at all hours of the day or night.

T. A. S. is proprietor of the COMPOUND ICELAND MOSS CANDY, so effectual a remedy for Coughs and Colds.

37 Main, near Park Street.

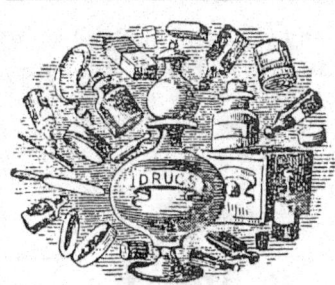

GEO. E. MEACOM,
DEALER IN
DRUGS & MEDICINES,
Fancy and Toilet Articles, &c.

126 MAIN STREET,
Nearly opposite Danvers Bank.

HENRY L. WHIDDEN,
PAINTER, GLAZIER,
AND
PAPERER,
CENTRAL ST., S. DANVERS,
Opposite South Church.

All orders promptly and faithfully executed.

E. S. HOWARD,
DEALER IN
West India Goods and Groceries,
81 MAIN, COR. WASHINGTON STREET,
SOUTH DANVERS.

Flour and Grain of all kinds must be CASH on delivery after January 1, 1856.

☞ Goods delivered to any part of the town free of expense.

GEORGE P. DANIELS,

DEALER IN

DRY GOODS, BROADCLOTHS,

CASSIMERES, DOESKINS, DRESS GOODS, ETC.

CARPETINGS AND READY-MADE CLOTHING.

ALSO,

Housekeeping Goods of every description; Hosiery, Gloves, Embroideries, Trimming Goods, Buttons, Fancy Goods, &c., &c.

83 MAIN ST., MONUMENT SQUARE,

SOUTH DANVERS.

SIMONDS HOTEL,

WASHINGTON SIMONDS, PROPRIETOR,

SOUTH DANVERS SQUARE.

Private and Select Parties accommodated on reasonable terms.

HOTEL, LIVERY, & SALE STABLE,

CHAS. SIMONDS,

PROPRIETOR,

S. DANVERS SQUARE,

PARTIES AND FUNERALS FURNISHED AT SHORT NOTICE.

NEWMAN & SYMONDS,

DEALERS IN

Flour, Grain, and Family Groceries,

AND

READY-MADE CLOTHING,

BOOTS, SHOES, ETC.

LOWELL STREET, SOUTH DANVERS, MASS.

CRESSEY & HALE,

DEALERS IN

CLOTHING & FURNISHING GOODS,

AND

BOOTS, SHOES, & RUBBERS,

AT THE LOWEST CASH PRICES.

TRASK'S BLOCK, 52 MAIN ST.,

NEXT TO PEABODY INSTITUTE,

SOUTH DANVERS, MASS.

BROWN & STANLEY,

LAST MANUFACTURERS

SPRING STREET, SOUTH DANVERS, MASS.

Orders solicited and promptly executed for all kinds of Men's, Women's, and Children's Lasts.

CLARK & GIDDINGS,
CARPENTERS & BUILDERS,
WALLACE STREET,
Near the Essex Railroad Depot,
SOUTH DANVERS.

AUGUSTUS HAMMOND,
Boot & Shoe Maker,
REAR OF POST OFFICE,

S. DANVERS SQUARE.

Custom work made to measure, and repairing done at short notice.

J. W. OSBORNE,
PLAIN & ORNAMENTAL
House & Sign Painter,
88 MAIN STREET,
SOUTH DANVERS.

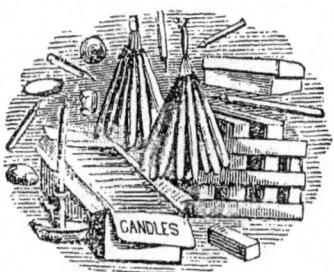

PAUL HILDRETH,
MANUFACTURER OF
SOAP & CANDLES,
142 MAIN STREET,
SOUTH DANVERS.

☞ Cash paid for Tallow. ☜

DRAIN, SOIL, AND WATER PIPE.

PRICE'S VITRIFIED
CLAY & STONE DRAIN & WATER PIPE,

The cheapest and best article now in use for Drains, Sinks, and for conveying Soil from Water Closets.

Also, Pipes from various other Manufacturers.

Can be had in any quantity of

J. F. BANISTER,

358 Federal St., cor. Mt. Washington Avenue, Boston.

ADVERTISING DEPARTMENT.

LYON'S PATENT
COPPER LIGHTNING CONDUCTOR.

The subscriber, Proprietor and Manufacturer of the above

LIGHTNING ROD,

For all the cities and towns in

ESSEX COUNTY,

Is prepared to put up said Rods in any place in the county. Orders addressed to the subscriber will be promptly attended to, and Rods set in the most recent improved scientific principles. Copper possesses greater advantages than any other metal that can be formed or used practically for a lightning rod. It possesses seven and one-half times the conducting power of Iron, in the opinion of all practical electricians.

A table showing the different conducting powers of several metals:

Silver.....100	Cadmium..24.5	Iron.....12.3
Copper....91.5	Zinc......24.0	Lead......8.2
Gold......64.9	Tin.......14.0	Platinum..7.9

The above rods will be put up at the following rates:

The 1¼ inch riveted rod for 15 cents per foot, cash.
The 1¼ inch continuous rod, without laps, one shilling per foot, cash.
The 1½ inch continuous, without laps, 22 cents per foot, cash.

THOMAS TRASK,
PROPRIETOR,
No. 50 MAIN STREET, SO. DANVERS.

☞ IRON RODS put up as follows: the Quimby Rod for 8 cents per foot; Spratt's, DeWolf, and the North American Rods (so called), for 10 cents per foot.   T. T.

SALEM DIRECTORY.

SMITH & CHAMBERLAIN,
MANUFACTURERS OF
RICH JEWELRY,
AND DEALERS IN
WATCHES, SILVER WARE, & FANCY GOODS.
No. 201 ESSEX STREET, SALEM,
FIVE DOORS EAST OF THE MARKET.

GEORGE B. APPLETON,
IMPORTER OF
GOLD & SILVER WATCHES,
AND DEALER IN
JEWELRY, SILVER SPOONS,
Plated & Silver Ware, and Spectacles,
AT LOW PRICES.
NO. 179 ESSEX STREET,
Nearly opposite } Essex House, }   SALEM.

~~~~~~

SILVER WARE—A large assortment, at as low prices as can be obtained in Boston or elsewhere—engraved gratis.
Watches and Clocks skilfully repaired and adjusted.
Jewelry and Spectacles manufactured and neatly repaired.

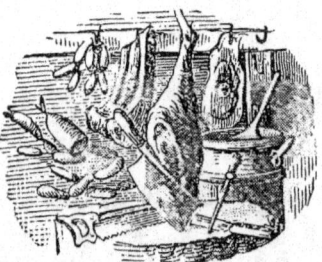

ASA HAYFORD,
DEALER IN
Beef, Pork, Mutton, Lamb,
HAM, POULTRY, ETC.,
91 ESSEX STREET,
SALEM.
☞ PATRONAGE SOLICITED. ☜

JAMES F. ALMY,

DEALER IN

SILKS, SHAWLS,

CLOAKS, & DRESS GOODS;

ALSO,

HOUSEKEEPING GOODS

Of every description,

156 ESSEX STREET (Bowker Block).

JAMES A. FARLESS,

IMPORTER OF

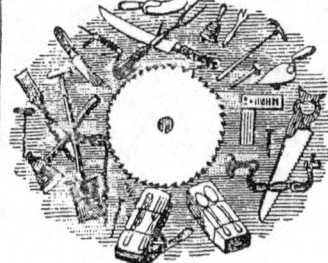

HARDWARE

AND

CUTLERY,

AND DEALER IN

Sporting Apparatus,

NAILS, LEAD, PAINTS, OIL, GLASS, ETC.

NO. 186 ESSEX STREET,

SALEM, MASS.

SOLD BY
ADAMS, RICHARDSON & CO.,

**FAIRBANKS'
SCALES,**
34 Kilby St., Boston.
GREENLEAF & BROWN,
AGENTS.

SALEM.

The wide-spread reputation of this Machine is eminently due to its peculiar merits, which are acknowledged by the best judges to surpass all others in the requisites for family use. It has become a domestic institution, and is justly looked upon as a household economy. In all the finer qualities of family sewing, on silk, linen, cotton, and broadcloth; in hemming, stitching, quilting, gathering, and all the innumerable ends to which female needlework is applied, the

WHEELER & WILSON
SEWING MACHINE

confessedly occupies a position of pre-eminence. Those who have not hitherto availed themselves of the advantages of this machine are invited to examine its operation, and obtain specimens of its work, at the salesroom,

228 Washington, cor. of Summer Street,

BOSTON.

J. E. ROOT, AGENT.

J. TREFREN, Agent,

FOR THE SALE OF

FAMILY AND MANUFACTURING

SEWING MACHINES,

Machine Silk,

Linen Thread,

Cotton Thread,

And Needles,

15 1-2 ST. PETER STREET,

UP STAIRS,

SALEM, MASS.

GEORGE B. APPLETON,
PRACTICAL AND SCIENTIFIC
WATCHMAKER,
No. 179 ESSEX STREET,

Nearly opposite Essex House.

SALEM.

CHRONOMETER BALANCES

Adjusted to heat and cold, also Chronometer Balances inserted in place of common Balances.

CLOCKS AND TIMEPIECES REPAIRED.

☞ This is the only Watchmaker's Store in Salem protected at night by a Watchman in the Store.

Mr. Appleton would state, that he has passed many years in the largest Watch Importing House in Boston, under the most competent instructors, *gentlemen of wide repute*, during which time the finer Escapements, Chronometer, Duplex, Triplex, Lever, and Lepine, received his *undivided* and *faithful* attention.

In addition to this experience he has had the charge of a *large amount* of Watch-work in a neighboring city, and was there appointed to the care of all the City, County, and Manufacturing Companies' Clocks.

All Time-keepers will be regulated by an

ASTRONOMICAL CLOCK

With Mercurial Pendulum, *adjusted to heat and cold*. The movement manufactured by the late EDMUND CURRIER, and used many years by him to regulate *Fine Watches*,—set up in a SUPERB MARBLE CASE. This Regulator shows *the exact mean time*, TO SECONDS.

FOR SALE!
FINE WATCHES

Of my own Importation.

GEO. B. APPLETON,

Nearly opposite Essex House,   179 Essex Street.

* Notice *

The following surname index covers:

Pages 196-256 for the first part of this book
&
Pages 1-101 for the second part.

Please note the South Danvers Directory is included in the second part of this book on pages 83-90.

INDEX

ABBE, 28 254
ABBOT, 88 205
ABBOTT, 86 88 199 201 205-206 241 243 246 248
ADAMS, 36 90 98 196 202 206 234 254-256
AGGE, 196
AGGEE, 47 253
AIKEN, 246
AKERMAN, 248
ALLEN, 84 198 208-209 217 231 234 236 249
ALLEY, 235
ALMON, 199 213 218
ALMY, 97 201 213 241 254
AMES, 198 205
ANDERSON, 202 230 233
ANDOVER, 235
ANDREWS, 13 51 86 196 198-199 210 213 219 228 230 241 247-249 253-255
ANNABLE, 87
APPLETON, 96 101 197 199 210 226 249 255-256
ARCHER, 35 196-198 201 203 205 217 225 237-238 249 253-254 256
ARNOLD, 203
ARRINGTON, 213 216
ASHBY, 66 196-197 212 214 253
ASHTON, 199
AUSTIN, 200 203 214 230
AVERELL, 196 213

AVERY, 212-213
BABBIDGE, 231
BABCOCK, 28 59 201-202 254
BADGER, 205
BAGNALL, 251
BAKER, 83-86 197 200 204 225 235
BALCH, 236
BALDWIN, 28 88
BALL, 196 201 234 249
BANCROFT, 84 89 196 199-200 249
BANISTER, 94 255
BARBER, 7
BARKER, 198 210
BARLOW, 197
BARNARD, 233
BARNES, 197 215
BARRETT, 14 254
BARRON, 205 215
BARSTOW, 199 227 249
BARTLETT, 198 202 214 248
BARTON, 196 203 232
BASCOM, 89
BASSETT, 206
BATCHELDER, 200-201 205 210 214 228 240
BATTIS, 46 55 198-199 253
BAXTON, 204
BEADLE, 197
BEAMAN, 198 218
BECKET, 197 237
BECKETT, 87
BECKFORD, 201-202 205

INDEX

BELL, 235
BENNETT, 82 199 202 220 253 256
BENSON, 231
BERG, 205
BERICK, 198 220
BERMINGHAM, 209
BERRY, 84 207 213 217 220 235
BERTRAM, 204 224 231-232 234 249
BIGELOW, 246
BISHOP, 246
BLACK, 86 88
BLAKE, 19 83 89 198 253-256
BLANCHARD, 217
BLANEY, 89-90
BLODGETT, 62 254 256
BOARDMAN, 202
BOMER, 89
BOND, 208
BOSSON, 197
BOTT, 81 87-89 197 200 208 253
BOUSLEY, 198
BOUTWELL, 217
BOWDITCH, 197 200 204 207 217 230 241
BOWDOIN, 79 200 228 254
BOWERS, 83
BOWKER, 60 201 207 229 254 256
BOWLAND, 209 216
BOWMAN, 197
BOYNTON, 43 84 207 235 248 256
BRADEN, 200
BRADFORD, 209 216
BRAY, 201 206 217
BRAYTON, 84-85 88

BREED, 200
BREWSTER, 200 208 211
BRICKETT, 235
BRIGGS, 198 213 217 228 246 249
BRIGHAM, 238
BRIGHT, 205
BRINE, 88
BROOK, 206
BROOKHOUSE, 204 230 232-233 235-236 243 249
BROOKING, 49 196 198 203 253-254
BROOKS, 60 63 87 89-90 196-202 205-206 209 212-214 228-229 236 238 242 253-256
BROWN, 42-43 53-55 88-90 93 196 198 202-206 208-210 212-216 218-220 223 225-226 228 231 234 236-239 241-242 248-249 253 255-256
BROWNE, 7 196 213 225 236 248-250
BRUCE, 205
BRYANT, 197 205
BUFFINGTON, 233
BUFFUM, 202-204 208
BURBANK, 205-206 208
BURBECK, 82 89 199 208 253 255
BURKINSHAW, 205
BURNHAM, 205 226 249
BURR, 231
BURRILL, 205
BURTON, 236
BUSH, 200
BUSHBY, 83
BUSWELL, 197 229

INDEX

BUTLER, 197
BUTMAN, 87 241
BUTTRICK, 223 249
BUXTON, 84 89 200 208 213
BYRNE, 196 209
CABEEN, 199
CABOT, 222 224 229 238 249
CALEF, 202 220
CALLER, 211
CALLEY, 205 212 214 225-226 249
CAMPION, 204
CARAWAY, 209
CAREY, 205
CARLETON, 200 208 219
CARLTON, 198 212 219 229 231 249
CARPENTER, 199
CARRUTH, 22 253
CARTER, 199 201
CARTY, 54 197 253
CARY, 248
CASSELL, 202
CATE, 205 213 218
CHADWICK, 223 249
CHAMBERLAIN, 40 63 96 196 199 201-203 207-208 218 224 226-227 254-256
CHAMBERLIN, 200 219
CHANCE, 202
CHANDLER, 197 202 205 213
CHAPMAN, 77 197 207 218 225 231 234 239 248 255
CHAPPLE, 213
CHARNCE, 206
CHASE, 8 202 209 213 217 224 230 233 236 238 250 254-255
CHEEVER, 89 205 231 240
CHESTER, 240

CHEVER, 199 213 249
CHILSON, 256
CHIPMAN, 43 200 209 256
CHISHOLM, 38 199 203 212-215 254 256
CHOAT, 243
CHOATE, 201 206 213 217 226-227 232 235-236 246-247 249
CHURCH, 196 215
CHURCHILL, 28 208
CHUTE, 207
CLAPP, 7 24 198 209 217 254
CLARK, 71 75 84 87 89-90 94 199 202-203 205 209 215 218 235 253-256
CLARKE, 203 225-226
CLEAVELAND, 218
CLEAVES, 225
CLEMENT, 205
CLEVELAND, 237 249
CLIFFORD, 240
CLOUGH, 200
CLOUTMAN, 208 212 236 247 249
COFFIN, 198 207
COGSWELL, 215
COLBURN, 205
COLBY, 209 213
COLE, 213
COLEMAN, 235
COLLINS, 17 197 205 207 212-213 253 255
COLMAN, 196 200 202 214
CONANT, 7
CONREY, 200 211
CONVERSE, 197
CONWAY, 200 208 225
COOK, 14 41 85 87 90 198 203 205 213 219 236-237 249

COOK, (Cont.) 254
COOKE, 228 235
COOMBS, 202
COOPER, 11 255
COOT, 201
COPELAND, 198 204
CORNELIUS, 208
COTTLE, 87
COTTS, 255
COWDREY, 84
COX, 196 205-206 224 236 249
CRAFTS, 203
CRAIG, 64 207 256
CRANDELL, 207
CRAWFORD, 88
CREAMER, 197 206 208 211
CREASY, 213 229
CRESSEY, 87-88 93 253
CRESSLEY, 89
CROCKER, 201 234 237
CROSBY, 6 23 73 197 205 217 235 253 255-256
CROSS, 199 213 215 227-228 235
CROWNISHIELD, 232
CULITON, 208
CULLITON, 200
CUNNINGHAM, 202
CURRAN, 211 237
CURRIER, 59 90 201 247 254-255
CURRIN, 221
CURTIS, 15
CURWEN, 204 223-224 226 249
CUSHING, 204 216
CUTLER, 201
CUTTER, 239
CUTTIS, 49
CUTTS, 196 203 253

DABNEY, 231-232
DAILEY, 209
DAKIN, 200
DALAND, 198 208
DALRYMPLE, 212-213 216 221
DALTON, 200 208 213 216 243 249
DALYRUMPLE, 199
DANA, 28
DANE, 84 86-87
DANFORTH, 54 198 207 253
DANIELS, 84-88 92 207 212 254
DANVERS, 205 225 234
DAVENPORT, 19-20 253-256
DAVIDSON, 44 206 253 255
DAVIS, 88 201 205 209 231 244 248
DAY, 198 211-213 225 236
DAYTON, 51 202 254
DEARBORN, 20 213 253-255
DEASE, 208
DENNIS, 46 198 248 253
DENNY, 28
DERBY, 196 205 221
DEVEREUX, 199 224 230-231 248-249
DEWEY, 246
DEWING, 200
DEXTER, 15 22 254 256
DIEHL, Patricia S 13
DIKE, 63 199 203 210 229 253-254
DIMOND, 200
DIX, 201 213 216 234 238
DIXEY, 248
DOCKHAM, 200 205
DODGE, 72 85 87 197-199 201-202 204-206 209-210

INDEX

DODGE, (Cont.) 214 217 221 232 234-235 241 248 254-255
DOLAN, 202
DOLAND, 241
DOLE, 87
DONALDSON, 207 229
DOWNING, 217 224
DOWST, 241
DRAPER, 4 89 204 254 256
DREW, 209
DRIVER, 197 211 229
DROWN, 203
DUDLEY, 6 255
DUKES, 200
DUMMER, 201
DUNCAN, 235
DUNCKLEE, 204
DUNHAM, 85 88
DUNLAP, 232
DUNN, 214
DUNTON, 23
DWINELL, 198 213 218 228
DWYER, 223-224 233 249
DYKE, 242
EASTON, 235
EATON, 196 209
EDGERLY, 213
EDWARDS, 53 198 206 208 255
ELLIOT, 87 90 243
ELLIOTT, 207
ELWELL, 198
EMERSON, 61 87 90 196 198 202 218 231 254
EMERTON, 196
EMERY, 205
EMMERTON, 217 239
ENDICOTT, 28 199 204 212 224-225 237 247 249
ENGLISH, 200
ESSEX, 88
ESTES, 199 205 209 239
ESTY, 205
EUSTIS, 87-88 216
EVANS, 200 225
EVERETT, 27 255
FABENS, 204 219 231 236 238
FAIRFIELD, 89 198
FANNING, 200
FARLESS, 97 196 199 202-203 206 242 254 256
FARLEY, 199
FARMER, 29 204 256
FARNHAM, 203
FARNSWORTH, 83
FARNUM, 200 214 219 240
FARRAR, 28
FARRELL, 90 197
FARRINGTON, 42 196 253-254
FAY, 235 238
FELLOWS, 197 201 218 225 241-242
FELT, 205-207 210 214 224 233 237 249
FELTON, 216
FENOLLOSA, 209
FERGUSON, 197 205
FERNALD, 90 247
FETTYPLACE, 231
FIELD, 204-205
FIELDS, 241
FIFIELD, 201 209 256
FILENE, 203
FISHER, 237
FISK, 200
FISKE, 85 87 232
FITZ, 204 206 211 214 243
FITZGERALD, 200

FLINT, 42 81 86 88-89 197 204 207 211 242 253 255-256
FLOTO, 206
FLOWERS, 212 235-236
FLOYD, 87 216
FOLEY, 205
FOLGER, 15
FOLSOM, 88
FOOTE, 207 238-239 248 255
FORBES, 28 243
FORBUSH, 207 240
FORTEN, 215
FOSTER, 80 196 202 204 206 213 223-226 229 237 243 249
FOWLER, 196 204 209
FOYE, 216
FRANCIS, 198 205 216 241
FRENCH, H P 251
FROTHINGHAM, 201 209 225 231
FRYE, 196 200 204 208 217 222 233
FULLER, 7 68 71 87 198-199 203 209-210 221 253 255
FULLERTON, 196 200
FULLINGTON, 248
GAGE, 205
GAHERY, 29 254
GALENCIA, 90
GANNET, 256
GANNETT, 3 253-254
GARDNER, 28 44 89 196 198 200 202 204 208 219 223 236 253
GARNDER, 212
GAVETT, 201 218 231
GEARY, 209
GENDROT, 29 254
GENTLEE, 235
GERSDORFF, 206
GETCHELL, 199 218 237
GIBNEY, 208
GIDDINGS, 87 90 94 240 253
GIFFORD, 197-198
GILBERT, 255
GILLESPIE, 197
GILLIS, 199-200 225 249
GILMORE, 241
GLAZIER, 196
GLONEY, 200
GLOVER, 197 209 212 220
GOLDTHWAIT, 84 87-88 90 198 201 235 243
GOMES, 197 202
GOODELL, 196 204 247
GOODESS, 203
GOODHUE, 72 196 200-202 204 207 218 223 225 253-256
GOODRIDGE, 89-90
GOODWIN, 197 202
GORDON, 213
GOSS, 45 58 196 201 205 207 209 218 253-256
GOULD, 221
GOVE, 206 217
GOWEN, 210
GRANT, 42 197 202 254
GRAY, 89 202 215 218 235 246 249
GREENE, 225 240
GREENLEAF, 256
GREENMAN, 70 209 256
GREENOUGH, 201
GRIFFEN, 199 207
GRIFFIN, 233 237-238
GRISWOLD, 67 207 256
GROVER, 71 199 205 253
GROVES, 249

INDEX

GUILFORD, 213 219 240
GUNNER, 198 220
GWINN, 202-204
HADLEY, 208
HAGERTY, 203
HALE, 37 62 87 89 93 196 202-203 218 240 253-255
HALEY, 198
HALL, 8 235 240-241 255
HALLETT, 10 253 255-256
HAM, 90
HAMMOND, 87 94 199 201 205 253
HAMOND, 54 198 219
HANMAN, 206
HANNAM, 208
HANSON, 196 202 204 208-209 226 229 236
HARADEN, 244
HARDING, 201 203
HARDY, 28 86-87 90 202 207 220
HARMON, 247
HARRINGTON, 200 208 211 222 224 226 234 239 249
HARRIS, 63 65 90 198 202 204 206 212-213 231 242 254-256
HART, 197 214
HARTNEY, 219
HASKELL, 52 73 198 200 202-203 207 209 219 247 249 254-256
HASKINS, 204 243
HASLAM, 209
HATCH, 63 199 203 210 225 253-254
HATHAWAY, 87 196 242
HATHORNE, 205
HAUSE, 209
HAVEN, 90
HAWES, 198
HAWKES, 201 209 216
HAY, 197
HAYFORD, 96 207 256
HAYWARD, 84 204 215 236 249
HAZLETON, 208
HEATH, 242
HEENEY, 199 210
HENDERSON, 197-198 201 205 209 234
HENFIELD, 199 241
HERRICK, 199 220
HEYLINGBERG, 88
HILDRETH, 28 89 94 256
HILL, 87 198 201 205 214 249
HILLS, 86 88
HILTON, 226
HINKLEY, 86
HOBART, 216 231
HODGES, 200 232 249
HODGKINS, 90
HOFFMAN, 204
HOLBROOK, 205
HOLLINGSWORTH, 28
HOLMAN, 89 236
HOLMES, 28 247
HOLT, 209
HOMAN, 205
HOMANS, 15
HONEYCOMB, 198 209 213 215
HOOD, 198 248-249
HOOPER, 250
HOPPIN, 199 219 227 229 231
HORTON, 200 207 219 255
HOUGHTON, 90
HOVEY, 5 24 48 202 206 232 253-254 256

HOWARD, 88 91 238 254
HOWE, 248 250
HOWES, 238
HUBBARD, 15 81 197 253
HUBON, 69 199 225 253
HUDSON, 3
HULL, 200 208
HUMPHREYS, 28
HUNT, 28 87 204 213 225-227 236
HUNTINGTON, 84 199 213 225 227 231-232 246 248
HURD, 79 200 204 254
HUSE, 200 211-212 223
HUTCHINS, 198
HUTCHINSON, 207 223
HYDE, 28 88-89
HYNES, 58 201 254
IDE, 198 201
INGALLS, 200
INGERSOLL, 199 248
ISACKSON, 205
IVES, 76-77 197 199 201 206-207 211 213 218 220 225 229 235-236 239 248 253 255-256
JACKSON, 243
JACOBS, 84 89-90
JANES, 197
JELLY, 196 215 231 237
JENKINS, 235
JENKS, 204 231
JEROME, 209
JEWETT, 9 89 211 218-219 223 225-226 249 253
JOCELYN, 209 216 239
JOHNSON, 199 206 209 228 233 243
JOHNTON, 86
JONES, 72 87 197-199 201 204

JONES, (Cont.) 206 208 213 220 254-255
JORDAN, 197
KEELEY, 235
KEELY, 85 88
KEENE, 223
KEHEW, 47 199 204 210 253
KELLEY, 204 208
KELMAN, 49 208 253 256
KEMP, 207
KENDALL, 208 212 240
KENNEY, 200 208 213 220 243
KENNY, 56 255-256
KIMBALL, 90 198-199 201 203 205-206 212 216 224-226 228 230-231 234 248-249
KING, 83-84 86 210 231 233
KINGMAN, 217
KINGSLEY, 221
KINSMAN, 200 218 230 233
KNAPP, 197
KNIGHT, 61-62 197 202 205 207-210 213 241 254 256
KNOWLES, 237
LACKEY, 198
LADD, 247 250
LAKEMAN, 231
LAMBERT, 220 249
LAMONT, 206
LAMSON, 210-212
LANDER, 202 207-208 239 256
LANE, 207 211 213
LANG, 206
LANGLEY, 4 255
LANGMAID, 240
LARRABEE, 90 197 202 213 236 241

LASKEY, 201 208
LAW, 197
LAWRENCE, 28
LEAVITT, 34 75 197-198 208-209 216 236-237 239-240 249 256
LEE, 197 205 220 223-224 227-229 250
LEECH, 197
LEEDS, 199 213 218
LEFAVOUR, 202 207-208 217
LEWIS, 213 220
LINCOLN, 28
LINDSEY, 202 225
LINEHAN, 210
LITTLE, 90 231 235
LITTLEFIELD, 84 197 205 213
LLOYD, 206
LOCKE, 14 18 198 254 256
LONGEE, 198
LOOBY, 200 208
LORD, 88-90 199 204 208 213-216 218 221 233 236 242 248
LORING, 46 198 233 235 249 253
LOUGEE, 52 254-255
LOVEJOY, 198
LOVERING, 198
LOVETT, 221
LOW, 231
LOWD, 205-206
LOWE, 30 199
LOWELL, 234
LUNT, 250
LUSCOMB, 203 206 210 213 216 235-236 240
LYNCH, 201 209
LYON, 95
MACINTIR, 207

MACK, 206 227 230 233
MACKINTIRE, 203 225 249
MACKLE, 209
MAGUIRE, 69
MAHONEY, 90 200
MALOON, 208
MANN, 202 209 216 242
MANNING, 89 205 208 219 221 225 229 242
MANSFIELD, 42 47 58 201 203-207 209 212-214 220 224 233 235 238 254-256
MARDEN, 198
MARKS, 243
MARSH, 21 84 253 256
MARSHALL, 85 88 209 243
MARSTIN, 84
MARTIN, 197 200-201 205 219 234
MASON, 11
MASURY, 16 249 254-255
MATTHEWS, 205
MAY, 201
MAYER, 41 201 203 254
MAYNARD, 235
MAYNES, 203 249
MCCALLEY, 200 208
MCCORD, 199
MCCURDY, 200
MCGEARY, 249
MCINTIRE, 198 208-209
MCINTYRE, 201 208
MCKENZIE, 208
MCKEY, 199
MCMULLAN, 204
MCNEAL, 205
MEACOM, 87 91 254
MECHANICS, 202
MEEK, 215 221
MEEKE, 214

INDEX

MELCHER, 198
MELLEN, 246
MELONEY, 200 208
MELZEARD, 241
MERRIAM, 235
MERRICK, 246
MERRILL, 83 85-86 88-90 211-213 244
MERRITT, 204 241 244 248
MESSER, 90
MESSERVEY, 232
MESSERVY, 205 223 225 227 230 249
METCALF, 201 218 246
METHUEN, 235
MILLER, 199 207 247-248
MILLET, 207 238
MILLETT, 59 196 201-202 217 233 254-255
MILLS, 199 218 231
MITCHELL, 209 226
MONROE, 90
MOODY, 197
MOORE, 204 211 225 241
MORELAND, 73 197 207 212 256
MORGAN, 204 216
MORRILL, 204
MORRIS, 205 246
MORRISON, 87
MORSE, 198 208 213-214 241
MORTON, 248
MOULTON, 196 198 200 204 209 240 244
MUCHMORE, 244
MUHLIG, 208
MULLET, 221
MUNROE, 84
MURPHY, 200 208
MURRAY, 84-85 88

NASH, 246
NEAL, 204 209 218
NEEDHAM, 84 196 199 201
NELSON, 90
NEWCOMB, 64 204-205 207 249 254 256
NEWELL, 207
NEWHALL, 83-84 90 200 210 212-213 222 225 228-229 233 237 249
NEWMAN, 84 87-88 93 254
NEWPORT, 205
NEWTON, 24 213
NICHOLS, 23 43 56 90 196-197 199-200 202-203 205 208 210 214 219-220 223-226 230 232 237-238 242 249 253 255-256
NICHOLSON, 52 197 253
NICKERSON, 201 209
NOAH, 200 210 214
NORFOLD, 202
NORRIS, 208 212-213 242
NORTHEAD, 199
NORTHEND, 248
NORTHEY, 226
NOURSE, 201 203 231
NOWELL, 205
NOYES, 63-64 202 254 256
O'CONNELL, 88 197
O'LEARY, 69 255
O'SHEA, 90
OAKES, 207
OBER, 198 207
OBY, 221
ODELL, 210 212-213 249
ODLIN, 205
OLIVER, 235 242
ORNE, 221
OSBORN, 84 86-88 90 201 202

INDEX

OSBORN, (Cont.) 213 214 235
OSBORNE, 83-85 89 94 203 216 226 255
OSGOOD, 84-85 89 199 203-204 206 208 231-232 235 247-249
OTTIGNON, 209
PAGE, 16 83 217-218 224-226 233 249 255
PAINE, 201 203-204
PALFRAY, 77 207
PALFREY, 239
PALFRY, 255
PALMER, 54 197 199 201 203 244 249 253
PARKER, 3 196 217 223-224 226 233 238-239 249 253-254 256
PARKS, 202
PARSONS, 88 201 210 254 256
PATCH, 208 210 249
PATTEN, 206
PATTERSON, 84-85 89 240
PAYSON, 23 223 225 232 234 249
PEABODY, 40 84 86 89 199 203 205 211-212 215 219 221 224 228-229 231-232 235 241 249 254
PEARCE, 12-13 256
PEASE, 76 196 209 225
PECK, 199
PEELE, 200 202 223-224 226 229 237 249
PEIRCE, 35 197 216 253
PEIRSON, 45 196 206 225 230-232 242 253 255
PEMBERTON, 89
PENDER, 89

PEPPER, 199 205 218
PERKINS, 35 53 86 88-89 196-200 203 206 208 212-213 219-221 223 225-226 232 234 237-241 244 246 248-249 253 255-256
PERLEY, 75 197 213 236 239 249 253
PERRY, 87 196-197 199 202 205-207 211-212 214 225 235 241 247 249
PETERSON, 205 213
PETTENGILL, 235
PETTINGILL, 7 213
PHELPS, 74 203 207 253
PHILLIPS, 15 87 199-201 204 209 219 221 225 228 240 246-249
PHIPPEN, 202-204 218 223-224 229 231
PHIPPS, 200
PICKERING, 207 209 243
PICKMAN, 204 218 223-224 232-233 238 240
PIERCE, 90 207
PIERSON, 203 234 239
PIKE, 220
PILLSBURY, 201
PINDAR, 90
PINEL, 233
PINGREE, 200 202 204 223 225 237 239 247 249
PINKHAM, 196 232 242
PINNOCK, 45 208 256
PIPER, 253 255
PITMAN, 200 205 215 220
PITTS, 209 213 241
PLANDER, 72 207 256
PLUM, 209
PLUMMER, 90 197 209 230

PLUMMER, (Cont.) 252
POLAND, 88
POND, 201
PONSLAND, 206
POOLE, 84 86 89-90 203
POOR, 83 85-86 90 224
POORE, 235
POPE, 205 208 212 241
PORTER, 73 90 207 208 221 256
POTTER, 198 212 219 234 238 244 248-249
POWER, 50 204 255
POWERS, 206
PRATT, 28 87 196 226
PRAY, 53 203 207 256
PRESBY, 201
PRESCOTT, 87 200 226 247-250
PRESTON, 84 86 88 196 209 211-212 235
PRICE, 41 48 89 196 201 203-204 208 219 226 229 254-256
PRIME, 56 202 204 208 210 255-256
PRINCE, 213
PROCTOR, 88 231 235
PULSIFER, 43 201 205-206 255
PUNCHARD, 197 236
PURBECK, 208 212 218
PUSLIFER, 198 207
PUTNAM, 71 84 86 88-90 196-198 200 202-205 208 210-213 219 224-226 231 233 235-236 238 241 249 253 255
QUIMBY, 206 209 242
QUINN, 208

RANDALL, 221 249
RANTOUL, 200 247 249
RAYMOND, 70 196 253
REA, 239
READ, 3 18 201 207 209 253 256
REDMOND, 200 202
REED, 83 89 197 205 213 220
REEVES, 202
RELIHAN, 90
REMON, 242
REMOND, 59 201 210 254
REYNOLDS, 15 67 202 204 254
RHODES, 206
RICH, 201
RICHARDS, 236
RICHARDSON, 22 36 98 196-197 202 205 213 226 232 237 254-256
RICKER, 204
RIDEOUT, 215 229
RIDER, 210 240
RILEY, 197 200
ROBBINS, 229
ROBERTS, 61 88-89 199-201 204 207 215-217 220 236 247-248 256
ROBERTSON, 208 211
ROBESON, 220
ROBINSON, 28 232 234 249
ROCK, 205
ROGERS, 199 201 205 220 232-233 248
ROLES, 201
ROLFE, 235
ROLLINS, 197
ROOT, 99
ROPES, 46 200-204 209 211-213 219 224-226 231-232

INDEX

ROPES, (Cont.) 249 256
ROSE, 201 231
ROSS, 12-13 202 256
ROUNDY, 199
ROWE, 202
ROWELL, 199 203 248
RUEE, 241
RUGGLES, 28
RUPP, 200 208
RUSE, 234
RUSSELL, 44 199 205 207 216 224 228 242
RUST, 90 196 213 217 231
RYAN, 199 221
SADDLER, 201
SAFFORD, 85 88 200 216 225 233 246
SALTONSTALL, 238
SANBORN, 199-200 208 210 213-214 241
SANDERSON, 198 203
SANGER, 74 83 88 196 198 236 246 253
SARGENT, 240
SAUL, 213 233
SAUNDERS, 201 205 209 223 225 235 241
SAVORY, 201 243
SAWSEY, 221
SAWYER, 9 87 207 215
SAXBY, 204 255
SCOTCHBURN, 201
SCRIBNER, 23
SEARL, 89
SEARLES, 90
SECCOMB, 39 205 255
SHACKELFORD, 60 210 254 256
SHACKLEY, 83 244
SHAHAN, 199 219-220

SHATSWELL, 197 204
SHAW, 80 90 206 214-215 246
SHELDON, 217
SHEPARD, 199-201 204 209 213 215 220 223 229
SHEPPARD, 57 255-256
SHILABER, 201
SHILLABER, 209
SHORES, 235
SHOVE, 87
SHREVE, 218 220 229
SHUTE, 25 254
SIBLEY, 51 197 199 207-208 253
SILSBEE, 204 211 213 217 223-224 226 229 234 238 242 248
SILVER, 228
SILVESTER, 86 226
SIMMONS, 32 253 255
SIMON, 199
SIMONDS, 39 89-90 92 200 202-203 206 212 219 254-256
SKERRY, 201-202 205 210 219 231
SKINNER, 55 198 243 253
SLEEPER, 212 219
SLOCUM, 204
SMALL, 39 202 254
SMALLEY, 208 213
SMITH, 21 26 31 52 68 77 87 96 198 201 203-205 208 210-213 216-217 219 225-226 231 233 239-240 248-249 253-256
SMOTHERS, 208
SNELL, 65 196 200 253 255
SNELLING, 205
SNOW, 7 200 207 216 254

SOUTH, 198
SOUTHARD, 215
SOUTHWARD, 198 206
SOUTHWICK, 88-90 197 205
SPALDING, 223 244
SPAULDING, 88 233
SPILLER, 70 88-89 210 248 253
STACY, 216
STANDLEY, 240
STANIFORD, 213 219
STANLEY, 89 93 197 208 255
STANTON, 205
STANWOOD, 204
STATEN, 80 202 225 242 254 256
STEARN, 23
STEARNS, 28 77
STEELE, 62 201 207 254 256
STEPHENSON, 209
STETSON, 10 51 197 253-255
STEVENS, 15 46 90 202 206 209 214 216 242 255
STEWART, 202
STICKNEY, 209 213
STILES, 198
STILL, 197
STIMPSON, 7 87 198 200 208 223 225 247 249
STIMSON, 2 86 256
STOCKER, 51 210 231 253
STODDARD, 248
STONE, 196 201 204 206 212 218 227-228 232 238
STORY, 199-200 219 226 233 247-249
STOW, 196
STRAW, 59 210 256
STREET, 223
STREETER, 213 228 249

SUMNER, 209
SUTTON, 83-84 90 214 223-224 235 237 239 241
SWAN, 7
SWASEY, 219 240
SWEET, 220
SWEETSER, 87 91 197 201 209 225 253
SYMONDS, 87-90 93 196-198 202 206 209 212-213 223 226 237 249 254
TAPLEY, 84
TAPPAN, 15
TAYLOR, 83-84 90 225 254
TEAGUE, 213
TEEL, 89-90
TEMPLE, 28
TESTE, 205
TETLOW, 38 197 253-254 256
THAXTER, 15
THAYER, 7 201 203 216 219 223 225 230
THOMAS, 246
THOMPSON, 90 196 199 219 248
THORNDIKE, 200
THORNER, 213
THURSTON, 214
TIBBETS, 215
TIBBETTS, 83-84 90 196 214
TILTON, 16 87
TITCOMB, 235
TODD, 226 235
TORR, 90
TORREY, 28 227
TOWER, 23
TOWLE, 198
TOWNE, 218 223-224
TOWNS, 205
TOWNSEND, 88

INDEX

TRAIN, 28
TRASK, 84 87-89 95 204 244 255
TREADWELL, 200 213 219
TREFREN, 100 207 256
TROFATTER, 208
TRUE, 198 231
TRUMBULL, 204
TUCKER, 212 218 237-238
TUFTS, 90 202-203 205-207
TURELL, 196
TURNER, 208 220
TURRELL, 90
TUTTLE, 70 198-201 203 206-208 213-214 218 239 254
TWOMBLY, 201
TYLER, 216
UPHAM, 249
UPTON, 84 90 198 204 207 209 211 214 216 219 221 223 225 229 240 248
VALENTINE, 2 231 256
VARNEY, 200 208 223 225 231
VENT, 213
VERR, 198
VERY, 90 199 212 214 216 218
VILES, 83-84
VINCENT, 197 204-205 208
WALCOTT, 83-84
WALDEN, 200 219 223 231
WALES, 28
WALKER, 84 87 198 204 208 219 224 249
WALLACE, 196 206
WALLIS, 57 198-199 201 206 214 224 253-255
WALTON, 196 198 202 212 241 248-249
WANT, 207
WARD, 87 201 204 216 220 231-233
WARDWELL, 213
WARE, 205 235
WARNER, 210
WARREN, 215
WASHBURN, 217
WATERS, 38 197 199-200 203-204 209 213 216 219 223-224 229-230 235 237 239 247-249 253-255
WATSON, 203 216 236 242
WATTS, 57 196 253
WEBB, 196 200 204 208 216-217 223 225 231 233 237 247-249
WEBSTER, 60 66 69 202-203 209 223 225 238 254 256
WEED, 247-248
WEEKS, 197 201 205-206 216
WEISSBERGER, 198
WELCH, 88 213
WELLS, 202
WELSH, 84
WENTWORTH, 201 209 211 214 256
WEST, 201 204 224-226 239
WESTON, 86 200 204 206 208 217 224 233 249
WHEATLAND, 200 206 218 222-223 227-229 236 247-249
WHEELER, 61 84-85 87-88 90 99 201 207 213 254 256
WHIDDEN, 89 91 255
WHINEY, 203
WHIPPLE, 197 202 204-205 207 212 214 218-219 223 231-232 235-236 248-249 253 256

WHITAKER, 198
WHITCOMB, 202
WHITE, 3 67 87 202 204 211 224 228 230 232 248 253-256
WHITNEY, 85 89 198
WHITTEMORE, 214
WHITTEN, 90
WHITTIER, 75 202 256
WIEDEMAN, 206
WIGGIN, 71 197 199 207 213-214 219 226 253-255
WILBUR, 68 256
WILDER, 15 28
WILEY, 88 242
WILKINS, 87 196 198 203 208 214 219
WILLEY, 220
WILLIAMS, 27 44 196 198 200 202 206 208-209 211-212 216 218 223 225 229 235 238 242 249 253 255
WILSON, 23 66 90 99 199 203 214 242 247 253-254 256
WINBERRY, 207
WINCHESTER, 47 198 208 213 243 256
WINDSOR, 24
WINN, 197 199 219 231 241
WINSOR, 206 212-213 227 248
WISE, 65 88 199 253
WOLCOTT, 83
WOOD, 28 206 209 216 235 243
WOODBERRY, 50 199 253
WOODBURY, 88-90 198 201 209
WOODFIN, 240
WOODFORD, 216
WOODMAN, 204
WOODS, 205 231
WOODWARD, 197 204
WORCESTER, 199 218 229 235 240 248-249
WRIGHT, 28 201 207
WUHR, 209
WYMAN, 209 236 249
YOUNG, 204
ZIMMERMAN, 198

www.ingramcontent.com/pod-product-compliance
Lightning Source LLC
Chambersburg PA
CBHW071950220426
43662CB00009B/1071